# Marx in the Field

# Marx in the Field

Edited by
Alessandra Mezzadri

ANTHEM PRESS

Anthem Press
An imprint of Wimbledon Publishing Company
*www.anthempress.com*

This edition first published in UK and USA 2023
by ANTHEM PRESS
75–76 Blackfriars Road, London SE1 8HA, UK
or PO Box 9779, London SW19 7ZG, UK
and
244 Madison Ave #116, New York, NY 10016, USA

First published in the UK and USA by Anthem Press in 2021

*British Library Cataloguing-in-Publication Data*
A catalogue record for this book is available from the British Library.

Library of Congress Control Number: 2023934809

ISBN-13: 978-1-83998-924-7 (Pbk)
ISBN-10: 1-83998-924-6 (Pbk)

Cover image: The image is based on the original painting 'Carlo Marx', by artist
Francesco Ghersina, photoshopped by Valentina D'Ettorre, with pictures by
Alessandra Mezzadri, Ben Cousins, and CITU Bengaluru archives.

This title is also available as an e-book.

# CONTENTS

# ILLUSTRATIONS

**Tables**

**Figures**

# ACKNOWLEDGEMENTS

This project is, at once, the result of years of reflection on Marxian political economy and its deployment during fieldwork and the intuition of a moment which crossed my mind as I was writing a paper for the conference Karl Marx @200 held in Patna, India, in the summer of 2018 and organized by the Asian Development Research Institute (ADRI). Perhaps, it is due to the double nature of its gestation, based both on my long-term experience and reflections as a fieldworker and on the intimacy of a quick moment of epiphany, that I feel so attached to it and grateful that it is finally becoming a book. It is also because of this dual nature that it is difficult to acknowledge all those I feel indebted to. Indeed, I want to thank ADRI and the organizing committee of 'Karl Marx @200' for their kind invitation and hospitality in Patna. I want to thank all the brilliant contributors to this volume, for having helped in turning a sketched idea into a rigorous and exciting intellectual enquiry. Among my colleagues, I want to thank with particular warmth the members of the SOAS Labour, Social Movements and Development (LSMD) research cluster. Several have contributed to this volume, but many others have shaped and sharpened my thinking during the years. Notwithstanding the multiple intellectual trajectories within the cluster, I hope the book does provide a glimpse of 'Marx at SOAS' – concrete, in conversation with other intellectual traditions, and engaged in the study of the many empirical manifestations of contemporary capitalism and its injustices. Among my past and current students, I want to thank Lorenza Monaco, Nithya Natarajan and Ayse Arslan, and the wonderful crowd of the Labour, Activism and Development (LADEV) Programme (previously LSMD). I also want to acknowledge the influence of an invited lecture on methods I delivered to students in the Doctoral School of Social and Behavioural Sciences at the University of Ghent, Belgium, in 2016, where I deployed the expression 'Marx in the Field' for the first time; thanks to the organizing committee, Itamar Shachar, Sigrid Vertommen (who has a chapter in this collection), Robin Thiers and Allan Souza Queiroz.

Thanks to Jairus Banaji for guiding my thinking on Marx and the world economy for many years. And thanks to Maria Mies and Silvia Federici – far more recent encounters along my academic and personal journey – and to Rohini Hensman and Naila Kabeer for inspiring and challenging me to further sharpen the feminist lens through which I today read, adjust and transgress Marxian categories and methods. Thanks also to Jessica Lerche for editorial support. I am grateful to Francesco Ghersina for letting me use a modified version of his painting 'Carlo Marx' as book cover. The pictures from the field used to dress 'his' Marx represent a textile factory in Shanghai, China (background, my own); a garment workers' mobilisation in India (right section of Marx's shirt, courtesy of CITU Bengaluru); and maize harvesting at Tugela Ferry, South Africa (left section of the shirt courtesy of Ben Cousins), and many thanks to my long-time friend Valentina D'Ettorre for the photo retouching. Sadly, Francesco's original painting – where Marx wears a floral red shirt – got stolen in the Prince Arthur Bar in Shoreditch, London, in 2019. If anyone spots it in a London home, please tell the hosts to return it, as Marx would have hated being objectified into private property through plunder, against which he wrote. They can get a free book copy instead, my treat. Finally, thanks to my family for coping with my thankless working rhythms. I dedicate my work on this collection to my son Leo Chico, whom, I hope, in ways of his choosing, will seek to understand this world and fight its injustices. And read Marx.

# Chapter One

# INTRODUCTION: MARX'S FIELD AS OUR GLOBAL PRESENT

## Alessandra Mezzadri

### Preamble: What Is Marx to the Process of Fieldwork?

By the summer of 2018, when this project was originally conceived, two hundred years had passed since the birth of Karl Marx. This date has been widely celebrated with talks, conferences, lectures and edited volumes. One of these many exciting projects, titled *Karl Marx's Life, Ideas, Influences: A Critical Examination on the Bicentenary*, edited by Shaibal Gupta, Marcello Musto and Babak Amini (2019), gathers the contributions to a conference held in July 2018 in Patna, India, at the Asian Development Research Institute (ADRI). I first wrote 'Marx in the sweatshop' – now a chapter in this collection – as a contribution to that conference. I conceived that paper as a fieldworker's celebration of the Marxian framework – a framework which, combined with feminist insights, has always strongly guided my research experience. As I wrote it, and prepared to fly to Patna, I realised that far more could and should be said about the potential benefits of deploying Marx and Marxian concepts and methods as a guide for today's 'radical fieldworkers' – those aspiring at 'doing' political economy across the world economy in practice, and committed to social and economic justice. By the time I landed in Patna, the idea of this volume – *Marx in the Field* – had already taken shape in my imagination, and I had contacted many of the contributors. I am excited that its final outlook looks spectacularly similar to my initial 'headnote'. As beautifully explained by Michael Taussig (2011), our attention as fieldworkers is often captured by 'fragments'; by encounters we suddenly experience and which are the outcomes of complex materialist explanations we then need to unpack and carefully analyse. To a certain extent, one could say this project was guided by an 'imagined fragment', an encounter between my conscious – unorthodox and feminist – use of Marxian methods of analysis and images from the field experiences that have shaped my concrete training as a social scientist through a continuous process of learning by doing.

This introductory chapter sketches the aims and rationale of the book and identifies three ways in which Marx can be brought 'to the field'. Obviously, these are hardly the only ways. However, they are *key ways* in which 'Marx' can guide us during field research, and in which the study of the concrete can in turn guide us to (re)read, use, adapt and at times 'transgress' and complement Marx's categories and methods of analysis. Following from this, it should be noted that this volume refers to and engages with issues of (Marxian) method(s) rather specifically, that is, in relation to the complex art (rather than science) of fieldwork – may this take place, as we shall see, in farms, among global exporters, farmers and/or traders; in factories and industrial units, focusing on employers and/or workers; across construction sites, medical clinics or prisons, tribal land or refugee camps; in homes, or inside public offices and dusty (or indeed, nowadays, online) archives. Hence, the 'field' here is primarily methodological, rather than geographical, as it refers to the concrete processes of conceptual development of research design, of deployment and adaptation of analytical categories for field research and/or data collection and analysis. The actual geography of the 'field' can vary widely. In fact, while several chapters here focus on the Global South, others either focus on the Global North or explore socio-economic relations connecting different regions of the world economy. Some focus on poor classes; others on elites or petty accumulators or intermediaries. The clarifications above are necessary to fully understand the ethos and scope of the volume, both in relation to the Marxian literature on methods and to the object of intervention in the development literature.

On the one hand, as argued by Henry Bernstein in his contributions here, there are already many brilliant historical analyses based on Marx's materialism, also instructing more general theoretical debates on method. While hopefully this book will stand as a useful complement to those reads, its primary scope remains becoming a far more practical guide on how to carry out concrete, meaningful Marxian analysis in specific contemporary settings. On the other hand, the geographical remit of *Marx in the Field* is far broader than that of 'classic' development studies research that tend to focus primarily on disadvantaged settings and classes. In fact, it is an attempt to 'globalise' the discipline, using concrete Marxian analysis as a lens. Notably, this intellectual project is carried out here by specifically showcasing the research of scholars linked – in several different ways – to political economy of development networks gravitating around SOAS, in London, where I was trained and still teach.

The list of topics covered here, while intended to be broad enough to convince readers of the many possible applications of Marxian methods for the successful study of the contemporary capitalist world in its concrete instantiations, is hardly exhaustive. There are a number of obvious lacunae, particularly in relation to ecology – increasingly a central contemporary concern of Marxist political economy (e.g. Bellamy-Foster 2002; Moore 2015; Saito 2017; Malm 2018) and always a key concern for feminist political economy and sociology (Merchant 1980; Mies and Shiva 1993; Salleh 1997; Barca 2019)[1] – or in relation to key geographical centres of accumulation within the world system, like China.[2] On the other hand, this volume hardly aims to cover all ground. Rather, it aims at winning the argument that one can draw extraordinarily productive connections between the study of Marx and its methods and categories and the concrete study of global capitalist development in its various facets. Hence, the study of

---

[1]   Point acknowledged by Dale (2018).
[2]   On methods for the study of labour in China, see Fuchs et al. (2019).

these methods and categories should be taught in each fieldwork methodology class across the social sciences. They are not only well equipped to unpack and challenge the complex power relations constituting the global economy. They can also propose field-work as a form of political practice in support of social and economic justice, rescuing it from technicistic and/or neocolonial classification tendencies. Hopefully, many other contributions will then follow in the footsteps of *Marx in the Field* and fill its many gaps while embracing its aims and objectives. The present and future fieldworkers of global capitalism, its multiple nodes of accumulation and gendered and racialised exploitation, plunder, inequality, poverty and injustice need many concrete roadmaps to facilitate their inquiries across the complexities of the world system. Marx was indeed a 'books person'. Still, my hope is that he would have liked this volume. After all, his work had a twofold aim: unveiling the limitations of classic bourgeois political economy, and illustrate the complex concrete workings of capitalism in his time – in order not only to interpret the world but, crucially, also to 'change it'. We are deep into this second business here. The next sections analyse three ways in which Marx can be productively 'brought to the field'; they further reflect on a number of key intellectual sources of inspiration behind this project and summarise some highlights from each contribution.

## *Marx in the Field*, Three Ways

Marx remains, at once, one of the giants of classical political economy and its fiercest critic. Many of Marx's observations – like capital's ever-rising appetite for commodi-fication and for the intensification of exploitation, or its drive towards concentration and the generation of inequality – remain extraordinarily relevant to the study of our global present. Processes of commodification continue being on the rise, multiplying the formation of new highly differentiated markets where even nature, ethics or life itself may be 'packaged' for personal consumption. The appropriation of nature for capitalist purposes and the globalisation of natural resource industries (Baglioni and Campling 2017) are leading to what George Monbiot (2014) has defined as 'The Pricing of Everything'. The rise of what Slavoj Žižek calls 'cultural capitalism' has precipitated processes of commercialisation of ethics, very profitable to a handful of corporations. In retail chains like The Body Shop, one can 'shop well to save the world' (Ponte and Richey 2011) and buy a fancy lipstick or soothing hand cream while financing the building of a hospital somewhere in Africa, or the purchase of HIV/AIDS medications. In food chains like Pret a Manger, buying a refreshing 'Lemon-Aid' is presented as an ethical act. Commodification is also having a profound effect on social reproduction, and life more broadly. Domestic and care work are increasingly commercialised (Mies 1986; Folbre 1996; Federici 2012; Fraser 2014), performed globally and nationally by underpaid migrants or ethnic minorities (Ehrenreich and Hochschild 2002; Yeates 2014; Grover et al. 2018). New reproductive technologies have enabled processes of commodification of the body and biological reproduction, epitomised, for instance, by the rise of global surrogacy (e.g. Pande 2014; Sangari 2015; Vora 2019; Vertommen 2016).

This rise in commodification and the escalating speed of global consumption is based on the persistence, spread and deepening of processes of exploitation. In China, the 'workshops of the world', and in many other economies engaged in labour-intensive manufacturing production for export, the exposure of workers to incessant working rhythms has the dark connotations of a proper Orwellian nightmare. Pun Ngai and Jenny Chan (2010) have documented the rise in suicide rates of Foxconn workers, unable to cope with the escalating pressures of the assembly line, as these spiral out of control taking over the whole of workers' reproductive time in dormitories and industrial hamlets, often also run by the company. The 2013 Rana Plaza disaster in Savar, a few kilometres from Dhaka, Bangladesh, exemplifies the destructive nature of current capitalism and the exploitation it implies for the labouring body (see Ashraf 2017). In that circumstance, the bodies of over one thousand workers were destroyed under a crumbling giant manu-facturing plant, as workers were locked inside its premises. Even when not posing such an immediate lethal danger, the 'abode of production' of many contemporary industries or farms scattered across the Global South – where the lion's share of global employment is located (ILO 2018) – clearly recalls the working conditions described by Marx in *Capital*. Child labour, to which Marx dedicated much space in the chapter on 'The working day' in *Volume I*, and in his description of the age of manufacture, is still widespread among many industries and in agriculture. According to official estimates, there are still over 200 million children working worldwide, and over 150 million can be classified as child labour. Of these, over 70 million work in hazardous occupations (ILO 2017). Across many sectors, like coffee, tea, garment or construction, the 'business of forced labour' (LeBaron 2018) or bonded labour practices (Shah et al. 2017; Guérin et al. 2013) thrive, often either through debt or payment retention mechanisms (Mezzadri and Srivastava 2015).

In terms of concentration, the astonishing rise in corporate profit rates that have taken place since the onset of neoliberalism has gone hand-in-hand with the rise of global and national monopolies and monopsonies (Durand and Milberg 2020). This is so, particu-larly, in the context of a 'retail revolution' driven by an international division of labour where Western economies sell and many emerging and developing economies produce, while their emerging middle classes also increasingly embrace high consumption rates. This has manifested in the growth and proliferation of complex global commodity chains stretching across the world economy and organised in complex production, labour and consumption networks and circuits (e.g. Bair 2009; Selwyn 2012; Neilson et al. 2014). At the same time, processes of financialisation – of markets, commodities and daily life – are increasingly subordinating the production of goods, services and people to the capricious forces of what Marx called 'fictitious capital' (i.e. 'non-productive' capital; see Banaji 2013) and debt. In countries like Brazil, financialisation is leading to the 'collaterisation of social policy', further entrenching debt into households' social reproduction via social schemes (Lavinas 2018).

Unsurprisingly, concentration is going hand in hand with hikes in inequality, both within and between countries. According to a now famous report by Oxfam (2015), a now infamous 1 per cent of the world owns the lion's share of all global resources and wealth. For the economist Thomas Piketty (2014), this is because *Capital in the 21st Century* has entered a patrimonial phase where returns to capital exceed growth rates, hence turning accumulation into a rent-based project steered by global elites. Worldwide, the social and economic outcomes of these rising inequalities impact upon women and ethnic minorities with particular harshness (Perrons 2014). Race and gender inequality co-constitute markets and class (Elson 1999; Bannerji 2011). In her recent prize-winning book, *Race for Profit* (2019), Keeanga-Yamahtta Taylor shows how banks and real estates in the United States undermined black ownership, reproducing a highly unequal access to property. On the other hand, in white settler states, property always had specific colonial features (Bhandar 2018). Accumulation under capitalism is *always* gendered and racialised (Davis 1983; Federici 2004; Bhattacharya 2017; Ferguson 2019; Bhattacharyya 2018). During the current COVID-19 pandemic – I am currently working at the final editorial tasks for this book in the midst of the global lockdown – the tragic implications of these inequalities are manifesting brutally, with ethnic minorities and context-specific vulnerable communities – like, for instance, Dalits or Muslims in India, refugees and migrants in Europe, BAME and black communities in the United Kingdom and United States – greatly over-represented among the sick and the dead and overexposed to starvation, violence or economic hardship, quite spectacularly confirming Achille Mbembe's (2012) observations on the necropolitics of capitalism (Lee 2020). In effect, the present pandemic is best represented as a unique crisis of social reproduction (Mezzadri 2020), turning inequalities into lethal socioeconomic weapons for expanding surplus populations.

Arguably, the crisis is also forcefully revealing Karl Marx's truth about global capitalism – that it is primarily based on the exploitation of human labour for the production of *all* value. Indeed, the generalised withdrawal of labour-power from the market during the lockdown has quickly led the world system on the brink of economic collapse. In fact, all the disquieting trends we are currently witnessing – pre- and post-COVID-19 – which structure the world economy while threatening many communities speak loudly about the broad, general relevance of Marxian insights for the study of our global present. However, to what extent do Marxian *categories of analysis*, as developed in *Capital* or elsewhere by Marx, may still work as a useful operational research framework? Could we use them productively for field-based research in, say, a global factory in India or China, a mine in tribal land in South Africa, a home-based workshop in Italy, a prison in the United States, or a large or small farm in Pakistan, Mozambique or Uzbekistan? Can we use them to understand the financialised features of today's global commodities like coffee or tea, the characteristics of merchant capital and petty trade in South Asia and their relation to the global and national economy, or the tight organisation and control of global migration in Europe or the Middle East? Moreover, how can we develop field and data collection methods that are coherent with such categories of analysis, and which are their features, strengths and limitations? And finally, how can we adapt Marxian categories of analysis in concrete fieldwork settings, where, as in Lewis Carroll's *Alice in Wonderland*, 'nothing would be what it is, because everything would be what it isn't'?[3] Should today's street vendors or gig-economy service deliverers be classified as (disguised) workers rather than micro-entrepreneurs, shifting policy focus from credit provision

---

[3]    Ben Fine (2010) deploys this quote from Lewis Carroll's tale in his Marxian analysis of *Social Capital*.

towards wage improvement? How do we investigate merchant capital, trade networks and petty commodity production, and their linkages with larger factories or industrial workshops? And in what ways can we use Marx when studying the home, reproductive activities and reproductive workers, and the global processes reconfiguring social and biological reproduction? In short, how *do we do* Marxian analysis in *practice*, in diverse sectoral and geographical contexts? How can we deploy *Marx in the Field*? These are some of the questions the contributions to this volume grapple with and aim to answer.

Marx's conceptual apparatus powerfully resonates with intellectuals, researchers, academics and activists worldwide. The concepts he introduced have already forcefully returned to haunt the mainstream social sciences. Somewhat amusingly, in the aftermath of the 2008 financial crisis, we had the pleasure to spot references to Marx even in the (hardly progressive) daily London tube newspaper *Metro*. Marxian insights are also proving useful to grapple with the terrible health and economic implications of the current COVID-19 crisis (Samaddar 2020) and the historical link between capitalism, ecology and pandemics (e.g. Wallace et al. 2020; Fasfalis 2020). Yet, the practical relevance of Marxian political economy for actual, concrete field-based research remains under-theorised and not systematically analysed. Strongly focused on concrete fieldwork and research cases, and aimed at filling this gap, this collection highlights three ways in which we can productively bring Marx into the field.

The first way is by showing the relevance of the Marxian research framework in practice by focusing on one or more key concepts, categories or processes highlighted by Marx in his critique of political economy and study of capitalist development. This line of contribution aims at illustrating how key Marxian tropes illuminate the ways in which contemporary capitalism unfolds in different settings and with which implications for processes of development, by reference to specific concrete cases. Examples of key themes discussed in different contributions to this volume are: the study of the commodity form and the concept of commodity fetishism; Marx's category of landed property; the distinction between absolute or relative surplus extraction or between formal and real subsumption of labour; the connections between production and circulation and the role of merchant capital; or the links between production, pauperisation, health depletion and/or nutrition. Notably, while discussing the methodological and explanatory relevance of these tropes, the essays in this collection may also highlight how we can rethink these concepts, categories and processes in relations to the cases analysed. This exercise may entail illustrating the distinct ways in which contemporary manifestations may depart from the classic Marxian explanation, or how Marxian concepts can be rehistoricised, complemented, reworked and deployed in combination with insights inspired by other progressive literatures like, for instance, feminism, critical realism or postcolonial analyses, effectively 'queering' methods and categories for concrete research. On the other hand, these shall never be congealed across time, but rather remain 'living' and contemporary analytical tools.

A second way to bring *Marx in the Field* is through a discussion of how Marxian categories may appear in 'disguised form' across the world economy, and how we can unveil and investigate them during fieldwork. If the previous line of contribution aims at underlining the great contemporary power of Marxian analysis for the methodological conceptualisation of our global present, this line of contribution is premised on showing the concrete steps needed to apply Marx's categories and concepts in settings where these may not appear in straightforward ways. An obvious example is the ways in which the labour process or indeed class – as well as class politics – may manifest in complex ways, apparently distant from the original Marxian formulation, obviously embedded in the contemporary history of its own time. Indeed, contemporary labour relations across the world economy, especially those involving women and marginalised groups – may appear as quite diverse and seem distant from the historical form of wage labour as studied by Marx. By the same token, also capital and its many representatives may appear under different historical guises and forms. Contributions to this second way of bringing *Marx in the Field* describe and illustrate how to distinguish between essence and appearance. On the other hand, the deconstruction of *fetishism* – of what appears – is a key insight of the Marxian method overall. Essays engaging with this second research agenda may also describe the difficulties in researching field settings, especially when structured by harsh power relations or dominated by ruthless elites.

A final line of contribution and a third way to bring *Marx in the Field* entails the description, discussion and analysis of which practical methods of data collection can guide a Marxian political economy approach to the field, again by refer-ence to concrete cases studies. Which data better illustrates some key processes analysed in the context of Marxian political economy? And which fieldwork strat-egies? And which concrete methods did Marx use, and to what extent can we still learn from and deploy them? Essays aiming at providing some answers to these questions discuss the ways in which distinct quantitative and qualitative methods, or indeed their combination, help us imagine concrete ways to oper-ationalise the study of production, labour or circulation, distribution, consump-tion and reproduction in ways consistent with Marxian thought and scope. Some analyses also dwell on the difficulties to develop these methods in practice, and/or on the operational limitations of doing research across the world economy. Others question the very possibility to identify data collection methods 'more appropriate' to a Marxian inquiry, or discuss how to concretely rethink Marxian methods – like workers' inquiries – when focusing on social relations not originally explored through a Marxian lens. Some contributions also briefly touch upon issues of ethics in the field, always complex in contexts defined by harsh relations of domination. Indeed, the Marxian analytical framework should never be divorced from political practice.

Obviously, there may be crossovers between these three lines of contributions, with some essays neatly fitting into one, addressing two or even covering all three. This depends on how contributors have interpreted the task of illustrating the interconnections between Marxian analysis and their own fieldwork experience. For instance, there may be overlaps between the difficulty in identifying Marxian categories in the field and the practical ways in which these can be researched and analysed. In fact, readers may also be able to spot further ways in which contributions bring *Marx in the Field*, and I strongly encourage them to try.

**Inspirations and Aspirations**

The concrete exploration of the world system has been the subject of fascinating analyses. George E. Marcus's (1995) influential paper on the different ways to conduct ethnography 'in' and 'of' the world system has triggered a productive debate on the different 'trails' and tropes field research may follow, and on the rise of multi-sited ethnography, its benefits and challenges, or difference, if at all, with classic anthropological methods (e.g. Shah 2017). The latter issue is also explored in Michael Burawoy's *Global Ethnography* (2000) in relation to the mutual shaping of local struggles and global forces (see also Chari and Gidwani 2005), while Anna Tsing's (2005) 'Friction' collapses the distinction between global and local altogether to explore the co-constitutive nature of global interconnections and their concrete instantiations in 'zones of awkward engagement' (useful comparisons in Gagnon 2019). *Marx in the Field* does not directly engage with these debates; it is not a book on ethnography. However, it cuts across some of their concerns, as its exploration of different avenues for Marxian political economy indirectly proposes a way to do research both 'in' and 'of' the world system, by deploying categories and methods stressing the global–local co-constitution of the socioeconomic processes shaping global capitalism.

Far more directly, *Marx in the Field* has taken inspiration from some key methodological texts in development studies, sociology and anthropology, and development economics, based on a political economy approach to development. One key text inspiring this project is undoubtedly *Fieldwork in Developing Countries* (1993), edited by Stephen Devereux and John Hoddinott. This collection, now 25 years old, still remains a unique reading in the development literature, for the honesty of its accounts, its operationalisation of political economy analysis and discussion of practical fieldwork issues and limitations. A second source of inspiration is represented by the text *Agricultural Markets from Theory to Practice: Field Experience in Developing Countries* (1999), edited by Barbara Harriss-White. This is a brilliant guide of how to navigate the vagaries of field research in practice, while accounting for the harsh power relations at work in rural settings. With its focus on agricultural markets, its scope is more circumscribed, aimed at scholars and students of agrarian change. Also, this text is almost 20 years old.

Besides these two volumes, a number of other useful articles have also addressed issues of political economy-inspired fieldwork, in terms of either method/s or research ethics. One is Jan Breman's powerful rejection of neutral accounts in contexts characterised by huge disparities in power, which he explains in 'Between accumulation and immiseration: The partiality of fieldwork in rural India' (1985). Another is Sharad Chari's reflection on developing a Marxian political economy approach to self-representation, to capture the ways in which workers may engage in acts of everyday resistance against the sheer power of capital in their daily lives, developed in 'Marxism, sarcasm, ethnography: Geographical fieldnotes from South India' (2003). A third is Michael Burawoy's generous discussion of the limitations of ethnographic methods due to 'inadequate theoretical reflection', in 'Ethnographic fallacies: Reflections on labour studies in the era of market fundamentalism' (2013). Finally, Henry Bernstein's essay, 'Studying development/development studies' (2006), highlights the fracture between the study of development as the process of capitalist penetration in developing regions – what Cowen and Shenton (1996) called 'immanent' development – and the evolution of development studies as a (neo)colonial discipline fostering an 'intentional' development project increasingly narrow and market-based. It also illustrates the explicatory power of Marxian political economy for the study of the global development process and its class- and state-based dynamics.

Influenced by these contributions and debates, this volume aims at more systematically exploring the relevance of a Marxian lens for the study of development. In fact, by highlighting the ways in which Marxian analysis can be operationalised *for the Field* across the world economy, this collection has the ambitious aim to mainstream the study of Marx, his concepts, categories and methods not only for *studying development* but also for *development studies*. If this discipline is to fully embrace its potential to speak about power and injustice, and to provide a key analytical lens for the study of global transformations learning from the experiences of developing regions and their trajectories, then it needs to overcome its narrower, technicistic tendencies and to be returned to the broader field of political economy. So, overall, the process of bringing *Marx in the Field* can be seen at once as the product of a long-standing tradition of studying capitalist development across the world through the lens of political economy, as well as a novel endeavour aimed at narrowing the gap between the theory and practice of development studies.

As I already mentioned in this introduction, SOAS, where I was trained and where I am still based, in London, remains a central academic institution for 'doing' Marxian political economy in practice – productively influenced by the insights of other radical intellectual traditions, like feminism, postcolonial theory and approaches to racial capitalism, crucial to 'decolonise' development. All contributors to this collection have links with SOAS – as alumni, academics, associates or friends. Some studied, worked or still work at SOAS. Others are engaged in debates on rural transformations featured in the *Journal of Agrarian Change*, or have/had links with the International Initiative for the Promotion of Political Economy (IPPE), or the Historical Materialism Conference, all SOAS-based. This is a key feature of this book; it codifies some of the specific ways in which critical development studies is interpreted at SOAS, influenced by Marxian political economy yet incorporating insights from other radical traditions and focusing on practical lessons for/from field research. Notwithstanding the circumscribed institutional 'catchment area', this collection includes a rather socially diverse group of authors engaging with Marx and fieldwork on the basis of distinct intellectual trajectories and focusing on varied case studies.

Finally, while this volume aspires at mainstreaming Marxian political economy for *thinking and doing* development studies in practice, it also tries to push the discipline beyond its original boundaries. First, the study of development today exceeds its original geographical focus on developing countries. The globalisation of processes of production, circulation, exchange and distribution entails the need to think about development as a global process and project. According to many contemporary Marxist scholars, Marx's framework was always meant to study the development of capitalist forces *globally* (e.g. Banaji 2010; Pradella 2014). Second, as facile linear and modernising narratives of development get increasingly disproven, due to mounting evidence that today it may be

'The West' following 'The Rest' (Breman and van der Linden 2014), insights from development studies can prove increasingly useful to investigate the socioeconomic changes taking place across the world economy. This is particularly evident with reference to the study of economic migration and the so-called refugee crisis, but also with regard to the spread of informal/ised work relations and economic activities, generally – erroneously – associated with developing settings. Indeed, as mentioned, not all essays contained in this collection focus geographically on developing regions. And while some address classic themes in development studies, like rural poverty, informal work or petty production, others analyse global financial markets, novel processes of global commodification, and focus on wealthy or emerging economies. However, they all show the productive ways in which it is possible to bring *Marx in the Field* in order to challenge rigid disciplinary boundaries and turn the study of development into a concrete exploration of our deeply interconnected global present.

## Contributions: Marx and Old and New Areas of Enquiry

As a significant number of chapters in this volume bring *Marx in the Field* in more than one way, it would make little sense to try to organise them into subsections merely based on the three lines of contributions I identified as central in previous sections. I have decided instead to organise the book based on content and context. Chapters engaging with 'older' or more classic concerns in Marxian political economy – such as exploitation; accumulation; capitalist elites; production, circulation and merchant capital; and the concrete workings of financialisation – appear first in this volume. These chapters are concerned with the usefulness of Marxian categories for the study of contemporary capitalism; some focus more on national processes of development, while others are concerned with either regional or global circuits of production, trade and finance (Chapters 2–7). A second bloc of chapters explores the key Marxian category of class *in the field*, its features and/or politics and institutions, and discuss fruitful ways in which it can and should be researched in practice, overcoming structural, rigid definitions (Chapters 8–10). Chapters focused on less explored themes in political economy – such as unfreedom, nutrition or health – follow (Chapters 11–13), and the collection ends with contributions which either further stretch the boundaries of Marxian political economy to explore novel areas of enquiry related to the global commodification of life and to 'marginal categories' in the study of political economy, or analyse the new extraordinary challenges of doing field research from 'afar' (Chapters 14–16). These contributions may engage with debates over the relevance of Marxian categories, or the ways in which they may appear in 'disguise' in the field. Greatly informed by feminism, a few contributions in the last two blocs also provide useful analyses of the empirical material used by Marx in his work and its relevance for contemporary studies on the bodily traits of working poverty, besides exploring possibilities for data collection and their challenges. With this simple reader in mind, let's now briefly present each contribution.

After this introduction, in Chapter 2 Henry Bernstein explores how some key questions central to all empirical research can be addressed in ways informed by Marxian categories, methods and approaches. His chapter also explores the challenges posed by

Marx's notion of what is 'visible' and empirically researchable and what is necessarily 'invisible' in capitalism; what is 'essence' and what 'appearance', based on Marx's conception of commodity fetishism. Drawing from Balibar, the chapter concludes with observations on researching class relations, dynamics, experiences, beliefs and practices, reflecting on the ways in which class encapsulates all social practices, without being the only one.

In Chapter 3, in an ambitious analysis contributing to all three lines of enquiry of *Marx in the Field*, Barbara Harriss-White reconstructs Marx's insights on merchant and commercial capital and shows how they shape debates on Indian capitalism. Drawing on decades of field research, the chapter outlines the features of existing commercial capitalism in India and explores the many methodological challenges of developing a concrete Marxian research agenda to study commercial capitalism in the twenty-first century.

Along compatible lines, in Chapter 4, Muhammad Ali Jan illustrates the features of a methodological approach aimed at grappling with diversity *within* capital by deploying an underexplored concept in Marx – that of 'fractions of capital'. Also drawing on Weber, the chapter identifies three dimensions along which fractions within a class can be identified: spatial, scalar and a social origin-based. Drawing from a variety of examples from the Global South, including his own fieldwork in rural and small-town Pakistani Punjab, Jan highlights how concrete studies of different forms of capital in different contexts must pay attention to the threads that bind social groups despite their diversities.

Chapters 5, 6 and 7 continue the concrete exploration of classic themes in political economy – exploitation, accumulation and finance – although they more heavily stress the global or regional features of such dynamics. In Chapter 5, my chapter, I identify three tropes of Marxian methodology relevant to the study of India's 'sweatshop regime' – namely, centring the analysis around 'the commodity' in order to illustrate the concrete workings of 'commodity fetishism'; the study of the distinct modes of surplus value extraction, their interplay and implications for the body; and the mapping of processes of subsumption of labour, resulting in various 'forms of exploitation'. The chapter illustrates the need to explore the social traits of exploitation and social reproduction drawing on the Marxist Feminist literature.

In Chapter 6, Adam Hanieh shows how Marx's extensive writings on class can deeply inform research in the Gulf. This chapter reflects on how Marxist conceptualisations of class help in grasping the specificities of labour, migration and capital accumulation in the Gulf, their regional social relations and dynamics. Particularly concerned with accumulation and drawing from many years of experience of researching capital–labour relations in the region, this analysis illustrates how Marx's work can turn into a powerful guide to doing fieldwork in the Gulf – revealing the right questions to ask and helping to unveil hidden connections.

In Chapter 7, Susan Newman discusses the relevance of *Volume II* of Marx's *Capital* for an integrated analysis of social relations of production, exchange and finance across global commodity circuits. Focusing on the global coffee commodity chain, the chapter examines the relationships between merchants, traders and workers, turning coffee into an object for consumption, as well as the roles of money-owners, money-lenders and money-managers operating on international financial exchanges and whose interests and operations impact other commodity chain actors.

In Chapter 8, Benjamin Selwyn reflects upon his experience in deploying Marxist class analysis to grasp the production and labour dynamics unfolding in export grape production in Brazil. Illustrating the forces at work encountered in the field, the chapter discusses a dual process of 'learning Marx by doing': first, related to moving from abstract and static to dynamic and experiential conceptions of class; and, second, based on using field-based knowledge on class struggle to re-theorise capital–labour relations. The analysis also discusses useful methods for mapping and recording field findings to identify concrete manifestations of class and power.

In Chapter 9, drawing on long-term fieldwork on trade unions and manufacturing across India, Satoshi Miyamura illustrates the contemporary relevance of Marx's analysis for the study of labour relations and struggles. Set against juridical and dualist approaches to labour institutions, and reductionist and conflict-free mainstream conceptions of labour relations based on methodological individualism, this analysis shows that Marx's method provides a productive framework to explore trade union politics in the subcontinent.

Chapter 10, by Farai Mtero, Brittany Bunce, Ben Cousins, Alex Dubb and Donna Hornby, analyses how Marx's conception of class as a 'concentration of many determinations' can inform fieldwork in rural South Africa, where class and livelihood strategies are co-constituted and differentiated along the lines of race, gender and generation, and households combine multiple income sources, including wage labour, self-employment and welfare payments. The chapter indicates which methods for data collection can be mediated by Marx's key concepts and theories, such as the production and appropriation of surplus value, accumulation and social reproduction, and describes how this approach – compatible with critical realism – informed research in four distinct fieldwork projects.

In Chapter 11, Lorena Lombardozzi unmasks the limitations of current studies on 'forced labour' and discusses how these often conceal the structural, concrete determinants of labour exploitation. Her chapter explores the case of agrarian labour in Uzbekistan post-Soviet independence and investigates the empirical, methodological and epistemological complexities underpinning the concept of labour freedom in this region through a Marxian lens. It also highlights the need for mixed methods for data collection to explore complex social relations and the contradictions of late capitalist accumulation.

In Chapter 12, Tania Toffanin illustrates the relevance of Marx's observations on health and exploitation for the study of more contemporary forms of homework and body depletion. Focusing on the Italian case, the analysis illustrates the interrelation between gendered exploitation in the home and adverse health effects. It underlines the benefits and challenges of deploying Marx's concrete methods of enquiry to connect health and work – based on labour inspectors' and doctors' reports – and it discusses the limitations of Marxian understandings of domestic labour's structural role in capitalist development.

In Chapter 13, Sara Stevano compares 'Marx's diet' in *Capital*, illustrating the malnourishment of Britain's working classes based on data from public health investigations, with the patterns of food consumption dominating among the poor in contemporary sub-Saharan Africa. Using primary data collected in Mozambique and Ghana, the chapter shows the similarities and differences in the poor's diets across time and space. It also stresses how concrete methods to analyse food consumption and its linkages with food systems must include multiple data sources and levels of analysis.

In Chapter 14, Sigrid Vertommen interrogates the usefulness of the Marxian method in capturing the features of commercial surrogacy in Georgia and highlights the processes of invisibilisation preventing Georgian surrogates from being considered 'real' workers despite their centrality in this rising global industry. While calling on Marx to focus the attention on the regimes of labour at the heart of processes of valorisation in the fertility industry, the chapter stresses the need to move beyond Marxist productivism to denaturalise the fictitious separation between productive and reproductive work. The chapter also discusses the possibilities and challenges of undertaking a workers' inquiry centred on reproductive work.

Originally concluding the collection, Chapter 15, in a preliminary way, interrogates the relevance of Marxian methods and categories for the study of what would appear as three 'marginal' figures in political economy, namely the tribal chieftaincy, the prisoner and the refugees. In the process of thinking about these figures, the chapter, which takes the narrative form of a collective conversation with Gavin Capps (chieftain), Genevieve LeBaron (prisoner) and Paolo Novak (refugee), we learn both what Marxian political economy can offer, analytically and politically, and what may be its main methodological constraints.

Finally, completing this introduction during the COVID-19 global lockdown, I felt the urge to also include an intervention focusing on the ways in which Marx's insights can guide us through a complex 'field' indeed – that of understanding the concrete implications and effects of this pandemic in specific regions of the world economy – while locked inside our homes. Drawing on evidence from India collected in the 'cyberfield', Subir Sinha brilliantly engages with this difficult task in Chapter 16. Here, focusing on migrant labour in India in COVID times, he highlights points of contact between Marxism and postcolonial studies and reflects on new avenues for 'field-based' analysis in the digital era. While this chapter concludes the collection, it hardly concludes the enquiry of what may be further productive ways in which Marxian insights may be deployed to study the 'margins' of political economy. Hopefully, the end of *Marx in the Field* is only the beginning. But let's now 'leave this noisy sphere' and follow Marx across the world economy, whose concrete secrets must 'be laid bare'.

## References

Ashraf, H. 2017. 'Beyond building safety: An ethnographic account of health and well-being on the Bangladesh garment shop floor'. In R. Prentice and G. De Neve (eds), *Unmaking the Global Sweatshop: Health and Safety of the World's Garment Workers*, pp. 250–74. Philadelphia: University of Pennsylvania Press.

Baglioni, E. and L. Campling. 2017. 'Natural resource industries as global value chains: Frontiers, fetishism, labour and the state'. *Environment and Planning A: Economy and Space* 49(11): 2437–56.

Bair, J. 2009. *Frontiers of Commodity Chain Research*. Stanford: Stanford University Press.

Banaji, J. 2010. *Theory as History: Essay Theory as History: Essays on Modes of Production and Exploitation*. Leiden: Brill.

———. 2013. 'Seasons of self-delusion: Opium, capitalism and the financial markets'. *Historical Materialism* 21(2): 3–19.

Bannerji, H. 2005. 'Building from Marx: Reflections on class and race'. *Social Justice* 32(4): 144–60.

———. 2011. 'Building from Marx: Reflections on "race", gender, and glass'. In S. Carpenter and S. Mojab (eds), *Educating from Marx*, pp. 41–60. New York: Palgrave Macmillan.

Barca, S. 2019. 'Labour and the ecological crisis: The eco-modernist dilemma in Western Marxism(s) (1970s–2000s)'. *Geoforum* 98: 226–35.

Bellamy-Foster, J. 2002. *Ecology against Capitalism*. New York: Monthly Review Press.

Bernstein, H. 2006. 'Studying development/development studies'. *African Studies* 65(1): 45–62.

Bhandar, B. 2018. *Colonial Lives of Property: Law, Land, and Racial Regimes of Ownership*. Durham: Duke University Press.

Bhattacharya, T. 2017. *Social Reproduction Theory: Remapping Class, Re-Centering Oppression*. London: Pluto.

Bhattacharyya, G. 2018. *Rethinking Racial Capitalism: Questions of Reproduction and Survival*. London: Rowman and Littlefield.

Breman, J. 1985. 'Between accumulation and immiseration: The partiality of fieldwork in rural India'. *Journal of Peasant Studies* 13(1): 5–36.

Breman, J. and M. van der Linden. 2014. 'Informalizing the economy: The return of the social question at a global level'. *Development and Change* 45(5): 920–40.

Burawoy, M. 2013. 'Ethnographic fallacies: Reflections on labour studies in the era of market fundamentalism'. *Work, Employment and Society* 27(3): 526–36.

Burawoy, M., S. O'Riain, J. A. Blum, S. George, Z. Gille, T. Gowan, L. Haney, M. Klawiter, S. H. Lopez and M. Thayer. 2000. *Global Ethnography: Forces, Connections, and Imaginations in a Postmodern World*. Berkeley: University of California Press.

Chari, S. 2003. 'Marxism, sarcasm, ethnography: Geographical fieldnotes from South India'. *Singapore Journal of Tropical Geography* 24(2): 169–83.

Chari, S. and V. Gidwani. 2005. 'Introduction: Grounds for a spatial ethnography of labor'. *Ethnography* 6(3): 267–81.

Cowen, M. P. and R. W. Shenton. 1996. *Doctrines of Development*. London: Routledge.

Dale, G. 2018. 'The emergence of an ecological Karl Marx: 1818–2018'. *Ecologist*, 5 May, https://theecologist.org/2018/may/05/emergence-ecological-karl-marx-1818-2018

Davis, A. Y. 1983. *Women, Race and Class*. New York: Random House.

Devereux, S. and J. Hoddinott, 1993. *Fieldwork in Developing Countries*. Boulder: Lynne Rienner.

Durand, D. and D. Milberg. 2020. 'Intellectual monopoly in global value chains'. *Review of International Political Economy* 27(2): 404–29.

Ehrenreich, B. and A. Hochschild. 2002. *Global Woman: Nannies, Maids, and Sex Workers in the New Economy*. New York: Henry Holt.

Elson, D. 1999. 'Labor markets as gendered institutions: Equality, efficiency and empowerment issues'. *World Development* 27(3): 611–27.

Fasfalis, D. 2020. 'Marx in the era of pandemic capitalism'. *Socialist Project*, 13 April, https://socialistproject.ca/2020/04/marx-in-the-era-of-pandemic-capitalism/

Federici, S. 2012. *Revolution at Point Zero: Housework, Reproduction, and Feminist Struggle*. Brooklyn: PM Press.

———. 2004. *Caliban and the Witch: Women, the Body and Primitive Accumulation*. Brooklyn, NY: Autonomedia.

Ferguson, S. 2019. *Women and Work. Feminism, Labour, and Social Reproduction*. London: Pluto.

Fine, B. 2010. *Theories of Social Capital: Researchers Behaving Badly*. London: Pluto.

Folbre, N. 1996. 'Hearts and spades: Paradigms of household economics'. *World Development* 14(2): 245–55.

Fraser, N. 2014. 'Behind Marx's hidden abode: For an expanded conception of capitalism'. *New Left Review* 86: 55–72.

Fuchs, D., P. Fuk-Ying Tse and X. Feng, 2019. 'Labour research under coercive authoritarianism: Comparative reflections on fieldwork challenges in China'. *Economic and Industrial Democracy* 40(1): 132–55.

Gagnon, T. 2019. 'Ethnography for a new global political economy? Marcus (1995) revisited, through the lens of Tsing and Nash'. *Ethnography* 20(2): 284–94.

Grover, S., T. Chambers and P. Jeffery. 2018. 'Portraits of women's paid domestic-care labour: Ethnographic studies from globalizing India'. *Journal of South Asian Development* 13(2): 1–18.

Guérin, I., B. D'Espallier and G. Venkatasubramanian. 2013. 'Debt in rural South India: Fragmentation, social regulation and discrimination'. *Journal of Development Studies* 49(9): 1155–71.

Harriss-White, B. 1999. *Agricultural Markets from Theory to Practice: Field Experience in Developing Countries.* New York: St. Martins.

ILO. 2017. *Global Estimates of Child Labour, Results and Trends 2012–2016.* Geneva: ILO.

———. 2018. *Women and Men in the Informal Economy: A Statistical Picture,* 3rd edn. Geneva: ILO.

Lavinas, L. 2018. 'The collateralization of social policy under financialized capitalism'. *Development and Change* 49(2): 502–17.

LeBaron, G. 2018. *The Global Business of Forced Labour.* Sheffield: SPERI.

Lee, C. J. 2020. 'The necropolitics of COVID-19', https://africasacountry.com/2020/04/the-necropolitics-of-covid-19

Malm, A. 2018. *The Progress of This Storm. Nature and Society in a Warming World.* London: Verso.

Marcus, G. E. 1995. 'Ethnography in/of the world system: The emergence of multi-sited ethnography'. *Annual Review of Anthropology* 24: 95–117.

Marx, K. 1990. *Capital.* London: Penguin Classics (reprint of Pelican Books edition, 1976).

Mbembe, A. 2012. *Necropolitics.* Durham: Duke University Press.

Merchant, C. 1980. *The Death of Nature: Women, Ecology and the Scientific Revolution.* New York: HarperCollins.

Mezzadri, A. 2017. *The Sweatshop Regime: Labouring Bodies, Exploitation, and Garments 'Made in India'.* Cambridge: Cambridge University Press.

———. 2020. 'A crisis like no other: Social reproduction and the regeneration of capitalist life under the COVID-19 pandemic'. *Developing Economics,* https://developingeconomics.org/2020/04/20/a-crisis-like-no-other-social-reproduction-and-the-regeneration-of-capitalist-life-during-the-covid-19-pandemic/

Mezzadri, A. and R. Srivastava. 2015. *Labour Regimes in the Indian Garment Sector: Capital–Labour Relations, Social Reproduction and Labour Standards in the National Capital Region (NCR).* ESRC Report. London: SOAS/CDPR.

Mies, M. 1986. *Patriarchy and Accumulation on a World Scale: Women in the International Division of Labour.* London: Zed.

Mies, M. and V. Shiva. 1993. *Ecofeminism.* London: Zed.

Monbiot, G. 2014. 'Put a price on nature? We must stop this neoliberal road to ruin'. *Guardian,* https://www.theguardian.com/environment/georgemonbiot/2014/jul/24/price-nature-neoliberal-capital-road-ruin

Moore, J. 2015. *Capitalism in the Web of Life: Ecology and the Accumulation of Capital.* London: Verso.

Neilson, J., B. Pritchard and H. Wai-Chun Yeun. 2014. 'Global value chains and global production networks in the changing international political economy: An introduction'. *Review of International Political Economy* 21(1): 1–8.

Oxfam. 2015. 'Wealth: Having it all and wanting more'. Oxfam Policy Paper.

Pande, A. 2014. *Wombs in Labor: Transnational Commercial Surrogacy in India.* New York: Columbia University Press.

Perrons, D. 2014. 'Gendering inequality: A note on Piketty's *Capital in the Twenty-First Century*'. *British Journal of Sociology* 65(4): 667–77.

Piketty, T. 2014. *Capital in the 21st Century*. Cambridge: Belknap Press.

Ponte, S. and A. M. Richey. 2011. *BrandAid: Shopping Well to Save the World*. Minneapolis: University of Minnesota Press.

Pradella, L. 2014. *Globalization and the Critique of Political Economy: New Insights from Marx's Writings*. London: Routledge.

Pun, N. and J. Chan. 2010. 'Suicide as protest for the new generation of Chinese migrant workers: Foxconn, global capital and the state'. *Asia Pacific Journal* 37(2): 1–50.

Saito, K. 2017. *Karl Marx's Ecosocialism: Capital, Nature, and the Unfinished Critique of Political Economy*. New York: New York University Press.

Salleh, A. 1997. *Ecofeminism as Politics*. London: Zed.

Sangari, K. 2015. *Solid: Liquid, A (Trans)national Reproductive Formation*. New Delhi: Tulika.

Selwyn, B. 2012. 'Beyond firm-centrism: Re-integrating labour and capitalism into global commodity chain analysis'. *Journal of Economic Geography* 12: 205–26.

Samaddar, R. 2020. *Borders of an Epidemic: COVID-19 and Migrant Workers*. Kolkata: CRG, http://www.mcrg.ac.in/RLS_Migration_2020/COVID-19.pdf

Shah, A. 2017. 'Ethnography? Participant observation, a potentially revolutionary praxis'. *HAU: Journal of Ethnography* 7(1): 45–59.

Shah, A., J. Lerche, R. Axelby, D. Benbabaali, B. Donegan, J. Raj and V. Thakur. 2017. *Ground Down by Growth: Tribe, Caste, Class and Inequality in 21st Century India*. London: Pluto.

Taussig, M. 2011. *I Swear I Saw This: Drawings in Fieldwork Notebooks, Namely My Own*. Chicago: University of Chicago Press.

Taylor, K. Y. 2019. *Race for Profit: How Banks and the Real Estate Industry Undermined Black Homeownership*. Chapel Hill: University of North Carolina Press.

Tsing, A. 2005. *Friction: An Ethnography of Global Connection*. Princeton: Princeton University Press.

Vertommen, S. 2016. 'From the Pergonal project to Kadimastem: A genealogy of Israel's reproductive-industrial complex'. *BioSocieties* 12(2): 282–306.

Vora, K. 2019. 'After the housewife: Surrogacy, labour and human reproduction'. *Radical Philosophy* 2(4).

Wallace, R., A. Liebman, L. F. Chaves and R. Wallace. 2020. 'COVID-19 and circuits of capital'. *Monthly Review*, https://monthlyreview.org/2020/05/01/covid-19-and-circuits-of-capital/

Yeates, N. 2014. 'Global care chains: Bringing in transnational reproductive labourer households'. In W. A. Dunaway (ed.), *Gendered Commodity Chains: Seeing Women's Work and Households in Global Production*, pp. 175–89. Stanford: Stanford University Press.

Žižek, S. 2014. 'First as tragedy, then as farce', https://www.youtube.com/watch?v=hpAMbpQ8J7g

# Chapter Two

# INTO THE FIELD WITH MARX

## SOME OBSERVATIONS ON RESEARCHING CLASS

### Henry Bernstein

**Abstract**

The way in which this chapter attempts to bring 'Marx in the Field' is through the exploration of how some key questions, central to all empirical research, can be addressed in ways informed by Marxian categories, methods and approaches. These key questions are what do we want to know? Why? How can we find out? In engaging with these questions, the chapter will address the tasks of 'problematisation' and the purpose of empirical investigation, that is, to generate new knowledge (versus 'verification'). In this process there are necessary protocols of what constitutes empirical evidence and assessing the quality/validity of evidence. Research inspired by Marx's ideas has to be disciplined by such protocols. The chapter will also explore the particular challenges posed by Marx's notion of what is 'visible' (observable, hence empirically researchable) and what is necessarily 'invisible' in capitalism (e.g. surplus value – or value more generally) – issues of essence and appearance. Notably, 'appearance' is no less 'real' than essence, and they are fundamentally connected as in Marx's conception of commodity fetishism; still their distinction should be acknowledged in empirical investigations. Finally, the chapter will conclude with observations on researching class, which is to say the ensembles of objective and subjective conditions encapsulated (and differentiated) as class (1) relations, (2) dynamics, (3) experiences, (4) beliefs and (5) practices. This follows Balibar's thesis that in a capitalist world, class relations are 'one determining structure, covering all social practices, without being the only one'.

## Introduction

There is no royal road to science, and only those who do not dread the fatiguing climb of its steep paths have a chance of gaining its luminous summits. (Marx 1976: 104)
Where things and their mutual relations are conceived not as fixed but rather as changing, their mental images, too, i.e. concepts, are also subject to change and reformulation; that they are not be encapsulated in rigid definitions, but rather developed in their process of historical or logical formation. (Engels, 'Preface' to Capital, Volume III, in Marx [1894] 1981: 103)
[For Marx] The concrete results of an investigation could not be predicted with a set of abstractions [...] The concrete study of reality always remains; the result is not given from the beginning. But a guide is needed. (Liedman 2018: 363, 376)

There are many ways to bring 'Marx in the Field', which is the scope of this volume. Here, I take 'in the field' to mean *empirical* investigation of social realities that will produce new knowledge of them, typically conducted today within university-based social science.[1] The design of empirical research is structured by three basic questions: (1) what do I want to find out? (2) why does it matter? and (3) how shall I find out? The first is the terrain of research questions, the second that of the motivation of research and the third that of research methods. There is also a fourth question: what are the uses of findings? Or at least researchers' hopes for their uses? This is informed by the first and second questions and should be disciplined by answers to the third.

This essay offers some brief observations on these questions but is not written directly from experiences of doing empirical fieldwork and its intellectual processes, which give other contributions to this timely collection their particular utility.

## What Do I Want to Find Out? Research Questions and Their Analytical Frameworks

Research questions are chosen for all kinds of reasons: intellectual, biographical, political, pragmatic and so on. Here I focus on drawing on Marx for inspiration in devising research questions and shaping analytical frameworks for investigating them. This throws up many issues, several of which I touch on.

For those who aspire to go in the field with Marx, this first question presents all the challenges in 'operationalising' his ideas, concepts and categories, otherwise provoked by his work and/or subsequent positions and debates, notably in recent times in academic social science. We all know that Marx's work can be extremely complex, was unfinished according to its own plan and subject to various tensions.[2] The coherence, validity and utility of Marx's

---

[1]  Moreover, empirical investigation of social realities in today's worlds of capitalism rather than historical research which is rich in instructive debates, including of theory and method. For a good exercise in historiography in this respect, see Suny (2017), and for remarkable syntheses of Marxist theoretical interpretation and historical debates, see Banaji (2010), on which see my review essay (Bernstein 2013b). I draw here on some parts of a previous article (Bernstein 2013a).

[2]  Only a small proportion of what Marx wrote was published during his life with his approval; the texts edited by others, not least Engels (*Capital, Volumes II* and *III*), are subject to major controversies in their posthumously published versions and their interpretations; the authoritative German edition of Marx and Engels's *Collected Works* is yet to be finished, if nearing completion. Further, Marx's writing was focused and inflected by the political conjunctures, struggles, advances and defeats that marked his time and the conclusions, explicit and implicit, he drew from them (Balibar 2014, among others). In a similar vein, Michael Burawoy (2011) suggests that 'optimism of the will' was the response of the young Gramsci to the Russian revolution and then the Turin factory occupations of 1919–20, while 'pessimism of the intellect' is the dominant register of his analyses of the conditions and prospects of socialist revolution in Western Europe, in the notebooks written in a fascist prison during the last period of his life (1926–37). This, I trust, does not suggest an ageist determinism. Rather, the differences between the younger and older Gramsci, as between different moments of Marx's life, are explicable by the political conjunctures which shaped their intellectual preoccupations: the what, why and how of their studies and analyses.

analyses, and of the legacies they have generated, remain massively contested, as much (or more?) by those who claim their inspiration than by those who reject them.

Most scholars who aspire to use Marx's work recognise that the forms of capitalism today are far more diverse than those presented in *Capital*; that is to say, forms of production and reproduction, hence of social relations, practices and beliefs within the worlds of contemporary capitalism shaped by class, gender, ethnicity and other differences, divisions and dynamics – which bring with them the challenges of what produces, connects and explains such diversity. In part this is due to the incompleteness, tensions and lacunae of Marx's great work, just noted, and also because of the 150 years plus of accelerated uneven and contradictory development of world capitalism since *Volume I* of *Capital* was published, even if we consider it an indispensable 'guide' (above) or 'guiding thread' (Sayer 1987) in investigating the worlds of capitalism.[3]

Exegesis and interpretation of *Capital*, not least in philosophical and theoretical debate of its method, remains a major industry. Sometimes overlooked in the heat of intense differences about Marx's epistemology (theory and method), and worth emphasis, is that his analyses incorporated massive amounts of empirical material, both historical and contemporary. This is evident, for example, in Chapters 10 and 15, and Part 8, of *Capital, Volume I* as well as in his writings on politics in France and elsewhere.[4]

Nonetheless, while investigation of empirical realities was so central to Marx's work, he 'was not an empiricist, as the term is usually understood, in that he did not reduce the real to the sensibly perceptible' (Sayer 1983: 186, note 26). Sayer's interrogation of *Capital* (1983, 1987) grasps the nettle of Marx's efforts to establish 'the real' through combining the 'invisible' and the 'visible' (the 'sensibly perceptible'). In the case of the capitalist mode of production, the 'invisible' is characterised as the 'essential relations' – for example, those of value, surplus value, abstract labour, the object of the most abstract chapters of *Capital* – which provide the 'conditions of existence' of the 'visible': their 'phenomenal forms' like the divisions of capitalist revenue (profit, interest, rent; Sayer 1983: chapter 3), social divisions of labour and indeed social classes. Of course, most

---

[3] It is sometimes remarked that mid-Victorian Britain had more domestic workers ('servants') than factory workers. In terms of today's concerns the most striking lacunae in *Capital* concern gender relations and ecology, both of which can affect how the 'law of value' itself is theorised. The centrality of gender relations to framing questions of social reproduction has been established by Marxist feminists; see, for example, the recent collection edited by Bhattacharya (2017). There is also a number of recent works arguing, in different ways, that the basis of a materialist ecology can be uncovered in, or adapted from, the work of Marx and Engels – among others Burkett (1999), Foster (2000), Moore (2015), Saito (2017).

[4] On France: 'The class struggles in France: 1848 to 1850' (written in 1850), 'The eighteenth Brumaire of Louis Bonaparte' (written in 1852), both in Marx (1973b), and 'The civil war in France' (written in 1871) in Marx (1974). While Marx did massive empirical research, it was not 'fieldwork' in the sense of primary empirical investigation, data collection and so on. The work of classic Marxism that approximates this sense of 'fieldwork' most closely was Engels ([1845] 1993) which added much personal observation of Manchester and Salford to the data he assembled from various official reports and other 'secondary sources'.

of *Capital* was concerned with exploring theoretically and illustrating empirically the mechanisms and moments of capital's 'laws of motion' and with critique of the 'bourgeois' political economy of the eighteenth and nineteenth centuries.

At the same time Sayer (1983: 11) rightly argued that Marx's 'derivation of essential relations' is itself empirically, which is to say historically, specific. The relation between 'invisible' and 'visible', essential and phenomenal, in *Capital* does not manifest a metaphysical position in which the latter term of each pair is simply the (more or less adequate) 'expression' of the former term. Phenomena are not 'expressions' of the essential 'hence their production must be explained', and the 'essential' does 'not exist independently' of its phenomenal forms (Gibbon and Neocosmos 1985: 168). Indeed, the 'sensibly perceptible' has its own fundamental reality in how capitalist social relations are *experienced* by those who live them, as presented in Marx's remarkable theorisation of 'the fetishism of the commodity' (Marx 1976: 163–77).[5]

As such extremely brief observations indicate, it can only be the 'visible' elements of Marx's constitution of capitalist reality (or realities) that are amenable to empirical investigation although, of course, how his theorisations of the 'invisible' (or 'essential') are grasped has critical effects for researching the empirically unknown.[6] One example is Marx's distinction between forms of the subsumption of labour by capital that produce 'absolute' and 'relative' surplus value, which can be investigated empirically through types of labour regimes in different branches of production (Marx 1976: appendix).[7]

---

[5]  The 'invisible'/'visible' distinction connects with, but it not identical to, familiar distinctions between 'content' and 'form' in social relations and practices, in which 'form' is not a simple 'expression' of content. The specificity of forms and their determinate effects likewise have to be investigated and explained. There are other senses of the 'invisible'/'visible' familiar in social science – for example, the investigation of social relations and dynamics that have been ignored (rendered 'invisible') in empirical research, both historical and contemporary, not least those centred on gender. Silvia Federici's novel reinterpretation of the transition from feudalism to capitalism (2004), centred on the remaking of gender relations, is an outstanding contribution to a project to make visible what had been 'invisible'. A different kind of example is James Scott's 'everyday forms of resistance' by oppressed groups, the ostensible efficacy of which rests on them remaining 'hidden' (Scott 1985). A third kind of example comes from notions of 'disguised wage labour' in studies of the economic sociology of capitalism, not least in connection with labour regimes where 'wage labour' in any formal or narrow sense is absent. This has been long debated in relation to petty commodity production subsumed by capital, but today has an additional political charge in the widespread ideological and legal fictions deployed on behalf of labour contracting, the 'gig economy', etc.

[6]  See Sayer's 'note on testing' (1983: 135–41). His case for an 'empirical Marx' continued through discussions of such central terms of the Marxist lexicon as 'productive forces', 'relations of production' and 'base/superstructure' (Sayer 1987) which he proposed should be deployed in an 'open-ended' manner amenable to empirical research (1983: 165–66).

[7]  'Results of the immediate process of production' was available for the first time in English as an appendix in Ben Fowkes's new translation of *Capital, Volume I*. Its previous publication history and significance is outlined in Ernest Mandel's 'Introduction' to it (Marx 1976: 943–47). A pioneering and provocative application of Marx's formal subsumption was Jairus Banaji's essay on the Deccan peasantry in the late nineteenth century (Banaji [1977] 2010: chapter 10).

A second kind of issue is that any field research inspired by Marx necessarily concerns parts of a larger whole, in both an analytical sense and a concrete/historical sense.[8] The former refers to Marx's theoretical analysis of the capitalist mode of production as a totality, moreover one with systemic qualities. The concrete/historical sense refers to the phases and mutations of capitalism on a world scale and the times and places it encompasses in all the definitive unevenness of its development. Thus, any field research *selects* particular concepts and categories, and their attendant issues, from the theory of the capitalist mode of production as a totality. At the same time, any field research must *locate* its object in a particular time and place within the histories of capitalism on a world scale. This does not assume, however, that world capitalism at any given moment determines any and every particular site and object of research within it in any direct, necessary and complete manner. Rather the nature and degree of such determination(s) are themselves an important matter of investigation.[9]

In a study of the maize *filière* (commodity chain) in twentieth-century South Africa I suggested as 'its underlying methodological stance' that

> South Africa necessarily manifests both the essential features, dynamics and contradictions of the capitalist mode of production and the historically specific forms of property, production, power and struggle through which capitalism has developed there. (Bernstein 1996b: 143, note 9)

Of course, this can only be a starting point and remains somewhat formulaic as a statement of intent. As always with an empirical analysis the proof of the pudding is in the eating: the test is how such formulations bear fruit in empirical investigation. The same article also observed that the advantages of a commodity chain approach

> in cutting a particular 'slice' from larger economic organisms to examine under the analytical microscope, may have corresponding disadvantages if we lose sight of the entities from which the 'slice' is extracted, how and where it fits into, and is shaped by, other elements of those entities. (Bernstein 1996a: 128)[10]

---

[8] In the section on 'The method of political economy' in the introduction to the *Grundrisse*, Marx contrasted his method, specifically relations between 'concrete' and 'abstract', with that of prior political economy and its deployment of a 'chaotic conception of the whole' (Marx 1973a: 100).

[9] There are dangers, of course, of 'world system determinism' as I have termed it (Bernstein 1996b: 50), a common effect of which is to downplay the significance of class formation and its effects within social formations. A recent study by Michael Levien (2018) of 'regimes of [land] dispossession' combines with unusual deftness the class dynamics of 'neoliberal India' with a local ethnography, arguing persuasively that 'land grabbing' in India today is not driven by world market forces and agents.

[10] Reiterated in Bernstein and Campling (2006: 444) which illustrates some of the empirical referents of 'commodity studies': 'The challenge, then, is to reinsert the "slices" identified by commodity studies – whether defined by, and to varying degrees combining, particular commodities, regions, forms of capital, corporate organization and strategy, systems of regulation, and so on – in the larger entities from which they are extracted.'

The object of any field research then is always delimited by the location of its object, or the 'slice' it addresses, with decisions that are partly intellectual and partly pragmatic about how much, and which aspects, of the wider totality – the uneven development of capitalism on a world scale – are incorporated in or otherwise inform its research questions. This might be broadly described as an issue of 'range' or scale. Mike Davis (2018: 22) warns that 'as the careful student of Marx eventually discovers, capitalism's "laws of motion" come with a lot of fine print', and refers to 'a middle landscape [...] where "secondary class struggles" over taxes, credit, and money are typically the imme-diate organizers of the political field' (2018: xix), and refers to Marx's 'middle level' concepts in his analyses of class politics in the France of his time (2018: 178). The design (and 'operationalisation') of research utilising Marx's concepts and categories always entails choices about scale in this sense, including different types of likely determinations and mediations, as Davis indicates.

A final issue here concerns possible problems of anachronism. While much can be inspired by Marx to identify research questions and analytical approaches to the study of capitalism today, it can also be misleading to extract particular passages from *Capital*, especially those that are framed empirically, as a 'model' to explore contemporary real-ities some 150 years later. On one hand, it can be suggested that few forms of labour regimes and exploitation have disappeared in capitalism since Marx's time. On the other hand, older forms are typically reconstructed and articulated in different ways with new forms of capital, and of its circuits of accumulation and reproduction (not least today of finance capital), in the continuous mutations and diversity of the uneven development of capitalism. Without doubt, some types of production and reproduc-tion – especially the most oppressive forms of 'household' production in 'putting-out' (outsourcing) arrangements – would look familiar to Marx, even across the long stretch of 'accelerated' historical change since his time, but others would not. Hence important research questions concern the conditions of reinvention and reproduction of osten-sibly 'archaic' (in Marx's term) social forms rather than viewing them through a lens of 'persistence'.[11]

## Why Does It Matter?

Much of the reasoning of answers to 'why does it matter?' is subsumed in answers to the first question whether explicitly or implicitly, in relation to existing literatures and

---

[11] Notions of 'persistence' typically evoke the ongoing significance of pre-capitalist relations and practices in the world of capitalism today, not least in studies of and debates about 'peasantry', for example, in the title of Boltvinik and Mann (2016). Some of the issues of changes in cap-italism since Marx's time, and their effects for understanding class relations and dynamics, are presented by Don Kalb (2015) who reflects on the connections, and tensions, between struc-tural determinants (of class 'position') and experiences of class; see also Breman and van der Linden (2014) and further below.

contentions about the specific contexts and processes addressed by research questions (their location in the uneven histories of capitalism, their places and times) and to selection from the corpus of theoretical ideas inspired by Marx (above) and the debates they have triggered. In some cases, the purpose of research may be formulated to contest, modify or elaborate selected ideas of Marx, or can shift a posteriori as a result of its findings, or a combination of both.

Answers to 'why does it matter?', like those to the first question, typically combine the intellectual, biographical, political, pragmatic and so on. However, here the political in a broad sense is further to the fore, explicitly or implicitly. That is because commitment to going into the field with Marx manifests opposition to, and critique of, other approaches 'on offer' in social science and in wider public discourse (including 'official' or quasi-'official' ideologies) that either deny or explain away the savage inequalities and contradictions of capitalism, whether on manifestly reactionary or liberal grounds, for example, in discourses of poverty and of 'mainstream' development studies which links so closely to them.[12]

## How Do I Find Out? Research Methods

My own position, simply stated, is that – unlike answers to the first and second questions – there are no methods of field research peculiar to Marx and that rules of evidence are necessary for any social science:

(1) while such rules can (and should) not emulate those claimed for the natural sciences, they must be as rigorous as possible in terms of reasoning and logic, deduction and inference and so on;[13]

(2) what constitutes 'evidence' in the social sciences rejects any fetishism of statistical and mathematical 'proofs', and their intrinsic superiority, and can encompass a wide range of materials;[14]

---

[12] There is an important political value in research that contests the empirical support claimed by ideologies like the quasi-'official' discourses of poverty and 'development' of the World Bank ('win win' within capitalism), and does so with or without the inspiration of Marx. A very different and potent recent example is Shlomo Sand (2009) who interrogates the biblical, historical and archaeological claims to 'the Land of Israel' central to Zionism, a quite recent (and originally secular) ethnonationalism.

[13] Thus free of any currently fashionable 'methodological nihilism' in the term of Andreas Malm's restatement of the philosophical realism of historical materialism applied to climate change *and* the social relations that produce it (2018: 122).

[14] Including on the 'subjective' side the creative analysis of novels and popular media and of dreams, for example, in the pioneering monographs of Pun Ngai (2005) and Yan Hairong (2008). Rejecting any fetishism of quantitative 'proofs' does not mean, of course, that statistical and mathematical methods cannot, and should not, be used in research inspired by Marx, exemplified, for example, in the work of Anwar Shaikh (2016).

(3) evidence in the social sciences can lead to analytically superior or inferior results, and in practice always leave space for interpretation and debate – social science research seldom generates conclusive evidence;

(4) there is a constant challenge to grasp the complex connections between material structures and relations (the 'objective') and how they are viewed and acted on by those who experience them (the 'subjective') – what connects the two is the notion of social practices.[15]

In short, just as research questions highlight that research should tell us something we didn't know before, that is, generate new knowledge of social existence, practice and struggle, likewise new knowledge, in part, depends on the quality of evidence used to investigate the research questions and to 'problematise' and test the theoretical framework used and its applications (if not 'testing' hypotheses in the narrow sense used in conventional Economics, for example). Empirical fact finding undertaken to demonstrate ('prove') a pre-given (political) stance – what I term 'verificationism', characteristic of most 'agit prop' literature – is not research in the sense used here and throughout this collection.

At the same time, thorny issues of method cannot be reduced to choice of 'technique' understood as the most 'efficient' ways of collecting particular kinds of data. All social science research is imbued with 'values' in the term associated with Max Weber or, to put it differently, inevitably infused with ideology and its contestations, in particular historical conditions. Weber's solution to this problem was to keep as separate as possible 'Politics as a Vocation' and 'Science as a Vocation' (the titles of lectures given near the end of his life, Weber 1948a, 1948b). Whatever the values that inevitably inform the choice of topic (the 'what?' and 'why?'), the investigation of its research questions (the 'how?') has to be disciplined by a commitment to method that is independent of the particular (political) values that motivate and frame the research. Weber was not endorsing a model of positivism, transposed (ostensibly) from natural science method, but emphasising the importance of agreed rules of evidence, as rigorous as possible, to distinguish social science knowledge from other expressions of 'values' or ideology ubiquitous in social life.[16]

This is important because some critiques of positivism would deny any validity of rules of evidence, hence the possibility of assessing opposing empirical claims and thus,

---

[15] As suggested in the epigrammatic formulations of Marx's 'Theses on Feuerbach' (1969) linking ontology, epistemology and politics. The 'Theses' proposed that producing knowledge of the worlds we inhabit – itself a practice or set of practices – involves investigating, through engaging with, the practices of social life and the social relations that generate them, in order to change/transcend those relations and practices. The 'Theses on Feuerbach' were written in 1845 and first published only in 1888 (after Marx's death); the original text was recovered still later in 1924.

[16] The tension is registered, with a certain poignancy, by Sand (2018: 197): 'I wander, and stray between, on one hand, analyses intended to confer a reasonable level of neutrality, free of value judgements, and, on the other hand, a strong incitement to participate, despite everything, in seeking rational and humanist alternatives to contradictions that currently have no solution, whether in terms of the capitalist economy or the question of planetary ecology.'

in effect, the possibility of any objective knowledge of social reality (Malm's 'methodological nihilism' in its various forms). In this sense, such philosophically radical positions abolish the 'how?' question of (empirical) research, often taking as their point of departure (and arrival!) the perceptions and values, identities, beliefs and 'imaginaries' (themselves often 'hidden') of the oppressed, 'subalterns', or whoever it claims to speak to or for.

## What Are the Uses of Findings?

There is no single answer to this question, almost by definition, although answers to it are likely to be empirical too. Perhaps it is easier to ask about researchers' hopes for the uses of their findings, which may fail to meet their expectations, of course. The bare fact is that most of what emerges from going into the field with Marx is destined to be read by other university-based social scientists, even though some researchers use their findings to contribute to anti-capitalist movements in various ways.

As already indicated, researchers who take to the field with Marx are making an intellectual, and typically political, commitment that helps shape their hopes for what the new knowledge they produce will reveal about the worlds of capitalism today. That is, they are not only anti-capitalist, a very loose designation to be sure, but believe that knowledge and use of Marx informs and enhances the intellectual basis of an effective anti-capitalist stance.

Much more could be raised here, for example, the long and conflicted histories of the places of intellectuals in socialist and communist parties and movements, but I move on to a final section that attempts to bring together some of the issues raised so far.[17]

## Researching Class

Social class and its contradictions in capitalism – above all that between capital and wage labour – is at the core of Marx's work and so it should remain for those who seek to follow him. That is my view while acknowledging the complexities of class relations, dynamics, beliefs and practices in capitalism today, compounded, as noted earlier, by the diversity of forms of production and reproduction, hence of social relations, practices and beliefs shaped by gender, ethnicity and other differences, divisions and dynamics as well as those of class.

So, some preliminary observations (or assertions). First, as Etienne Balibar put it: in a capitalist world, class relations are '*one determining* structure, covering *all* social practices, without being the *only* one' (as quoted by Therborn 2007: 88, emphases in original).

---

[17] One can note briefly, as further complications, the intellectual respect accorded to Marx by some eminent social scientists without any connection to left politics, like Claude Lévi-Strauss and Emmanuel Le Roy Ladurie; the important contributions that continue to be made by former Marxists like Maurice Godelier and Shlomo Sand; and more generally, as indicated by Alessandra Mezzadri in her introduction to this collection, work by non-Marxist researchers and theorists that may contribute to enriching the means of intellectual production available to those inspired by Marx.

In sum, class relations are *universal but not exclusive* determinations of social relations and practices in capitalism. They combine with other social differences and divisions of which gender is the most widespread and which can also include oppressive and exclusionary relations of race and ethnicity, religion and caste – all of which demand serious research.[18] At the same time, in Marx's framework these complex combinations of social relations are not adequately conceptualised in an additive manner as 'class plus' or 'gender plus' or 'race plus' and the like, as in current conceptions of 'intersectionality'.[19]

Second, what I term the 'economic sociology' (Bernstein 2010) of class in today's globalised capitalism and its (increasingly) uneven development is marked by a series of complexities concerning, on different scales, forms of production and labour regimes, social divisions of labour, labour migration, rural–urban divisions and connections, organisational forms of capital and markets, state policies and practices and their effects.[20]

Third, as a result of problematising widespread notions of 'small' or 'family' farmers or 'peasants', I suggested that many, perhaps most, of those so designated in capitalism today belong to classes of labour, in that they have to reproduce themselves in large part through wage labour.[21] They are extremely heterogeneous in their composition and characteristics, not least because of the immensely varied ways in which very different

---

[18] See, for example, Jens Lerche and Alpa Shah's use of Philippe Bourgois's conception of 'conjugated oppression' to conceptualise combined relations of tribe, caste and class in India (Lerche and Shah 2018; Bourgois 1988) and their reflections on the politics marked by 'conjugated oppression' (Shah and Lerche 2018). Bourgois's study of a banana plantation in Central America shows key differences between the ways its Amerindian workers were able (Kuna) or unable (Guaymi) to act on the ethnic hierarchy of its labour regime.

[19] On this see the sympathetic and precise critique by McNally (2017). Gender and race relations and their social differences and divisions are not necessarily explicable by 'the interests of capital'. The same applies to generation, on which see the illuminating introduction to rural social relations by Ben White (2020). Note too that there is an important difference between thinking that whatever exists in the world of capitalism does so because it serves the 'interests of capital' (a functionalist explanation), and exploring how what exists is produced as effects of the contradictory dynamics of capitalist social relations. Those contradictory dynamics include the *unintended consequences* of, on one hand, particular paths of accumulation and strategies of political rule by capital and, on the other hand, the pursuit of reproduction by classes of labour (later in this chapter) and their challenges to the rule of capital.

[20] This observation touches on that central and problematic tendency of 'classic' Marxism to identify 'the' working class primarily as the full-time (and mostly male) industrial proletariat. A major reconsideration of this inheritance is provided by Marcel van der Linden (2008), among others; see also notes 11 above and 21 following.

[21] In effect an empirical generalisation that prompted theoretical rethinking. I have come to prefer the term 'classes of labour' to the inherited vocabulary of proletarianisation/proletariat (and semi-proletarianisation/semi-proletariat), as it is less encumbered with problematic assumptions and associations in both political economy (e.g. functionalist readings of Marx's concept of the reserve army of labour) and political theory and ideology (e.g. constructions of an idealised [Hegelian] collective class subject). For further development of the notion of 'classes of labour' through empirical research, see Pattenden (2016).

types of 'self-employment' and wage employment can be combined and thus are structurally fragmented. To paraphrase Lenin (1964: 34), 'infinitely diverse combinations of elements of this or that type of labour are possible' – and, one can add, types of reproduction of labour.

Fourth, this means that identifying and characterising class positions confronts great fluidity in the forms and combinations of social relations and is not satisfied by a desire to find the correct 'label' (which blights some class analysis claiming the inspiration of Marx). Rather those forms and combinations are 'subject to change and reformulation' (Engels in Marx 1981: 103). This is especially apt today as globally 'informal' workers are rapidly growing in relative terms while 'formal' workers, more closely approximating inherited notions of proletarians, are perhaps declining absolutely, generating 'radically changed conditions of contemporary class conflict' (Davis 2018: 21; see also Davis 2006 and note 11 above).

Finally, this suggests to me that an initial methodological step in researching class is to identify class *dynamics*, that is, resulting from those 'laws of motion' operating in the various spaces of capitalism with all their concrete diversity (the 'fine print' in Davis's term, above). Only then do the research questions follow: whether, in what ways and to what extent such dynamics are manifested in class identities, practices and struggles. An example from my own area of interest is Lenin's analysis of the class differentiation of the peasantry in late nineteenth-century Russia (Lenin [1899] 1964: chapter 2). Its mistakes 'included the methodological: the use of surveys at single points in time to deduce trends' and 'the empirical: exaggerating the extent of differentiation' (Bernstein 2018: 1131).[22] At the same time, Lenin's analysis illuminated 'a tendency of differentiation that can be identified from the contradictory unity of class places in petty commodity production' (Bernstein 2010: 109), that is, a class dynamic that can be applied and tested in other contexts without assuming that 'it will be evident in identical *trends*, mechanisms, rhythms or forms of class differentiation everywhere' (ibid.).

A third mistake of Lenin's original analysis and 'perhaps of greatest import' was 'the political: deriving the expectation of "class struggle in the village" from a socioeconomic analysis of peasant class formation (itself flawed)' (Bernstein 2018: 1131). This points towards the passage from 'the economic sociology' of class to its 'political sociology' (Bernstein 2010) which involves a series of further factors and determinations that affect political agency.

In making this move, it is important to emphasise that the economic and social power of capital, rooted in a system of property and commodity relations, has to be secured through its political and ideological rule, exercised – again universally but not exclusively – through the state. We should not assume that the rule of capital works through any simple unity and instrumentality of purpose, nor that it is necessarily coherent in how it seeks to justify itself ideologically as a moral order or in its political strategies and

---

[22] Even so Lenin, together with Plekhanov, 'provided valuable evidence about peasant indebtedness, rents and tax rates' and 'the economic pressures underlying peasant (wage) labour in agriculture and industry' in the Russia of their time (Kingston-Mann 1991: 10–11).

practices. There are no guarantees of unity, coherence and effectiveness in how capital perceives, anticipates, assesses, confronts and tries to contain the social contradictions of capitalism in order both to pursue profit and accumulation and to secure legitimacy for, or at least acquiescence in, how it does so.

Concerning classes of labour, a central issue is indicated by Mahmood Mamdani's observation that the 'translation' of 'social facts' into 'political facts' is always contingent and unpredictable.[23] This is especially so because of 'the many ways in which power fragment[s] the *circumstances* and *experiences* of the oppressed' (Mamdani 1996: 219, 272, emphasis added). The great variation in *circumstances* can be investigated, in part, by research of the complexities of the economic sociology of class.[24] For the political sociology of class, a crucial next step is how those circumstances are *experienced*, as Mamdani suggests. Existentially, they are not experienced (self-)evidently and exclusively as class exploitation and oppression *in general* but in terms of specific identities like 'urban/rural dwellers, industrial workers/agricultural labourers, urban craftsmen and women peasants, men/women, mental/manual labour, young/old, black/white, regional, national and ethnic differences, and so on', in the list of examples given by Peter Gibbon and Michael Neocosmos (1985: 190).[25]

To conclude: Barbara Harriss-White and Nandini Gooptu (2000: 89) restate a central issue of the political complexities of class thus – that 'struggle over class' precedes and is a condition of 'struggle between classes'. In 'mapping India's world of unorganized labour', they explore how struggles 'over class' by the working poor are inflected, and restricted, by gender, caste, religious and other social differences and divisions. They suggest that the overwhelming majority of Indian classes of labour 'is still engaged in the first struggle' (Harriss-White and Gooptu 2000: 89) over class, while Indian classes of capital are engaged in the second struggle through their offensives against classes of labour – an argument that can be tested elsewhere, of course.

---

[23] In his remarkable reconstruction of the history of the United Farm Workers in California, Frank Bardacke (2011: 239) refers to 'the improbable chains of causality that constituted the politics of the time' – and most times? He further observes (ibid.: 331) that 'Historical thinking – considerations of the whys and wherefores of the past – tends to mask the uncertainties and anxieties of human action.'

[24] As Davis remarks: 'the principal problem with most Marxist analyses of nationalism – or, for that matter, of politics in general – has *not* been a refusal to acknowledge the autonomy of the discursive, the cultural, or the ethnic but rather the failure to map comprehensively the entire field of property relations and their derivative conflicts. Although it is heresy to say so, we need *more* economic interpretation, not less' (2018: 178, emphases in original). His book contains a sweeping periodisation of class struggle and its principal dimensions, primarily in the North, from 1838 to 1921, which concludes rather abruptly (2018: 26–154).

[25] It is common, of course, for particular capitals to seize on relational differences/divisions – of gender, of generation, of place (town and countryside) and of ethnicity and nationality – in how they recruit labour and organise it in production and in how they deal with resistance from classes of labour.

## References

Balibar, E. 2014. *The Philosophy of Marx* (reprint edition). London: Verso.

Banaji, J. 2010. *Theory as History. Essays on Modes of Production and Exploitation.* London: Verso.

Bardacke, F. 2011. *Trampling Out the Vintage. Cesar Chavez and the Two Souls of the United Farm Workers.* London: Verso.

Bernstein, H. 1996a. 'The political economy of the maize *filière*'. In H. Bernstein (ed.), *The Agrarian Question in South Africa*, pp. 120–45. London: Frank Cass.

———. 1996b. 'Agrarian questions then and now'. In H. Bernstein and T. Brass (eds), *Agrarian Questions*, pp. 22–59. London: Frank Cass.

———. 2010. *Class Dynamics of Agrarian Change.* Halifax, Nova Scotia: Fernwood.

———. 2013a. 'Doing committed social research: What are the dangers?' *China Journal of Social Work* 6(1): 69–81.

———. 2013b. 'Historical materialism and agrarian history'. *Journal of Agrarian Change* 13(2): 310–29.

———. 2018. 'The "peasant problem" in the Russian revolution(s), 1905–1929'. *Journal of Peasant Studies* 45(5–6): 1127–50.

Bernstein, H. and L. Campling. 2006. 'Commodity studies and commodity fetishism II: Profits with principles?' *Journal of Agrarian Change* 6(3): 414–47.

Bhattacharya, T. (ed.). 2017. *Social Reproduction Theory. Remapping Class, Recentering Oppression.* London: Pluto Press.

Boltvinik, J. and S. A. Mann (eds). 2016. *Poverty and Persistence of the Peasantry in the Twenty-First Century.* London: Zed Books.

Bourgois, P. 1988. 'Conjugated oppression: Class and ethnicity among Guaymi and Kuna banana workers'. *American Ethnologist* 15(2): 328–48.

Breman, J. and M. van der Linden. 2014. 'Informalizing the economy: The return of the social question at a global level'. *Development and Change* 45(5): 920–40.

Burawoy, M. 2010. 'From Polanyi to Pollyanna: The false optimism of global labor studies'. *Global Labour Journal* 1(2): 301–13.

Burawoy, M. 2011. 'On uncompromising pessimism: Response to my critics', *Global Labour Journal* 2(1): 73–77.

Burkett, P. 1999. *Marx and Nature. A Red and Green Perspective.* New York: St Martin's Press.

Davis, M. 2006. *Planet of Slums.* London: Verso.

———. 2018. *Old Gods, New Enigmas. Marx's Lost Theory.* London: Verso.

Engels, F. 1993. *The Condition of the Working Class in England.* Oxford: Oxford University Press.

Federici, S. 2004. *Caliban and the Witch: Women, the Body and Primitive Accumulation.* New York: Autonomedia.

Foster, J. Bellamy. 2000. *Marx's Ecology: Materialism and Nature.* New York: Monthly Review Press.

Gibbon, P. and M. Neocosmos. 1985. 'Some problems in the political economy of "African socialism"'. In H. Bernstein and B. K. Campbell (eds), *Contradictions of Accumulation in Africa: Studies in Economy and State*, 153–206. Beverly Hills: Sage.

Harriss-White, B. and N. Gooptu. 2000. 'Mapping India's world of unorganized labour'. In L. Panitch and C. Leys (eds), *The Socialist Register 2001*, pp. 89–118. London: Merlin Press.

Kalb, D. 2015. 'Introduction: Class and the new anthropological holism'. In J. Carrier and D. Kalb (eds), *Anthropologies of Class: Power, Practice and Inequality*, pp. 1–27. Cambridge: Cambridge University Press.

Kingston-Mann, E. 1991. 'Peasant communes and economic innovation: A preliminary inquiry'. In E. Kingston-Mann and T. Mixter (eds), *Peasant Economy, Culture, and Politics of European Russia, 1800–1921*, pp. 23–51. Princeton: Princeton University Press.

Lenin, V. I. [1899] 1964. 'Collected Works', Volume 3: *The Development of Capitalism in Russia. The Process of the Formation of a Hoe Market for Large-Scale Industry.* Moscow: Progress.

Lerche, J. and A. Shah. 2018. 'Tribe, caste and class – New mechanisms of exploitation and oppression'. In A. Shah, J. Lerche, R. Axelby, D. Benbabaali, B. Donegan, J. Raj and V. Thakur (eds), *Ground Down by Growth. Tribe, Cate, Class and Inequality in Twenty-First-Century India*, pp. 1–31. London: Pluto Press.

Levien, M. 2018. *Dispossession without Development. Land Grabs in Neoliberal India*. Oxford: Oxford University Press.

Liedman, S.-E. 2018. *A World to Win. The Life and Works of Karl Marx*. London: Verso.

Malm, A. 2018. *The Progress of This Storm. Nature and Society in a Warming World*. London: Verso.

Mamdani, M. 1996. *Citizen and Subject. Contemporary Africa and the Legacy of Late Colonialism*. Cape Town: David Philip.

Marx, K. 1969. 'Theses on Feuerbach'. In K. Marx and F. Engels (eds), *Selected Works, Volume 1*. Moscow: Progress.

———. 1973a. *Grundrisse*. Harmondsworth: Penguin.

———. 1973b. *Political Writings, Volume 2. Surveys from Exile*. Harmondsworth: Penguin.

———. 1974. *Political Writings, Volume 3. The First International and After*. Harmondsworth: Penguin.

———. 1976. *Capital, Volume I*. Harmondsworth: Penguin.

———. 1981. *Capital, Volume III*. Harmondsworth: Penguin.

McNally, D. 2017. 'Intersections and dialectics: Critical reconstructions in social reproduction theory'. In T. Bhattacharya (ed.), *Social Reproduction Theory*, pp. 94–111. London: Pluto Press.

Moore, J. W. 2015. *Capitalism in the Web of Life. Ecology and the Accumulation of Capital*. London: Verso.

Pattenden, J. 2016. *Labour, State and Society in Rural India: A Class-Relational Approach*. Manchester: University of Manchester Press.

Pun, N. 2005. *Made in China: Women Factory Workers in a Global Workplace*. Durham: Duke University Press.

Saito, K. 2017. *Karl Marx's Ecosocialism. Capital, Nature, and the Unfinished Critique of Political Economy*. New York: Monthly Review Press.

Sand, S. 2009. *The Invention of the Jewish People*. London: Verso.

———. 2018. *The End of the French Intellectual. From Zola to Houellebecq*. London: Verso.

Sayer, D. 1983. *Marx's Method. Ideology, Science and Critique in 'Capital'*, 2nd edn. Brighton: Harvester Press.

———. 1987. *The Violence of Abstraction. The Analytic Foundations of Historical Materialism*. Oxford: Basil Blackwell.

Scott, J. C. 1985. *Weapons of the Weak*. New Haven, CT: Yale University Press.

Shah, A. and J. Lerche. 2018. 'The struggles ahead'. In A. Shah, J. Lerche, R. Axelby, D. Benbabaali, B. Donegan, J. Raj and V. Thakur (eds), *Ground Down by Growth. Tribe, Cate, Class and Inequality in Twenty-First-Century India*, pp. 203–15. London: Pluto Press.

Shaikh, A. 2016. *Capitalism: Competition, Conflict, Crises*. Oxford: Oxford University Press.

Suny, R. G. 2017. *Red Flag Unfurled. History, Historians and the Russian Revolution*. London: Verso.

Therborn, G. 2007. 'After dialectics. Radical social theory in a post-communist world'. *New Left Review* 43: 63–114.

van der Linden, M. 2008. *Workers of the World. Essays toward a Global Labour History*. Leiden: Brill.

Weber, M. 1948a. 'Politics as a vocation'. In H. H. Gerth and C. Wright Mills (eds), *From Max Weber. Essays in Sociology*, pp. 77–128. London: Routledge & Kegan Paul.

———. 1948b. 'Science as a vocation'. In H. H. Gerth and C. Wright Mills (eds), *From Max Weber. Essays in Sociology*, pp. 129–56. London: Routledge & Kegan Paul.

White, B. 2020. *Agriculture and the Generation Problem*. Halifax: Fernwood.

Yan, H. 2008. *New Masters, New Servants. Migration, Development, and Women Workers in China*. Durham: Duke University Press.

# Chapter Three

# MARX'S MERCHANTS' CAPITAL

## RESEARCHING AGRARIAN MARKETS IN CONTEMPORARY INDIA

### Barbara Harriss-White

## Abstract

After analysing Marx's many insights on merchants' and commercial capital, and on circulation more broadly, this chapter shows how these have crucially shaped debates on Indian capitalism. It outlines the features of existing commercial capitalism in India, and it explores the many methodological challenges of concretely researching 'Marx's merchants' on the ground, effectively suggesting a Marxian research agenda on commercial capitalism for the twenty-first century.

## Introduction

In this market, open auctions are conducted directly from covered platforms, where a small number of bullock carts and a much larger number of tractor trolleys filled with produce from the surrounding villages are lined up by farmers for sale [...] Much is at stake here at this site of transfer, technique, vigilance, manipulation, exploitation and resistance. And yet none of this is easily apparent except to those routinely involved in the making and managing of grain heaps from day-to-day and across marketing seasons. (Mekhala Krishnamurthy describing Harda Mandi in Madhya Pradesh, 2019: 94)

In the midst of an era of monopoly capital and rampant commodification without much by way of brakes lies a set of concepts that are highly relevant to the study of political economy. They call out to be dragged to the centre-stage from the wings, as they never seem to capture quite enough spotlight in the study of development. These are merchants' capital (MC) and commercial capital (CC) (Banaji 2016, 2020; Jan 2017). What did Marx have to say about these concepts, and what is it about them that demands engaging with them in the twenty-first century?

Drawing from decades of field research in India, this chapter outlines questions about theories and research on MC through a Marxian lens. It analyses Marx's engagement with the categories of MC and CC. It reveals the relevance of Marxian analysis for early and more recent debates on Indian capitalism and points to ways they may be developed. Finally, the chapter introduces methodological research challenges associated with conducting fieldwork on MC and CC.

An understanding of Marx's approach to merchants involves exploring spheres of analysis ranging from the micro-scale of the firm through the meso-scale of circuits and processes of capital, to Marx's macro-theory of history. Let us start with the passages in which Marx attempts to grapple with merchants, their features and roles under capitalism. Then we reflect on their relevance for contemporary Indian capitalism and on the methods which can be deployed to investigate merchants and their markets.

## Merchants' Capital and Commercial Capital

### Concepts and theories

In Marxist scholarship, MC has largely been seen in the abstract as capital used for buying and selling (Marx 1887: chapter 5) – the market of mainstream economics – while CC has been usefully understood as the actually existing form (Jan 2017; Sanyal 2007). However, in *Capital, Volume III*, Marx does not start with MC but with CC. In fact, throughout *Volume III*, he uses MC/CC interchangeably. In addition, he invokes a lexicon of synonyms: 'dealers', 'salesman', 'commercial agents', 'buyers', 'sellers', 'traders', 'shopkeepers', 'traffickers', even a 'hybrid form' for the small trader (Jan and Harriss-White 2019). In particular, in *Volume III*, Part IV, chapters 16 and 17, Marx theorises – at the micro and meso level – the necessity and the efficiency of commodity markets for capitalist society. They constitute the essential process of circulation through which value is realised for the sphere of production/industrial capital. The specialist merchant converts the producer's commodity to money – and perhaps this conversion is iterated several times as the commodity passes through a series of what he calls 'productive consumers' who add use value to it at each step – before it reaches the 'private end consumer'. Only at this point of final sale and purchase, does the commodity realise use value. So, in saving the producer from all the interruptions imposed by distribution, the commercial capitalist allows him to deploy a correspondingly greater proportion of his capital productively with less needed for his money reserve. Specialised MC speeds up both the distribution and the creation of surplus value in production because both processes can occur simultaneously. The velocity of consumption acts as the ultimate constraint.

Crucially, in Marx's schema, there is meshing between circulation and production. While CC appears as a distinct form of the social division of labour, in fact it has two theoretical components – money capital used for buying and selling and capital circulated through money advances from traders to producers. Further, if the velocity of payment by merchants to producers is slow, commodity capital from producers will metamorphose into the market.

Further, non-mercantile activity can penetrate circulation. Insisting that the process of circulation by itself – buying and selling – does not create surplus value, Marx then tackles the fact that productive additions of value in the sphere of distribution may take place not simply between firms – as in a classic value chain (Kaplinsky and Morris 2006) – or through subcontracting activity to owners of mills and trucks – but also within a multifunctional commercial firm. Marx conflates stores and transport as components of the constant capital needed in circulation in order to realise value, calling them 'heterogeneous functions' for which a merchant may even have to pay by advancing fixed or circulating capital. They are distinguished from the costs of buying and selling ('accounting, bookkeeping, marketing, correspondence'), from constant capital (costs of offices and materials like paper) and from variable capital (wage labour costs). Marx argues in two ways about these heterogeneous functions. First, he berates a list of bourgeois economists for claiming that transport is productive arguing that, since use values are realised only in consumption, merchants when they transport commodities are appropriating the use value created in production, not creating use value in circulation. Yet, second, he is found repeatedly stressing that such costs are the costs of processes of production subsequent to the first, 'industrial branches'. 'The express company owner, the railway director, and the ship-owner, are not merchants.' Marx's model of MC is the wholesaler, leaving 'entirely out of consideration all possible processes of production which may continue in the process of circulation' (all quotations from chapter 17). As costs of circulation, such processes are part of the total process of reproduction.

## Costs and profits

In chapter 17, Marx is at further pains to signal that the time spent by the commodity in circulation is vital to the production of value and surplus value in the sphere of production itself. Stripping all productive activity meshed with marketing from his model, merchants' profits are not got on a cost-plus basis. They are calculated in relation to general rates of return but must be got, first, by buying below the price of production, thus deducting from the profits of the producer, and, second, by accelerating the pace of turnover.

Though buying and selling in circulation are necessary but do not add value, the merchant's labour costs, since they substitute for the distributive activity that would otherwise have to be performed by the producer, simply substitute for industrial capital. But as the 'act of circulation' lengthens – with the growing size/reach of markets and their increasing organisational complexity – industrial capital forfeits profit to CC which funds the 'secondary operations', centralising their costs and reducing them through scale economies per unit of sale. As CC accumulates, the wage labour it hires does not create surplus value but it does create profit for the merchant who appropriates it in several ways. First, through the underpayment that the merchant made on the first purchase from the producer; second, through the component of unpaid work of the merchant's 'clerks' (their exploitation, although not for surplus value) and third, through the realisation of surplus value in the merchant's sale – which is how the process of reproduction contributes to total capital. It is in this sense that only for the merchant, and not for society or industrial capital, wage labour in a commercial firm is productive. Marx then develops a mathematical proof for this paradox. He concludes that the slower the turnover, the larger the ratio of merchants to productive/industrial capital and the lower the latter's rate of return.

## Role of MC in the development of capitalism

Marx's macro-historical theory of MC, focused on capital used for buying and selling, is grounded along with usurers' or moneylenders' capital in 'antediluvian' capitalist pre-history (Marx 1887, chapter 4). Its application to the transition to capitalism means that it is set at a scale and scope which at first sight has little relevance to contemporary society and is far removed from field research.

Marx can be read as arguing that MC plays a fundamental role in the development of capitalism. But it is a category and a process full of contradictions. First as seen earlier here, it is necessary but by itself unproductive of use value. Second, MC embodies ambivalent progressive and retrogressive roles. On the one hand,

> the development of commerce and merchant capital gives rise everywhere to a tendency towards the production of exchange values, increases its volume, multiplies it, makes it cosmopolitan and develops money into world money. Commerce therefore has a more or less dissolving influence on the producing organisation which it finds at hand, and whose different forms are mainly carried on with a view to use value. (Marx 1894: chapter 20)

Another progressive aspect of the role of MC is to enable the concentration of capital to be invested in production. This is a process 'logically' prior to the development of capitalist production; investment capital is necessary for plant, raw material and wages, before production is able to happen.[1]

On the other hand, MC cannot evade having a retrogressive role because – as Lenin, writing later about the development of capitalism in Russia, explained (1899) – it is unable to avoid being dependent on pre-capitalist labour processes to generate the production it devours. Furthermore, insofar as MC reinvests resources got from buying cheap and selling dear into markets and speculation, it clearly does not reinvest in expanding production. 'The independent development of merchants' capital is inversely proportional to the degree of development of capitalist production' (Marx 1894: chapter 20). It is productive investment rather than MC which revolutionises capital. MC is but an obstacle to the 'real capitalist mode of production' (ibid.).

So, the way Marx argues about the balance of contradictory effects is to privilege production relations: 'to what extent it (commerce) brings about the dissolution of the old mode of production depends upon its solidity and internal structure, and whither this process of dissolution will lead, in other words what new mode of production will replace the old, does not depend on commerce, but on the character of the old mode itself' (ibid.). Productive industrial capital is also privileged in Marx's historical prediction that the development of capitalism would force MC to be progressively subordinated to the role of a passive 'wing of industrial capital' (ibid.). And, even while subordinating other classes to its interests, MC was and is unable directly to intervene in class formation.

---

[1]   It differs from primitive accumulation, which also entails destroying the connection between labour and land, freeing labour up for wage-work (Perelman 2000; Adnan 2015).

## The Relevance of MC to Contemporary India

Why are Marx's insights important when pure wholesalers are so thin on the ground, when in practical – and accounting – terms it is tantamount to impossible to disentangle the costs of tendrils of productive activity in the process of circulation from profits from buying and selling, and when so very few mercantile corporations suffused with productive activity that is either subcontracted 'in' or internalised show signs of subordination to industrial capital (e.g. Krishnamurthy and Vijayshankar 2012; Jan and Harriss-White 2012)? Despite contradictions in Marx's approach, the processes he describes resonate with concrete realities.

In spite of the specificity of Marx's model of nineteenth-century British capitalism, Marx's concept of MC was influential in India for reasons simultaneously both good and bad. First, Marx's model of MC as unproductive but necessary found resonance in many of the pre- and peri-Independence investigations into wide marketing margins (price differences between commodities at 'farm-gate' and retail). These reports revealed the exploitation of impoverished producers by strikingly wealthier traders and commission agents. Their culmination was surely the Reserve Bank's *All India Rural Credit Survey* published in 1951, which concluded that the root problem of agrarian backwardness was the 'colonial-cum-commercial-cum urban domination over the rural economy' to such a degree that 'private trade can be tolerated only if the government does not have viable alternatives' (Chattopadhyay 1969: 221–22). If MC could be seen as unproductive but, contrary to Marx's theorising, also as *not necessary*, at least not in the form of the mercantile firm, then many state interventions aimed at 'eliminating middlemen' and bypassing private MC altogether could be justified.

Second, Marx's conclusion that the independent development of MC is inversely proportional to industrial capitalist development seemed able to explain backward forms of production in agriculture as well as industry and the sluggish development of both. It found fertile ground in rural Indian empirical conditions. For example, in West Bengal, 'the 'merchants'' ability to dominate the commodity market through stocking and price manipulation implies a deduction from the returns of producers, the real income of wage and labour income earners as well as from consumers' (Chattopadhyay 1969: 234). Locked together with land rent and interest-bearing capital, it was seen as able to delay or block the process of agrarian transformation (Bhaduri 1983).

Third, debates in peasant studies have grappled with the concrete form of Marx's 'commerce' – money used for buying and selling in combination with money advances for production. These debates engage with the question whether the indirect control of small-scale production by moneylending from merchants does or does not proletarianise producers who are dependent on such relations for their reproduction (Banaji 1977, 2016). In fact, small-scale production (petty commodity, small-scale producer or family forms) were strongly expected to be eradicated: 'Their position is absolutely hopeless as long as capitalism holds sway [...] capitalist large scale production is absolutely sure to run over their impotent antiquated system of small production as a train runs over a pushcart', wrote Engels in *The Peasant Question* (2001: 472). Yet these are remarkably persistent forms of production throughout agrarian societies (Harriss-White 2018; Jan and Harriss-White

2019). By the twenty-first century they had been relabelled as 'self-employment', 'micro-enterprise' and outright entrepreneurs by government commissions, aid agencies and scholars and presented as worthy aspirations and objectives of the ironically fashionable 'pro-poor development'. Petty commodity production (Marx 1894: chapter 17) has developed analytically as a catch-all category for petty activity involving trade, services and finance alongside production. However, a small agent embodying capital and labour and engaged in petty trade, whose profit from buying and selling may be equal to or less than that of a wageworker, still differs from the latter to the extent they are independent from exploitation through the wage relation.

Fourth, Marx's formulation of circulation as an independent sphere – though one which is progressively stripped of independence with the development of capitalism in production – and of MC as having an unavoidably ambivalent role – carries strong implications for a developmental state faced with a backward agricultural sector. Both agrarian transformation and the disempowerment of agricultural MC must be effected through changing *production*, an argument giving legitimacy both to land reform and to the technology of the Green Revolution (Rogaly et al. 1999). It is only more recently that MC is actually credited with financing and directing productive investment in post–land reform periods and regions of India, in contexts lacking 'adequate supply of formal credit' (Rawal 2005: 300).

Overall, while MC is a necessary theoretical concept, Marx can hardly be blamed for failing to anticipate or to theorise the development of the composite forms of capital that have proved to be so persistent in India's economy, as elsewhere. Banaji puts it like this: 'it is logically absurd to imagine a history of capital using a notion of commerce that was developed by Marx for the kind of capitalist economy that evolved only in the 19th century. In practice that is largely what has happened [...] There is a methodological impasse at work here, a staggering confusion of history and of logic' (2010: 256).

Actually existing CC is not an autonomous independent force floating above production relations and about to be subordinated to industrial capital. It is deeply rooted in production and exerts indirect control over production. In India, even though the incidence of compulsive exchange and distress commerce seems to have declined over recent decades, the mass of agricultural producers are involved in markets from which they cannot possibly withdraw under any circumstances, barring a crisis of destitution. The mechanisms of control remain money advances and the state's protection of the power of agro-processing, which includes its support through banks for the roles of these 'heterogeneous productive functions' as net contributors of money capital to the cascade of rural credit and as net recipients of the stream of marketed surplus destined for rural–urban trade. My own work on rice production in West Bengal has unveiled how these mechanisms work in practice (Harriss-White 2008). Indian rural CC is closely involved with productive activity. Trade cannot take place without processing ('an interruption of the process of circulation for productive purposes'), transport ('the use value of things is materialised in their consumption and their consumption may require a change of location') or storage (productively preventing deterioration in the way Marx conceived repair of factory machinery) (Marx 1885: chapters 6, 17). Overall, the intertwining of production and circulation is a general phenomenon in rural/small-town India (Harriss-White 2016a).

## A Marxian Agenda for CC for the Twenty-First Century

So, Marx's theories set an agenda of questions concerning the role of CC in the formation of rural–urban classes and the means whereby the relations driving their evolution can be studied. In fact, in forming classes, actually existing CC performs three roles (Jan and Harriss-White 2012). They all need field study.

The first is the progressive and constantly expanding role of the efficient movement of commodities and surplus mediated by prices. Mainstream research on agricultural markets confines itself to this role often reducing it to what can be known about efficiency through the analysis of price behaviour (Palaskas and Harriss-White 1993), despite David Bateman's (1976) exhaustive demonstration that to evaluate efficiency there is no substitute for business accounts. Marx meanwhile stressed the roles of turnover speed in circulation and the simultaneity of production and marketing for the efficient expansion of production.

The second is the role CC performs in relation to exploitation and class formation and the extent to which relations of exploitation also depend on (pre-existing) forms of non-economic social authority. This in turn depends on whether and how CC forms and protects monopolies and/or enables multiple modes of surplus value extraction; on whether CC can prevent petty trade from accumulating even while it cannot prevent it from multiplying and on the social segmentation of accumulation and commodification.

The third role of actually existing CC relates to resource transfers. The capacity of CC to lengthen 'acts of circulation' and complexify both global and domestic supply chains and markets, implies the transfer of resources not only between spheres of production and circulation, but between sectors. The mechanism is commonly called the terms of trade (Mitra 1977). It is simplified as the long-term relation between agricultural and non-agricultural prices. As the relative power of capital and labour in agriculture and non-agriculture shape the form taken by this resource transfer, the roles of CC in this process are of paramount importance. Yet they are considerably neglected.

A Marxist agenda for field research framed around CC also needs to include other aspects of class formation, including, for instance, the roles of commercial labour and of non-economic relations in circulation; it needs to investigate the extent to which circulation can be researched independently from production; and it should explore the possibility for comparative research.

Last, in *Volume III*, Marx theorised MC and CC without reference to the state. While Marx's vivid description of primitive accumulation evoked a state able to be subdued or to have its domains alienated, to experiment and at times fail, it also sketched a state able to enforce 'bloody legislation' and underwrite capitalist development (Marx 1887: chapters 25–28). Indeed, for the guarantee and protection of capital, the state must raise and allocate revenues and must support the victims of these processes so as to prevent their becoming a threat to capital (Khan 2005). In the Indian case the informal unregistered economy was deliberately created so that only the largest factory labour forces qualified for state protection (Dietrich Wielenga 2019). As for commodities, the Indian state has imposed on CC direct control and indirect regulative obligations embodying contradictory evaluations. Even in a neoliberal era, the Indian state controls and may de-commodify products in the process of circulation (as for civil supplies, cotton and cloth, essential food, energy). This direct intervention is justified by failures of competence of CC, or by the need to protect producers and/or consumers when commercial profit rises above the general rate of return. At the same time, the state also regulates sites, transactions, contracts, information, rent and bank credit for private CC. Indeed, also these contradictory roles and relations between the state and rural markets should be included in a Marxian research agenda for the study of CC in the field. Hence, this agenda should really involve a vast range of types of evidence and of scales – of firms, of time and of space. While the practical difficulty of researching it explains the small number of scholars engaged in it, there is no doubt about its relevance to contemporary political economy.

## Researching Actually Existing MC and CC

### The mandi as the field

Merchants and commodity markets are rarely studied in the field. It is production that has marginalised circulation analytically. Even in mainstream economics, 'the market' is replete with romantic assumptions about efficiency and competition which 'residualise' real markets. Marx himself preferred to use stylised evocations of what might now be called value chains for linen and cloth. In face to face encounters, merchants are thought tight-lipped and evasive, for reasons which range from fear of the state (due to commonplace fraud and adulteration), through hoarding in search for windfall profits, to the evasion of taxes, the avoiding of grounds for jealousy and reluctance to betray the secrecy of their trade records.

In the words of Mekhala Krishnamurthy (2010: 6), there is an element of inevitability in the rhythms and pace of the *mandi* (here marketplace), which make it an extraordinarily fascinating research field site.

> So, on a scorching April afternoon, when the yard was filled with great dunes of wheat, and Yadavji, the vastly experienced *mandi* superintendent, listening to the rumble of tractors signalling the restarting of the auction after a break, described the *mandi* as a process that cannot be postponed or put off, a daily act as inevitable as the rising and setting sun, as natural and necessary as one's morning routine of waking up, washing one's face, brushing one's teeth and doing the all-important 'latrine-bathroom,' I could understand quite precisely what he meant. (2010: 6)

How to research such 'inevitability'? While Krishnamurthy develops ethnography as a field tool to excavate a mine of case material, in this part of my essay I draw on the experience of over four decades of face-to-face interviews whose purpose has been to record business histories in order to activate a Marxist analysis in which case studies are integrated with quantitative material (see Harriss-White 1999).

## *Fixing the size and importance of CC*

Most official data is useless for a Marxist analysis because it has been collected to serve specific regulatory objectives for the state that are path-dependent even when well out of date. In the census and economic censuses for instance, the category of trade is bundled with hotels, restaurants and transport and none but the crudest classification is permitted for caste or gender. Published annual reports of state or private corporations are set at levels of abstraction which mask the day-to-day operations through which accumulation does or does not occur. Without recourse to Marx's imagined linen market, there is no alternative to the field – and therefore to the restrictions on generalisation resulting from local level enquiry.

While Marx himself theorised from a chain-like model of commodity transactions, the systemic approach required by Marx's concept of CC is extremely hard to piece together and exceeds both vertical chain-based approaches and industrial organisation frameworks centred horizontally on institutions shaping transactions.[2] Finding merchants is difficult. India has several sources of local lists of possible traders – all identifying different firms. Factories Acts only cover the largest trade-cum-processing units; Chambers of Commerce list the locally powerful; Commercial Taxes and Excise registers include those known to be taxable so they exclude petty trade (while their vernacular labels also prove unreliable indicators of operational functionality). In an era where increasing volumes of commodity trade bypass physical marketplaces, the Regulated Markets confines their records logically enough to traders transacting in the regulated market yard.

Random sampling from combined lists reveals many obstacles in contexts of informality: multiple firms sharing one licence, one listed firm with multiple branch shops and commodities, firms as hubs for many unlicensed and unlisted firms, untraceable firms with fictitious names and addresses, firms trading intermittently, firms controlled by others sited outside the area and listed elsewhere and absentee firms. Rules for randomised replacements need organising in advance for firms which are discovered not to exist.

In addition, Indian research cannot avoid the existing body of literature on agro-commerce indicating economic, social and operational differentiation, a great range of assets, place-to-place idiosyncrasy in market structure, the coexistence of many forms of technologies, labour organisation, control over firms, farms and families, spatial sites and capacities for mobility (e.g. Olsen 1996). Sample sizes ought to be guided by population variances, but we are faced not only with a large set of variables to research but with multiple variances, with variances unknown in advance and with unknown unknowns. The idea of sampling is a defensible approach to embarking on field knowledge but, granted that it can never be rigorous, it is an art rather than a science.

One way of approaching sampling an unknown population is by mapping a settlement on foot – not forgetting upper levels of commercial buildings and interiors of

---

[2]  Both discussed in Harriss-White (2016b).

yards – prior to stratifying by quarters or commercial clusters evident from maps and then moving to random sampling. Or firms may be selected along transects inside market towns, also keeping in mind the possibility of itinerant and/or period markets (Harriss 1976). Snowball sampling ensures networks of contacts are used (Sinha 2017), as do willing key informants (Amirali 2018), though both these choices risk exclusivity. When field insights are added to schedules of questions incrementally as they occur, most field research is left not with neat random samples from which extrapolations can be confidently made, but with case studies. And while Flyvbjerg (2006) has convincingly argued for case studies as ways of knowing, the great diversity of MC/CC constituting marketing systems means that Marxist questions on the roles of MC in capitalist transformations may only be answered provisionally – in constant need of refinement.

### A field agenda from Marxist political economy

Business histories can be mobilised for the central questions of class formation and accumulation at two time-scales – the long term and the day-to-day. Life histories tell of socialisation to business, forms of asset ownership, origins and destinations of capital/investments, estimates of current assets values, risks, losses and bankruptcies, accumulation, concentration and centralisation or alternatively expansion by multiplication. Seasonal – and more detailed – profiles of activity combinations, costs, price formation, types of transactions, production credit, other money advances and payment behaviour, and the complexities of the labour process suggest rates of return and reveal distinct processes of class formation. Olsen (1996), Crow (2001), Jan (2017 and in this volume) and Sinha (2017) deserve mention as rare cases of combined field research on production and circulation and their relation to class formation. Appendix 1 outlines a schedule that has survived over two thousand applications from 1973 to 2013.[3]

Obviously, the quality of evidence varies with the field encounter. And the 'business encounter' is often a difficult one, embedded in many paradoxes. While the social origins of the insider-researcher are easy for the merchant to know, those of the outsider are not. The plus of being a confidant for working lives devoted to competition is balanced by the minus of the outsider's unfamiliarity with commercial language, which may be exacerbated when language assistance is needed. Assumed ignorant, the researcher's idiocy is constantly put to the test in interview. By the end of fieldwork, the right questions, the correct language and the range of meaningful answers will have become apparent, but the answers are never complete. Notably, while independence from the state is paramount, local legitimacy may need to be established by prior blessing from a local official and business leaders. To minimise the damage of sequencing socially divisive fieldwork, the detail of public policies and official data

---

[3]   The archives on rural exchange, markets and merchants and market towns are held by the Centre of South Asian Studies Cambridge and Ashoka University, India. Grey material on rural development (1970–2010) is in the French Institute, Pondicherry.

must be collected only after the phase of private business interviews – with Trade Union leaders last of all.

## Minimising errors and managing multiple stories

In the interviews with merchants, *multiple stories* must be managed, through an approach structured through errors, while aimed at minimising such errors. Preparation needs engagement with scholarship from clashing paradigms outside the comfort zone of political economy. It also needs introductions to local business associations, advance letters which explain objectives and assure confidentiality. Despite the easy availability of internet bios, a local-language factsheet helps the consistency of rumours about the field-worker. Interviews have to be outside busy seasons, weekdays and times of day, yet traders are still too busy to converse in mangled language. Recordings and schedules are unwelcome. So assistance in a three-way interview may smooth its performance. Questions need to be learned, rehearsed, reverse translated and piloted in advance. The order of questions can be shaped by the interviewee. The default social setting is interviewing 'up' and it is as respectful to ask at the end about what has been missed out as to answer merchants' own questions throughout. Since local knowledge requires trust as well as scholarly preparation, extensive fieldwork is needed, enriched if iterated over long time-spans. Self-presentation matters and local and transparent domestic arrangements are passports to interviews. The privacy and confidentiality that must be assured are at the mercy of the merchant interviewed; workers, family members, other traders, even passers-by, remind the researcher of the cultural specificity of sensitive questions. Expert in the liar's truth, the trader has an interest in underestimating output, credit and profits, overestimating costs and debts and evading the detail of portfolio-building. The means of dealing with the conflicts of outcomes of this conflict of interest may include (1) a positive construction of the merchant's role in society which naturalises the inevitability of exploitation, evasive and corrupt relations with the state; (2) multiple cross-checking questions about different aspects of his sensitive activities (in-built redundancy); (3) conversation weaving between the general, the local and the particular; (4) accepting a scale of vagueness in orders of magnitude appropriate to the scale of theory, prioritising consistency. Key informants may provide a vital yardstick to evaluate plausibility in interviews with others.

In reactive situations stories will change. The story of the account book (if ever offered) will be supplemented with that of the interviews. The size of business, assets, returns and income will grow with time and familiarity in the field – resulting from the evolving mutual sensibilities of researcher and merchants. Evidence of social relations of crime, corruption and influence with agents of the state based on class and kin emerge. It helps to set out with a mindset intent on refuting the starter hypothesis that such behaviour exists.

A map of trade will be triangulated with quantitative information reaching the highest resolution possible while a rich periphery will be idiosyncratic. The story will be more complete than the evidence for it. The (random) sample is a useful organisational algorithm but it rarely exists in the field.

## The office and archive as the field

While much of the state's data rides roughshod over Marxist questions about MC, its data on prices are so abundant as to have transformed the study of markets into that of prices. Prices alone have permitted inferences about competition, integration and efficiency. The central government's Department of Statistics (DoS) processes extensive sedimentary deposits of price data, destined for consumer price indices and inflation monitoring, but stacked in strata thick with dust and nibbled by mice and silver fish. Local prices do not only add to the regression industry, they reveal seasonal reversals, potentiate fine-grained analysis of local terms of trade and the valuation of local consumption baskets relevant to measuring poverty outcomes of exchange relations. But, since the DoS employs data collectors, these data are subject to the same three sources of error threatening scholarly researchers. Official prices are often stylised; stocks underestimated, commodity flows (from which the development of regional and national markets might be indicated) go unrecorded or are periodically guestimated. Banks may also permit access to data on deposits and loans from which intersectoral resource transfers and allocations may be suggested. These corroborate the stories of portfolio-building and accumulation trajectories of local merchants. Long hours of office fieldwork copying official data may generate unofficial insights of 'office ethnography'. Gossip and meetings overheard while copying – missed if data is speedily photographed – alert the fieldworker to new knowledge: for example to the question of the *competence* of the merchant capitalist class and to the use of court cases to reveal the relative competences in policy implementation of merchants and the local state.

## Conclusions

'Marx's merchant' remains a fascinating if underdeveloped figure in political economy. Yet, its relevance for our understanding of contemporary capitalism, mapping patterns of accumulation, inequality and poverty, and grasping the intimate interrelation between production and circulation is paramount. After reconstructing Marx's theorisation of MC and CC, this analysis has indicated how these insights have guided debates on capitalism in India and have sketched some key components of a Marxist agenda for researching CC in the twenty-first century, highlighting its many perils and methodological challenges. While the field is full of elephant traps, these must be negotiated if contributions are to be made to theories grounded in logic and in history and if extrapolations are not matters of wishful thinking. Long ago, Greenhalge (1896) warned that the practical is the political. However, the reverse also holds, and nowhere more so than in the field of the market place, the political is the practical.

## References

Adnan, S. 2015. 'Primitive accumulation and the "transition to capitalism" '. In B. Harriss-White and J. Heyer (eds), *Indian Capitalism in Development*, pp. 23–45. London: Routledge.

Amirali, A. 2018. *Market Power: Traders, Farmers and the Politics of Accumulation in the Pakistani Punjab.* DPhil thesis, Oxford University.

Banaji, J. 1977. 'Capitalist domination and the small peasantry: Deccan districts in the late nineteenth century'. *Economic and Political Weekly* 12(33/34): 1375–404.

———. 2010. *Theory as History: Essays on Modes of Production and Exploitation.* Oxford: Blackwell.

———. 2016. 'Merchant capitalism, peasant households and industrial accumulation: Integration of a model'. *Journal of Agrarian Change* 16(3): 410–31.

———. 2020. *A Brief History of Commercial Capitalism.* Chicago: Haymarket.

Bateman, D. 1976. 'Agricultural markets: A review of the literature of marketing theory and of selected applications'. *Journal of Agricultural Economics* 27(2): 171–226.

Bhaduri, A. 1983. *The Economic Structure of Backward Agriculture.* London: Academic Press.

Crow, B. 2001. *Markets, Class and Social Change: Trading Networks and Poverty in Rural South Asia.* London: Palgrave-Macmillan.

Dietrich Wielenga, K. 2019. 'The emergence of the informal sector: Labour legislation and politics in South India, 1940–1960'. *Modern Asian Studies.*

Engels, F. 1894. 'The peasant question in France and Germany', https://www.marxists.org/archive/marx/works/1894/peasant-question/index.htm (accessed 30 March 2018).

Flyvbjerg, B. 2006. 'Five misunderstandings about case study research'. *Qualitative Inquiry* 12(2): 219–45.

Greenhalge, F. 1896. 'Practical politics'. *North American Review* 162(471): 154–59.

Harriss, B. 1976. 'Social specificity in rural weekly markets – The case of northern Tamil Nadu'. In E. Gormsen (ed.), *Market Distribution Systems*, pp. 39–48. Heft 10: Mainzer Geographische Studien.

Harriss-White, B. 1996. *A Political Economy of Agricultural Markets in South India: Masters of the Countryside.* New Delhi: Sage.

———. 1999. *Agricultural Markets from Theory to Practice.* London: Macmillan.

———. 2008. *Rural Commercial Capital: Agricultural Markets in West Bengal.* New Delhi: Oxford University Press.

——— (ed.). 2016a. *Middle India and Urban-Rural Development: Four Decades of Change.* Heidelberg: Springer.

———. 2016b. 'From analysing "filieres vivrieres" to understanding capital and petty production in rural South India'. *Journal of Agrarian Change* 16(3): 478–500.

———. 2018. 'Awkward classes and India's development'. *Review of Political Economy* 30(3): 355–76.

Jan, M. A. 2017. *Rural Commercial Capital: Accumulation, Class and Power in Pakistani Punjab.* DPhil, Oxford University.

———. 2019. 'The complexity of exchange: Wheat markets, petty-commodity producers and the emergence of commercial capital in colonial Punjab'. *Journal of Agrarian Change* 19(2): 225–48.

Jan, M. A. and B. Harriss-White. 2012. 'The three roles of agricultural markets: A review of ideas about agricultural commodity markets in India'. *Economic and Political Weekly* XLVIL(52): 39–52.

———. 2019. 'Petty production and India's development'. In S. Gupta, M. Musto and B. Amini (eds), *Karl Marx – Life, Ideas, Influence: A Critical Examination on the Bicentenary*, pp. 345–67. New York: Palgrave-Macmillan.

Kaplinsky, R. and M. Morris. 2006. *The Structure of Supply Chains and Their Implications for Export Supply.* Kenya: African Economic Research Consortium.

Khan, M. 2005. 'The capitalist transformation'. In K. S. Jomo and E. Reinert (eds), *The Origins of Development Economics: How Schools of Economic Thought Have Addressed Development*, pp. 69–80. London: Zed Press.

Krishnamurthy, M. 2010. 'Mandi Times'. Paper presented at 'Rethinking Global Workplaces: Polychrony and Uncertainty', London School of Economics, May.

———. 2015. 'The political economy of agricultural markets: Insights from within and across regions'. In IDFC Rural Development Network (ed.), *India Rural Development Report 2013–2014*, pp. 59–79. New Delhi: Orient Blackswan.

———. 2019. 'Fields, markets and agricultural commodities'. In S. Srivastava, Y. Arif and J. Abraham (eds), *Critical Themes in Indian Sociology*. New Delhi: Sage.

Krishnamurthy, M. and P. S. Vijayshankar. 2012. 'Understanding agricultural commodity markets' introduction to special issue of the *Review of Rural Affairs*'. *Economic and Political Weekly* XLVII: 34–37.

Lenin, V. 1899. 'The development of capitalism in Russia: The process of the formation of a home market for large-scale industry', https://www.marxists.org/archive/lenin/works/1899/devel/index.htm (accessed 30 March 2018)

Marx, K. 1885. *Capital, Volume II*, https://www.marxists.org/archive/marx/works/1885-c2/ (accessed 30 March 2018).

———. 1887. *Capital, Volume I*, https://www.marxists.org/archive/marx/works/download/pdf/Capital-Volume-I.pdf (accessed 30 March 2018).

———. 1894. *Capital, Volume III*, https://www.marxists.org/archive/marx/works/download/pdf/Capital-Volume-III.pdf (accessed 30 March 2018).

Mitra, A. 1977. *Terms of Trade and Class Relations: An Essay in Political Economy*. London: Cass (republished by Routledge in 2005).

Olsen, W. 1996. *Rural Indian Social Relations*. New Delhi: Oxford University Press.

Palaskas, T. and B. Harriss-White. 1993. 'Testing marketing integration: New approaches with case material from the West Bengal food economy'. *Journal of Development Studies* 30(1): 1–57.

Perelman, M. 2000. *The Invention of Capitalism: The Secret History of Primitive Accumulation*. Durham: Duke University Press.

Rawal, V. 2005. 'Banking and credit relations in rural West Bengal'. In V. K. Ramachandran and M. Swaminathan (eds), *Financial Liberalization and Rural Credit in India*, pp. 279–325. New Delhi: Tulika Books.

Rogaly, B., B. Harriss-White and S. Bose. 1999. *Sonar Bangla: Agricultural Growth and Agrarian Change in West Bengal and Bangladesh*. New Delhi: Sage.

Sanyal, K. 2007. *Rethinking Capitalist Development: Primitive Accumulation, Governmentality and Post-colonial Capitalism*. New Delhi: Routledge.

Sinha, S. 2017. *Agrarian Accumulation in Liberalised India: A Study of Capitalist Farmers in Punjab*. PhD thesis, SOAS.

# Appendix 1

## Default Order of Questions Used in Field Interviews in Tamil Nadu and West Bengal, 1973–2013

*Section one: Background and history*
### 1.1 History
Family details, occupational history, caste, native place
Date of start of firm, reasons
Skill acquisition/mobilisation of labour/finding of contacts/licence(s)/premises, etc.
Starting capital (SC)/fixed and working capital
Spatial location of SC
Sectoral origin of SC

### 1.2 Control over resources
Organisation of ownership of firm/changes/reasons
Organisation of family/size and composition/changes/reasons
Organisation of family land/size (units): wet/dry/changes/reasons
Organisation of family non-land businesses
Changes/reasons

### 1.3 The town and region
At DoS, the types/numbers/size structures/and operational functions of firms and the flows of sampled commodity through the area

### 1.4 The firm
History of growth of firm: commodities/geography of flows/organisation of transport/sites of transactions/clientele – sellers and buyers/labour/finance/technical change (diversification/concentration)
Now: quantities (seasonal profiles): Origins/destinations/intermediaries/transport/storage/processing/other activities/by-products
Size now: Assets/gross output (profiles per day, per season/storage patterns)

### 1.5 Role of family and gender
Female and male family labour in firm/kinship/inheritance – close kin and occupations

### 1.6 Land relations: reforms in the region/tenurial changes
Own land and impact/crops marketed/marketed surplus/no. of intermediaries/dependence on other traders (information/transport/credit/storage/processing/other)/credit relations/rents

### 1.7 Market infrastructure
Physical locations of market transactions/changes over time/seasonally/geographically at times of crisis (concentration? if not why not?); other infrastructural changes in the area
*Section two: Organisation of markets*
Diversity and regulation/rules of the game

### 2.1 Operational functions/local labels and meanings in sampled commodity:
Buy/sell/broker/store/transport/process/finance trade/finance production/other activity; reasons for combinations; flexibility

## 2.2 Types of contract/transactions

Proportion of sales/purchases large farmer/small farmer/landless producer
Contracts: spot/open auction/attached/closed negotiation/delayed price dispersions
Forward/kin/caste
Weights/measures
Payment systems
Linked contracts/places/seasons (credit/labour/crop/water/land/other/other seasons)
Velocities of storage
Trade (repeat) (max/min/qty/time)

## 2.3 Uncertainty

Losses and crises
Means of enforcement of contract
Disputes and means of resolution: costs
Crime: theft, adulteration, differences in weights and measures, other

## 2.4 Transactions costs

Travel and entertainment
Salaries of enforcement staff and costs (%)
Information
Media
Prices and quantities
Places
Institutions/intermediaries
Changes over time of information base
Bulletin/post and stat/telegrams/telephone/clerks/contacts/internet/other
Clients (questions about setting up a new client); costs
Other intermediaries (setting up contacts); costs
Clerks and employees (selection)

## 2.5 Other costs (not disaggregated here but details required)

Rent, fuel, lube, electricity, spare parts, labour: permanent, casual, contract (wages, perks,
emergency costs), interest on loans borrowed (details of loans in and out); political costs

## 2.6 Government regulation

How are the following organised? licensing/price information/place for transactions/storage
(location/quantities/time)/contracts/technical change/payment/finance/fee (for market/for
transaction)/security/hygiene/transport/subordinate labour
*Section three: Accumulation*
Control over production, economic mobility and portfolio development, the relation between
agriculture, trade and business
Turnover/gross output by profile
Assets
Local/regional development and merchant's portfolio/patterns of investment/disinvestment over
the history of the firm/locations/types/sectors (reasons/organisation)
Savings (stocks/shares/human capital/education/dowry, etc.)
Spatial and social mobility
Land in last generation and now
Businesses in last generation and now
Own landholding, mode of operation and decision-making
Mode of operation and decision-making on land of clients/advice

Finance-in (maximum/minimum/sources/terms and conditions/seasons and places)
Finance-out (max totally/min totally/max to individual/min to individual)/variety of terms and conditions/borrowers (traders/agents/large farmer and small farmer archetypes) (no. of large farmers/no. of small farmers/means of repayment/terms and conditions: interest formation/losses/default and outstanding
Ties with marketing and ensuring supplies of commodities and credit

*Section four: Labour in firm*
Family (check roles and stipends/rewards)
Permanent male (*m*) female (*f*) jobs/pay per unit time/wage negotiations/perks
Casual *m*: max/min/rates/jobs/dispersion of contracts/type of payment/bonding through loans/other/perks
 *f*: max/min/rates/jobs/dispersion of contracts/type of payment/bonding through loans/other/perks
 Child: max/min/rates/jobs/dispersion of contracts/type of payment/bonding through loans/other/perks
Changes/technological change and labour process/contract labour

*Section five: New crops and marketing problems*
Last 10 years
Changes in cropping patterns
Needs of crops for marketing: quality standards/perishability
Technical problems/decentralisation/processing/transport/perishability
Information (price/place/intermediaries/organisation of subordinate markets/spatial flows)
Technology and technological change
Finance
Exchange relations (entry/dependence and flexibility of transactions/dependence of intermediaries upon each other)

*Section six: Policy/the state*
Lobbies
Associations/DoS/reasons/history (TUs/labour/state controls/auto-regulation/crime, etc.)
Other associations
Politics
Parties (finance/election funding/affiliation and action through parties/policies towards trade)
Other activity (temple/Lions/Red Cross/Rotary/panchayat/co-operative/school and hospital governing, etc.)
Contact with state
Price and procurement (state trading/related policies, e.g. NMS/FFW)
Regulation of storage/processing/transport/cooperation/licensing/commercial taxation/finance of trade/finance of production/small-scale industry/other schemes/IRDP/regulated market
Biggest problems with marketing/operation of firm
Solutions from respondent's perspective

*Section seven: Profits*
Rough estimated net profit (per bag/time unit, specify unit) and extrapolate
Per year/in bands as appropriate to income distribution, e.g. under Rs 50,000/50,000–100,000/100,000–400,000/400,000–1,000,000/1,000,000–10,000,000/>10 m

# Chapter Four

# THE TIES THAT DIVIDE

## MARX'S FRACTIONS OF CAPITAL AND CLASS ANALYSIS IN/FOR THE GLOBAL SOUTH

### Muhammad Ali Jan

**Abstract**

Capital exists in a great variety of forms and configurations both historically and in the contemporary period. Yet, appropriate concepts and frameworks for capturing this diversity remain underdeveloped. This chapter argues that a fruitful methodological approach to grapple with this diversity of capital is by deploying a key but underexplored concept in Marx of 'fraktions' – fractions of capital. This concept highlights a relatively cohesive group within a class having a comparatively distinct location within the process of capitalist social reproduction and concrete sociopolitical interests which may be contradictory to other strata, even as it shares with them the same relationship to productive property and the process of accumulation. The chapter proposes three dimensions along which fractions within a class can be identified: a spatial dimension which identifies capital-accumulating classes in various locations; a scalar dimension which highlights the existence of capital at different scales of operation and a social origin dimension, which recognizes that modern capitalist classes transmute from prior social groups and that their origins stamp their current form in determinate ways. Using this framework and drawing from a variety of examples from the Global South, including the author's own fieldwork in rural and small-town Pakistani Punjab, the analysis highlights how a more concrete study of the different forms of capital can be undertaken which is sensitive to both the specificities of capital in different contexts as well as the threads that bind social groups despite their diversities.

## Introduction

One of the main criticisms levelled against Marx's conception of class is its highly abstract nature. Throughout much of the three volumes of *Capital*, as well as in his most widely read works, he simplifies the class structure of capitalist society to the bourgeoisie and proletariat, sometimes including 'landowners' as a separate group. This simplified schema was obviously created as a necessary abstraction since the subject matter of *Capital* is not the concrete class structure of specific capitalist societies but an analysis of the 'laws of motion' – to use his own expression – of capital in general. However, this has not prevented critics from using it as an example of why his framework is not applicable to a study of the actual diversity of class relations under capitalism (Parkin 1979).

It would nonetheless be a mistake to believe that Marx did not appreciate the considerable complexity and heterogeneity that was inherent in terms such as 'capital', 'bourgeoisie' and labour. Far from homogenizing classes, his works demonstrate a keen appreciation of the cleavages within them and an effort to grapple with the resultant complexities. Whether it be the rise of Louis Bonaparte due to the frictions between different segments of French capital, or his views on the compact between landed and financial interests to explain food policy in England, his writings show that classes in concrete settings are more complex and layered than the analysis emanating from value theory in *Capital*.

While Marx's political writings are full of arresting insights about contradictions within and between different classes, they are also highly unsystematic, disjointed and often self-contradictory. How then can scholars undertaking empirical research on class relations in the Global South utilize the richness of Marx's works on the subject and derive more systematic concepts from them?

This chapter argues that a useful way of proceeding is by building on Marx's work elucidating the diversity *within a particular class*. This stems from the empirical observation that although capital and labour are the fundamental classes of capitalist society and their antagonism central to explaining social change, both are internally segmented along different lines and illuminating these axes of differentiation within a class are as crucial as understanding relations between classes. This is done by drawing on the concept of 'fractions' that Marx uses repeatedly in his work but without any systematic detail. The concept refers to a relatively cohesive group within a class having a distinct location in the process of social reproduction and concrete sociopolitical interests which may be at odds with other strata – even as it shares with them the same relationship to productive property and accumulation.

It further proposes three dimensions along which this concept can be developed to study segmentation within the capitalist class by drawing on observations from field-based studies of capitalists in the Global South: first, a *scalar* dimension which highlights the important differences between international, national and local capitalist blocs in terms of scale of operation as well as the organizational forms associated with it; second, a *spatial* dimension which identifies different fractions according to their location within a particular production process or sectors of the economy and the contradictions that arise from this; finally, a *social origin* dimension which recognizes how capitalist classes evolve out of prior social groups and how their origins impact their subsequent trajectory in determinate ways. This final dimension also points out the necessity of combining Marx's concept of class with Max Weber's work on 'status groups' in order to understand the complex co-evolution of class with other relations such as caste, gender and ethnicity, which have been central to the work of Marxist scholars in different contexts of the Global North and South. Therefore, the chapter proposes a synthesis of Marx and Weber when studying class fractions.

I begin by locating the origins of Marx's conception of fractions not in his abstract theoretical works but in his political and journalistic writings. I show how Marx was well aware that class was an insufficiently precise concept for understanding political economy and that a concrete analysis required unveiling the existence of heterogeneity within dominant and dominated social groups. At the same time, I argue that Marx was unable to define the concept of 'fractions' coherently and in order for it to be useful for research in developing countries, it needs to be developed more systematically. I then propose three dimensions along which the concept of fractions can be developed to uncover class heterogeneity in specific social contexts, explaining their underlying reasons. Finally, I draw upon the literature from South Asia and beyond to show how scholars have identified the existence of fractions among the bourgeoisie and what the contradictions between fractions and the dominance of certain factions means for the trajectory of capitalist development, the ways in which labour is exploited as well as for political struggles.

## Marx on Fractions: Capital as Unity in Difference

Despite the centrality of 'class' to his framework it is notable that Marx never defined the concept in any coherent manner. The chapter titled 'Classes' where Marx appears to be laying down the contours of the concept in a more consistent way only appears at the very end of *Volume III* of *Capital*. Marx begins by asking the question 'what is a class?' and answers it by making the claim that 'wage labourers, capitalists and landowners' are the 'three great classes of modern society based on the capitalist mode of production' (Marx 1981: 1025). However, as soon he starts to explain his rationale for the class categories, the manuscript abruptly breaks off, never to be completed again.

Of course, in these two pages, as in a few other parts of *Capital*, there is a clear recognition of the difference between class relations at the level of the abstract mode of production and those in concrete social formations. Marx writes, for example, that even in England, where his tripartite class structure finds its closest approximation, it is found in 'far from pure form' (ibid.). Instead, he highlights the existence of 'middle' and 'transitional' levels whose boundaries with the other three are highly fuzzy (ibid.). There is also a detailed analysis of merchant capital as a historically distinct form that has a determinate impact on the nature and pace of industrial development (Marx 1981: chapter 20). These rare references show an awareness not only of groups difficult to categorize either as capital or labour but also the existence of diversity within the fundamental class categories. However, the dynamics of capital in general and not class relations in the specific societies remain the focus of his magnum opus.

It is in Marx's political and journalistic writings that the concepts appropriate for a concrete analysis of class relations can be found, albeit in a scattered and somewhat confusing form. The most important one is the concept of 'fraction' – sometimes referred to as 'faction' – which Marx uses to highlight the existence of different interest groups within the bourgeoisie itself. The concept is coined and deployed most extensively in his works on the social struggles in France where it is used to understand the rivalries between contending political parties as well as the rise of Louis Bonaparte. It is also found is his writings on Britain and America, to explain internal class cleavages and their impact on specific domestic policies and on overseas colonial adventures. In these works Marx emphasizes the decisive political role of the 'rival fractions and factions of the appropriating class' highlighting the unity in difference that exists within the bourgeoisie (Marx and Engels 1986: 329).

This dialectic of unity and difference within the bourgeoisie is outlined along both economic and political lines. Marx writes, for example, about the 'economic foundations' of various parts of the bourgeoisie 'held together by great common interests and marked off by specific conditions of production' (Marx and Engels 1979: 112). Furthermore, Marx points out the existence of 'different kinds of property' among whom it is necessary to advance 'the common class interest without giving up their mutual rivalry' (Marx and Engels 1978: 95). A classic example of economic contradiction is between 'financial' and 'industrial' fractions which may have different interests in concrete contexts despite the many threads that inextricably bind them together.

Referring to 'big bankers and moneylenders' in France, Marx argues how the credit system led to enormous centralization in their hands and thus made this class of 'parasites', who 'despoil industrial capitalists' and 'interfered' in production, 'extremely powerful' (Marx 1981: 678–79). On another occasion, describing the coalition of interests involved in the British conquest of India, he shows the existence of cooperation and antagonism between the 'moneyocracy' which financed the endeavour, the 'aristocracy' that deployed its army and the 'millocracy' that sold its cloth (Marx and Engels 1980: 154–55). Finally, despite listing landowners as a separate class in *Volume III*, in the *Eighteenth Brumaire* he refers to 'the two great interests into which the bourgeoisie is split – landed property and capital'. 'We speak of landed property,' Marx writes 'for large landed property, despite its feudal coquetry and pride of race, has been rendered thoroughly bourgeoisie by modern society' (Marx and Engels 1979: 128).

But Marx also makes references to 'fractions' in more explicitly political terms, where it is not the economic foundations, but the quest for political hegemony that defines various strata. He repeatedly asks which sections of the bourgeoisie rule and legislate through the formal state institutions and which segments are excluded. This is closely tied to the idea that the general interests of the dominant class are organized under the political control of a segment of that class, a view expounded further by later Marxists such as Gramsci and Poulantzas, but already contained in Marx's own thought.[1] The hegemonic segment of the dominant class is one where other segments 'find their natural mainstays and commanders' (ibid.).

For example, he explains how under Louis Philippe, political power was concentrated in the hands, not of the entire bourgeois class, but of one fraction of that class, the financial aristocracy, which itself was composed of multiple interests such as banking, railways, construction, and so on. On another occasion, he refers to a coterie of 'lawyers, writers, officers and officials' as leaders of the anti-Louis Bonaparte fraction of the French bourgeoisie, which included industrial interests as well (Marx 1979: 112–13). This signifies how groups located in different parts of the production process can be organized under the same fraction at particular political conjunctures (Davis 2015: 66). Marx's repeated recourse to 'fractions' highlights an awareness that class on its own is not a sufficiently

---

[1]   See, for example, Poulantzas (1978: 77–79) for a useful discussion of the concept.

precise concept for explaining the dynamics of social struggles and change in concrete contexts.

However, as stated at the beginning of the section, the category of 'fractions' remains relatively underdeveloped in Marx's political writings. First, the range of terms he uses to explain the phenomenon leads to a lot of confusion. Marx uses interchangeably, 'part', 'section', 'party', 'stratum' among other terms when referring to divisions between capitalists. Second, the rationale behind the usage is neither clear nor always consistent; for example, Marx uses the term 'fraction' not only for different parts of the same class but sometimes also for parts of the same political party, as in his analysis of the Party of Order in France. On some occasions, he also refers to each party itself as a fraction.

Nor does Marx's logic behind the use of these terms remain confined to political and economic contradictions. He also occasionally finds religious cleavages underlying distinct class fractions; he writes, for example, how alongside the industrial, financial and landed factions was the 'fourth faction' of the Party of Order, the Catholic (Marx and Engels 1980: 156). Further, he speaks of a politically organized part of the bourgeoisie that does not rest on common economic foundations as a mere 'collection' or coterie but usually also calls such a group a faction. These different usages highlight both the importance Marx attaches to the concept for a concrete analysis of class relations but also his inability to theoretically organize it during his lifetime, a task that fell on subsequent generations of scholars.

Nonetheless, the importance of the concept for researchers working on class relations in particular regions of the Global South – that is, those aiming to study economic cleavages from the bottom up – is undeniable. Before that, however, it needs to be developed in a clearer and more systematic manner. The next section draws on some important theoretical and empirical work by scholars of class relations to present both a definition as well as three dimensions along which the concept can be developed for empirical research.

## The Dimensions of Differentiation: Fractions of Scale, Space and Social Origin

In a brilliant critique of Rostow's stages of economic growth, Paul Baran argued that 'historical configurations must be studied concretely' which does not mean jettisoning theory in favour of 'ploddy empiricism' but the interpenetration of theory and concrete observation, of theoretical work which draws its 'lifeblood from historical study' (Baran 1969: 65). In other words, classes must be treated as historical, rather than structural facts, the outcomes of agency and struggle, of experience and the consciousness of social groups. An important starting point is to ask how classes, rooted in a concrete set of economic relations, take on historically specific forms? Closely related is a recognition that class formation is a protracted process, constantly negotiated by struggles both within and in opposition to other groups (Fantasia 1995: 275).

The historical formation of classes out of the struggles of the past means that they are never a homogeneous entity but have great diversity and differentiation within them.

Such an approach militates against sterile formulations which treat classes as purely logical abstractions, to be read a priori from an already given 'mode of production'.[2] Such analyses take categories such as 'peasants', 'merchant', 'landlords' to be external to one another and are unable to appreciate both their historical incorporation into capital as well as their specific locations in the overall process of social reproduction. In order to avoid such formulations, scholars need to disaggregate the bourgeoisie, historicize the emergence and interrelation of different segments of capital and study the implications of their mutual cooperation and antagonism for dominated groups as well as for state formation.

At this point it would be pertinent to define more precisely what we mean by the term 'fraction'. The chapter uses Maurice Zeitlin and Richard Ratclif's work who define what they call 'class segment' (used interchangeable with 'fraction') as a 'relatively cohesive group within a class having a comparatively distinct location within the process of social reproduction and consequently, its own specific political economic requirements and concrete interests that may be contradictory to those of other fractions. Nonetheless, it shares with the other fractions essentially the same relationship to ownership of productive property' and the overall process of accumulation (Zeitlin et al. 1976: 1009). Using this framework, they identify large landowners as a distinct segment within the capitalist class of Chile that has also historically been the political representative of the bourgeoisie (Zeitlin and Ratcliff 1988).

The next question is how exactly should different fractions be identified in concrete political economic formations? The first dimension proposed by the chapter is the *scale* of economic production, closely tied to which is the mode of ownership, organization and management. While the possession and non-possession of 'property' – or 'means of production' in a more a comprehensive Marxian sense – is crucial in separating different classes, it is important to remember that the size and mode of possession of these resources vary in different spatial and historical contexts and has significant implications for class formation and struggle. In other words, the degree and extent of ownership or control over 'means of production' can be big enough so as to create qualitative, not merely quantitative differences between capitalists.

This difference has long been recognized in the Marxist and neo-Marxist literature on 'national', 'comprador' and 'foreign' capital emerging from the Dependency theory literature, even if the political and ideological positions underpinning their analyses have been highly problematic (Friedmann and Wayne 1977). A clearer way to proceed is by keeping the differences in scale between 'foreign', 'national' and 'local' fractions of the bourgeoisie without the ideological baggage of the dependency school. Moreover, researchers should be cognizant that differences in scale are closely linked to the modes of ownership, control and management of capital which can themselves be the basis of cleavages. Evidence shows, for example, that 'foreign' capital has corporate ownership and management structures with managerial jobs created for 'middle classes' in the South (e.g. Evans 1979). By contrast, 'local capital' tends to be organized around family

---

[2]   See Rahman (2012) as an example of such theoretical formalism.

and kin relations and regulates accumulation through interpersonal ties. 'National' capital could be somewhere in the middle, relying on both family and corporate forms of organization. In addition, many countries in the Global South contain large sectors of 'state capitalism' around key industries where bureaucracy and capital are merged into one and have a distinct identity and interest in the social formation.

The segmentation along scale is also closely tied to the second dimension along which 'fractions' of capital can be identified and studied: the *spatial/regional* location of the capitalist class. Much of the literature tends to speak of capital as if it were equally divided across the length and breadth of a social formation. However, one outstanding feature of capital is the immense regional and spatial differentiation created through its operation, what scholars refer to as 'uneven development' (Harvey 2005). Capital tends to operate in regional configurations concentrated in particular areas, which simultaneously integrates it to other parts of a social formation, which can also create distinct interest groups within the capitalist class with profound implications for the trajectory of development.

Spatial fractions can arise due to the concentration of a capitalist class in a particular region around a certain sector or industry, allowing it to create a unified economic and political identity against those without such advantages. Finance capital in the United States organized around Wall Street (Ho 2009) or industrial cluster capitalists in Italy (e.g. Trigilia and Burroni 2009) are merely two instances. Spatial fractions can also arise from the contradiction between capital located in the metropolitan capitals of a country and in the provincial towns and villages away from the centre, what is referred to as 'provincial', 'rurban' or 'small-town' capitalism. In multi-ethnic societies the existence of regional pockets of capital gains added significance. Moreover, such fractions could be restricted to a particular form or sector (e.g. industrial, commercial, agrarian and so on) or be more comprehensively interlocked as part of a portfolio of investments by the same group of capitalists (Zeitlin and Ratcliff 1988: 54).

A final dimension along which the fractions of capital can be ascertained is what the chapter calls 'social origins'. With the exception of when a society is invaded and a new class of rulers created by external conquest, capital stems from those groups already in existence. Historically, the crystallization of capitalist classes has taken place when new technologies, forms and rationales of production are taken up by existing social groups. A rich literature on the 'origins' of capital and the subsequent character of capitalist development has long dealt with these issues (e.g. Banaji 2007, 47–70; Dobb 1947). The location of new classes is often linked to the activities they pursue prior to the transformation, for example, landlord, peasant, merchant, artisan and so on, which shape the contours of their modes of organization of production and the trajectories of accumulation in determinate ways. As Schumpeter brilliantly observed, 'classes co-existing at any given time bear the marks of different centuries on their brow' (Schumpeter 1955: 111).

However, it is also important to note that in most pre-capitalist societies, one's position in the overall social division of labour is not simply a neutral fact but closely tied to the status of the individual in that society. As Max Weber noted, social differentiation exists not only on 'economic class' lines but also by the ranking of groups along a social estimation of 'honour' gauged through the specific 'style of life' that members of the same status are expected to have (Weber 1978: 305–7). In general, status group membership is

**Table 4.1** Identifying fractions within the capitalist class

| Dimensions | Features | Examples |
|---|---|---|
| Scalar | Degree and extent of ownership + organizational form | Corporate capital versus family enterprise |
| Spatial/regional | Concentration in a particular region or location | Industrial clusters with distinct regional identity and interests |
| Social background | Pre-capitalist status distinctions reconfigured by capitalist relations | Ethnic, racial or caste divisions |

based not on wealth but on social prestige, particularly for traditionally dominant groups with inherited privilege. Such privilege could come from a variety of sources such as 'military', 'bureaucratic' or 'religious' leadership, often tied to landownership.

Therefore, many capitalist classes emerge out of traditional forms of privilege rooted in status groups. This could mean traditional landlords and aristocrats transforming themselves into capitalists by reorienting their production for the market, as recounted by Weber himself for the Prussian Junkers (Weber 1979: 179). It could also mean members of erstwhile royalty, military and bureaucracy moving into industry. On the other hand, when capitalists emerge from social groups considered lower in the status hierarchy, there is always a tendency of fractionalization of the bourgeoisie along the lines of social status, especially if existing elites are closely knit together and resent the entrance of newer groups. Moreover, status considerations and distinctions are not cast away by the rise of capitalist development – instead, what one finds is a reconfiguration of identities linked to caste, race, religion and gender reconfigured with class relations – resulting in complex trajectories of social struggles, state formation and capital accumulation. Table 4.1 gives a summary of the axes along which the concept of fractions explicated in this chapter can be explored.

It must be clarified that definitions are merely guides to empirical research and ultimately, a concrete analysis would have to constantly re-assess conceptual categories in relation to concrete empirical investigations. First, while the concept of 'fractions' is meant to highlight the dialectic of similarity and difference within a concrete social class, these differences are not limited to the three axes listed above. Depending on the case study, scholars can identify the existence of fractions along lines different from those elaborated in this chapter. Second, it is important to remember that these dimensions of differentiation are not necessarily separate from one another in concrete situations and can be strongly interlinked. By the same token, a fraction may be distinguished from another along one axes but can be interlinked with it along another. Finally, while the chapter deals with different fractions of capital, the analysis can be extended to labour and its lines of segmentation. However, the multiplication of criteria for delineating fractions can only be done through theoretically reflexive empirical work and can never be a purely logical analysis.

In the final section, the chapter briefly reviews some examples – mainly from South Asia – of research using class fractions to explain social and political change.

## Fractions of Capital and Social Change in South Asia and Beyond

Evidence for the existence of fractions along all three dimensions has long been established in the literature on capitalist development in South Asia – and the Global South in general – even if it has not been articulated in those terms and even if there has been vigorous debate on the exact composition and behaviour of these factions. This can be seen from the important literature on 'intermediate classes' in South Asia. Scholars working with the concept highlight the existence of a group of a smaller, 'non-monopoly' fraction composed of merchants, rich peasants, small-scale manufacturers and retailers, with its own forms of organization and set of interests, distinct from large, 'monopoly' capital (Harriss-White 2003: chapter 3).

More importantly, the difference is not merely one of degree but also qualitative in terms of social organization. Large capital tends to have a nation-wide reach and is organized along corporate, managerial lines, while 'intermediate' capitalists deploy labour through informal contracts as well as through caste and gender hierarchies and most importantly, their firms are rooted in the structure of the patriarchal family. Furthermore, their distinct interests manifest themselves in the form of their contradiction against large scale capital on a range of issues, from labour laws to credit disbursement, as well as their explicitly political opposition to large capital in critical historical junctures (e.g. Banaji 2016; Harriss-White 2013; Parthasarathy 2013).

In Pakistan, for example, many small- and medium-scale capitalists were at the forefront of the movement against the military dictatorship of the 1960s which was seen as too closely tied to a handful of big business conglomerates whom they saw as monopolizing business activity (Jones 2003: 120). Once the new left-leaning government of Bhutto came to power, this fraction bitterly and successfully fought against the imposition of labour laws on their 'family-owned' enterprises, something the large-scale capitalists were unable to prevent. A clear division emerged in the bourgeoisie where small- and medium-scale capitalists with more flexible labour practices and local rootedness were able to undercut the old, large-scale capital and many of today's large national business capitalists emerged from their ranks.

Like fractions along the scalar dimension, there is evidence of regional/spatial concentration of capital resulting in the formation of distinct fractions at particular historical conjunctures. In South Asia, the existence of capital emerging not from the metropolitan trading capitals but from 'provincial' towns and regions, is well documented. Anita Weiss highlights the emergence of a distinct stratum of industrialists in three provincial districts of Pakistani Punjab whose origins lie in the growth of small-scale, labour-intensive industries rooted in kinship and family relations (Weiss 1991). Stanley Kochanek shows further how this fraction coalesced around the leadership of Mian Nawaz Sharif, the most successful prime minister in Pakistan's history. The rise of this stratum led to considerable opposition from the entrenched bourgeoisie, which was regionally situated in the port towns of Karachi and was ethnically different from the challengers (Kochanek 1997: 55).

The close connection between the rise of new regional fractions of the bourgeoisie and political change is also described by Sanjaya Baru for many states in India. Reviewing the literature on Andhra Pradesh, Gujarat, Tamil Nadu and Maharashtra, he shows that during the 1970s and 1980s an increasing number of new capitalists emerged in these 'post-Green revolution' centres of dynamism, covering several industries, such as textiles, cement, sugar, chemicals, fertilizers, pharmaceuticals (Baru 2000: chapter 7). Moreover, instead of throwing in their weight with the ruling Congress Party, like the fraction of capital which arose during the national liberation struggle, these entrants decided to back ethno-regional parties in exchange for various benefits, thereby contributing to the serious decline of the Congress and the growing strength of regional political dispensations.

Nor are these interconnections limited to South Asia alone – a very important example comes from the rise of a new 'devout bourgeoisie' in the Anatolian region of Turkey (Gumuscu 2010: 845). This group, historically marginalized by the Ankara-based establishment during the import substitution regime, was provided new opportunities during the liberalization phase, which resulted in export-oriented industrialists with roots in small and medium enterprises experiencing remarkable growth in their wealth and power. Culturally, this stratum was more devout and considered the secular ethos of the Kemalist military, bourgeoisie and middle classes as alien to both Islam and Turkish history. It therefore decided to back the pro-business Islamism of the Justice and Development Party (AKP) headed by Tayyip Erdogan, playing a critical role in his rise to dominance in Turkish politics.

Finally, the most obvious dimension along which economic and political fractions emerge is that of 'social origins', which covers not simply a Marxian emphasis on particular places in the division of labour, but also a Weberian view of what an individual or group's location in such a division means in terms of status hierarchy. There is a rich literature on the existence of fractions of capital emerging not simply from merchants, peasants and artisans, but also how these translate into the status categories of caste. For example, Sharad Chari has traced how a section of the *Gounder* peasant caste in Tiruppur district of Tamil Nadu, transformed into textile and knitwear capitalists, utilizing 'fraternal' caste solidarity in developing horizontal ties with other capitalists and for controlling labour that belonged to the same caste (Chari 2004).

Carol Upadhya's work on the 'farmer-capitalists' of coastal Andhra Pradesh belonging to the *kamma* caste tells a similar story of how the rich peasant segment of this caste used its agrarian surpluses and caste networks to diversify their investment portfolios and emerge as the leading business elite of the region (Upadhya 1988: 1436). Another case of the rise of *Patidar* castes of farmer industrialists in Gujarat is documented by Mario Rutten in his work (Rutten 2003: chapter 2). In both cases, the accumulation of capital by these new elites was politically and culturally articulated in different ways. In the case of the *kammas* who were traditionally considered lower caste, this was done by backing anti-Brahmin/upper-caste parties and associations while in the case of the *Patidars*, who were also traditionally considered inferior by upper castes, it found expression first through the rise of Hindu nationalism of the Bhartiya Janata Party and most recently under *Patidar* rights associations.

Perhaps the most insightful use of the concept of fractions for concrete sociopolitical analysis which subtly combines segmentation along spatial and social origin lines is Jeffery Paige's classic work on coffee elites and democratic transitions in Central America (Paige 1998). Through extensive archival work and primary data collection, Paige demonstrated the existence of two distinct factions emerging from the key commodity of the region, that is, coffee. The first fraction was the large landowners in coffee, and later in cattle, cotton and sugar who were closely tied to the banking system and utilized a labour repressive regime for their accumulation. The second was the agro-industrial fraction consisting of processors of these commodities, who employed wage labour and was more concerned with export and quality maintenance. In terms of social origins, the former fraction was largely composed of Spanish colonial nobility while the latter were mostly immigrant families, which created another layer of friction between the two.

Paige shows how this division resulted in the two fractions taking diametrically opposed positions during the socialist assertions from below that Central America experienced throughout the 1970s and 80s. The landowners resolutely backed authoritarian military regimes bent on crushing the popular mobilization from below while the agro-industrial elite which was located in a more productive node within the agro-commercial chain and could afford to offer concessions, became disillusioned with the authoritarian regimes and their conservative backers and joined the pro-democracy movement, playing a critical role in the transition to democratic rule along with some concessions for workers and peasants, even though, ironically, the end-result was the establishment of neoliberal democracies in the region.

Thus, a fractions of capital approach to class analysis can 'sensitize' researchers to the diversity and heterogeneity within actually existing capitalist classes, fieldwork can then illuminate the precise contours of segmentation in specific, concrete settings and a constant conversation between the two allows for a richer analysis. My own work on the interactions between farmers, traders and processors in two regions of small-town and rural Punjab – what I term 'rurban' Punjab – revealed that the leading local capitalists were mostly partition refugees from eastern Punjab who had migrated in 1947. A majority were from lower caste and small farmer backgrounds who had used their surpluses from trading and cultivation in the aftermath of the Green revolution, to invest in factories and thereby emerge as the dominant industrial capitalists of both regions.

Moreover, the institution of the joint family, their tightly knit kinship connections, as well as the feelings of solidarity emerging from refugee status allowed them to establish business partnerships and credit relations among themselves across the rural–urban divide in a way that was not possible for the more dispersed and factionalized (though in one region numerically greater) local population. This distinct and more organized identity vis-à-vis the locals allowed them greater leverage in their dealings with the state, which was much more partial towards their demands. Finally, despite the recent emergence of capitalists from the local population, the character of local capitalism in both areas is clearly stamped by the accumulation strategies of the diversified rural commercial from refugee backgrounds (Jan 2017). Thus, although the concept of fractions allows researchers to recognize diversity, their contours are always an empirical question that varies greatly in different places. Finally, since the formation of such axes of differentiation takes place over time, such research is by definition historical.

In conclusion, while Marxist scholars have paid a lot of attention to the relationships between different classes, the same has not been done for identifying heterogeneity within classes themselves. As the chapter has sought to demonstrate, many of the central planks on which capitalist societies rest, such as the structure of economic growth, the regimes under which labour is deployed and exploited as well as the political form the state in capitalist societies take, are deeply tied not simply to class struggles from below, but to how these struggles are articulated with the views and interests of different fractions of the capitalist class. In other words, the purported unity of capital at the level of the abstract mode of production hardly ever reproduces itself at the level of the concrete social formation and 'actually existing capitalist' classes remain deeply divided on many of these key questions. Therefore, scholars and activists need to understand these divisions in order to identify greater openings for labour rights and democratization.

## Conclusion

This chapter has proposed a more nuanced approach to class analysis by paying attention to divisions within the dominant class. Drawing on the concept of 'fractions' it has demonstrated the origins of the concept in Marx's own political and journalistic writings. While these writings reveal a keen awareness that classes and their struggles are more complex at the level of a concrete social formation than the more abstract study of capitalist dynamics in *Capital*, it has also argued that Marx was unable to give the concept the coherence of his most famous works, which is perhaps why it has been ignored to some extent. However, 'fractional' analysis is highly relevant to researchers working on the empirical complexities of class relations in many countries of the Global South and should be developed in the same way as his better known concepts of 'real and formal subsumption' of labour to capital, or the dialectic of production and circulation (e.g. Das 2012).

In order to develop it further, the chapter has drawn upon theoretical and empirical works by Marxist and non-Marxist scholars to highlight three interconnected dimensions along which fractions within the capitalist class can exist, namely scale, space and social origins. It further argues that the social origin dimension is closely associated to Max Weber's concept of status groups, highlighting divisions in society on estimations of social honour and prestige, something that becomes extremely important in many countries of the South where inherited privilege based on caste, gender and religion articulates with class in all sorts of complex ways.

Finally, it shows the efficacy of the concept in concrete class analysis by drawing on the literature from South Asia and beyond. These works show how in key aspects of society, such as state and political form, structure of economic growth as well as the regulation and exploitation of labour, the existence of fractions within the capitalist class are critical and by understanding and utilizing these, scholars and social movements can further progressive and radical praxis and create openings for a more democratic and egalitarian society.

## References

Banaji, J. 2007. 'Islam, the Mediterranean and the rise of capitalism'. *Historical Materialism* 15(1): 47–74.

———. 2016. 'Merchant capitalism, peasant households and industrial accumulation: Integration of a model'. *Journal of Agrarian Change* 16(3): 410–31.

Baran, P. A. 1969. 'A non-communist manifesto'. In J. O' Neil (ed.), *The Longer View: Essays Towards a Critique of Political Economy*, pp. 52–67. New York: Monthly Review Press.

Baru, S. 2000. 'Economic policy and development of capitalism in India: The role of regional capitalists and political parties'. In F. Frankel, Z. Hasan, R. Bharagawa and B. Arora (eds), *Transforming India. Social and Political Dynamics of Democracy*, pp. 207–30. Delhi: Oxford University Press.

Chari, S. 2004. *Fraternal Capital: Peasant-Workers, Self-Made Men and Globalization in Provincial India*. New Delhi: Permanent Black.

Das, R. J. 2012. 'Reconceptualizing capitalism: Forms of subsumption of labor, class struggle, and uneven development'. *Review of Radical Political Economics* 44(2): 178–200.

Davis, M. 2015. 'Marx's lost theory: The politics of nationalism in 1848'. *New Left Review* 93: 45–66.

Dobb, M. 1947. *Studies in the Development of Capitalism*. New York: International.

Evans, P. 1979. *Dependent Development: The Alliance of Multinational, State, and Local Capital in Brazil*. Princeton: Princeton University Press.

Fantasia, R. 1995. 'From class consciousness to culture, action and social organization'. *Annual Review of Sociology* 21(1): 269–87.

Friedmann, H. and J. Wayne. 1977. 'Dependency theory: A critique'. *Canadian Journal of Sociology* 2(4): 399–416.

Gumuscu, S. 2010. 'Class, status, and party: The changing face of political Islam in Turkey and Egypt'. *Comparative Political Studies* 43(7): 835–61.

Harriss-White, B. 2003. *India Working: Essays on Society and Economy*. Cambridge: Cambridge University Press.

———. 2013. 'West Bengal's rural commercial capital'. *International Critical Thought* 3(1): 20–42.

Harvey, D. 2005. *A Brief History of Neoliberalism*. New York: Oxford University Press.

Ho, K. 2009. *Liquidated: An Ethnography of Wall Street*. Durham: Duke University Press.

Jan, M. A. 2017. *Rural Commercial Capital: Accumulation, Class and Power in Pakistani Punjab*. PhD dissertation, Department of International Development, University of Oxford.

Jones, P. E. 2003. *The Pakistan People's Party: Rise to Power*. Karachi: Oxford University Press.

Kochanek, S. 1997. 'Interest groups in Pakistan: The growing power of business'. *Journal of South Asian and Middle Eastern Studies* 20(3): 46–71.

Marx, K. 1981. *Capital: A Critique of Political Economy, Volume III*. London: Penguin.

Marx, K. and F. Engels. 1978. *Marx-Engels Collected Works, Volume X*. London: Lawrence and Wishart.

———. 1979. *Marx-Engels Collected Works, Volume XI*. London: Lawrence and Wishart.

———. 1980. *Marx-Engels Collected Works, Volume XII*. London: Lawrence and Wishart.

———. 1986. *Marx-Engels Collected Works, Volume XXII*. London: Lawrence and Wishart.

Paige, J. M. 1998. *Coffee and Power: Revolution and the Rise of Democracy in Central America*. Cambridge: Harvard University Press.

Parkin, F. 1979. *Marxism and Class Theory: A Bourgeoise Critique*. London: Tavistock.

Parthasarathy, D. 2013. 'Rural, urban, and regional: Re-spatializing capital and politics in India'. In T. Bunnel, D. Parthasarathy and E. Thomspon (eds), *Cleavage, Connection and Conflict in Rural, Urban and Contemporary Asia*, pp. 15–30. New York: Springer.

Poulantzas, N. 1978. *Political Power and Social Classes*. London: Verso.

Rahman, T. 2012. *The Class Structure of Pakistan*. Karachi: Oxford University Press.

Rutten, M. 2003. *Rural Capitalists in Asia: A Comparative Analysis on India, Indonesia and Malaysia*. New York: Routledge Curzon.

Schumpeter, J. 1955. *Imperialism and Social Classes*. New York: Meridian.

Trigilia, C. and L. Burroni. 2009. 'Italy: Rise, decline and restructuring of a regionalized capitalism'. *Economy and Society* 38(4): 630–53.

Upadhya, C. 1988. 'The farmer-capitalists of coastal Andhra Pradesh'. *Economic and Political Weekly* 23(28): 1433–42.

Weber, M. 1978. *Economy and Society: An Outline of Interpretive Sociology* (ed. G. Roth and C. Wittich). Berkeley: University of California Press.

———. 1979. 'Developmental tendencies in the situation of east Elbian rural labourers'. *Economy and Society* 8(2): 177–205.

Weiss, A. M. 1991. *Culture, Class, and Development in Pakistan: The Emergence of an Industrial Bourgeoisie in Punjab*. Lahore: Vanguard.

Zeitlin, M., W. L. Neuman and R. E. Ratcliff. 1976. 'Class segments: Agrarian property and political leadership in the capitalist class of Chile'. *American Sociological Review* 41(6): 1006–29.

Zeitlin, M. and R. E. Ratcliff. 1988. *Landlords & Capitalists: The Dominant Class of Chile*. Princeton: Princeton University Press.

# Chapter Five

# MARX IN THE SWEATSHOP

## EXPLOITATION AND SOCIAL REPRODUCTION IN A GARMENT FACTORY CALLED INDIA

### Alessandra Mezzadri

**Abstract**

In *Volume I* of *Capital*, Marx takes us on an odyssey through the secrets of the world of commodities produced under capitalism – their 'real' value, the exploitative nature of the labour process and the dark abode of production. His contribution to studies of early capitalism and working poverty is seminal, but how is Marx still relevant for the study of contemporary globalised production? This chapter identifies three tropes of Marxian methodology relevant to the study of India's 'sweatshop regime': first, the initial framing of the analysis around 'the commodity', to illustrate the concrete workings of 'commodity fetishism' and its links to regional comparative advantage; second, the study of different modes of extraction of surplus-value, their interplay and implications for the labouring body; and lastly, the mapping of distinct processes of subsumption of labour into capitalist circuits, resulting in various 'forms of exploitation'. While celebrating the relevance of the Marxian method for the concrete analysis of contemporary sweatshops, the chapter also reflects on the need to complement it with insights on the social traits of exploitation and social reproduction, drawing from the feminist literature.

## Introduction: From *Volume I* of *Capital* to the Indian Sweatshop

One hundred and fifty years after its publication, *Das Kapital* remains relevant for the study of capitalist production. Marx's analysis of the 'abode of production' developed in *Volume I* still powerfully resonates with many issues facing the labouring classes worldwide, especially the developing world. First, many of these classes experience unacceptable rhythms, intensity and length of working hours, while remuneration often remains below what is defined as a 'living wage'. Second, these classes remain exposed to high occupational risk, industrial 'disasters' and health conditions linked to overwork and exhaustion. The labouring body strains under the intense pitch and speed of work imposed by the ever-increasing velocity of circulation of raw materials, goods and delivery times characterising today's global economy. However, the most important reason *Volume I* should still be considered a vital reading to interpret key aspects of our contemporary global economy is for Marx's *method*. The very structure of the volume, in this sense, offers a crucial research framework.

Marx starts from an investigation of the commodity form, then proceeds to reveal the 'dark secrets' behind its value, which lie in the process of surplus labour extraction and exploitation of the worker. Several chapters are dedicated to analysing how labour surplus can be extracted, in *absolute* or *relative* terms, that is, either through ruthless strategies to extend the working day or by increasing work intensity and/or productivity. Different modes of labour surplus extraction have distinct implications for the labouring body. We don't encounter the processes that initiated the whole system until the end of *Volume I* – the mechanisms of dispossession that threw workers onto the market to sell the only commodity they had left, labour-power: a commodity that, if kept for personal consumption, will not save the worker from starvation, but, once sold to and consumed by the capitalist, will instead generate surplus-value and reproduce the worker simultaneously.

Different typologies of labour surplus extraction are not the only ways in which exploitation can differ in practice. Exploitation can have different features and manifestations and crucially, as argued by Jairus Banaji, different *forms*. For instance, depending on the 'degree' of dispossession and divorce of people from their means of production (land, but also work tools and access to markets outside the clutches of the capitalist), exploitation can manifest in more or less pure or disguised forms of wage work (e.g. Bernstein 2010). Labour can be subsumed into the capitalist process in either *real* or *formal* terms (Banaji 2010). Under generalised capitalist production, even those not fully divorced from their means of production may still be fully divorced from the means of survival outside the market and subsumed *formally* into the capitalist circuit as units of labour.

In this chapter I argue that these three 'tropes' within the Marxian method of analysis as developed in *Volume I* – namely the initial framing of the analysis around the commodity; the observation of different modes of labour surplus extraction; and the mapping of different processes of labour subsumption – are crucial to understanding key features of contemporary production in labour-intensive industries. This viewpoint is supported taking the case of India's 'sweatshop regime' (Mezzadri 2017). Here it allows for an investigation into the features of 'the garment' as a commodity and into the multiple processes of labour surplus extraction and 'forms of exploitation' (Banaji 2010) behind the 'made in India' label. While deploying the Marxian method, the analysis also complements it with insights from feminist theorists, particularly Maria Mies (1982, 1986) and Silvia Federici (2004, 2012). This deepens our understanding of contemporary social features of value and exploitation, of the mechanisms of surplus extraction and of the distinct patterns of social reproduction of the workforce within India's sweatshop regime. The empirical narrative draws on many years of extensive fieldwork in India, across garment export hubs, industrial hamlets and peri-urban/rural outposts (Mezzadri 2017).

The section which follows discusses the relevance of adopting the commodity as the starting point of analyses of production and explains how global and regional capitalists fetishise India as a giant sourcing factory specialising in distinct garment 'commodities'. It will also expand on the relation between physical and social materialities of production and work and on the social features of exploitation. The third section discusses the processes of labour surplus extraction across the sweatshop regime and compares them to those described by Marx. It insists on their mutually reinforcing nature and on their highly socially differentiated aspects and impacts on distinct labouring bodies. The fourth section highlights the multiple 'forms of exploitation' within the sweatshop regime and reflects on how they shape social features of today's garment proletariat. It also expands on how social reproduction sustains different forms of exploitation. The concluding section reflects on what India's sweatshop regime suggests about the contemporary nature of exploitation and value.

## The Commodity and the Sweatshop

In the nineteenth century, capital already appeared as 'an immense collection of commodities' (Marx 1990: 125). The opening chapter of *Volume I* highlights the double nature of the value of all 'things' produced under capitalism. Capitalist things are defined; they have a use-value, on the basis of their utility, and an exchange-value, based on which they will be exchanged in the market. While the latter is naturalised as linked to the former, this is hardly the case. Under capitalism the exchange-value of commodities – their real value – is given by the quantity of labour, or labour-time, needed to produce them. From this point of view, everything that surrounds us and that we purchase and use today – our furniture, cars, i-Pads and indeed our clothes – incorporates different quantities of 'congealed labour-time', conferring distinct values beyond their mere sensuousness. Marx is quite clear about this (ibid.: 163).

> A commodity appears at first sight an extremely obvious, trivial thing. But its analysis brings out that it is a very strange thing, abounding in metaphysical subtleties and theological niceties. So far as it is a use-value, there is nothing mysterious about it [...] But as soon as it emerges as a commodity, it changes into a thing which transcends sensuousness.

This is a key insight. Indeed, the value of a garment has little to do with its use-value. If this was true when Marx was writing, it is even more so today. Western wardrobes – but also increasingly those of the rising middle classes in emerging economies like India – bulge with cheap garments. Their usefulness as 'sensuous things' is therefore greatly limited. The value of these garments, unfortunately, does reflect the perceived value of labour-time congealed in them, a value that is greatly depressed by the cheapness of services provided by the poor labouring masses in garment-producing economies. It is only for those garments that command high prices due to 'branding' that exchange-value reflects not only congealed labour-time in production but also intangible 'rents' based on the vast consumer power of global actors. But let's stay focused on the commodity and its twofold value form.

The fact that the real value of commodities under capitalism transcends their usefulness has been largely interpreted as an indication that their physical features do not really matter. Marx (ibid.: 165) writes:

> The commodity form, and the value-relation of the products of labour within which it appears, have absolutely no connection with the physical nature of the commodity and the material relations arising out of this.

Ways to interpret this vary. One is that the physical properties of commodities have no relation to the social process deployed to produce them. Another is, instead, that in the process of becoming commodities, things should not be seen as simply linked to their physical status but *primarily as an expression of the social relations deployed to produce them*. These are crucially different explanations; one suggests that physical and social 'materialities' fundamentally differ; the other highlights the presence of multiple, different types of 'materialities' epitomised by the commodity form.

An enquiry into the world of garments clearly supports the second explanation. The word 'garment' can refer to different commodities – jeans, jackets, t-shirts, blouses. Product differentiation is astonishing, currently further boosted at a global level by the Zara business model, which is increasing the speed of production, circulation and, crucially, withdrawal from circulation – a strategy designed to push consumers to frenetically buy and discard in a process which can be dubbed 'economic consumption bulimia' and which generates massive waste. While this amazing product specialisation raises key questions about today's consumerism, it also needs to be accounted for when thinking about the garment as a commodity defined by its exchange-value, in turn given by the labour-time necessary to produce it.

If we look at the features of distinct sets of garments, they all differ and entail distinct processes of production. Their physical properties do not necessarily matter in terms of use-value; however, they do matter in terms of the *quantity and type* of congealed labour-time they are likely to incorporate. An order for 100,000 basic jeans will be produced on an assembly line, with a specific organisation of production, at a given pace, by a labour force at a specific level of productivity and intensity of work. Meanwhile, an order for a small batch of embroidered blouses will be realised under different conditions. In short, different physical properties of commodities, here garments, entail different social processes of production.

This is another reason why it is crucial to begin with the commodity, and the Marxian method is still greatly useful in this respect. While this intuition has been followed up by commodity studies, especially in their early conceptualisation within World System Analysis (Hopkins and Wallerstein 1986; Bair 2009), attention to the interplay between physical and social materialities of production has not been systematically developed. In fact, it has been developed mainly with reference to nature and land (e.g. Coronil 1997; Castree 2003) or farming differences (Watts 1994), but not necessarily to the complex world of 'man-made things'. If these things have a complex 'social life' (Appadurai 1986) across circuits of distribution and consumption, their distinct features also shape a fairly diverse 'social life' across the labour process.

In India, within what I call the 'sweatshop regime', the correspondence between physical and social materialities of production is striking. Product specialisation is highly localised. Interviews with sourcing actors, global and regional buyers, retailers and manufacturers clearly reveal how the whole country is 'made' into a giant department store, with different garment collections on different floors. Delhi (NCR) and Jaipur produce embellished ladieswear; Ludhiana, woollens; Bengaluru and Chennai, basic garments like jeans, jackets or shirts; and Tiruppur, t-shirts. Kolkata, in industrial decline since Partition, specialises in low-end nightwear, kidswear and workwear. Mumbai is a hub for fashion trade and design – the cash register of the India store. There are historical reasons behind each pattern of product specialisation, and global and regional actors continue reproducing them by placing differentiated orders across export hubs based on past performance (Mezzadri 2017).

The garment department store metaphor represents how sourcing actors have fetishised India based on garment commodities. The physical properties of these commodities differ substantially, as do the social processes of production, both in quantity of labour-time needed and type of labour deployed. In northern India and Kolkata, production is in networks of small and medium factories and workshops, and value addition is decentralised to armies of artisan-workers. Within this organisation of production, useful for niche products made on semi-assembly lines, group systems or artisanal tailoring systems, the factory labour force is mainly male migrants from the Hindi belt. Ancillary activities take place in home-based settings. Embroidery, for instance, is organised by labour contractors and scattered across peri-urban and rural outposts like Bareilly in Uttar Pradesh, where different types of home-based workers often perform these tasks under relations of neo-bondage or patriarchal unfreedom (Mezzadri 2017).

In the southern garment centres of Chennai and Bengaluru, where factories aiming at mass-producing basic items are larger and organised in assembly line production, the workforce is mainly factory workers and is feminised. Here, women are considered the best labour force to contain industrial costs. Tiruppur, which is characterised by a combination of Fordist and post-industrial landscapes (De Neve 2014), adopts a system whereby both male and female migratory labour coexist (Chari 2004; Carswell and De Neve 2013). This product specialisation of the Indian garment store is realised through a process whereby the whole country is turned into a massive 'global factory' (Chang 2009) – a sweatshop regime, where distinct 'labours' perform distinct tasks and produce different garments.

Indeed, each garment in India can be conceived as an expression of the labour-time needed to produce it. However, the varying social profile of the workforce involved in producing garments also suggests that, as distinct commodities, different garments conceal *qualitatively different* types of labour-time and not simply homogenous units of labour. In short, while the case of India's sweatshop regime reaffirms the need to start our analysis from the commodity, it also suggests the need to pay attention to the processes of social differentiation of the labour deployed to make the commodity. While, at a more abstract level, the real value of commodities rests on the labour-power contained, in turn the value attributed to that labour-power changes with the social profile of the workers who sell it.

The relevance of the social profile of labour is stressed by feminist analyses, which have illustrated the racialised and gendered features of 'global shop-floors' and 'global farms' (Elson and Pearson 1981; Mies 1982; Salzinger 2003; Fernandes 1997; Novo 2004; Caraway 2005; Bair 2010; Ruwanpura 2011). In India, the social differentiation of the workforce operates as a 'Social Structure of Accumulation' (Harriss-White 2003). Our case reveals how such social differentiation is also strongly connected to commodity differentiation. Complementing the Marxian method with feminist insights, we gain an in-depth understanding of how things are made and by whom. Let us now examine labour surplus extraction across the sweatshop regime. Once complemented with feminist approaches, the Marxian method again provides key insights that unveil salient features of contemporary exploitation.

## The Labour Process, the Working Day and the Sweatshop

The labour process is that in which the labour, through different 'systems' and 'tools', transforms raw materials into new use-values. Under capitalism, the tools and raw materials are owned and provided by the capitalists, as is the labour-time of workers, and hence the use-value produced (chapter 7). In the act of labouring, workers consume their labour-power as sold to the capitalist, transferring its value and that contained in the raw materials onto the new products (chapter 8). In the process, workers both transfer 'old' value and generate a 'new' one; the difference between the labour-time *necessary* to workers' reproduction and surplus labour-time gives the rate of surplus-value. 'Made' in production, this surplus can only be realised in the sphere of circulation/ exchange (chapter 9). Capitalists aim at expanding the share of surplus labour-time at the expense of necessary labour-time. This despite the fact that labour-power and its 'container' (Federici 2012) – the labouring body – need to regenerate and replenish to be able to continue being sold. In the absence of legal boundaries imposed by the state, or economic ones imposed by profitability (like tight labour markets), capital is uninterested in workers' fate.

> Capital asks no questions about the length of life of labour-power. What interests it is purely and simply the maximum of labour-power than can be set in motion in a working day. It attains this objective by shortening the life of labour-power, in the same way as a greedy farmer snatches more produce from the soil by robbing it of its fertility. (Marx, 1990: 376)

In this light, the working day, to which Marx dedicates a long chapter (chapter 10), becomes not only the rhythmic cycle of the labour process, and the arena of struggle between workers and capitalists over the appropriation of labour surplus, but arguably also the theatre where the labouring body can be robbed of more labour-time than that initially sold by the worker and be inexorably depleted. In short, the working day is the theatre of exploitation. Marx describes two types of surplus-value appropriation, *absolute* and *relative*. The former is generally characterised as based on attempts to extend the working day beyond its limits. The second is linked to reducing necessary labour-time, that is, the time needed to reproduce labour. This is either via a cheapening of commodities (meaning they absorb less labour-time) or rises in productivity, for instance, through a deployment of new tools of labour, like machinery.

Some analyses of absolute and relative surplus extraction processes consider the latter more virtuous/less pernicious. However, both can be ruthless. If absolute surplus extraction entails exhausting working hours and rhythms with the implications that Marx describes (epidemics, low life expectancy, child mortality), processes of relative surplus extraction are not necessarily kinder. First, the cheapening of commodities can lead to cuts in wages. Second, the deployment of new machinery and deepening of the division of labour triggers deskilling that, by reducing workers to 'living appendages' of a 'lifeless organism' (Marx 1990: 548), cheapens the value of the commodity labour-power, hence de facto reducing workers' share of overall surplus (Braverman 1974). It also makes the workers ever more dependent upon the labour market to survive, as they lose craftsmanship skills.

Marx is also clear that absolute and relative surplus extraction can proceed hand-in-hand (ibid.: 438). Indeed, today, sweatshops see both. Absolute and relative forms of surplus extraction are not only inextricably and intimately linked; they also reinforce each other, producing dark synergies. Take the cases of factory shopfloor production in Delhi and Bengaluru. In factories and workshops in Delhi, production is flexible and often requires a continuous adjustment to changing deliveries and orders. Overtime is inbuilt in such a system; many are compelled to work beyond their shifts. Workers in and around Delhi generally work 10–12 hours daily in factories and up to 16 hours in workshops (Mezzadri and Srivastava 2015). The majority are male migrants, so they may not protest against this practice if linked to an increase in take-home wages (see also Breman 2013). In fact, labour circulation can reinforce these overtime practices. Here, the extension of the working day cannot be solely classified as a device for absolute surplus extraction, as fluctuating worktimes become a key part of both the organisation of production and of workers' strategy at reproduction via labour circulation. As overtime is rarely compensated at overtime rates as set by Indian labour laws, the extension of the working day and cheapening of labour are realised simultaneously.

On Bengaluru's feminised shopfloors, Fordist assembly line production dominates. The larger size of industrial units and product specialisation in basic garments entails a cheapening of labour-power based on the technical division of labour and deskilling (e.g. Jenkins and Blyton 2016). Overtime also becomes necessary here during busy periods. Women workers are far less keen on overtime than their male counterparts in Delhi. However, the majority report that they cannot refuse overtime. A significant portion of this overtime is not paid at legal rates; in fact, it may not be paid at all, presented as extra work that women need to do to meet their targets (Peepercamp 2018); targets often set well beyond reasonable productivity levels. Here it is also impossible to disentangle absolute and relative surplus extraction, as the two processes are organically intertwined. A rise in the rate of absolute surplus extraction is obtained through the imposition of a technical organisation and management of production aimed at extending the share of relative surplus – namely batch, target-based production. Notably, both in Delhi and Bengaluru, as in other garment hubs, the cheapening of labour is also linked to rising living costs. A study on wages in Tiruppur shows that while nominal wages have risen since the 1980s, real wages have stagnated (Sivakumar 2017).

Both the exhausting length of the working day and the harsh intensity of work in the sweatshop lead to systematic depletion of the labouring body, a process described in detail by workers. Delhi workers revealed the high incidence of chronic illnesses and fatigue. Those in large factories reported waves of fainting during the unbearably hot summer months, while homeworkers suffered loss of eyesight (Mezzadri and Srivastava 2015). It is impossible to isolate the contributions of the distinct modes of surplus extraction to health depletion; they also work through dark synergies. Similar findings are encountered in other garment centres (De Neve and Prentice 2017).

The processes of absolute and relative surplus extraction are also enabled by discursive practices naturalising and deepening social inequalities and structural differences in labour markets. For women factory workers, for instance, exploitation is both an economic and social experience, nurtured not only by the mechanisms of the assembly line and overwork but also by the mobilisation of gender stereotypes reproducing their work as of lower value (Wright 2006). For them, the fight for higher wages and the containment of the working day is indivisible from that against patriarchal norms. For low-caste workers like Ansari Muslims engaged in embroidery, stereotypes embedded in structural oppression are also mobilised to expand exploitation rates. Their experience calls for the development of a 'labour theory of stigma' (John 2013), as the traits of their lived exploitation transcend traditional (Marxian) debates on labour surplus extraction. Their bodies, trapped within regimes of stigma, cannot valorise their labour-power. For them, labouring is also a *performance* in subordination and humiliation.[1]

A number of Marxian analyses identify a third mode of appropriation of labour surplus (which Marx excluded ex ante from his analysis), namely paying labour below its reproductive cost, or below the value of necessary labour-time, leading to 'super-exploitation' or 'immiseration' (Higginbottom 2012; Selwyn 2017). Some of these analyses link super-exploitation to imperialism (Smith 2016). While representing important contributions to our understanding of the contemporary global division of labour, these studies may downplay the role of national and local factors in setting the differences in the value of labour-power across the world (Fine and Saad-Filho 2018). Moreover, modes of surplus extraction have always been *experienced differently*. The feminist literature has illustrated this point at length, showing that modes of surplus extraction are always relational – in particular, gendered and racialised – hence dependent on the distinct social traits of labouring bodies. For many categories of vulnerable workers, harsher forms of absolute surplus extraction involving wages below the value of necessary labour power – and the cost of social reproduction – have been the norm, rather than the result of 'super-exploitation' (or indeed 'modern slavery'). The next section will dwell more on exploitation and its multiple *forms* (Banaji 2010), proposing a Marxian feminist approach centred on social reproduction.

## Forms of Exploitation and Social Reproduction in the Sweatshop

The distinction between formal and real subsumption of labour is the third key feature of the Marxian method crucial to the analysis of the sweatshop. Marx addresses the distinction between formal and real subsumption in the appendix to *Volume I*, on the *Result of the Immediate Process of Production*. We have the formal subsumption of labour when capital subsumes the labour process 'as it finds it', in the context of a pre-capitalist or 'archaic' mode of production (Marx, 1990: 1021). In this case, the penetration of capitalism

---

[1]    Shah et al. (2017) explore these issues as 'conjugated oppression' in India.

manifests with the takeover of reproduction, but not of the means of production. Labour may still own these means, but is deprived of the possibility to reproduce outside the logic of the market where it must sell its labour-power to survive.

The real subsumption of labour manifests when capital revolutionises the mode of production and imposes its own labour process. As Marx describes in the chapters on the labour process, the age of manufacture and cooperation and of large machinery (chapters 7–15), real subsumption involves (1) the restructuring of the labour process according to a new division of labour, progressively deskilling workers; (2) the provision of all tools of work and machinery by the capitalist; (3) the progressive transformation of the worker into an 'appendage' of the machine. Moreover, the initial enabling condition for the process of real subsumption is the dispossession of the worker from both the means of production and reproduction, so that she must return to the market to sell labour-power again and again. In short, selling one's labour becomes, under capitalism, the only dynamic compulsion ensuring survival.

> Capitalist production therefore reproduces in the course of its own process the separation between labour-power and the conditions of labour. (ibid.: 723)

There is a clear relation between the different ways surplus is extracted and the ways in which subsumption of labour manifests. Marx highlights that within processes of formal subsumption, surplus-value can only be produced in absolute terms (ibid.: 1021). On the other hand, Marx also links relative surplus extraction with processes of real subsumption.

> If the production of absolute surplus-value was the material expression of the formal subsumption of labour under capital, then the production of relative surplus-value may be viewed as its real subsumption. (ibid.: 1025)

Modes of value extraction and forms of labour subsumption, while related, are not the same thing. The former indicates the strategies through which capital obtains surplus. The latter indicates the particular *form* that the labour relation can take under capitalism – the *forms of exploitation* (Banaji 2010). Indeed, across the sweatshop regime, the subsumption of labour takes place in both real and formal terms, and exploitation takes various forms.

Re-examining the complex labour processes of the sweatshop regime – varying with the physical materiality of production – one can clearly appreciate the distinct ways in which labour subsumption can take place and exploitation manifest. Factories host armies of wage-workers with varied social profiles and positions on the employment ladder. A significant part of the labour process takes place in non-factory or home-based settings. Garment areas like Delhi, which need armies of embroiderers, have progressively incorporated peripheral colonies and villages into their orbit, requisitioning traditional artisanal putting-out networks (Mezzadri 2017).

Contrary to Marx, however, in the sweatshop regime, processes of formal subsumption of labour are not transitory. Forms of 'unfree labour' (Banaji 2010) are continuously reproduced by capital to resolve pressing issues of profitability, while also performing key, non-factory tasks central to value addition. In fact, even dispossession, central to the formation of processes of real subsumption of labour, does not take place as Marx depicts. In India, as in many other parts of the world, dispossession is a 'partial' if ongoing process (Mies 1986; Harvey 2004), which may leave workers with some means of production – tools or land – but which ensures their inability to subsist outside the capitalist law of labour surplus extraction. It is first and foremost dispossession from alternative modes of living outside capitalism. Evidence from Delhi suggests that a significant proportion of garment workers still own some land. However, this is hardly crucial to their survival (Mezzadri and Srivastava 2015). Despite being only partially dispossessed, the contemporary garment working class is neither 'semi-proletarianised' (e.g. Zhou et al. 2015 on China) nor 'deproletarianised' (e.g. Brass 1990). Their process of proletarianisation is complete in its aim to divorce producers from subsistence. In this context, expropriation from the means of production becomes irrelevant; indeed, partial dispossession is handy for capital, as it guarantees the externalisation of all costs for the social reproduction of the workforce (Mezzadri 2017).

The exposure of the garment proletariat to multiple forms of exploitation is enabled by patterns of social reproduction that are equally multiple and complex. While Marx primarily observed the features and forms of exploitation at the point of production, illustrating the varied ways in which labour surplus can be extracted and labour subsumed into the capitalist relation, feminist literature has compellingly shown how these features and forms are moulded across *realms of social reproduction*. This is because exploitation is co-constituted through forms of social oppression crossing reproductive realms (Mies 1982, 1986). Indeed, the social (reproductive) profile of labouring classes is no secondary complication to the study of how things are made and value created and extracted. The Muslim Ansari embroidery workers of the sweatshop regime, for instance, are likely to continue being included into processes of formal subsumption of labour by virtue of their social profile as low-caste workers engaged in traditional occupations. Capital benefits greatly from these units of labour 'in disguise' – hidden and easily disposable.

Forms of social oppression shaped by patriarchy and racism contribute directly to expanding rates of exploitation. The cost of the commodity labour-power varies for distinct labouring bodies. Labour commodification is a highly differential process, crucial to the generation of distinct forms of exploitation, and workers come with different 'price-tags' on their bodies (Mezzadri 2017). Women workers arrive at garment factory gates already moulded as 'inferior labour' within the realm of social reproduction, where their unpaid labour is naturalised as a personal service and 'act of love' (Federici 2012). Hence, women's labour enters production valued by its historical disadvantage rather than priced for its socially necessary value.

Reproductive realms are the very foundation of capitalist processes; they generate and regenerate the commodity labour-power. Federici (2004) argues that capitalism starts from the kitchen and the bedroom. Domestic, reproductive and care work all serve the purpose of regenerating the commodity labour-power (Fortunati 1981). These activities nurture the labouring body as the 'first machine' ever invented by capitalism (Federici 2004). Given its constitutive role in processes and rates of exploitation, social reproduction should be considered as directly contributing to value generation (Mezzadri 2019). While this point is contentious (e.g. Ferguson 2019), it is fundamental to capturing the workings of exploitation in contemporary times and avoiding rigid distinctions between productive/value-producing circuits and reproductive/non-value-producing circuits.

Across the sweatshop regime, the contribution of reproductive realms and activities to value generation is paramount. While in India the 'dormitory' features of the labour regime (see Pun and Smith, 2007) are far less structured and centralized than in China, also here industrial hamlets and other workers' reproductive sites perform key functions of control and surplus value extraction (Mezzadri, 2019). The chaotic, dirty and exhausting life of workers who live there, ruled by housing brokers often connected to labour contractors (Mezzadri and Srivastava 2015), curtails workers' capacity to resist and expands exploitation rates. Realms of intergenerational reproduction – for example, villages of origin of migrant workers – subsidise capital. They reabsorb unemployed workers and internalise the social costs of labour externalised by capital – long-term housing, health provision, and care for children or the elderly generally left behind. The deployment of these reproductive realms as social 'buffer zones' decreases the value of what is considered socially necessary labour-time. Moreover, across all reproductive realms, unpaid *reproductive activities*, mainly performed by women and involving the execution of both individual and collective care and domestic duties, further depress the cost of socially necessary labour-time and with it its value. If Marx provides us with a research framework for studying the world of production and the 'secrets' behind the generation of its value, the lens of social reproduction exposes the broader theatre in which this production and its secrets unfold.

## Conclusions: The Many Struggles over Value

This chapter argues that the Marxian method developed in *Volume I* of *Capital* remains valuable for the study of contemporary, globalised production. Marx's framing of the analysis around the commodity and its distinctive value form, and his illustration of mechanisms of surplus extraction and exploitation under capitalism, still constitutes a key framework for understanding the world we inhabit. It is deployed here to explore India's sweatshop regime and yields key insights. Highlighting how the commodity (garments) reflects and incorporates labour-time illustrates the interrelation between physical and social materialities of production. The analysis shows the relevance of Marx's distinction between modes of surplus extraction – absolute and relative; and it indicates how they not only coexist in the sweatshop regime but also reinforce each other. Finally, it shows the relevance of Marx's identification of differential processes of subsumption of labour under capitalism – formal and real; and the different 'forms of exploitation' (Banaji 2010) at work across the sweatshop regime are mapped.

While committed to the Marxian method, the analysis also highlights the need to complement it, drawing on insights from radical feminist literature on the co-constitution of social oppression and exploitation and the role of social reproduction in production and extraction of value. This shows that while commodity values are clearly based on labour-time, this labour-time is valued, devalued and revalued following the distinctive social traits of different categories of labourers. Processes of absolute and relative surplus-value are also structured and their interplay examined on the basis of labourers' social identities, and these identities, in some cases, carry regimes of 'stigma' (John 2013) that intensify the work and push the price of labour well below the cost of its regeneration and replenishment.

Moreover, the feminist lens allows a deeper analysis of the forms and features of exploitation that coexist under capitalism. Indeed, it partially explains the continuation of certain forms of exploitation and their stable (non-transitory) role in the processes of surplus generation. It also illuminates the role that social reproductive realms and activities play for the very creation of value (Mezzadri 2019). Through the deployment of a Marxian feminist lens focused on social reproduction, exploitation appears as a complex socioeconomic process and experience, which is not merely moulded at the point of production, but extends far beyond the social or physical boundaries of any place of work. While manifesting in production, its roots and rationale far exceed this sphere and originate in a co-constitutive relation with social oppression. Reproductive realms and activities form key parts of the complex architecture within which distinct forms of exploitation survive and reconstitute. Ultimately, through the lens of social reproduction – in its more radical analytical sense – exploitation appears as a collection of struggles over the fruits of labour, the share of surplus and over the recognition of who contributes to this process and how.

## References

Appadurai, A. 1986. 'Introduction: Commodities and the politics of value'. In A. Appadurai (ed.), *The Social Life of Things: Commodities in Cultural Perspective*. New York: Cambridge University Press.

Bair, J. 2009. *Frontiers of Commodity Chain Research*. Stanford, CA: Stanford University Press.

———. 2010. 'On difference and capital: Gender and the globalization of production'. *Signs: Journal of Women in Culture & Society* 36(1): 203–26.

Banaji, J. 2010. *Theory as History: Essays on Modes of Production and Exploitation*. London: Haymarket.

Bernstein, H. 2010. *Class Dynamics of Agrarian Change*. Canada: Fernwood, Pluto and University of Michigan Press.

Brass, T. 1990. 'Class struggle and the deproletarianisation of agricultural labour in Haryana (India)'. *Journal of Peasant Studies* 18(1): 36–65.

Braverman, H. 1974. *Labour and Monopoly Capital: The Degradation of Work in the Twentieth Century*. New York: Monthly Review Press.

Breman, J. 2013. *At Work in the Informal Economy of India, A Perspective from the Bottom-Up*. New Delhi: Oxford University Press.

Caraway, T. L. 2005. 'The political economy of feminization: From "cheap labor" to gendered discourses of work'. *Politics and Gender* 3: 399–429.

Carswell, G. and G. De Neve. 2013. 'Labouring for global markets: Conceptualising labour agency in global production networks'. *Geoforum* 44(1): 62–70.

Castree, N. 2003. 'Commodifying what nature?' *Progress in Human Geography* 27(3): 273–97.

Chang, D. 2009. 'Informalising labour in Asia's global factory'. *Journal of Contemporary Asia* 39(2): 161–79.

Chari, S. 2004. *Fraternal Capital: Peasant-Workers, Self-Made Men, and Globalization in Provincial India*. New Delhi: Permanent Black.

Coronil, F. 1997. *The Magical State*. Chicago: University of Chicago Press.

De Neve, G. 2014. 'Fordism, flexible specialization and CSR: How Indian garment workers critique neoliberal labour regimes'. *Ethnography* 15(2): 184–207.

De Neve, G. and R. Prentice. 2017. *After Rana Plaza: Rethinking Garment Workers' Health and Safety*. Philadelphia: University of Pennsylvania Press.

Elson, D. and R. Pearson. 1981. 'The subordination of women and the internationalisation of factory production'. In K. Young, R. McCullagh and C. Wolkowitz (eds), *Of Marriage and the Market: Women's Subordination in International Perspective*. London: CSE Books.

Federici, S. 2004. *Caliban and the Witch: Women, the Body and Primitive Accumulation*. Brooklyn: Autonomedia.

———. 2012. *Revolution at Point Zero: Housework, Reproduction, and Feminist Struggle*. Brooklyn: PM Press.

Ferguson, S. 2019. *Women and Work: Feminism, Labour, and Social Reproduction*. London: Pluto.

Fernandes, L. 1997. *Producing Workers: The Politics of Gender, Class and Culture in the Calcutta Jute Mills*. Philadelphia: University of Pennsylvania Press.

Fine, B. and A. Saad-Filho. 2018. 'Marx 200: The abiding relevance of the labour theory of value'. *Review of Political Economy* 30(2): 1–16.

Fortunati, L. 1981. *L'Arcano della Reproduzione: Casalinghe, Prostitute, Operai e Capitale*. Venezia: Marsilio Editori.

Fraser, N. 2014. 'Behind Marx's hidden abode: For an expanded conception of capitalism'. *New Left Review* 86: 55–72.

Harriss-White, B. 2003. *India Working. Essays on Society and Economics*. Cambridge: Cambridge University Press.

Harvey, D. 2004. 'The "new" imperialism: Accumulation by dispossession'. *Socialist Register* 40: 63–87.

Higginbottom, A. 2012. 'Structure and essence in "Capital I": Extra surplus-value and the stages of capitalism'. *Journal of Australian Political Economy* 70: 251–70.

Hopkins, T. and I. Wallerstein. 1986. 'Commodity chains in the world economy prior to 1800'. *Review* 10(1): 157–70.

Jenkins, J. and P. Blyton. 2016. 'In debt to the time-bank: The manipulation of working time in Indian garment factories and "working dead horse" '. *Work Employment and Society* 31(1): 90–105.

John, M. E. 2013. 'The problem of women's labour: Some autobiographical perspectives'. *Indian Journal of Gender Studies* 20(2): 177–212.

Novo, C. 2004. 'The making of vulnerabilities: Indigenous day laborers in Mexico's neoliberal agriculture'. *Identities: Global Studies in Culture and Power* 11(2): 217–41.

Marx, K. 1990. *Capital, Volume I*. Penguin Classics (reprint of Pelican Books edition, 1976).

Mezzadri, A. 2017. *The Sweatshop Regime: Labouring Bodies, Exploitation and Garments Made in India*. Cambridge: Cambridge University Press.

———. 2019. 'On the value of social reproduction: Informal labour, the majority world and the need for inclusive theories and politics'. *Radical Philosophy* 2(4): 33–41.

Mezzadri, A. and R. Srivastava. 2015. *Labour Regimes in the Indian Garment Sector: Capital–Labour Relations, Social Reproduction and Labour Standards in the National Capital Region (NCR)*. London: SOAS.

Mies, M. 1982. *The Lace Makers of Narsapur: Indian Housewives Produce for the World Market*. London: Zed.

———. 1986. *Patriarchy and Accumulation on a World Scale: Women in the International Division of Labour*. London: Zed.

Peepercamp, M. 2018. *Labour without Liberty. Female Migrant Workers in Bangalore's Garment Industry*. Report by the Indian Committee of the Netherlands, Clean Clothes Campaign, and Global Labour Union, http://cividep.org/wp-content/uploads/2018/02/LabourWithoutLiberty.pdf

Pun, N. and C. Smith. 2007. 'Putting transnational labour process in its place: The dormitory labour regime in post-socialist China'. *Work, Employment and Society* 21(1): 27–45.

Ruwanpura, K. N. 2011. 'Women workers in the apparel sector: A three-decade (r)evolution of feminist contributions?' *Progress in Development Studies* 11(3): 197–209.

Salzinger, L. 2003. *Genders in Production*. Berkley: University of California Press.

Selwyn, B. 2017. *The Struggle for Development*. Cambridge: Polity.

Shah, A., J. Lerche, R. Axelby, D. Benbabaali, B. Donegan, J. Raj and V. Thakur. 2017. *Ground Down by Growth: Tribe, Caste, Class and Inequality in 21st Century India*. London: Pluto.

Sivakumar, S. 2017. *Towards a Living Wage: A Study of the Minimum Wages Struggle of Workers in Tiruppur's Garment Sector*. Tiruppur: SAVE.

Smith, J. 2016. *Imperialism in the 21st Century. Globalization, Super-Exploitation and Capitalism's Financial Crisis*. New York: Monthly Review Press.

Watts, M. J. 1994. 'Life under contract: Contract farming, agrarian restructuring, and flexible accumulation'. In P. D. Little and M. J. Watts (eds), *Living Under Contract: Contract Farming and Agrarian Transformation in Sub-Saharan Africa*. Madison: University of Wisconsin Press.

Wright, M. 2006. *Disposable Women and Other Myths of Global Capitalism*. New York: Routledge.

Zhou T., Fan Y. L. and Gao M. 2015. 'Semi-proletarianization of the peasantry: The impact of transferring capital to countryside on rural production relationship'. *Anthropologist* 21(3): 565–72.

# Chapter Six

# THINKING ABOUT CAPITAL AND CLASS IN THE GULF ARAB STATES

## Adam Hanieh

**Abstract**

The study of the Middle East, and of the Gulf monarchies in particular, is generally dominated by institutionalist and neo-Weberian approaches focusing on religious identity, sectarianism, authoritarianism or natural resource endowment as key explanatory factors underlying social processes in the region. In these accounts, the notion of class often disappears from view or is loosely elided with anachronistic or imprecise labels such as 'merchants' and 'elites'. This chapter reflects on how Marxist conceptualisations of class can help in grasping the specificities of labour, migration and capital accumulation in the Gulf – not least in thinking about how the social relations underlying these categories extend across national borders with profound implications for the surrounding region. This is much more than simply an issue of theory; Marx's work can be a powerful guide to doing field research in the Gulf – revealing the right questions to ask and helping unearth surprising connections that might otherwise have gone unnoticed. The analysis draws on the author's experience of several years of living and research in the Gulf; conducting interviews with businesspeople, migrant workers and other key informants; teaching Gulf women citizens and, overall, trying to grasp – in the field, with Marx – the nature of capitalist accumulation in the Gulf.

## Introduction

My work has largely focused on the Middle East, where I explore questions of political economy and class formation. With a few significant exceptions, Marxist writing on the Middle East has long been eclipsed by institutionalist and neo-Weberian approaches that emphasise factors such as religious identity, sectarianism, authoritarianism or natural resource endowment as key explanatory factors underlying social processes in the region. This is particularly true for academic research on the Gulf monarchies – my main area of interest – where categories such as class and capitalism are largely absent or loosely elided with anachronistic or imprecise labels such as 'merchants' and 'elites'. Counter to this marginalisation of Marxist categories, I hope to show in this chapter how Marx's extensive writings provide a powerful lens for understanding the dynamics of the region and to illustrate the ways in which they have informed my own work. This is much more than simply an issue of theory; Marx's work has been a profound help to me in conducting fieldwork and primary research – revealing the right questions to ask and helping unearth surprising connections that might otherwise have gone unnoticed.

My principal research interests have been twofold: first, an attempt to theorise and map the nature of accumulation and the circulation of capital in the Gulf and, second, to analyse how this relates to forms of labour exploitation and migration flows to the region. But before discussing the specificities of this research, I want to begin with a few observations on Marx's general method. To my mind, a lot of writing about Marx – not only from critics but also some adherents of Marxism – tends to adopt a very one-dimensional picture of his work that leads to misleading caricatures and 'straw-men' arguments. Claims that Marx was a crude technological determinist or class reductionist, for example, bear little resemblance to what he actually wrote and how he approached the study of history and society. It is true that some of Marx's followers have been guilty of such problems – and we should certainly avoid approaching Marx's writing as some kind of revealed truth, in which debate is reduced to philological exegesis of a sacred text – but any honest engagement with Marx uncovers a fluid and dynamic thinker, willing to change his mind in the face of new evidence and whose method was far removed from any formulaic or teleological thought.

In this spirit, there are several overarching features of Marx's method that are particularly important to highlight and which have been essential to my own thinking. The first of these is his close and scrupulous attention to empirical detail as the necessary prerequisite and ultimate root of any 'theory building'. This is often poorly appreciated, but Marx had a lifelong commitment to accumulating, processing and understanding the latest in scientific and historical evidence, material that he then integrated into his understanding of economic and social processes. As part of this, Marx showed immense interest in a wide array of topics beyond those we normally consider as 'social science' and also had a deep concern with the long-term history of specific countries and regions beyond the borders of Europe.[1] Indeed, in the last years of his life, Marx was engaged in a massive study of 'Asia Minor [...] the Near East and Middle East, the Islamic world, the Americas, and Asia (with three centres of focus: India, China, and Central Asia)' as part of a chronology of world history that ran to over 1,500 pages in print (Kratke 2012: 14).

All of this is immediately relevant to thinking about fieldwork, where a commitment to primary data, historical specificity and the interpretation of direct experience is paramount. But as much as Marx took clear delight in the latest empirical discoveries and historical research, he stridently rejected any empiricist or positivist approaches to the study of society. In his often quoted statement that 'all science would be superfluous if the form of appearance of things directly coincided with their essence' (Marx 1981: 956),

---

[1]   These included, for example, his close attention to the latest debates in soil science (Saito 2017), which were to inform his analysis of the relationship between town and countryside and continue to shape discussions around today's ecological crises. Likewise, Marx's enthusiastic study of Charles Darwin's *Origin of the Species* was marked by a sophisticated appreciation of the non-teleological and contingent aspects to evolution – a feature that remains widely misunderstood in popular accounts of Darwin today (Sayer and Corrigan 1987: 66).

Marx's method was carefully focused on establishing not simply how conceptual categories worked, but *why* reality took these forms in the first place. This was most clearly
expressed in his decades-long exploration and critique of political economy, culminating
in his magnum opus *Capital*. Throughout this work, Marx sought to trace the connection
between capitalist social relations and their social forms (most centrally, that of value).
As numerous authors have emphasised, underlying this approach is a distinctive methodological framework rooted in a theory of commodity fetishism, where social relations
under capitalism take the form of material things that then appear to possess an autonomous and independent power over human beings (Rubin 1972; Sayer 1987; Ollman
2003). By digging below surface appearances and reconstructing the nature of these
social relations, we are thus able to understand the particular ideological forms through
which the world appears to us (Sayer 1987). As Dorothy Smith notes, Marx's epistemology thus sees 'the concepts foundational to political economy as expressions or
reflections of the social relations of a mode of production' and, from this standpoint, 'the
difference between ideology and science is the difference between treating those concepts
as the primitives of theory and treating them as sites for exploring the social relations that
are expressed in them' (Smith 2004: 446).

Essential to this epistemology is starting with the concrete, lived experience of people –
a point that has been particularly emphasised by Marxist feminists (Smith 2004; Bannerji
1995). In this, Marx and Engels are insistent that consciousness cannot be understood
separate from the real-life activity of human beings (Smith 2004: 448). This is very
different from the caricature of Marx sometimes advanced, in which 'superstructural'
phenomenon are said to exist as a distinct and separable level that reflects economic
being. Instead, by foregrounding 'real living individuals' as the basis of his theory of history, Marx was not simply asserting the primacy of the material over the ideal, but rather
insisting that 'the material existence of [...] individuals can no longer be conceptualised
in ways which exclude their consciousness' (Sayer 1987: 87) – in other words, it makes
as much sense to conceive of human beings without consciousness as it is to conceive of
consciousness without human beings. Once again, this holds implications for fieldwork,
not least of which is the importance of uncovering the ideas and beliefs that people hold
about themselves and their social situation and connecting this to their 'activity and their
material conditions under which they live' (Marx and Engels 1845: 163).

This standpoint is closely related to a final feature of Marx's method: the deep
connection between his theory building and political practice. Marx and Engels were of
course lifelong revolutionary actors and played leading roles in the radical movements
of the mid-nineteenth century. Their political commitment is often illustrated through
the famous 11th Thesis on Feuerbach (later inscribed on Marx's gravestone), where
they assert that 'The philosophers have only interpreted the world, in various ways; the
point is to change it' (p. 123). But I think it is a mistake to read this pithy sentence as
simply a pledge to political activity. Rather, as the theses that precede no. 11 make abun-
dantly clear, Marx's real target here is an abstract and ahistorical German philosophy
that separated thoughts and conceptions from the concrete life activity of human beings
(Thesis 1). Marx was actually making a profound epistemological point: it was human
beings in action that produced forms of thought, and thus it was only through actively

participating in changing their social circumstances that people change themselves and their forms of thought. Theory and practice are here conceived as an inseparable unity – which he describes in Thesis 3 as 'revolutionary practice' – and it is thus really only possible to fully understand the world through our attempts to change it. Framed in this manner, political activity is not simply a moral commitment but actually part of Marx's 'method'; in this sense, Marx was always 'in the field'.

## Marx and the Gulf

I want to illustrate some of these broader methodological points more concretely through reflecting on my own work on the political economy of the six Gulf Arab states: Saudi Arabia, the UAE, Qatar, Bahrain, Oman and Kuwait. I have a long-standing interest in the Gulf that originally stemmed from political activism around Palestine. Following several years living and working in Palestine during the Oslo process and throughout the Second Intifada, I became increasingly convinced that dynamics in Palestine could not be understood without a deeper investigation of the wider Middle East and the particular role of the Gulf states. This was evident, for example, in the strong dependency of leading Palestinian capitalists on their investments in the Gulf, as well as the considerable involvement of Gulf-based firms in major Palestinian companies and financial institutions (Hanieh 2011). Gulf governments also played an influential role in Palestinian politics through the provision of aid and financial support to the Palestinian Authority, and many friends and relatives spoke of time they had spent as workers in the oil and other industries in Saudi Arabia, the UAE and other Gulf states. At a political level, it was clear that US strategy in the Middle East was partially driven by an attempt to establish economic and political relationships between Israel and the Gulf – a trend that has become strikingly apparent over recent years. Yet, despite all these varied connections, there was little satisfactory analysis of the political economy of regional capitalism and the particular weight of the Gulf within this.

From my own perspective, Marx's work has been absolutely essential to thinking through these regional patterns, beginning with an understanding of capitalism in the Gulf itself. Much of the academic literature on the Gulf is framed by Rentier State Theory (RST), which attempts to explain the political, social and economic features of the Gulf through the massive financial rents arising from the sale of hydrocarbons (oil and gas) on the world market (Beblawi and Luciani 1987; Mahdavy 1970; Skocpol 1982; Ross 2001). While there are a variety of different versions of RST, most start from the assumption that the availability of oil rents has fostered a pronounced *autonomy* of the Gulf state (and hence ruling families) from society, which has allowed the state to overshadow all other social groups. According to this assumption, Gulf monarchies, freed by oil revenues from the constraints of taxation and the need to respond to societal demands, constitute an archetypal 'strong state', with a particularly enhanced capacity 'to penetrate society, regulate social relationships, extract resources, and appropriate or use resources in determined ways' (Migdal 1998: 4). In this manner, RST approaches tend to deny the utility of class as a conceptual category, depicting private capital as weak and underdeveloped and downplaying the importance of labour and the structure of working classes. The analysis in these accounts thus tends to focus on the personalities and internal intrigues of ruling families and the ways in which states deploy and distribute oil rents throughout society.

There is a lot that can be said about RST that goes beyond the scope of this chapter, but in my opinion a perceptive critique is provided by Marx's approach to understanding the state and its relationship to class formation. Marx conceived the state not as a 'thing' or collection of individual social actors, but rather as a particular expression of class power – with the latter understood as a set of social relations that is continually in the process of coming-into-being. From this perspective, the state is not a separate sphere of politics that stands apart from the economic sphere; it is a social relation, or, as Bertell Ollman describes it, 'the set of institutional forms through which a ruling class relates to the rest of society' (Ollman 2003: 202). The relationship the ruling class holds with the state is actually part of what constitutes it as a class; state and class need to be seen as mutually reinforcing and co-constituted, with the latter providing the conditions of existence for the former. An analysis of the state, therefore, must begin with an 'examination of the "anatomy of bourgeois society"', that is, an analysis of the specifically capitalist mode of social labour, the appropriation of the surplus product and the resulting laws of reproduction of the whole social formation, which objectively give rise to the particular political form' (Hirsch 1979: 58). Approached in this way, class formation – the ways in which classes emerge around the production, realisation and appropriation of profit – becomes the central starting point to understanding any social formation.

What is important to highlight here is that Marx's emphasis on the social relations of class sets up a whole different set of questions than those arising from RST and other conventional approaches to the Gulf. Instead of a surface-level focus on oil wealth, ruling family intrigues or tribal and religious factors, a focus on class formation raises questions such as: how do classes of capital and labour emerge, and how do they relate to one another? What are the specificities of different moments of capital accumulation (production, commodity exchange, finance and so on) and how are these connected? What are the spatial dynamics of this accumulation, that is, how does it extend across national, regional and global circuits? How do these dynamics relate to the specific role of the state in the Gulf? How can we conceptualise ruling families vis-à-vis the capitalist class, and migrant labour vis-à-vis the citizen population? Questions such as these bring out the distinctive features of a Marxian compared to institutionalist and neo-Weberian approaches (such as RST); the kinds of questions we ask, and the insights we can potentially draw, shift dramatically when we foreground questions of class formation and capital accumulation.

## Capital in the Gulf

Guided by these kinds of questions, my work on class in the Gulf has taken two key directions. The first of these has been an attempt to understand the nature of the capitalist class in the Gulf, its different moments of accumulation, the way this class connects to the state and ruling families, and – something that became most apparent to me through an extended period of living, research and working in the Gulf – the specific ways that this accumulation was organised spatially. I have employed a variety of different methods throughout this research, including fieldwork interviews, studies of different economic sectors and policies and a detailed mapping of share ownership, cross-border capital flows and corporate structures in the Gulf.

Through my initial phases of fieldwork, I met with numerous businesspeople and state officials. This was often difficult to organise due to the quite closed nature of Gulf society, but opportunities presented themselves through an extended period of teaching at a university for Emirati students in Dubai. Many insights emerged in the course of these discussions. First, it was very clear that the leading corporate sectors in the Gulf very much conceived their accumulation across a variety of diversified business activities – productive, commercial and financial – that were organised through conglomerate or holding group structures. Time and time again, formal and informal conversations with businesspeople in the Gulf emphasised the way that they sought to extend investments through different but closely related sectors. An employee of a well-known retail firm that I spoke with in 2009, for example, stressed his company's deep involvement in aluminium, steel, cement, construction, as well as banking interests. The significance of this interweaving of accumulation across the circuit of capital – an expression of the increasing concentration and centralisation of capital ownership that Marx pointed to in his work – was not something that I had really given much thought to previously. But these kinds of comments led me to investigate and attempt to trace more comprehensively the ownership structures of large conglomerates in the Gulf. Through interviews and a close analysis of stock exchange data, company websites and other data sources, I attempted to reconstruct the concrete nature of the capitalist class in the Gulf (Hanieh 2011).

Other features of the capitalist class also emerged through this fieldwork. One of the most interesting aspects to this was the repeated manner in which businesspeople described members of the ruling family as corporate or economic actors – not simply through their political domination of the state. Ruling family members held *private* interests in a vast array of business activities – again largely organised through diversified, conglomerate structures. The line between the 'state' and 'capital' in other words, was not one of sharp demarcation, rather ruling families needed to be conceptualised as leading members *of* the private capitalist class. This blurring of the lines between public and private capital was highlighted by one Abu Dhabi-based informant who perceptively pointed to the presence of government ministries that were specifically tasked with managing the private wealth of the ruler. Viewing ruling family members as capitalists and not simply authoritarian leaders recasts how we think of capital and the state in Gulf, upsetting standard RST models that posit a 'strong state' suspended over a 'weak' private business community. In this manner, Marx's understanding of the state form as fundamentally expressing the nature of capitalist class power is confirmed.

A further useful insight that strongly emerged through this fieldwork was the importance of the internationalisation of capital within business strategies, with large conglomerates clearly focusing on expanding their accumulation across national borders (Hanieh 2011; 2018). This was true at a number of different spatial scales. Most immediately, expansion into neighbouring Gulf markets was widely identified as a key aspect of future growth. As part of this process, there are increasing interdependencies between

**Table 6.1** GCC involvement in banking sectors of selected Arab countries

| Country | Total no. of banks | No. of GCC-related banks | Share of total country bank assets held by GCC-related banks (%) | Share of total non-government bank assets held by GCC-related banks (%) |
|---|---|---|---|---|
| Jordan | 18 | 12 | 86 | 86 |
| Palestine | 6 | 2 | 63 | 63 |
| Egypt | 37 | 17 | 30 | 59 |
| Lebanon | 35 | 26 | 51 | 51 |
| Algeria | 19 | 7 | 5 | 45 |
| Tunisia | 36 | 11 | 18 | 25 |

*Source*: Adapted from Hanieh (2018: 187).

Gulf capital from different national origins, expressed in joint investments, pan-Gulf licensing and agency rights, and the emergence of new forms of financial capital such as private equity firms that tended to be controlled by a variety of investors from different Gulf countries. This interlocking of accumulation across the pan-Gulf scale – what I came to term Khaleeji Capital – is highly hierarchical and largely organised around a Saudi–UAE axis (Hanieh 2011). This also helps us understand the nature of the Gulf's regional integration project – the Gulf Cooperation Council – as something much more than simply an outcome of security or military coordination against perceived external threats.

A final aspect to this internationalisation is the growing reach of Gulf conglomerates beyond the Gulf itself. This is evident throughout global markets such as North America, Western Europe and, increasingly, East Asia, but I have been particularly interested in what this might mean for the nature of capitalist development in Arab countries in the wider Middle East. From the 2000s onwards, we can observe the rising weight of Gulf conglomerates in key economic sectors across neighbouring states, including real estate and urban development, agribusiness, telecommunications, retail, logistics, banking and finance (see Table 6.1).

This region-wide expansion of Gulf capital raises a series of important issues regarding how we understand neoliberal processes and class formation in the rest of the Middle East: the interiorisation of Gulf capital in the class structures of other Arab states means that the political economy of the wider region is being increasingly pulled around the dynamics of accumulation in the Gulf (Hanieh 2018).

## Labour and Migration in the Gulf

Again, inspired by Marx, something that I have continually sought to keep upfront in my work is the necessity of viewing capital as a social relation, one formed through its particular relationship with labour. It is not possible, in other words, to understand Gulf capital (or the Gulf state) without also examining the conditions and forms of labour.

In my opinion, one of the weaknesses of much work on the political economy of the Gulf is a tendency to ignore labour altogether, or relegate it to a secondary aspect or outcome of RST models. This is particularly problematic in the case of the Gulf, where a majority of the labour force is made up of temporary migrant workers who are denied all political and civil rights and lack any viable route to permanent residency or citizenship.

The latest available statistics record the percentage of non-nationals in the labour force as ranging between 56 and 82 per cent in Saudi Arabia, Oman, Bahrain and Kuwait, to around 93–94 per cent in Qatar and the UAE. Non-nationals represent 70 per cent of the total labour force across the Gulf as a whole, a figure larger than anywhere else in the world.[2] The overwhelming majority of these migrant workers – around 88 per cent – are located in the Gulf's private sector.[3] All of this give the region a distinctive position in patterns of migration at the global level; indeed, the Gulf hosts more migrants than any other region in the Global South, with Saudi Arabia alone ranking as the second largest source of remittances in the world (after the United States).

The entry of migrant workers to the Gulf is managed through the infamous *kafala* system, a work permit arrangement that ties the worker to a sponsor (known as a *kafil*), forbids them from seeking alternative employment and formally prevents departure from the country without employer permission (Dito 2014). These legal structures strengthen the power of employers over migrant workers and help underpin chronically low wages and hazardous work conditions. As noted, the vast majority of migrant workers are located in the private sector, where there are no minimum wages. At a discursive level, Gulf media outlets and government officials frequently employ a highly racialised language that cast migrants as security, demographic, cultural or sexual threats (Buckley 2014).

I have conducted interviews with migrant workers in the Gulf whose stories provide a consistent account of the methods of their recruitment and the types of working conditions they face. During a recent trip to Dubai, for example, a 28-year-old former construction worker explained how he had initially responded to a newspaper advertisement in Pakistan from a labour agency that was recruiting for a well-known Emirati construction firm. Encouraged by his brother, he paid 7,000 UAE dirham (just under US\$2,000) for a work permit and plane ticket. On arrival in Dubai the firm took his passport from him, and he was housed in a labour camp with movement to and from

---

[2]   Gulf Labour Markets and Migration, 'Percentage of nationals and non-nationals in employed population in GCC countries', http://gulfmigration.eu/percentage-of-nationals-and-non-nationals-in-employed-population-in-gcc-countries-national-statistics-latest-year-or-period-available/ (accessed 20 April 2020).

[3]   Gulf Labour Markets and Migration, 'Percentage of non-nationals in government sector and in private and other sectors', http://gulfmigration.eu/percentage-of-non-nationals-in-govpercentage-of-non-nationals-in-government-sector-and-in-private-and-other-sectors-in-gcc-countries-national-statistics-latest-year-or-period-available (accessed 20 April 2020). This figure does not include the UAE for which figures are unavailable but are likely of a similar magnitude.

work organised through employer-mandated transportation. Working 14 hours every day, except Friday, his income was only 1,000 dirhams/month, meaning that it would take a minimum of seven months to repay all his initial costs.

For many people, one of the most memorable moments in visiting Dubai is the opportunity to see Burj Khalifa, the world's tallest building, which reaches a towering 830 m in height. But as my interviewee commented to me, 'Who do the tourists think built this? They see the building, but the people who made it are invisible.' I was immediately reminded of Marx's comments about how commodities – in this case the spectacle of the built environment – appear to possess a power in and of themselves, independent of human beings. We are awed by the staggering cityscapes of the Gulf, but remain oblivious to the actual people who built them. Marx once observed that if we are to move away from the self-image projected by 'our friend Moneybags', we must delve 'into the hidden abode of production' where we discover 'not only how capital produces, but how capital is produced' – this 'secret' as he termed it, is one that hundreds of thousands of workers in the Gulf are acutely aware of every day (Marx 1887: 121).

The invisibility of labour is something continually reinforced in the Gulf's public sphere, where low-paid migrant workers are completely absent from city branding campaigns that emphasise extravagant architecture, endless shopping opportunities and a unique cultural pastiche of modernity and Islamic tradition. One illustration of this can be seen in the spatially segregation of labour camps, where much of the low-paid worker population in the Gulf is housed. The reality of this struck me once during an attempt to visit one of these camps with a friend. Driving around in circles looking for a camp that was marked clearly on the map but didn't seem to be where it should be, we commented how nice it was that there was a dense row of lush trees along the side of a dusty highway. It then dawned on us that these trees were actually meant as a physical barrier, one aimed at hiding the labour camp from the view of citizens or tourists. Located in these kinds of distant areas, the prohibitive cost of transport prevents workers from freely moving about in the city or interacting with the rest of the population. At times this circumscription of movement is legally enforced – in 2011, for example, Qatari authorities barred male migrant workers (mostly involved in construction) from living in established residential areas (Kovessy 2014). Female domestic workers are particularly affected by such restrictions on their movement, as they typically live with their employer who may bar them from leaving the house (Gamburd 2009).

Ultimately, such patterns of labour control constitute a powerful means to discipline the migrant workforce. Importantly, however, they also underpin the particular nature of citizenship in the Gulf. With the right to import migrant workers granted to citizens by the state, local firms take on responsibility for the day-to-day monitoring and management of non-citizen labour (Longva 1997: 100). This provides both lucrative income streams for the citizen population (through the sale of work permits) and also deepens the vulnerability of migrants to violence, abuse and poor working conditions (Khalaf 2014). Precisely because the *kafala* system personalises the day-to-day control of migrants in the hands of local citizens and firms, a deep logic of securitisation is generalised throughout much of the wider citizen population (Dito 2014). Migrant domestic workers – mostly women and among the most isolated of all workers in the Gulf – play an essential role in reproducing Gulf households and have been a key factor enabling the growing visibility of women citizens in the workplace, educational institutions and public life. In this manner, the institutional structures governing migration in the Gulf shape much more than just the lived experience of migrants – these structures are fundamental to how Gulf citizens themselves are integrated into their societies.

At the same time, the citizen population itself is also sharply divided. The unemployment rate among citizens – particularly youth and women – is very high in some Gulf states (notably Saudi Arabia and Oman), where private firms have generally preferred to employ significantly cheaper migrant labour rather than citizens (Hanieh 2018). Wealthier citizens – particularly those linked to the large conglomerates or ruling family – occupy a much more privileged position, with access to government contracts, state-backed investments and high-ranking official appointments. There are also significant ethno-sectarian divisions in the Gulf, which have their historical roots in the divide-and-rule techniques of population control developed under British colonialism and continue to form an important element to how ruling families maintain their power (Alshehabi 2019).

All of this points to the complexities of class relations in the Gulf, which can only be unpacked through a concrete analysis of the forms of capital accumulation and the specificities of a sharply hierarchical, racially stratified and mostly migrant working class. Critical to this is Marx's insistence that capital and labour are internally related; we need to keep both sides of this relationship in view when attempting to understand the ways that class has come into being in the Gulf. Such an approach means that it is not enough to identify (as many NGOs and international organisations do) inadequate migration policies, a lack of effective labour regulations, or a weak understanding of international norms as the root causes of the poor conditions of migrant labour in the Gulf. The deeply exploitative forms of labour found throughout the region – and the ways these are shaped through migration and the construction of citizenship – are *systemic* features of how Gulf capitalism reproduces itself.

## Conclusion

These class dynamics are not simply a matter of concern to those whole live in the Gulf itself. In the aftermath of the Arab uprisings that erupted in Tunisia in 2010 and which spread rapidly across the entire Middle East, it has become patently clear how important the Gulf is to the future of the region as a whole. From the wars in Syria and Libya – where different Gulf powers have supported an ever-shifting range of factions – to the catastrophic bombing of Yemen, the Gulf has been the main Arab protagonist involved in the region's current conflicts. Outside these areas of open war, the Gulf also increasingly shapes the political and economic policies of other Arab states. In partnership with international financial institutions such as the World Bank, IMF and European Bank for Reconstruction and Development, billion-dollar funding packages from the Gulf states have insisted on the standard tropes of market-led development – prioritising privatisation, opening up to foreign investment, and cuts to subsidies and social spending (Hanieh

2018: 255–65). Politically, this has been closely entwined with hardening authoritarianism and repression of social protest through the years that followed 2011. All of these processes are reflected in the growing linkages between the political economy of various Arab countries and the dynamics of Gulf capitalism itself.

In the initial phase of the 2011 uprisings, a number of leading scholars reflected on the current state of Middle East studies and the apparent inability to predict the extraordinary surge of region-wide popular protest and the rapid overthrow of authoritarian regimes in Tunisia and Egypt (Bellin 2012; Gause 2011; Valbjørn and Volpi 2014). Some of the more perceptive accounts in these discussions noted the way that questions of political economy had been relatively marginalised in recent academic work on the region, and that one of the positive consequences of the uprisings was that 'political economy issues [were placed] front and center' united around the essential question of 'where has the money gone?' and thus helping to counteract 'much of the popular media's fixation on violence, terrorism, and sectarianism' that too often shapes how the Middle East is perceived (Moore 2013: 225). Since that time, numerous accounts of the political economy of the uprisings have emerged, drawing attention to the tight linkages between authoritarianism and class power and highlighting the significance of labour and other social movements in both the laying the ground for the uprisings and shaping their subsequent trajectories (Beinin and Vairel 2013; Beinin 2015; Achcar 2013; Hanieh 2013; Alexander and Bassiouny 2014; Abdulrahman 2015).

In many ways, this welcome resurgence of interest in Middle East political economy precisely confirms Marx's approach to knowledge production – where the objects and forms of knowledge cannot be separated from the active struggles of people against structures of power and domination. But we must always remember that Marx intended his project as a *critique* of political economy, not simply as an extension of the classical political economy tradition embodied in the works of Ricardo, Smith, Say, Malthus and Mill. It is in a fundamental and truly radical sense that Marx urged us to go beyond the simple surface appearances of the 'economy' and interrogate the *why* that sits underneath the concepts and categories in which we usually conduct conversations about the world. This is a task that remains incomplete for the study of the Middle East, but it is one in which Marx's framework – and perhaps most importantly, his method – holds enduring utility.

## References

Abdulrahman, M. 2015. *Egypt's Long Revolution: Protest Movements and Uprisings.* London: Routledge.

Achcar, G. 2013. *The People Want: A Radical Exploration of the Arab Uprising.* Berkeley: University of California Press.

Alexander, A. and M. Bassiouny. 2014. *Bread, Freedom, Social Justice Workers and the Egyptian Revolution.* London: Zed.

Alshehabi, O. 2019. *Contested Modernity: Sectarianism, Nationalism, and Colonialism in Bahrain.* London: Oneworld.

Bannerji, H. 1995. *Thinking Through: Essay on Marxism, Feminism and Anti-Racism.* Toronto: Women's Press.

Beblawi, H. and G. Luciani (eds). 1987. *The Rentier State: Nation, State and the Integration of the Arab World*. London: Croom Helm.

Beinin, J. 2015. *Workers and Thieves: Labor Movements and Popular Uprisings in Tunisia and Egypt*. Stanford: Stanford University Press.

Beinin, J. and F. Vairel (eds). 2013. *Social Movements, Mobilization, and Contestation in the Middle East and North Africa*. Stanford: Stanford University Press.

Bellin, E. 2012. 'Reconsidering the robustness of authoritarianism in the Middle East: Lessons from the Arab Spring'. *Comparative Politics* (January): 127–49.

Buckley, M. 2014. 'Construction work, bachelor builders and the intersectional politics of urbanisation in Dubai'. In A. Khalaf, O. AlShehabi and A. Hanieh (eds), *Transit States: Labour, Migration and Citizenship in the Gulf*, pp. 32–152. London: Pluto Press.

Dito, M. 2014. 'Kafala: Foundations of migrant exclusion in GCC labour markets'. In A. Khalaf, O. AlShehabi and A. Hanieh (eds), *Transit States: Labour, Migration and Citizenship in the Gulf*, pp. 79–100. London: Pluto Press.

Gamburd, M. 2009. 'Advocating for Sri Lankan migrant workers'. *Critical Asian Studies* 41(1): 61–88.

Gause III, G. F. 2011. 'Why Middle East studies missed the Arab Spring: The myth of authoritarian stability'. *Foreign Affairs* 90(4): 81–84, 85–90.

Hanieh, A. 2011. *Capitalism and Class in the Gulf Arab States*. Basingstoke: Palgrave Macmillan.

———. 2013. *Lineages of Revolt: Issues of Contemporary Capitalism in the Middle East*. Chicago: Haymarket Books.

———. 2018. *Money, Markets, and Monarchies: The Gulf Cooperation Council and the Political Economy of the Contemporary Middle East*. Cambridge: Cambridge University Press.

Hirsch, J. 1979. 'The state apparatus and social reproduction: Elements of a theory of the bourgeois state'. In J. Holloway and S. Picciotto (eds), *State and Capital: A Marxist Debate*, pp. 57–107. London: Edward Arnold.

Khalaf, A. 2014. 'The politics of migration'. In A. Khalaf, O. AlShehabi and A. Hanieh (eds), *Transit States: Labour, Migration and Citizenship in the Gulf*, pp. 39–56. London: Pluto Press.

Kovessy, P. 2014. 'Crackdown on partitioned homes continues with amended Qatar law', http://dohanews.co/crackdown-partitioned-homes-continues-new-law/ (accessed 7 February 2020).

Kratke, M. 2012. 'Marx and world history'. *International Review of Social History* 63(1): 91–125.

Longva, A. N. 1997. *Walls Built on Sand: Migration, Exclusion and Society in Kuwait*. Boulder: Westview.

Mahdavy, H. 1970. 'The patterns and problems of economic development in rentier states: The case of Iran'. In M. Cook (ed.), *Studies in the Economic History of the Middle East*, pp. 428–67. London: Oxford University Press.

Marx, K. 1981/3, *Capital, Volume III* (trans. David Fernbach). London: Penguin.

———. 1887. *Capital, Volume I: A Critique of Political Economy* (trans. Samuel Moore and Edward Aveling). Moscow: Progress.

Marx, K. and F. Engels. 1845/6. 'The German ideology'. In *MECW Volume 5*, pp. 19–539. London: Lawrence and Wishart.

Migdal, J. 1998. *Strong Societies and Weak States: State-Society Relations and State Capabilities in the Third World*. Princeton: Princeton University Press.

Moore, P. 2013. 'The bread revolutions of 2011: Teaching political economies of the Middle East'. *PS: Political Science & Politics* 46(2): 225–29.

Ollman, B. 2003. *Dance of the Dialectic: Steps in Marx's Method*. Urbana: University of Illinois Press.

Ross, M. 2001. 'Does oil hinder democracy?' *World Politics* 53(3): 325–61.

Rubin, I. 1972. *Essays on Marx's Theory of Value*. Detroit: Black and Red.

Saito, K. 2017. *Karl Marx's Ecosocialism: Capital, Nature, and the Unfinished Critique of Political Economy*. New York: Monthly Review Press.

Sayer, D. 1987. *The Violence of Abstraction*. Oxford: Basil Blackwell.

Sayer, D. and P. Corrigan. 1987. 'Revolution against the state: The context and significance of Marx's later writings'. *Dialectical Anthropology* 12(1): 65–82.

Skocpol, T. 1982. 'Rentier state and Shi'a Islam in the Iranian revolution'. *Theory and Society* 11(3): 46–82.

Smith, D. E. 2004. 'Ideology, science and social relations: A reinterpretation of Marx's epistemology'. *European Journal of Social Theory* 7: 445–62 .

Valbjørn, M. and F. Volpi. 2014. 'Revisiting theories of Arab politics in the aftermath of the Arab uprisings'. *Mediterranean Politics* 19(1): 134–36.

# Chapter Seven

# MARX ON THE BOURSE

## COFFEE AND THE INTERSECTING/INTEGRATED CIRCUITS OF CAPITAL

### Susan Newman

**Abstract**

There has been a tendency in academic scholarship of the contemporary capitalist system not only to limit analyses to the confines of specific disciplines with established concepts, analytical categories and methods, but also to focus on realms of production, exchange and finance as distinct from each other. This decoupling is clear within economics with the distinction between the 'real' and the 'financial'. By contrast, the integrated nature of production, exchange and finance is stressed by Marx in *Capital, Volume II* as he examines economic reproduction in its totality. While *Volume II* is centred on the market place, as opposed to production in *Volume I* or finance in *Volume III*, it has at its heart the notion of the commodity as the unity and contradiction between use-value and exchange-value. *Volume II* develops Marx's reproduction schema by examining the constant intertwining of appearance and disappearance of money capital, productive capital and commodity capital from the sphere of circulation into the sphere of production and back again. In doing so, this schema highlights the unity and contradiction between the two spheres and provides clear guidance for identifying both sites and subjects of research that have largely been analysed separately. This chapter elucidates the influence of *Volume II* on recent analyses of the changing social relations of production of coffee commodity chains that examine not only the relationships between merchants, traders and workers that transform and transport coffee into an object for consumption, but also the money-owner, money-lender and money-manager operating on international financial exchanges as their interests and operations interact with those of commodity chain actors.

## Introduction

Marx begins his analysis in *Capital, Volume I* with the commodity. The commodity, or more precisely its production by commodified and exploited labour, has been the subject of much study by scholars inspired by Marx's analysis. Notable are contributions inspired by world systems approaches that have tackled the historical political economy of capitalism through in-depth studies in the evolution of the ways in which the production and exchange of single commodities have been organized globally. Notable are the epic works of Sidney Mintz (1986) on sugar and the more recent contribution by Sven Beckert (2015) on cotton.

Like sugar and cotton, coffee production in the Global South has its origins in colonial conquest and surplus extraction by colonizers in the Global North. At the time of independence, the economic structures of former colonies were heavily skewed, with capitalist relations concentrated within export commodity sectors, typically within a narrow range of commodities. This was recognized in the policies of independent nation states as well as development policies of the Global North. Economic development would require the development of surplus generating sectors and the channelling of surplus towards productive accumulation more widely. At the same time, structuralist ideas were informing the development policies of the Global North with the Prebish–Singer hypothesis of a long-run declining terms of trade to commodity exports from developing countries underpinning a critical focus on industrial development and the need to stabilize commodity prices. In this way, commodity price policies and agreements served as development policy in the 1960s and 70s.

The continued dependence of developing countries, particularly in sub-Saharan Africa on a narrow range of primary exports for foreign exchange income, has been noted by UNCTAD (2019). At the same time, the notion of Global Value Chain Development has gained influence among international financial institutions as a private sector oriented development strategy prompting numerous critiques of the approach as overly optimistic based upon limited understanding of power relations, wider social and political contests and development processes themselves (Bair and Werner 2011; Neilson 2014).

Coffee and other 'soft commodities' have received increasing interest from financial investors over the last decade-and-a-half as part of a phenomenon referred to as the 'financialization of commodities'. The share of non-commercial open interest on futures markets serves as a conservative estimate for financial investment on these markets. Between 1986 and 2008, this ratio increased from 20 per cent to over 60 per cent for the coffee 'C' contract traded on the New York Intercontinental Exchange. There is now relative agreement that the trading practices of money managers have acted to shift prices occurring on these exchanges away from the fundamentals of supply and demand for the underlying commodity (van Huellen 2018; 2019; Edere et al. 2016; Tang and Xiong 2012). How changes in price formation on international exchanges relate to prices on the ground and the organization of production is still largely under researched.

Within the wider scholarship of the contemporary capitalist system there has been a tendency not only to limit analyses to the confines of specific disciplines with established concepts, analytical categories and methods, but also in the focus of analytical lens to realms of production, exchange and finance as distinct from each other. This decoupling is clear within economics with the distinction between the 'real' and the 'financial'. Within the orthodox Marxist tradition, the tendency has been to focus upon the social relations of capitalist production and to view exchange, or the market, as a passive reflection of these (Clarke 1995). Clark observed that the understanding of the market was central to Marx's analysis of the capitalist mode of production and of his critique of political economy since it is the market that imposes its capitalist character on each individual capital. 'This means that Marx's account of the market cannot be divorced from his critique of capitalism as a whole' (ibid.: 3).

The integrated nature of production, exchange and finance is stressed by Marx in *Capital, Volume II* as he examines economic reproduction in its totality. While *Volume II* is centred on the marketplace, as opposed to production in *Volume I* or finance in *Volume III*, it has at its heart the notion of the commodity as the unity and contradiction between use-value and exchange-value. *Volume II* develops Marx's reproduction schema by examining the constant intertwining of appearance and disappearance of money capital, productive capital and commodity capital from the sphere of circulation into the sphere of production and back again. In doing so, Marx highlights the unity and contradiction between the two spheres and provides clear guidance for identifying both sites and subjects of research that have largely been analysed separately. This chapter elucidates the influence of *Volume II* on recent analyses of the changing social relations of production of coffee commodity chains that examines not only the relationships between merchants, traders and workers that transform and transport coffee into an object for consumption, but also the money-owner, money-lender and money-manager operating on international financial exchanges as their interests and operations interact with those of commodity chain actors (Newman 2009a; Bargawi and Newman 2017).

## Marx and the Market

### *Production and exchange*

While *Volume I* of *Capital* exposes capitalisms 'hidden abode of production' and the origins of value that are obscured by the focus of bourgeois economists on the commodity form itself and the centrality of market exchange, *Volume II* sets value in motion extending the analysis to temporal dynamics and spatialized nature of production and exchange. Marx introduces the building block to his integrated reproduction schema, the money circuit of capital expressed in the famous formula $M - C \ldots P \ldots C' - M'$. He identifies three stages in the circular movement of capital, in moving from one stage to the other, capital changes form, it undergoes metamorphosis from money capital to commodity capital to productive capital as it enters production and then to a qualitatively different commodity and quantitatively different money capital increased by surplus-value. The three stages are described in at the start of *Volume II* as follows:

*First Stage*: The capitalist appears as a buyer on the commodity- and the labour-market; his money is transformed into commodities, or it goes through the circulation act $M - C$.

*Second Stage*: Productive consumption of the purchased commodities by the capitalist. He acts as a capitalist producer of commodities; his capital passes through the process of production. The result is a commodity of more value than that of the elements entering into its production.

*Third Stage*: The capitalist returns to the market as a seller; his commodities are turned into money; or they pass through the circulation act $C - M$. (Marx 1992: 109)

The circuit is divided into two spheres, the sphere of circulation that is necessary for the valorization of capital and the sphere of production that is necessary for the creation of value but appears from the vantage point of money capital as an interruption to a process of making more money from money. The appearance and disappearance of money capital, productive capital and commodity capital are in a process of constant intertwining from the sphere of circulation into the sphere of production and back again.

By highlighting the unity and contradiction between the two spheres, this schema immediately reveals the limitations of focusing research on practices and outcomes on international commodity exchanges as distinct from production or studying the conditions of production in isolation of, or abstracted from, the market. In relation to the study of changing social relations in the production and exchange of coffee, the reproduction schema provides clear guidance for identifying both sites and subjects of research that had largely been analysed separately.

The 'commodity chain' construct of World Systems Theory (WST) was developed and deployed with the articulation between the sphere of circulation and the sphere of production somewhat in mind, understood as 'a network of labour and production processes whose end result is a finished commodity' (Hopkins and Wallerstain 1986: 159). The commodity chain within WST serves as an intermediate unit of analysis for studying the world system from a long-range, macro-historical perspective (Bair and Werner 2011). Commodity chains, in their totality then make up the world system, or the global production system more precisely. While the analytical focus is on the organization of production and the labour process this is inseparable from the articulation between units of production along the chain that take place in the sphere of exchange.

### *Production, exchange and finance*

Financialization, as the rise of financial power and logic in economic decision-making, has become an accepted term within critical scholarship to describe the character of the world economy over the last three decades. Variously defined, financialization refers to different scales of economic and social processes: at the level of the firm or corporation in the transformation of business models (Lazonick 2010; Lazonick and O'Sullivan 2000); at the level of individuals and households in the operations of everyday life (Langley 2004, 2008; Montgomerie 2006; Froud et al. 2002); and at the level of the world economy in structural change in the defining logic of capitalism as a coherent macro-system of accumulation, albeit one that is inherently contradictory and uneven in its manifestation (Arrighi 1994).

With some notable exceptions, there has however been a tendency to conceptualize the financial and the real as accommodated in discrete spheres that are in tension/zero-sum competition. For example, post-Keynesian inspired scholars who conduct income/money-oriented analyses at the level of the nation state often conclude that financialization manifests as the 'crowding out' of real investment (e.g. Stockhammer 2010).

Mainstream economics has also long separated the 'financial' from the 'real' economy as exemplified by the distinct subfield of financial economics that deals with financial markets while other branches of economics tend to assume the role of financial markets as unproblematic intermediaries/allocators of resources through the invocation of the efficient market hypothesis.

From the perspective of *Volume II*, financialization, as a systemic feature of contemporary capitalism, can be located within the circuit of capital but also understood in relation to the unity of production and exchange, where finance plays an integrated and integral role, as well as contradictory tendencies. A number of Marxist scholars have noted the subordination of production in financialized accumulation (e.g. Lapavitsas 2014; Fine 2012) and located their analysis of financialization in the integrated circuit of industrial capital, there has been a tendency to focus upon the rise of interest-bearing capital (IBC) and characterizing financialization as the dominance of the sphere of circulation over the sphere of production. These literatures have primarily drawn from Marx's analysis in *Volume III* where emphasis is placed on finance (as opposed to production in *Volume I* and exchange in *Volume II*). While recognizing the position of production in the creation of value and surplus-value, the focus has been on the sphere of circulation to the relative neglect of the sphere of production to which it is critically joined.

Marx differentiates two forms of merchant capital: commercial capital and money-dealing capital, and finance capital is the articulated combination of the two forms of merchant capital and industrial capital. The motive of money-dealing capital is to advance credit in return for a share of the profits from the activity that it finances. So-called interest-bearing capital might be utilized as money capital that might finance the (expanded) reproduction of capital or it can derive a share of profits from non-surplus producing activities such as financing capital in exchange which is also integral to the industrial circuit of capital. In this way, finance and industrial capital are symbiotic. Financialization, has thus, been viewed as the dominance of the accumulation of IBC over productive capital. However, the accumulation of IBC can never fully break free from productive capital as an attempt to make profit without the link to production would result in a speculative boom which eventually crashes when the economy is brought back to the reality of the need for production.

Production is necessary for the generation of surplus, created by the purchase of labour power below labour-time which can be accumulated as (productive) capital to extend the same circuit or spun off into a different circuit (the production of a different commodity). While it is possible to profit from the exchange of commodities (in the sphere of circulation), as in the case of merchant capital, no surplus is created in this activity and returns to merchant capital is a share of value, the amount being determined by the prevailing social distributional relations. Financialization can thus be defined as the process of capital restructuring (commercial, money dealing, and industrial capital and their articulation) for the expansion of financialized accumulation.

A study of the social relations of coffee production thus requires the study of a range of actors that work to produce and turn coffee into an object for consumption that include the workers and the industrialists that are the *dramatis personae* of *Volume I* as well as the money-owner (and the money-lender), the wholesale merchant, the trader and the entrepreneur or 'functioning' capitalist that are the players of *Volume II*. These actors operate in different locations within, and without, the chain, in different nation states and at different scales as they interact directly and indirectly with one another.

## Contradictions between the Integrated Spheres of Production and Circulation: The Case of Coffee

The analytical bridge between *Volume I* and *Volume III* provided in *Volume II* can be deployed in the study of contemporary commodity chains as they are historically structured. By operationalizing the intertwining of the circuits of capital, we can reveal the relationship between financialization and the restructuring of production along commodity chains and the contradictions that this throws up (Newman 2009a; Bargawi and Newman 2017; Staritz et al. 2018). Other recent approaches to investigating the flow of finance that intertwine commodity chains and act to appropriate and channel surplus towards wealth creation include the notion of Global Wealth Chains (Seabrooke and Wigan 2014) and the call by economic geographers to extended the Global Production Networks (GPN) framework via the addition of Global Financial Networks with the idea of studying these in relation to GPNs as they are overlaid and intersect (Coe et al. 2014).

In the study of coffee chains discussed in this chapter, two operational definitions of the financialization of commodity chains that are informed by an analytical location of financialization within Marx's circuit of capital are deployed. The first definition, which has been harnessed by economics and financial scholars in investigating the 'financialization of commodities', relates to the increase in activities on commodity derivatives markets driven purely by financial interests through the large-scale entry of financial investors with the emergence of commodities as an asset class in portfolio investment (Ederer et al. 2016; Tang and Xiong 2012); and the second involves changes in the business strategies of international commodity traders as they increasingly place commodity derivatives markets at the centre of their trading activities and profit-generation strategies (Staritz et al. 2018).

The long economic slowdown since the end of the post-war boom has initiated the neoliberal restructuring of capital. This has involved a process of withdrawal of the state from provisions for health, social security and old age that has precipitated the rise of private provisioning and the promotion of financial investment in general and the rise of commodities as an asset class, like stocks and bonds, in portfolio investment in particular (Domanski and Heath 2007). Falling rates of profit for productive investment has also spurred corporations to refocus investments towards financial interests (Lazonick 2010). In this way commodities have become an asset class under 'money manager capitalism', or accumulation from the perspective of money capital (Wray 2008). The notional volume of coffee derivatives in the sphere of circulation are several times that of physical coffee in exchange and very little coffee is delivered via the international exchanges.

While rising interest by financial investors in commodity markets is now widely recognized as affecting price behaviour beyond those that would be informed purely by underlying supply and demand conditions, the 'financialization of commodities' literature has remained the statistical analysis of prices on exchanges themselves. For example, Ederer et al. (2016) found a significant effect of long trading positions held money managers in coffee derivatives markets on prices and Tang and Xiong (2012) found the greater co-movement of prices across unrated commodities following the entry of index investors on the markets.

Commodity derivative markets were first formed as a way for farmers and traders to hedge against risks that come from price changes that can occur between the signing of a contract, that might occur prior to harvest, and the delivery date for the contracted commodity. In reality, small-holder production is dominant in many coffee-producing regions, and given the size of their crop compared with the lot sizes on commodity exchanges, and the financial resources required to maintain positions on derivatives markets, farmers rarely hedge against price risks on coffee exchanges (Gibbon and Ponte 2005; Newman 2009a; Bargawi and Newman 2017; Breger-Bush 2012).

The intersection between coffee derivatives and physical markets is located with international commodity traders in the sphere of circulation. The coffee industry at the international trader[1] level is highly concentrated. The largest trading houses hedge all green[2] coffee trades routinely. In doing so, the price at which they purchase coffee from local suppliers is tied to prices on the international exchange in the way described in Bargawi and Newman's (2017: 176) study of price formation along coffee chains:

> International trading companies purchase coffee from local exporters, subsidiaries, or companies in their trading group located at origin. For coffee from a particular origin, the international trader decides on a differential to the international exchange at which it is willing to purchase coffee on that day. This differential reflects the difference in quality of the contracted coffee compared with minimum quality deliverable on either of the international exchanges. The trader then contacts its suppliers with this offer price, and the negotiation proceeds based on local market conditions. It is up to the seller to decide to fix the price at a particular time. The actual price at which the coffee is exchanged will be the futures price at the point of fixing, plus or minus the agreed differential under the so-called price-to-be-fixed contract. Since the international trader hedges by offsetting its position in physicals with futures contracts, the time at which the price is fixed is of little importance. On the other hand, local exporters tend not to be hedged so the time at which they fix can be critical. A seller may hold off fixing the price if it expects the futures price to rise further; losses are made if the futures price falls below the price at which coffee was purchased.

Historically, coffee trading houses operated as commercial capital. They profited from the activity of buying cheap and selling dear $(M - M')$. This was made possible by the highly uneven power relations that shaped the emergence of coffee production systems, introduced to the tropics through colonial conquest and subjugation. Plantation production relied upon coerced and enslaved labour that facilitated high rates of surplus appropriation. For several decades after the independence in coffee-producing countries, coffee trading houses continued to profit from their market position and power vis-à-vis producing countries although economic development policies that included single state marketing channels for coffee exports and the multilateral system of agreed commodity

---

[1] International traders occupy the position along coffee chains between local coffee markets in producer countries and coffee roasters based in the Global North. In 2011, the top five companies accounted for 55 per cent of global market share (International Trade Centre 2011).

[2] Green coffee refers to dry coffee beans yet to be roasted.

coffee prices under the International Coffee Agreement (1962–89) engendered a balance of power that was relatively equal by historical comparison. At the same time, shift to small-holder production took place in a number of coffee-producing regions that has reshaped the social relations of production on the ground. From the 1980s onwards, structural adjustment policies saw the liberalization of coffee marketing systems in many producer countries that involved removal of parastatals and other state marketing institutions, shifting market power in favour of coffee trading houses as domestic marketing systems became more fragmented.

With greater scope for profit from derivatives trading, with the 'financialization of commodities', coffee trading houses have actively participated in derivatives trading beyond considerations of hedging against volatile prices. Newman (2009a) observed that coffee trading houses have integrated futures trading into their profit strategies. The study found evidence of trading houses engaging in 'speculative' hedging in order to reap financial rewards as well as greater alignment in the trading strategies of coffee trading houses. Coffee trading houses thus operate both as merchants and money managers where they can profit from price movements as coffee traders and as financial speculators.

The transmission of volatile prices that evolve on international commodity exchanges upstream along coffee chains has profound implications on the patterns of appropriation and hence distribution. Coffee trading companies have always been able to profit from their appropriation of surplus-value from primary produces but the mechanisms through which this appropriation takes place have expanded with financialization.

The way that prices are experienced by small-holder producers is mediated by local institutions of marketing that vary between and within countries. In Tanzania, a centralized coffee auction operates alongside a direct export channel that provides an institutional barrier between domestic sellers and international trading companies. Between 60 and 90 per cent of coffee goes through the auction although this can vary dramatically from year to year (Baregu et al. 2013). Locally, there are four main channels through which coffee is marketed: (1) a purely private marketing channel consisting of private coffee buyers to purchase partially processed coffee from farmers at trading posts or at the farm gate and transfer these to mills for processing before it is sold at the auction; (2) the traditional cooperative channel involves farmers depositing their semi-processed coffee to the primary society to be processed at the union-owned mill. Here a fee is deducted for milling and farmers receive a first payment. Possession of the coffee remains with the farmer who receives a second payment equal to the difference between the auction price and their initial payment after it is sold; (3) non-union farmers groups operate in a similar way to cooperative unions in terms of marketing but cooperation is for marketing purposes only; and (4) direct export channel coordinated by producer support organizations (Bargawi and Newman 2017). By contrast, liberalization of the coffee system in Uganda in 1991 further reaching and it remains as the most liberalized coffee market in East Africa. The cooperative marketing channel in Uganda has virtually disappeared and there is very limited regulation of coffee exporters (Newman 2009a). The ways in which coffee prices are transmitted/realized along different marketing channels differ accordingly with profound implications for accumulation within production.

The weekly auctions during coffee marketing season in Tanzania limit the rapidity with which prices evolving on the international exchange are transmitted through the auction to local actors. The two-payment system of the cooperative union marketing system also acts to smooth the income received by coffee growers and overall and does not disadvantage them in terms of within season price variability. Here coffee producers receive the bulk of the export price for coffee. Coffee growers in Tanzania that sell through private channels benefit from the price stabilization and information functions provided by the auction but will not be able to benefit from potential price increases within a season as they sell at the prevailing auction price.

In Uganda, both local exporters and international trading houses purchase coffee for export. Unlike in Tanzania where processors are located close to coffee growing areas, exporter processors in Uganda are primarily based in Kampala. Subsidiaries of international trading houses all hedge. They frequently take into account their expectations on how prices will evolve in the London and New York markets when deciding on the timing with which to place an order of futures or options contracts. International exporters do not, however, fully transmit changes in the international exchange price upstream. International exporters will themselves cushion the short-term volatility to some extent to make the procurement of coffee practical in the Ugandan context by maintaining a purchasing (or factory) price throughout a day, and for longer periods if world price fluctuations are not too severe (Newman 2009a).

Local exporters in Uganda do not hedge using derivatives contracts because of their lack of access to the required finance. They work to limit their exposure to international price fluctuations by using forward contracts for a portion of their expected sales to lock in a transaction price ahead of a delivery date, and by engaging in back-to-back selling – where they sell as rapidly as possible after purchasing coffee to limit the time period of exposure to price variability. While forward contracts would act to limit the transmission of price fluctuations upstream, back-to-back selling passes along price fluctuations. The local coffee marketing system in Uganda involves a range of intermediaries or middlemen, who are to some extent shielded from very short-term movements in futures prices. They are, however, still exposed to inter-day or weekly swings in the purchasing price of exporters in Kampala. Middlemen buy and sell coffee on the spot. They have no access to contractual arrangements that can limit their exposure to short-term price movements and try to ensure large margins that can contain the price volatility by purchasing semi-processed coffee at the farmgate at stable but low prices. This is reflected in the very low levels of investment in coffee production by smallholders who do not seek to expand their coffee production. Smallholders in Uganda tend but one or two trees on plots where they produce food crops in the main. Coffee is produced for cash income required for expenditure on marketized aspects of social reproduction such as the purchase of school uniforms (Newman 2009b).

The contradiction between circulation and production is expressed with practices in the sphere of circulation acting to undermine conditions for the sustainability and expansion of production in Uganda. In Tanzania, growers in the Kilimanjaro region are better positioned to plan and reinvest in coffee production as the coffee auction provides an institutional shield from the worst of price variation. Small holders marketing through cooperative structures in Tanzania have the possibility of profiting from short-term price increases at the international level since they are able to maintain ownership of their coffee until the auction. In addition, profits from the value addition associated with the processing of coffee into export grades accrue to the farmers who are members of cooperative unions partly limiting the appropriation of surplus-value downstream along the chain (Newman 2009b). Overall, financialized accumulation along coffee chains exerts pressure to limit productive accumulation at the site of surplus-value creation while reliant upon the sustained production of coffee.

## Conclusion

The collapse of the International Coffee Agreement in 1989 fundamentally changed the way in which coffee prices were determined, removing the institution that provided a partial barrier against the exertion of power by coffee trading companies in price negotiations. The unevenness in power relations between producers and traders in producing countries on the one side and international traders on the other was made more acute with the abolition of state marketing structures as part of structural adjustment programmes. As trading houses began to act as both merchant and finance capital, they were able to utilize mechanisms of valuation that amount to technologies of appropriation along coffee chains. This insight has been gained by deploying the analytical framing provided by Marx's reproduction schema in *Volume II* that takes us beyond the majority of studies that seek to identify financialization, on one side, or identify direct mechanisms of exploitation and appropriation along commodity chains, on the other. By understand the inseparability of finance and financialization from productive restructuring and the social relations of production as connected through the sphere of exchange, the study of price formation on the ground thus serves as the concrete form with which the relations of production and exchange are played out across national boundaries.

The approach discussed in this chapter complements Marxist critiques of Global Value Chains that draw from the analytical categories developed in *Volume I* in order to highlight the systemic nature of appropriation of these chains, focusing on capital as a class relation of surplus-value appropriation by highlighting the tools of valuation that arise in the sphere of circulation in order to divorce 'value addition' from 'value creation' along commodity chains that works to create a highly unequal distribution of income in favour of capital and the Global North (Selwyn 2019; Quentin and Campling 2018; Mezzadri 2014).

The schema laid out in *Volume II* is particularly instructive in investigating interconnectedness and interdependencies across forms of capital and types of actors, contradictions and their overall macro-implications that link micro-constituent processes to the crisis prone tendencies of the system elucidated in *Volume III*.

# References

Arrighi, G. 1994. *The Long Twentieth Century: Money, Power, and the Origins of Our Times*. London: Verso.

Bair, J. and M. Werner. 2011. 'Commodity chains and the uneven geographies of global capitalism: A disarticulations perspective'. *Environment and Planning A: Economy and Space* 43: 988–97.

Baregu, S., J. Barreiro-Hurle and F. Maro, F. 2013. *Analysis of Incentives and Disincentives for Coffee in the United Republic of Tanzania*. Rome: Food and Agriculture Organization.

Bargawi, H. K. and S. A. Newman. 2017. 'From futures markets to the farm gate: A study of price formation along Tanzania's coffee commodity chain'. *Economic Geography* 9(2): 162–84.

Beckert, S. 2015. *Empire of Cotton: A Global History*. New York: Vintage.

Bush, S. B. 2012. *Derivatives and Development: A Political Economy of Global Finance, Farming, and Poverty*. Basingstoke: Springer.

Clarke, S. 1995. 'Marx and the market', http://homepages.warwick.ac.uk/~syrbe/pubs/LAMARKW.pdf (accessed 1 May 2019).

Coe, N. M., K. P. Y. Lai and D. Wójcik. 2014. 'Integrating finance into global production networks'. *Regional Studies* 48(5): 761–77.

Domanski, D. and A. Heath. 2007. 'Financial investors and commodity markets'. *BIS Quarterly Review* (March): 53–67.

Ederer, S., C. Heumesser and C. Staritz. 2016. 'Financialization and commodity prices: An empirical analysis for coffee, cotton, wheat and oil'. *International Review of Applied Economics* 30(4): 462–87.

Fine, B. 2012. 'Financialisation and social policy'. In P. Utting, S. Razavi and R. Varghese Buchholz (eds), *The Global Crisis and Transformative Social Change*. London: Palgrave Macmillan.

Froud, J., S. Johal and K. Williams. 2002. 'Financialisation and the coupon pool'. *Capital & Class* 26(3): 119–51.

Gibbon, P. and S. Ponte. 2005. *Trading Down: Africa, Value Chains, and the Global Economy*. Philadelphia: Temple University Press.

Hopkins, T. K. and I. Wallerstein. 1986. 'Commodity chains in the world-economy prior to 1800'. *Review (Fernand Braudel Center)* 10(1): 157–70.

International Trade Centre. 2011. *The Coffee Exporter's Guide*. Geneva: International Trade Centre.

Langley, P. 2004. 'In the eye of the "perfect storm": The final salary pensions crisis and financialisation of Anglo American capitalism'. *New Political Economy* 9(4): 539–58.

———. 2008. *The Everyday Life of Global Finance: Saving and Borrowing in Anglo-America*. Oxford: Oxford University Press.

Lapavitsas, C. 2011. 'Theorizing financialization'. *Work, Employment and Society* 25(4): 611–26.

———. 2014. *Profiting without Producing: How Finance Exploits Us All*. London: Verso.

Lazonick, W. 2010. 'Innovative business models and varieties of capitalism: Financialization of the US corporation'. *Business History Review* 84(4): 675–702.

Lazonick, W. and M. O'Sullivan. 2000. 'Maximizing shareholder value: A new ideology for corporate governance'. *Economy and Society* 29(1): 13–35.

Marx, K. 1992. *Capital: A Critique of Political Economy, Volume II*. London: Penguin Books.

Mezzadri, A. 2014. 'Backshoring, local sweatshop regimes and CSR in India'. *Competition & Change* 18(4): 327–44.

Mintz, S. W. 1986. *Sweetness and Power: The Place of Sugar in Modern History*. London: Penguin.

Montgomerie, J. 2006. 'The financialization of the American credit card industry'. *Competition & Change* 10(3): 301–19.

Neilson, J. 2014. 'Value chains, neoliberalism and development practice: The Indonesian experience'. *Review of International Political Economy* 21(1): 38–69.

Newman, S. A. 2009a. 'Financialization and changes in the social relations along commodity chains: The case of coffee'. *Review of Radical Political Economics* 41(4): 539–59.

———. 2009b. *Futures Markets and Coffee Prices*. PhD dissertation, University of London, SOAS.

Quentin, D. and L. Campling. 2018. 'Global inequality chains: Integrating mechanisms of value distribution into analyses of global production'. *Global Networks* 18(1): 33–56.

Seabrooke, L. and D. Wigan. 2014. 'Global wealth chains in the international political economy'. *Review of International Political Economy* 21(1): 257–63.

Selwyn, B. 2019. 'Poverty chains and global capitalism'. *Competition & Change* 23(1): 71–97.

Staritz, C., S. Newman, B. Tröster and L. Plank. 2018. 'Financialization and global commodity chains: Distributional implications for cotton in sub-Saharan Africa'. *Development and Change* 49(3): 815–42.

Stockhammer, E. 2010. 'Financialization and the global economy'. *Political Economy Research Institute Working Paper* 242: 40.

Talbot, J. M. 2004. *Grounds for Agreement: The Political Economy of the Coffee Commodity Chain.* Lanham: Rowman and Littlefield.

Tang, K. and W. Xiong. 2012. 'Index investment and the financialization of commodities'. *Financial Analysts Journal* 68(6): 54–74.

UNCTAD. 2019. *Commodity Dependence: A Twenty-Year Perspective.* Geneva: United Nations.

van Huellen, S. 2019. 'Approaches to price formation in financialized commodity markets'. *Journal of Economic Surveys* 34(1): 219–37.

———. 2018. 'Too much of a good thing? Speculative effects on commodity futures curves'. *Journal of Financial Markets*: 100480.

Wray, L. R. 2008. 'The commodities market bubble: Money manager capitalism and the financialization of commodities', No. 96. Public Policy Brief, The Levy Economics Institute of Bard College.

# Chapter Eight

# LEARNING MARX BY DOING

## CLASS ANALYSIS IN AN EMERGING ZONE OF GLOBAL HORTICULTURE

### Benjamin Selwyn

**Abstract**

The interior of North East Brazil has emerged over the last three decades as a fast-expanding zone of export grape production. Its growth is based upon fast-changing class relations. This chapter reflects upon the author's attempts to deploy Marxist class analysis to comprehend these dynamics. Illustrating the forces at work in the case and field-sites analysed, the chapter discusses a dual process of 'learning Marx by doing'. First, it describes the author's process of learning how to move from abstract, static and structural conceptions of class relations, to dynamic and experiential ones, in order to decipher the region's social transformations. Second, it illustrates how field observations on the rising self-organisation of the export sector's labour force and its achievement of significant concessions from employers were informed by, but also informed, the author's understandings of capital–labour relations. The chapter also addresses the relevance of methods aimed at carefully mapping and recording field findings, as these greatly help in identifying key features of class and power in their concrete manifestations in given settings.

## Introduction

*The modern bourgeois society [...] has simplified class antagonisms. Society as a whole is more and more splitting up into two great hostile camps, into two great classes directly facing each other – Bourgeoisie and Proletariat. (Marx and Engels 1969: 14)*

This conception of class – of two 'great classes directly facing each other' – informed my early PhD research. Yet, after contact with empirical reality, I realised how it represents a theoretical abstraction that rarely exists in empirical reality. I found that really existing class relations are complex, dynamic and multistranded.

This chapter discusses processes of social transformation in North East Brazil's fast-expanding export grape sector and, interrelatedly, considers how they can be comprehended from a class-relational perspective by reflecting upon the author's field-work in the region during the 2000s. Part of this account entails a discussion of how, upon encountering and trying to decipher the region's social transformations, the author's conception of class itself underwent significant modification. In a sense, this should not surprise anyone attempting to deploy theoretical concepts and categories to understand real social processes. The latter are always far more complicated, complex and contradictory than the former. Nevertheless, the act of reflecting upon how researchers (need to) confront their own limitation is potentially a valuable one, as such confrontation and resolution is often part and parcel of gaining a better comprehension of material reality.

The chapter is organised as follows. The second section provides a brief background to the expansion and global integration of North East Brazil's export grape sector. The third section discusses the author's attempts to deploy a conception of class adequate to the task of illuminating evolving social relations in the region. The fourth section outlines the interactions of the sector's labour process and workers' bargaining power, while the fifth outlines and discusses how these impacted upon changing gender divisions of labour in the valley. The sixth section summarises and concludes the chapter.

## Export Grape Production in North East Brazil

The interior of the North East, commonly referred to as the *Sertão* is perhaps best associated with chronic poverty, mass unemployment, regular and crushing droughts and a very strong culture of machismo. However, from the 1960s onwards the then military dictatorship and subsequent civilian governments began investing heavily in energy generation (power plants) and after that in irrigating the region to stimulate food production for the domestic market. Between 1960 and 1988 the publicly irrigated area in the North East expanded from around 52,000 hectares to 619,000 hectares. By the early 2000s in the region's São Francisco (SF) valley alone, around 40,000 public and 60,000 private irrigated hectares of land had been established (Selwyn 2012).

The SF valley (see Figure 8.1) emerged during the 1990s and 2000s as a region of dynamic export horticulture. Between 1997 and 2007, table grape export volumes and earnings increased from 3,700 tons and US$4.7 million to over 78,000 tons and over US$170 million (Valexport 2008). Table grapes are the most labour-intensive crop cultivated in the region, and by the mid-2000s there were more than 50,000 workers employed in the grape sector alone, the majority of whom were women (Selwyn 2012).

The table grape sector is organised through four 'chains' – bottom- and top-end domestic (ranging from open street markets to large retailers) and EU and UK export markets (where the latter are the most demanding). Exporting farms exist within increasingly competitive global markets, dominated by northern retailers such as Tesco and Carrefour. Retailers impose strict demands upon suppliers, requiring the latter produce grapes to highly specified standards (e.g. achieving accurate berry and bunch size and fruit colour) (Reardon et al. 2001). This necessitates an increasingly scientific approach to grape production, with exporting farms employing agronomists and using sophisticated techniques to manage an ever more skilled workforce (Selwyn 2007)

With the initial establishment of irrigated agriculture in the SF valley in the mid- to late 1960s, mostly small-scale family farmers (*colonos*) were settled on the projects and began cultivating basic food crops. However, from the early 1980s, the federal state's

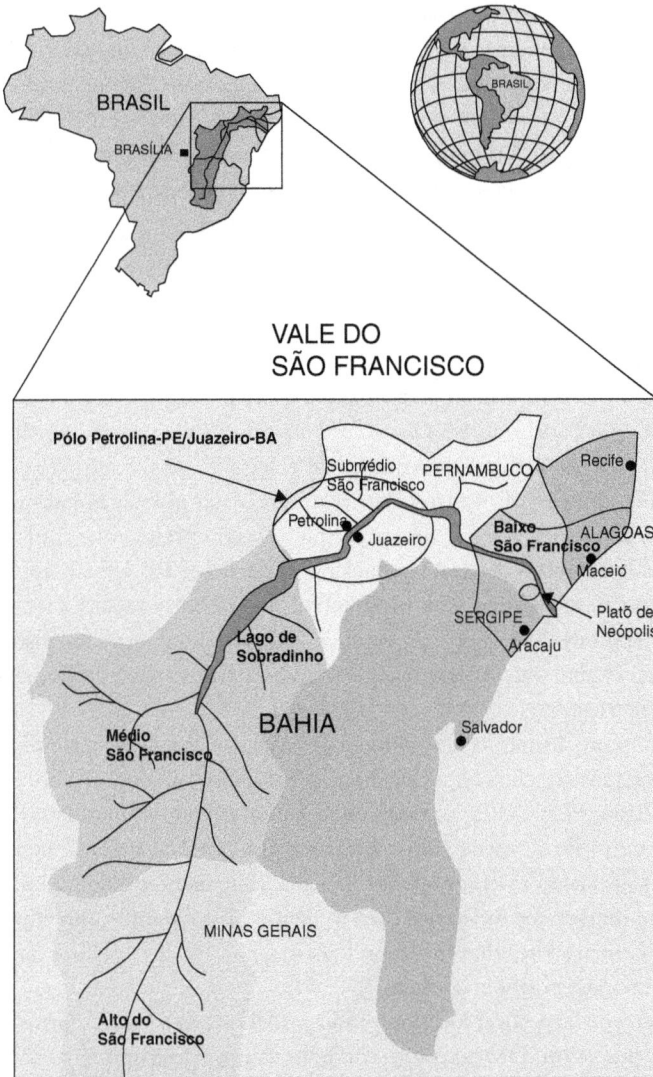

**Figure 8.1** São Francisco valley in Brazil.
*Source*: Nilo Coelho Irrigation District (2002).

development agencies – *Commisão do Vale do São Francisco* (CODEVASF) and *Empressa Brasileira de Pesquisa* (EMPBRAPA) – began recruiting more highly capitalised agricultural firms to the region, with the aim of promoting higher value export agriculture and generating foreign exchange. Medium- and large-scale firms and agricultural cooperatives arrived in the region and began cultivating crops such as melon, banana, mango and grape.

These shifts were underpinned by fast-changing class relations – entailing formation of new classes, dynamic relations between capital and labour, intertwined with changing gender divisions of labour. Very significantly, the sectors labour force was able through collective action to win better wages and conditions, thus impacting positively on regional developmental dynamics. What was particularly important for me to understand was (1) why and how the balance of power between capital and labour shifted, relatively, in favour of labour, (2) how this impacted upon distributional and developmental dynamics in the valley and (3) how these two processes worked their way through evolving gender relations.

## Challenges of Class Analysis

According to Lenin the 'living soul of Marxism' is the 'concrete analysis of a concrete situation' (1965: 165–67). When I arrived in the SF valley my conception of class reflected my reading of Marx and Engels's *Communist Manifesto*. While a useful starting point, such a perspective does not provide the conceptual categories or methodology necessary for comprehending nuances of evolving class relations under global capitalism.

As my research progressed – documenting and comprehending findings – I found that my initial conception of class was lacking. What I needed was an approach to class that could illuminate dynamics of exploitation and resistance and how they involved other social relations, like gender. I wanted to understand how the balance of class power between capital and labour changed and how this impacted upon developmental dynamics in the region.

In these attempts I first needed to identify pitfalls of overly structuralist conceptions of class – that portray class as a 'location' or 'position' as opposed to a relationship. G. A. Cohen's assertion that a 'person's class is established by nothing but his objective place in the network of ownership relations' captures a structural element of class. However, it is ill-placed to comprehend how class relations evolve and are constituted by other social markers of difference such as gender. For example, directly following the above quote, Cohen writes that 'his consciousness, culture, and politics do not enter the definition of his class position' (Cohen 1978: 73).

Such a focus on structural location privileges 'class' over 'other' forms of social distinction and oppression. During my research, however, it became increasingly apparent that race class and gender are 'social relations and forms [that] come into being in and through each other' (Bannerji 2005: 149). My own research focussed on the intertwining of the latter two.

An exclusive focus upon class position is problematic for other reasons. As E. P. Thompson argued, such a conception of class generates misleading political expectations. '"It", the working class, is assumed to have a real existence, which can be defined almost mathematically … Once this is assumed it becomes possible to deduce the class-consciousness which "it" ought to have (but seldom does have)' (Thompson 1963: 9). Structuralist definitions of class effectively de-emphasise collective political action as a determinant of class relations. Class is something 'which in fact happens (and can be shown to have happened) in human relationships' (ibid.: 8). It is not, then, only an 'objective place in the network of ownership relations'.

An 'experiential' conception of class starts from the understanding that class relations are structured. But it then immediately enquires into how those structured relations are reproduced. It incorporates, analytically, an element of indeterminacy or open-endedness, where structured relations are contested and evolve. Such contestations and shifts in power relations between capital and labour, their distributional and developmental implications (i.e. developmental processes and outcomes) become as central to class analysis as the identification of different class positions. Being aware of such dynamics requires a toolbox of concepts and categories that illuminate them. Elements of Marxist labour process and labour regime theory are potentially useful here.

Because firms relate to each other through constant competition, the labour process is characterised by an endless productivity drive designed to maximise the speed and intensity of the performance of tasks and the 'precision, predictability and quality of transformations being worked' (Brighton Labour Process Group 1977: 13; Braverman 1974). Capital therefore continually reorganises 'a system of power relations the function of which is to define and enforce the discipline of the labour process' (Brighton Labour Process Group 1977: 13). However, much labour process theory has been criticised for a 'connectivity problem' – not explaining adequately how workplace-based labour processes are co-constituted by broader (non-workplace-based) social relations such as gender (Thompson 2010; Newsome et al. 2015). In reality, labour processes exists within broader labour regimes, which encapsulate the 'interrelation of (segmented) labour markets and recruitment, condition of employment and labour processes, and forms of enterprise authority and control' (Bernstein 2007: 7).

Part of this controlling process is the (sub)division of tasks within the workplace and the division of labour (often by gender) in response to evolving external and internal pressures: competition by other firms and the extent to which workers acquiesce to management. However, that capital seeks to maintain control over the labour process does not always mean that it does. Such barriers to total control constitute, in turn, new moments at which the reproduction of class relations is indeterminate and partially open-ended.

One way of illuminating this open-endedness is to investigate when and how workers are able to collectively represent themselves and win tangible gains vis-à-vis capital. The late Erik Olin Wright's (2000) distinction between workers' associational and structural power enables such an investigation. The former is a product of workers' collective (usually trade union and political party) organisation, comprising 'the various forms of power that result from the formation of collective organization of workers' (ibid.: 962). By contrast, structural power accrues to workers on the basis of their position in the economic system, that is, the specific power conferred on them derived from their position in the production process and their ability to disrupt it.

The following sections discuss how these aspects – labour process, gender division of labour, worker's structural and associational power – combine in and through an evolving labour regime and the subsequent impacts upon development in the SF valley.

**Labour Process and Workers' Bargaining Power**

The SF valley's export table grape sector emerged in the context of an ongoing global retail revolution with direct implications for the export sector's labour process and broader class relations. The transformations associated with the increasing power of giant retailers is leading to increased standardisation and regulation of global and domestic food chains (Reardon et al. 2003). This revolution has come about through a number of shifts:

(1)    a huge concentration of retailer power across the global north and now, increasingly, across the Global South;

(2)    increased use of global sourcing by these retailers as competitive strategy;

(3)    the emergence of new zones of 'non-traditional' agricultural exports to supply northern retailers and consumers;

(4)    the penetration of northern retail capital across the Global South and simultaneously a response by southern retail capital to these pressures through adopting up-to-date techniques utilised by northern retailers; and

(5)    increasingly strict 'governance' of global supply chains by northern retailers to ensure that southern suppliers meet their quality and other requirements.

The consequences for SF valley grape producers was a rapid increase in product quality requirements, which amplified the complexity of grape production. An indication of the complexity is the relatively high number of operations involved in the cultivation cycle. Table 8.1 shows the operations necessary to meet the standards for the four main market destinations noted above. In the table, dark horizontal stripes denote operations always carried out, dark grey denotes operations sometimes but not always performed, and those not shaded denote operations not performed. Column two refers to the timing of operations with numbers signifying weeks before, during or after the major cutting back of branches.

Table 8.1 shows that the number of operations per cultivation cycle that are always performed is determined primarily by export destination. Farms producing for the top-end UK market usually require 34 operations per cultivation cycle, grapes destined for mainland Europe require 24, top-end domestic require 20 and bottom end domestic just 9 operations. The increasingly complex labour process required more workers, raising the labour density on export farms with impacts on relations between capital and labour. Put differently, processes of commodity production (in this case the same commodity for diverse markets) are intertwined with class and power relations in highly specific and contingent ways.

Not carrying out operations on time, or without sufficient attention, results in lower quality fruit. A farm owner explained that 'a bad pruning delays the whole cycle, leaves bunches too tight and can spoil the whole bunch. Also, with bunch thinning the berries may be touched too much by the workers, which leaves them with stains later on, and you have lower quality berries' (Selwyn 2007: 536). Farms have detailed production calendars, variations in each plant cycle, depending on climatic conditions, mean that agronomists and managers must continually monitor plant, berry and bunch growth in order to ensure the operations are carried out at the optimal moment of the cycle.

**Table 8.1** Operations and timing of the cultivation cycle according to market destination

| Operation | Timing (weeks) | Market destination | | | |
|---|---|---|---|---|---|
| | | 1 | 2 | 3 | 4 |
| 1) Soil analysis | −1 | | | | |
| 2) Soil aeration | −1 | | | | |
| 3) Chemical fertilisation | −1 | | | | |
| 4) Organic fertilisation | −1 | | | | |
| 5) Major cutting back of branches | 1 | | | | |
| 6) Painting shoot stubs | 2 | | | | |
| 7) Collecting the branches | 2 | | | | |
| 8) Breaking branches | 2 | | | | |
| 9) Agro-toxin application | 2 | | | | |
| 10) Dry-tying | 2 | | | | |
| 11) Dry-tying | 3 | | | | |
| 12) Cutting back shoots | 4 | | | | |
| 13) Application of gibberellic acid | 4 | | | | |
| 14) Tying back shoots | 5 | | | | |
| 15) Application of gibberellic acid | 5 | | | | |
| 16) Cutting back shoots | 5 | | | | |
| 17) Leaf analysis | 5 | | | | |
| 18) Deleafing/freeing bunches | 5 | | | | |
| 19) Application of gibberellic acid | 6 | | | | |
| 20) Cutting back of shoots | 6 | | | | |
| 21) Retying of shoots | 7 | | | | |
| 22) Application of gibberellic acid | 7 | | | | |
| 23) Thinning young berries | 7 | | | | |
| 24) Application of gibberellic acid | 8 | | | | |
| 25) Freeing the bunches + selection | 8 | | | | |
| 26) Cutting back shoots | 9 | | | | |
| 27) Application of gibberellic acid | 9 | | | | |
| 28) Pruning | 9 | | | | |
| 29) Chinese hat | 11 | | | | |
| 30) Cutting back shoots | 11 | | | | |
| 31) Repeat major bunch pruning | 12 | | | | |
| 32) Pre-harvest cleaning | 15 | | | | |
| 33) Brix analysis | 16 | | | | |
| 34) Harvest | 16 | | | | |

*Source*: Observations and interviews from farms in the SF valley (2002, 2003).

**Key:**

| | Always performed | | Sometimes performed | | Never performed |
|---|---|---|---|---|---|

## Structural to Associational Power

The main trade union representing workers in the SF grape branch is the Sindicato de Trabalhadores Rurais (STR), originally formed in 1963 to represent small-scale farmers in the SF region. From the 1970s onwards, the SF valley's STR activities centred on providing welfare to dryland family farmers. STR's activities shifted with the expansion of fruticulture production, the emergence of an export agriculture sector employing significant numbers of workers on permanent contracts, and the ending of the military dictatorship in the mid-1980s. These processes contributed to the STR reorienting its principal activities towards improving the wages and work conditions of workers in the irrigated agriculture sector. As a lawyer from the STR described how:

> Before we had the collective agreement, working on grape farms could be very dangerous. Workers were transported to the farms on top of lorries, they had to apply insecticides without using protective clothing, they might hurt themselves at work and not be able to continue working, and then the boss would sack them. Lunch breaks were not specified, with workers sometimes being forced to work throughout the day without a break, and safe drinking water was not provided. (Interview with Sidrone da Silva Neto, Petrolina, July 2002)

STR's president explained how the union had sought to mobilise its rural constituency:

> Throughout 1992 and 1993 we held many meetings with rural workers explaining why we wanted collective bargaining and how we wanted to win a *convensão colletiva* [collective agreement] for our members. In January 1994 we convened a mass meeting with 500 workers, and later that month we were able to get the bosses [organised within VALEXPORT] to sit down with us and discuss the contents of the agreement. In February 1994 we were able to sign the first collective agreement. (Interview with Francisco Pascal, Petrolina, July 2003)

Some of the most noteworthy guarantees of the early agreements included: Early gains in the collective agreement included pay 10 per cent above the minimum wage, an overtime wage established at 50 per cent higher than the hourly rate for extra work after normal hours and 70 per cent higher for work during holidays and weekends, a 25 per cent higher wage and provision of protective clothing and masks to workers applying or working with pesticides, the guarantee of at least one hour for a lunch break and the right of trade union officials (*delegados* – delegates) to enter farms during lunch breaks to meet with workers. These were significant achievements by the STR compared to the previous conditions faced by workers, but also within the national context, where the Collor and then Cardoso administrations confronted the Brazilian labour movement head-on, and the latter also succeeded in pushing down the minimum wage (Berg 2010).

Once the agreement was signed the STR continued to mobilise its membership in order to improve further their conditions. A trade union official from the STR's umbrella organisation explained how they brought their already successful strategy from Pernambuco's coastal sugar zone to the SF valley:

> We developed a strategy of making demands on the farm owners [in the coastal sugar zone], and if they didn't meet them we would go on strike on the same day ... So we already had

a strategy of fighting for better conditions for rural workers when we confronted the need to improve the *São Francisco* collective agreement. (Interview with João Griba da Silva, Petrolina, July 2003)

The first strike in the SF valley was in 1997, and in 2001 the STR organised a 10-day strike to protect workers' gains, during which 'we blocked the roads with rocks and fires to stop the buses taking the workers to the farms, and we blocked the entrances to the farms' (Selwyn 2007: 548).

The ability of workers in the SF valley's export grape sector to win and defend significant concessions from their employers is rooted in their ability to disrupt significantly the production of export quality grapes (structural power) and their effective organisation within the STR (associational power). While the former exists independently of the latter, it is the former that enables workers to realise and enhance their bargaining capacity with employers. In turn, however, STR's bargaining capacity does not stem directly and unproblematically from workers structural power in the grape sector. Rather, as we have seen, the STR has reorientated itself several times from the 1980s onwards. These transformations in the balance of power between capital and labour had unforeseen impacts upon the gender division of labour with a particular bearing upon many women workers in the sector.

## Evolving Gender Divisions of Labour

In the late 1980s and early 1990s, women made up 65 per cent of the total workforce on exporting grape farms (Collins and Krippner 1999: 522; see also Collins 1993). By the time of the author's research in the valley, the gender division of labour was evolving. By the early 2000s, the majority of employed workers were still women, but their position vis-à-vis male workers had changed significantly in two ways. First, farm managers and owners confirmed that they were gradually reducing the numbers of women employed on permanent contracts. For example, while during the mid- to late 1990s women comprised the overwhelming majority of permanently employed workers, by the early 2000s they made up only between 40 and 50 per cent (Selwyn 2007). A second and interlinked change is that women workers have been allocated to different tasks, and their status as skilled workers has been downgraded.

In the historical division of labour in the SF valley, men were required to do heavier tasks such as cutting back branches and cracking vines (to regulate vine growth) and more hazardous tasks such as chemical applications (Collins 1993, 2000; Collins and Krippner 1999). Manual fertilisation, where the workers have to carry sacks of fertiliser and distribute it by hand, the digging of deep fertilisation holes and cutting grass were also the preserve of male workers. Female workers carried out tasks such as deleafing, tying bunches back to the trellis, selecting bunches and bunch pruning. There were a number of reasons for this gender division of labour. First, managers tend to grade women's skills differently than men's: 'What would ordinarily be construed as skill, grafting of grape vines, is coded instead as manual dexterity, delicacy and nimbleness of fingers' (Collins 1993: 105; Elson and Pearson 1981). Hence, skilled work is redefined as 'natural' to women workers, thus not a skill per se but an attribute, thus reducing pressures on farms to remunerate skilled workers more favourably. Second, in the 1980s and early 1990s, women were perceived to be less active politically in the SF valley. Third, women are also perceived by firms to be less bothered by the close supervision exercised by the field managers. While these reasons were valid during the late 1980s and early 1990s, important changes to social relations within the grape branch led many employers to begin changing their view of the benefits of hiring women workers.

The above rationale changed during the 2000s as a partial response to the shifts in the balance of class power noted above (see Table 8.2). Managers were less emphatic about women's 'innate' abilities, as described above, and talked more about how work previously carried out by women was increasingly being transferred to men. Table 8.2 highlights a number of key operations within grape production that were previously the preserve of women workers but are increasingly carried out by both men and women. Column two illustrates the historical division of labour on exporting farms and shows a clear gender division of labour between tasks that are considered suitable for men and women, by farm managers as well as privately hired agronomists and irrigation district staff, corresponding to the period of the late 1980s and early 1990s (see Collins 1993). Column three shows changes in the gender division of labour taking place on many farms. Under the traditional gender division of labour, tasks such as bunch thinning, deflowering and bunch selection pruning were all allocated to female workers, but it is now increasingly common to see men working alongside women workers performing these tasks. No tasks that were previously the preserve of male workers have been allocated to women.

In the earlier stages of grape production, it was commonplace on farms for labour to be organised according to the historical and relatively rigid division of labour. In the new work teams, workers are trained to carry out a greater number of tasks. In this way farms are able to increase the percentage of permanently employed male workers as they are able to carry out both 'heavy' and 'dexterous' tasks, while reducing the numbers of permanently employed women and thus reducing their non-wage social costs.

There are a number of reasons for these changes. The first reason relates to increasing work intensity as farms use new production methods to increase worker productivity. For example, exporting farms moved away from daily task targets and towards a combination of daily task targets plus piece rate systems, to ensure that farms gain the full eight hours of labour from each worker. Under these circumstances, managers increasingly value workers' ability to labour at high intensity for the full working day. They tell how male workers are stronger, can work for longer periods in the heat and are less prone to injury.

> Working with men is better than working with women. He is free from family responsibilities every day, culturally he will not be the one taking his child to the doctor, he doesn't get sick as much as a woman, he doesn't have the same number of problems at home ... our medical certificates show that women are absent more than men. (Interview of manager of Logos Butia, Curaçá, 22 July 2003)

**Table 8.2** Changes in the gender division of labour in export grape production

| Operation | Historical gender division of labour (late 1980s–early 1990s) | New gender division of labour (late 1990s–early 2000s) |
| --- | --- | --- |
| Cutting back branches | Male | No change |
| Deleafing | Female | Female/male |
| Major cutting back of branches | Male | No change |
| Cracking branches | Male | No change |
| Application of dormex | Male | No change |
| Dry-tying | Female | Female/male |
| Application of gibberellic acid | Male | No change |
| Deleafing/freeing bunches | Male/female | No change |
| Bunch thinning | Female | Female/male |
| Selection of bunches | Female | Female/male |
| Pruning | Female | Female/male |
| Chinese hat | Female/male | No change |
| Pre-cleaning | Female/male | No change |
| Harvest | Female/male | No change |

*Source*: Author's observations/interviews with managers, SF valley (2002, 2003).

The same manager explained that through training farms are able to employ male as opposed to female workers. 'There are many men who if you train them properly, will work as well as if not better than women – the quality of the work is the same' (ibid.). From the perspective of this manager, these advantages to hiring men are contrary to the more traditional division of labour, as workers' skills are redefined in relation to their on-farm training, and supervision (more on this in a later section), as opposed to their innate abilities.

Another aspect of this shift is related to the number of tasks a worker can perform. Once male workers are trained to perform operations such as bunch thinning, selection and pruning, they can combine the 'delicate' alongside heavier tasks. While there is a trend towards labour specialisation through the creation of new work teams (more on this in a later section ) this does not eliminate the need for general workers. General tasks include cutting grass, digging holes, maintaining the trellis, applying fertilisers and agrotoxins, loading and unloading grape crates onto tractor pulled carts, clearing the ground of cut vines and burning and disposing of rubbish.

The second reason concerns non-wage costs borne by employers. Participation in trade unions, particularly by women workers has brought about the range of benefits noted above. In response, many farms are looking for ways of reducing these costs. One way is to hire male workers to do the work previously done by women. One manager explained:

The problem with hiring women under Brazilian law is that they have the right to stay at home for three months per year when they are pregnant, if you add another month for holidays, then she is away from work for four months of the year ... but we are changing and many men are already doing the bunch pruning process. Since they only have one month of holidays, it is better for us to hire them. (Interview with manager of JMM farm, Petrolina, 3 June 2002)

A third factor contributing to these transformations relates to farm's ability to hire workers during the harvest cycle. For many farms these changes have not come about through a clear thought-out strategy. Some reached the conclusion that they could substitute men for women based on trial and error.

> We reached the time to carry out the bunch pruning, but since there are other grape farms in the region we found that there were very few skilled women to employ, as they had already employed them. From this point we employed both men and women who did not have experience, and then we were surprised that those men were able to learn as fast as the women. This taught us that it was not essential to have women workers carrying out certain operations and men carrying out others. After a few months of this we realised that there was no point having this barrier that interfered with our hiring practices ... it is only a question of training the new workforce. Then we started trying to put men to do other operations that were previously designated for women. (Interview with manager of Brazil Uvas, Curaçá, June 2003)

During the early expansion of the grape branch women were widely employed, became skilled in the various elements involved in grape branch pruning. These skills in turn enabled them to move between jobs on different farms. However, the changes in the gender division of labour reduced these relative opportunities, as part of a broader attempt by exporting farms to reorganise the capital–labour relation in their favour.

The kinds of one-sided structuralist conceptions of class, discussed above, are ill-placed to trace how the subtleties of shifting gender relations are constitutive of capital–labour relations more generally. Combining structural and experiential features of class provides a methodological-theoretical way to approach such complex, dynamic and interactive processes.

## Conclusion

The formation, global integration and expansion of the SF valley's export table grape sector has been based upon new and evolving class relations and, unsurprisingly, escapes the simplifying schema proposed by Marx and Engels, noted at the start of this chapter. However, that initial schema is still useful in posing the questions of who benefits, how and to what extent from capitalist expansion/development.

In the SF valley, a new rural labour force emerged from late 1980s onwards. It began mobilising, under the leadership of the regions rural trade union, the STR. Unlike in many other world regions of export horticulture, its mobilisations proved relatively successful, to the extent that by the mid-1990s collective bargaining and rights over pay and conditions were established. Workers were able to use their associational power, articulated through the STR, to draw upon their emerging structural power, derived from an increasingly complex labour process, to win these rights through threats of and actual strike action. These victories benefitted female workers because they won a range of wage and non-wage rights (related to maternal responsibilities).

As with all class relations, however, these early victories for the valley's labour force were not the end of the story. On the contrary, these gains pushed the valley's employers to look to other ways to maintain profitability. They did so through restructuring the gender division of labour by reorganising the labour process, making men undertake tasks previously considered as women's work. This enabled employers to reduce the numbers of women employed on permanent contracts while increasing the percentage of women employed on temporary contracts (Selwyn 2010).

The author's experience of conducting this fieldwork and deploying class-relational concepts and categories to understand the dynamics of regional change were reflected upon. Commencing with a relatively simple and structuralist approach, the author found it necessary to adopt a more relational and experiential conception of class. This shift enabled him to incorporate gender into his class analysis more satisfactorily than a narrow structuralist concept of class would have allowed. As the late Ellen Wood noted, 'Class formation [is] a[n] historical process shaped by the "logic" of material determinations ... Class, in other words, is a phenomenon which is visible only in process' (1995: 81: Bannerji 1995; Elson and Pearson 1981).

Class analysis requires simultaneously a conception of the relative solidity of class structure and of the relative fluidity of class experience. Grasping these two dialectically constituted elements of class analysis is necessary in order to avoid overemphasising one element at the expense of the other. Notably, for this purpose, documenting one's findings during the fieldwork phase represents a demanding, yet necessary method and practice. First, it is a way of testing the utility of using relatively abstract concepts to illuminate empirical reality. Second, it does inform the ways in which theory needs to guide, but not constrain a fruitful Marxian analysis for the twenty-first century. For instance, the mapping of production and labour activities and the changing gendered features of the labour process provides key information on both class and power. Understanding the particularity of these dynamics (whether due to local or commodity-specific factors) is, in turn, key to comprehending possibilities for successful labouring class collective action.

## References

Bannerji, H. 1995. *Thinking Through: Essays on Feminism, Marxism and Anti- Racism*. Toronto: Women's Press.

———. 2005. 'Building from Marx: Reflections on class and race', *Social Justice* 32(102): 144–60.

Berg, J. 2010. *Laws or Luck? Understanding Rising Formality in Brazil in the 2000s*. Brasilia: International Labour Office, https://www.ilo.org/brasilia/publicacoes/WCMS_227064/lang--pt/index. htm (accessed 10 October 2010).

Bernstein, H. 2007. 'Capital and labour from centre to margins'. Keynote speech at the conference 'Living on the Margins', Stellenbosch University, 26–28 March, http://pdf.steerweb.org/WFP%20ESSAY/Bernstein_dsi.pdf (accessed 8 December 2019).

Braverman, H. 1974. 'Labor and monopoly capital', *New York Monthly Review*.

Brighton Labour Process Group. 1977. 'The capitalist labour process'. *Capital and Class*, 1: 3–42.

CODEVASF. 2001. *Censo Fruticultura 2001 do Vale do São Francisco*. Brasilia: CODEVASF.

Cohen, G. 1978. *Karl Marx's Theory of History*. Oxford: Oxford University Press.

————. 2000. *Karl Marx's Theory of History: A Defence*. Oxford: Clarendon.

Collins, J. 1993. 'Gender, contracts and wage work: Agricultural restructuring in Brazil's São Francisco valley', *Development and Change* 24(1): 53–82.

————. 1995. 'Farm size and non-traditional exports: Determinants of participation in world markets', *World Development* 23(7): 1103–14.

————. 2000. 'Tracing social relations in commodity chains: The case of grapes in Brazil'. In A. Haugerud, M. Priscilla Stone and P. D. Little (eds), *Commodities and Globalization: Anthropological Perspectives*, pp. 97–109. Lanham: Rowman and Littlefield.

Collins J. and G. Krippner. 1999. 'Permanent labor contracts in agriculture: Flexibility and subordination in a new export crop', *Comparative Studies in Society and History* 41(3): 510–34.

Elson, D. and R. Pearson. 1981. 'Nimble fingers make cheap workers: An analysis of women's employment in third world export manufacturing'. *Quarterly Feminist Review* 7: 87–101.

Lenin, V. I. 1965. *Collected Works, Vol. 31*, 4th English edition. Moscow: Progress.

Marx, K. 1990. *Capital: A Critique of Political Economy, Vol. 1*. London: Penguin.

Marx, K. and F. Engels. 1969. *Marx/Engels Selected Works, Vol. I*. Moscow: Progress.

Newsome, K., P. Taylor, J. Bair and A. Rainnie. 2015. *Putting Labour in Its Place: Labour Process Analysis and Global Value Chains*. Basingstoke: Palgrave Macmillan.

Nilo Coelho Irrigation District. 2002. *Internal Report*. Petrolina: Nilo Coelho Irrigation District.

Reardon, T., C. M. Timmer, C. B. Barrett and J. Berdegue. 2003. 'The rise of supermarkets in Africa, Asia, and Latin America'. *American Journal of Agricultural Economics* 85(5): 371–88.

Selwyn, B. 2007. 'Labor process and workers' bargaining power in export grape production, North East Brazil'. *Journal of Agrarian Change* 7(4): 526–53.

————. 2010. 'Gender, wage work and development in North East Brazil'. *Bulletin of Latin American Research* 29(1): 51–70.

————. 2012. *Workers, State and Development in Brazil: Powers of Labour, Chains of Value*. Manchester: Manchester University Press.

Smith, C. 2006. 'The double indeterminacy of labour power: Labour effort and labour mobility'. *Work, Employment and Society* 20(2): 389–402.

Thompson, E. P. 1963. *The Making of the English Working Class*. New York: Vintage.

Valexport. 2008. *Há 20 Anos Unindo Forças Para o Desenvolvimento do Vale do São Francisco e da Fruticultura Brasileira*. Petrolina: Valexport.

Wood, E. 1995. *Democracy against Capitalism*. Cambridge: Cambridge University Press.

Wright, E. O. 2000. 'Working-class power, capitalist-class interests, and class compromise'. *American Journal of Sociology* 105(4): 957–1002.

# Chapter Nine

# UNDERSTANDING LABOUR RELATIONS AND STRUGGLES IN INDIA THROUGH MARX'S METHOD

Satoshi Miyamura

## Abstract

This chapter illustrates the contemporary relevance of Marx's analysis of labour relations and struggles with reference to India. It argues that Marx's method provides an alternative to the methodological individualistic, reductionist and conflict-free mainstream conception of labour relations. It also challenges the juridical and dualist approach to labour. Marx's method is deployed to understand labour relations and struggles with reference to the long-term fieldwork on trade unions in various regions of India.

## Introduction

In a widely quoted passage in the *Eighteenth Brumaire of Louis Bonaparte*, Marx (1852) wrote that:

> Men make their own history, but they do not make it as they please; they do not make it under self-selected circumstances, but under circumstances existing already, given and transmitted from the past.

This chapter illustrates the contemporary relevance of Marx's analysis of labour association and class struggle with reference to debates on labour reforms in India. As reflected in the above quote, Marx's method can be used to understand class relations and struggles as being shaped by material conditions in their social and historical specificities, which in turn reflect struggles past and present. Marx's approach is contrasted with the methodological individualism and reductionism inherent in the orthodox conception of labour relations, which underlies debates on labour flexibilisation. It is argued that Marx offers a method to understand labour relations and struggles in a way that overcomes dichotomous and juridical perspectives, drawing on case studies from long-term fieldwork on trade unions and labour movements in various regions of India.

It does so by first engaging with debates on labour market reforms in India and interrogates the conception of labour and labour markets underpinning these debates. This provides the backdrop to the outlining of Marx's method, and his analysis of class and class struggle, elaborated through fieldwork observations from India in the following two sections. The chapter concludes by drawing policy and political implications of the methodological discussion.

### Debates on Labour Reforms in India: A Conceptual Critique

It is hard to guess how Marx would engage with contemporary debates on 'jobless growth' and accusations of labour populism raised against union militancy in areas of the world characterised by working poverty and weak institutionalised power of labour. However, he emphasised how associations of labour need to focus on issues beyond those in the immediate workplaces. His advice to the First International makes clear how Marx (1866: 92) saw the potential role of trade unions to engage with broader social and political movements as an important driver of class struggle:

> Apart from their original purposes, they must now learn to act deliberately as organising centres of the working class in the broad interest of its *complete emancipation*. They must aid every social and political movement tending in that direction [...] They must convince the world at large that their efforts, far from being narrow – and selfish, aim at the emancipation of the downtrodden millions.

There has been intense debate on labour market policies in India over the past three decades (Haldar and Deakin 2015; Lerche 2015; Miyamura 2012; Sharma 2006; Shyam Sundar 2005). Part of the debate emerged through the concern over the so-called jobless growth since the mid-1980s, in which employment growth in the formal sector has been slower than output growth. As the Indian economy increasingly 'liberalised' over the 1990s, legislations such as chapter V-B of the Industrial Dispute Act (IDA) – which stipulates firms of certain size to obtain permission from governments to layoff or retrench workers, or close down establishments – have recurrently been criticised for discouraging firms in India from generating sufficient employment and compelling them to operate at a 'suboptimal' scale and a higher degree of capital and skill intensity (Besley and Burgess 2004; Debroy 2005; Fallon and Lucas 1991; Kochhar et al. 2006; Government of India 2002; World Bank 2000), even while evidence for these arguments have been systematically contested (Papola 1994; Singh 1995; Bhalotra 1998; Jenkins 1999; Bardhan 2002; Bhattacharjea 2006; Teitelbaum 2011; Shyam Sundar 2016). The latest iteration of this debate has been recited around the Indian government's ongoing pursuit of labour flexibilising reforms by consolidating various labour laws into four codes on wages, industrial relations, social security, and safety and working conditions (Jayaram 2019; Shyam Sundar 2019).

Both proponents of labour flexiblisation policies and those who contest them share a methodologically individualistic, reductionist and conflict-free conception of labour relations. This is exemplified in the framing of mainstream labour economics in which positive as well as negative roles of labour laws and trade unions are explained in a choice theoretic framework of individual behaviour with the benchmark being the equilibrium point in the labour market between labour supply and demand. Proponents of labour flexibilisation policies criticise trade unionism and labour legislations for the 'distortion' they cause in diverting the economy away from efficient resource allocation by increasing labour costs and lowering labour demand. Institutional forms of trade unions are explained and modelled as particular aggregation of individual member's interests such as through 'median votes' (Booth 1995). But those who defend positive roles of institutions, labour laws and trade unionism also draw on their efficiency-enhancing effects by mediating information (Freeman and Medoff 1984) or moderating incentives for 'labour militancy' (Calmfors and Driffill 1988). As outlined in section 3, this is in contrast to Marx's approach to the labour market as reflecting inherently antagonistic social relations of production, which includes not just exploitation in the labour process but also the whole circuit of capital.

This then gives rise to a juridical and institutional conception of labour relations that is also shared by both camps of the mainstream debates on labour market reforms. For example, the IDA and many other labour legislations in India apply only to 'workmen' (Ministry of Labour and Employment 2015). Employees are then divided into formal and informal sectors according to the status of their workplace as well as contractual status.[1] Accordingly, both proponents and critiques of labour market reforms presume duality in labour relations between employed and unemployed, paid and unpaid, formal and informal, regular and irregular, unionised and non-unionised, among many other dichotomies. And yet, despite the juridical and formalistic conception, the state rarely features as either a site for struggles or as an active agent in shaping labour relations. Again, as discussed in the next section, this is in contrast to Marx's method in which these conceptual dualities have to be understood as steps in abstraction, rather than as formal demarcations for actual existing social relations. In particular, in the current historical juncture in India, it is precisely capital's strategy to enhance its control over labour in and through all of these different domains, and as a result, labour struggle takes place across boundaries, including productive and reproductive spheres. In the process of fieldwork, Marx's method and his conception of class can be deployed to research struggles that cut across many of the conventional boundaries assumed in studies of industrial relations and labour economics.

## Understanding Class Struggles through Marx's Method

Marx analysed class and class struggles throughout his various writings, particularly in his studies of historical and political developments, but without famously giving a definitive definition of the concept. Yet, as demonstrated by Bensaïd (2002: 97–121) and elaborated in Campling et al. (2016), Marx's conception of class and class struggles unfolds through the three volumes of *Capital* following his 'method of rising from the

---

[1]  According to the Indian law, workers are categorised across two dimensions. On the one hand, the site of employment is distinguished between organised and unorganised sectors depending on the size of employment, while, on the other hand, workers are also categorised to be either formally or informally employed depending on whether the employer provides employment and social security benefits, with overlap between the two categorisations.

abstract to the concrete' (Marx 1993: 101). The purpose of this section is to provide a sketch (rather than a comprehensive overview) of Marx's method and analysis of class struggles, in order to then contrast them with the conceptual features of mainstream approach to labour relations as highlighted in the next section.

In *Volume I* of *Capital*, Marx unfolds his labour theory of value and focuses on the source of surplus-value, abstracting from other 'determinations and relations' (Marx 1993: 100). In chapter 1, by starting from commodity production and characterising the aspect of capitalism as general commodity production, Marx introduces the notion of abstract labour as corresponding to the value embodied in commodities (Marx 1976: 128). As abstract labour is based on the *socially necessary* labour-time, relations of exploitation are conceived, from the outset, as *social* relations, which 'inevitably involves tension and conflict between the classes' (Ste. Croix 1981: 49), that is, *class struggle*. This is in contrast to the methodological individualistic, reductionist and conflict-free conception of labour relations that characterise the mainstream debate outlined in the next section.

It also means that in the analysis of exploitation in *Volume I*, determinations and relations introduced in subsequent volumes are already presupposed, which include the labour market, social division of labour through capitalist competition, social reproduction of labour and class struggle. That Marx conceives class not solely defined by the employment relation in the labour process but as a synthesis of all social relations becomes apparent by chapter 10, 'The working day'. Marx illustrates how the time duration of work is determined through 'a struggle between collective capital, i.e. the class of capitalists, and collective labour, i.e. the working class' (Marx 1976: 344), which is also simultaneously struggles over the capitalist subsumption of labour as well as over the reproduction of labour-power. *Volume II* then extends determinations in conflictual relations over the selling and buying of labour-power as commodity in circulation, which 'brings about an ever growing division of social labour' (Marx 1992a: 119). These analyses in the labour process and in the circuit of capital are then integrated in the overall capitalist competition in *Volume* III, adding further determinations in which 'each individual capitalist [...] participates in the exploitation of the entire working class by capital as a whole' (Marx 1992b: 298). Thus, Marx's conception of class articulated through the logic of three volumes of *Capital* offers an alternative to understanding labour relations and struggles that are co-constitutive of '"many determinations" within the whole array of social relations' (Campling et al. 2016: 1747), as opposed to the mainstream analysis of labour relations confined to a particular sphere of economic activities, workplace or institutions, detached from broader relations of domination and subordination.

Towards the end of *Volume I*, chapter 32, 'The historical tendency of capitalist accumulation', Marx discusses 'the immanent laws of capitalist production itself' and then suggests that 'with this there also grows the revolt of the working class, a class constantly increasing in numbers and trained, united and organized by the very mechanism of the capitalist process of production' (1976: 929). But this does not mean that labour relations and struggles are to be directly read off from 'immanent laws' of the mode of production. This is because 'class relations articulate cultural and social as well as political and economic dimensions' (Campling et al. 2016: 1748). In the final and famously incomplete chapter 52 of *Volume III*, 'Classes', Marx introduces 'wage-labourers, capitalists and landowners' as 'the three great classes of modern society' and then notes that 'even' in England 'this class articulation does not emerge in pure form' (Marx 1992b: 1025). As Thompson (1963: 8) argued, class is 'a historical phenomenon, unifying a number of disparate and seemingly unconnected events, both in the raw material of experience and in consciousness' and therefore 'is a historical experience'. Wood (1995: 83) goes further and argues that 'class struggle therefore precedes class, both in the sense that class forma-tion *presuppose* an experience of conflict and struggle arising out of production relations, and in the sense that there are conflicts and struggles structured "in class ways" even in societies that do not yet have class-conscious formations' (original emphasis). While not all forms of struggles against domination and subordination are class struggles, they are nevertheless 'in part mutually constituted with it' (Campling et al. 2016: 1748; see also Harriss 1990; Merchant 1990; Mies 2014; Moore 2015; Federici 2017; Banaji 2012). Therefore, using Marx's method and deploying his conception of class allows struggles to be encountered in places and contexts beyond the conventional gaze of industrial relations and labour economics.

## Understanding Labour Relations and Struggles in India

Understanding labour relations and struggles through Marx's method means deploying the concept of class in its social and historical specificities. The process of fieldwork turns this observation into a lived experience, highlighting what applied historical materialism looks like in practice. I have a two-decade-long experience of field-based research in India, focusing on industrial hubs, relations, labour movements and unions. In my fieldwork-based research on industrial restructuring and labour movements, class relations are found to interact with diverse forms of social domination and subordination.

For example, a fieldwork carried out in 2001 in a jute textile mill near Kolkata in West Bengal revealed that workers in the whole of the weaving section were recruited from a single village in the neighbouring state of Odisha (formally Orissa). The recruitment was based on religious and caste identities, and a 'jobber' from the region was able to exercise strong control over the labour process to the extent that an absent weaver could not be replaced by a substitute or temporary worker on the day without the jobber's consent. In another jute textile mill researched during the 2001 fieldwork, settling of disputes over wages and working conditions involved not just managers and trade union organisers but also intervention from a 'religious leader' who was said to have a strong influence over workers (Miyamura 2010: 385). These observations reinforce Fernandes's (1997) con-tention that broader social dimensions are central to class relations in Kolkata jute mills despite being suppressed by centralised trade union politics. Parallels can also be drawn with studies in other sectors, including Parry (1999) who observed the importance of 'primordial loyalties' in labour relations in a public sector steel plant.

Another field-based study carried out in 2019 focused on a union fighting for the regularisation of waste collectors in Mumbai, which also reveals complex ways in which class and caste, communal and regional identities interact. All waste collectors are Dalits – those who are subjugated at the bottom or outside of the caste hierarchy; and their sense of social subordination has been identified as an initial barrier to unionisation as well as a strength of subsequent mobilisation. At the same time, while all waste collectors are Dalits, those with permanent contracts are differentiated from those who are subcontracted, including being allocated to different entrances to the dumping ground. Also, waste collectors from different regions and linguistic backgrounds were assigned to different waste collection routes within the city, further complicating the ways in which trade union mobilisation draws on multilayered identities and consciousness. Interesting parallels can be drawn between these field observations and Gill's (2009) work on informal scrap trade in Delhi as well as perhaps a more romanticised vision in Boo (2013), both of which show how class relations are articulated in caste identities.

In 2019, during a round of research on a trade union organising domestic workers in Mumbai to demand enforcement of minimum wages, workers revealed that being a part of the union has been instrumental in changing their perceptions about their class position. Prior to unionisation, these women identified themselves as housewives, mothers, carers or as 'maids and servants' (in their socially derogatory connotations), but after joining the union, these women have come to see themselves as workers (Miyamura 2019). These observations corroborate with a wide range of studies revealing various ways in which class intersects with gender, race, religion, caste and various other forms of social domination (James 1989; Breman 1999a, 1999b; Hensman 2011; Selwyn 2012; Pattenden 2016; Mezzadri 2016; Shah et al. 2017; Baglioni 2018, among others).

Deploying the Marx's method also means understanding a collective action not merely as a representation of aggregated individual interests or 'median votes' but as a reflection of shared experiences of exploitation and domination. As reflected by the quote in the opening of this chapter, this does not mean that individuals do not have choices or 'freedom' to act (in the liberal sense, of course) or indeed individual agency to try to actively modify their own material conditions (Miyamura 2020). However, at the same time, Marx's method makes explicit how material conditions, which are the result of human activities past and present, in turn shape opportunities, constraints and capacities for a collective action (Sartre 1976). This framework allows for an understanding of trajectories of labour movements and unionisation that avoids simplistic individual voluntarism.

Indian industry has been undergoing substantive restructuring over recent decades, which has proceeded in varying forms and degrees of technological change, outsourcing, informalisation of employment, intensification of the labour process and relocation/consolidation of production. Undoubtedly, industrial restructuring and labour struggles shape each other in diverse and context-specific ways (Silver 2003; Anner 2008, 2015). While, in many cases, industrial restructuring was carried out as part of employers' attempt to bypass negotiating with established trade unions, situations have been observed where retrenched workers in the closed production site succeeded in coordinating with and organising workers around unionisation in the relocated site. For example, a research on a multinational soap and detergent manufacturing firm in India has revealed how union activists who lost their jobs after the closure of the factory in Mumbai subsequently linked up with workers in relocated sites across India to maintain extra-plant solidarity through a company-based union federation (Miyamura 2016b: 1931–33). Similarly, cases have been observed where mobilisation received support by building solidarity with workers across different employment statuses as well as in other production sites at local, national and international levels. For example, automobile manufacturing workers in Pune formed a region-based trade union federation to link and support struggles of unions at the plant level, many of whom relocated from Mumbai after closure (Miyamura 2016a: 1279). Permanent workers in some auto sector factories in the National Capital Region (NCR) around Delhi have also mobilised contract workers in their attempt to form trade unions (Miyamura 2016b: 1933–35; see also Monaco 2015; Nowak 2017). These cases do not, of course, indicate that shared class consciousness or mobilisation is inevitable, or that narrow 'economic' interests of individual workers do not matter. Indeed, even in cases where extra workplace solidarity was extended, sustaining it beyond the initial momentum around unionisation has often been challenging, as I have observed in my recent fieldwork in 2019. As an example, many of the unions of the soap and detergent manufacturing firm that formed in relocated sites have come under attack by the company management as well as local provincial states. The regional federation of unions in Pune subsequently split due to disputes among the leaderships. In my recent fieldwork in 2019, I found that the solidarity between permanent and contract workers in the NCR auto factories has also been undermined by trade unions negotiating solely on behalf of permanent workers. These various cases, nevertheless, suggest the need for open-ended ways in which class relations are experienced.

Studying the diversity of trade unions and labour movements also illustrates the importance of moving away from the conventional focus on organisational forms of trade unions and, instead, evaluating them in their specific sociohistorical contexts. For example, in many regions and sectors, industrial restructuring has led to undermining of traditional collective bargaining institutions characterised by industrial or regional bargaining involving central trade union organisations typically affiliated to political parties and with the state playing coordinating or mediating roles. But where state-coordinated collective bargaining mechanisms and established forms of trade unions have remained resilient – for example, in some of the formal sector manufacturing firms in Kolkata – 'accepted' institutionalised recourse for dispute resolution has dampened overt forms of strikes. For example, in the aforementioned case of Kolkata jute textile manufacturing, party-affiliated unionism and industry-wide collective bargaining dominate and continue to be relatively stable (Miyamura 2016a: 1277). But party-affiliated unionism has also been observed to maintain its stability in an electric fan manufacturing plant in Kolkata, indicating that organisational forms of labour associations reflect regionally and historically specific developments of labour movements (Miyamura 2016b: 1928–30). These observations contest presumptions that associate party-political forms of trade unions with labour militancy and unstable industrial relations (Banerji et al. 1995; Pencavel 1995). At the same time, it has been found that the resilience of established unions in Kolkata has sometimes limited the scope for alternative forms of mobilisation, particularly in mobilising workers in informal employment, while in other regions, it was observed that party-affiliated unions have been instrumental in linking struggles that interweaves formal and informal employment status as well as productive and reproductive issues (Miyamura 2016a).

An example of the latter comes from a trade union that traditionally organised formal sector workers in cotton textile manufacturing in Mumbai, where most of its mills closed down over the past three decades (Bhattacherjee 1989; Pinto and Fernandes 1996; Kulkarni 1999; Krishnan 2000). As mills shut down, the focus of many unions shifted away from protesting against closure and redevelopment of mill land to negotiating compensations and securing housing for the retrenched workers. However, there have also been attempts by some unions to draw on their organisa-tional capacity to mobilise workers in informal employment, including the afore-mentioned mobilisation of domestic women workers, some of whom are based in communities closely connected to the mill workers. The union's hierarchical and entirely male-dominated organisational structure, built up through many decades of struggles in the textile mills, contrasts with another union mobilising domestic and home-based workers in a slum in Mumbai, which is organised more horizontally and currently has a leadership entirely of female; all except one are domestic and home-based workers themselves.

Attempts to link struggles across formal and informal employment can be found in the latter union too. Domestic workers have attempted to mobilise workers in other occupations residing in the same slum, including mobilising their husbands who work as construction workers to secure their welfare payments. However, the different tra-jectories in which these different struggles are linked appear to also shape the agenda and strategies of collective action. While the former textile mills-based union focuses primarily on the enforcement of minimum wages for domestic workers, the latter slum-based domestic workers' union pursues forms of mobilisation that more explicitly link workplace struggles with home- or community-based issues, including gender-based harassment and violence, alcoholism, among others. These observations echo those of Agarwala (2013) in the diverse and uneven ways in which issues around informality are mobilised in India.

In yet another case researched during my 2019 fieldwork, a settlement to force a multinational company to pay compensation and clean up the toxic wastes left after the 2001 closure of a thermometer factory in Kodaikanal, Tamil Nadu, was achieved by a close collaboration between its trade union and local environmental groups, including using tactics such as an online release of a rap song video depicting the impact of mercury poising on the workers and the environment. Collaboration between trade unions and citizen groups was also instrumental in sustaining the nine-day strike of public sector bus drivers in Mumbai in January 2019, which involved community organising to prevent authorities from entering the workers' quarters and removing striking bus drivers. The latter case also reveals that employers and the state equally attempt to control not just the labour process in the workplace but also the reproductive processes in households and communities. Automobile manufacturing firms in the industrial 'corridor' in the NCR have actively utilised community-based disciplining mechanisms, including collusion with 'goons' (Miyamura 2016b; see also Monaco 2015). These examples once again highlight how struggles in practice challenge formalistic and juridical boundaries such as between 'workmen' and others, formal and informal, regular and irregular, productive and reproductive, among others. Echoing Marx's address to the First International cited earlier, spaces for labour struggles are curved out in diverse ways even (and perhaps especially) where the scope for wage bargaining is limited or where traditional forms of trade unions have proven to be ineffective.

## Conclusion

This chapter has taken on the concept of labour relations and struggles by contrasting Marx's method with the framework common in the mainstream debate on labour-flexibilising reforms in India. It has argued that Marx's method is in sharp opposition to the methodological individualistic and reductionist approach to labour relations that assumes conflict-free allocation of revenues and with juridical and dualist framing. Deploying Marx's method means understanding labour relations as class struggles in all their complexities, context specificities and interactions with various forms of social dominations and subordinations. It also means challenging conceptual boundaries of formal versus informal, regular and irregular, productive and reproductive and other demarcations, and finding struggles across these different spheres. In concrete terms and with reference to my own fieldwork experience on industrial relations and labour movements and unionism in India, this has meant understanding class and class struggles in their diverse forms of articulations.

It should be noted that despite their apparent complexity, the conceptions of labour relations and struggles, which are derived from Marx's method and applied in their concrete social and historical specificities, have the potential to strongly inform an alternative policy agenda on labour that moves the debate beyond flexibilising reforms. Moreover, in India, debates on 'jobless growth' and the perceived need to 'ease industrial relations' and 'simplify labour codes' (Jayaram 2019; Shyam Sundar 2019) must be located in the broader patterns of capitalist development in the current historical juncture experienced in the subcontinent, and could motivate a more fundamental debate on the potential for an alternative trajectory, including a labour-led development (Selwyn 2017).

Finally, Marx's method also informs an agenda for research and political mobilisation that focuses on struggles beyond the gaze of conventional analyses and debates, including mobilisation that links productive and reproductive struggles (Agarwala 2013; Breman 1999a, 1999b; Federici 2017; Hensman 2011; Miyamura 2019). As outlined in the previous section, there is increasing space for workplace struggles to engage with social reproductive issues around homeplace-based relations, housing, healthcare, environment and others. This also gives rises to state and institutional mediation as sites for labour struggles (Pattenden 2016). Again, ways in which productive and reproductive struggles are linked have been observed to be contingent upon the specific history and context of mobilisation. Deploying Marx's method in the field offers a first step to addressing these issues.

# References

Agarwala, R. 2013. *Informal Labor, Formal Politics, and Dignified Discontent in India*. Cambridge: Cambridge University Press.

Anner, M. 2008. 'Meeting the challenges of industrial restructuring: Labor reform and enforcement in Latin America'. *Latin American Politics & Society* 50(2): 33–65.

———. 2015. 'Labor control regimes and worker resistance in global supply chains'. *Labor History* 56(3): 292–307.

Baglioni, E. 2018. 'Labour control and the labour question in global production networks: Exploitation and disciplining in Senegalese export horticulture'. *Journal of Economic Geography* 18(1): 111–37.

Banaji, J. 2012. *Theory as History: Essays on Modes of Production and Exploitation*. Chicago: Haymarket Books.

Banerji, A., J. E. Campos and R. H. Sabot. 1995. 'The political economy of formal sector pay and employment in developing countries'. *World Bank Policy Research Working Paper* 1435 (March).

Bardhan, P. 2002. 'Political economy of reform in India'. In Rakesh Mohan (ed.), *Facets of the Indian Economy: The NCAER Golden Jubilee Lectures*, pp. 123–35. New Delhi: Oxford University Press.

Bensaïd, D. 2002. *Marx for Our Times: Adventures and Misadventures of a Critique*. London: Verso.

Besley, T. and R. Burgess. 2004. 'Can labor regulation hinder economic performance? Evidence from India'. *Quarterly Journal of Economics* 119(1): 91–134.

Bhalotra, S. R. 1998. 'The puzzle of jobless growth in Indian manufacturing'. *Oxford Bulletin of Economics and Statistics* 60(1): 5–32.

Bhattacharjea, A. 2006. 'Labour market regulation and industrial performance in India: A critical review of the empirical evidence'. *Indian Journal of Labour Economics* 49(2): 211–32.

———. 1989. 'Evolution of unionism and labour market structure: Case of Bombay textile mills, 1947–1985'. *Economic and Political Weekly* 24(21): M67–76.

Boo, K. 2013. *Behind the Beautiful Forevers: Life, Death and Hope in a Mumbai Slum*. London: Portobello.

Booth, A. 1995. *The Economics of Trade Union*. Cambridge: Cambridge University Press.

Breman, J. 1999a. 'The study of industrial labour in post-colonial India: The formal sector: An introductory review'. In J. P. Parry, J. Breman and K. Kapadia (eds), *The Worlds of Indian Industrial Labour*, pp. 1–42. New Delhi: Sage.

———. 1999b. 'The study of industrial labour in post-colonial India: The informal sector: A concluding review'. In J. P. Parry, J. Breman and K. Kapadia (eds), *The Worlds of Indian Industrial Labour*, pp. 407–32. New Delhi: Sage.

Calmfors, L. and J. Driffill. 1988. 'Bargaining structure, corporatism and macroeconomic performance'. *Economic Policy* 3(6): 14–61.

Campling, L., S. Miyamura, J. Pattenden and B. Selwyn. 2016. 'Class dynamics of development: A methodological note'. *Third World Quarterly* 37(10): 1745–67.

Debroy, B. 2005. 'Issues in labour law reform'. In B. Debroy and P. D. Kaushik (eds), *Reforming the Labour Market*, pp. 37–76. New Delhi: Academic Foundation.

Fallon, P. R. and R. E. B. Lucas. 1991. 'The impact of changes in job security regulations in India and Zimbabwe'. *World Bank Economic Review* 5(3): 395–413.

Federici, S. 2017. *Caliban and the Witch: Women, the Body and Primitive Accumulation*. New York: Autonomedia.

Fernandes, L. 1997. *Producing Workers: The Politics of Gender, Class, and Culture in the Calcutta Jute Mills*. Philadelphia: University of Pennsylvania Press.

Freeman, R. B. and J. L. Medoff. 1984. *What Do Unions Do?* New York: Basic.

Gill, K. 2009. *Of Poverty and Plastic: Scavenging and Scrap Trading Entrepreneurs in India's Urban Informal Economy*. Oxford: Oxford University Press.

Government of India, Ministry of Labour. 2002. *The Second National Commission on Labour Report*, http://labour.nic.in/lcomm2/nlc_report.html (accessed 23 July 2014).

Haldar, A. and S. Deakin. 2015. 'How should India reform its labour laws?' *Economic and Political Weekly* 50(12): 48–55.

Harriss, B. 1990. 'Another awkward class: Merchants and agrarian change in India'. In H. Bernstein, B. Crow, M. Mackintosh and C. Martin (eds), *The Food Question: Profits Versus People?*, pp. 91–103. London: Earthscan.

Hensman, R. 2011. *Workers, Unions and Global Capitalism: Lessons from India*. New Delhi: Tulika.

James, C. L. R. 1989. *The Black Jacobins: Toussaint L'Ouverture and the San Domingo Revolution*. New York: Vintage.

Jayaram, N. 2019. 'Protection of workers' wages in India: An analysis of the Labour Code on Wages, 2019'. *Economic and Political Weekly* 54(49). https://www.epw.in/engage/article/protection-workers-wages-india-labour-wage-code (accessed 12 February 2020).

Jenkins, R. 1999. *Democratic Politics and Economic Reform in India*. Cambridge: Cambridge University Press.

Kochhar, K., U. Kumar, R. Rajan, A. Subramanian and I. Tokatlidis. 2006. 'India's pattern of development: What happened, what follows?' *Journal of Monetary Economics* 53(5): 981–1019.

Krishnan, S. 2000. *The Murder of the Mills: A Case Study of Phoenix Mills*. Mumbai: Girangaon Bachao Andolan.

Kulkarni, S. 1999. 'Impact of restructuring of the Bombay textile industry on labour and labour institutions'. *Indian Journal Labour Economics* 42(4): 865–71.

Lerche, J. 2015. *Making India? The Labour Law Reforms of Narendra Modi's Government*. London: SOAS South Asia Institute. https://www.soas.ac.uk/south-asia-institute/events/file107716.pdf (accessed 11 March 2016).

Marx, K. 1852. *The Eighteenth Brumaire of Louis Bonaparte*, https://www.marxists.org/archive/marx/works/1852/18th-brumaire/index.htm (accessed 5 September 2018).

———. [1866] 1973. 'Instructions for delegates to the Geneva Congress'. In *The First International and After, Vol. 3. Political Writings*. London: Penguin.

———. 1976. *Capital: Critique of Political Economy, Volume I* (trans. Ben Fowkes). London: Penguin Classics.

———. 1992a. *Capital: Critique of Political Economy, Volume II* (trans. David Fernbach). London: Penguin Classics.

———. 1992b. *Capital: Critique of Political Economy, Volume III* (trans. David Fernbach). London: Penguin.

———. 1993. *Grundrisse*. London: Penguin.

Merchant, C. 1990. *The Death of Nature: Women, Ecology and the Scientific Revolution*. New York: Bravo.

Mezzadri, A. 2016. *The Sweatshop Regime: Labouring Bodies, Exploitation, and Garments Made in India*. New York: Cambridge University Press.

Mies, M. 2014. *Patriarchy and Accumulation on a World Scale: Women in the International Division of Labour*. London: Zed.

Ministry of Labour and Employment. 2015. 'Industrial relations FAQ', 25 November, https://labour.gov.in/faqs/industrial-relations-faq-0 (accessed 11 February 2020).

Miyamura, S. 2010. *Labour Market Institutions in Indian Industry: A Comparison of Mumbai and Kolkata*. PhD thesis, University of London.

———. 2012. 'Emerging consensus on labour market institutions and implications for developing countries: From the debates in India'. *Forum for Social Economics* 41(1): 97–123.

———. 2016a. 'Rethinking labour market institutions in Indian industry: Forms, functions and socio-historical contexts'. *Journal of Peasant Studies* 43(6): 1262–84.

———. 2016b. 'Diverse trajectories of industrial restructuring and labour organising in India'. *Third World Quarterly* 37(10): 1921–41.

———. 2019. 'Labour organising across productive and reproductive relations in India: A comparative labour regime perspective'. Paper presented at the AFEP-IIPPE Conference in Political Economy, Lille, 3–5 July.

————. 2020. 'Are we all rational, optimising agents?' In K. Deane and E. Van Waeyenberge (eds), *Recharting the History of Economic Thought*, pp. 13–29. Basingstoke: Palgrave Macmillan.

Monaco, L. 2015. *Bringing Operaismo to Gurgaon: A Study of Labour Composition and Resistance Practices in the Indian Auto Industry*. PhD thesis, SOAS, University of London.

Moore, J. W. 2015. *Capitalism in the Web of Life: Ecology and the Accumulation of Capital*. New York: Verso.

Nowak, J. 2017. 'Mass strikes in India and Brazil as the terrain for a new social movement unionism'. *Development and Change* 48(5): 965–86.

Papola, T. S. 1994. 'Structural adjustment, labour market flexibility and employment'. *Indian Journal of Labour Economics* 37(1): 3–16.

Parry, J. P. 1999. 'Lords of labour: Working and shirking in Bhilai'. *Contributions to Indian Sociology* 33(1&2): 107–40.

Pattenden, J. 2016. *Labour, State and Society in Rural India*. Manchester: Manchester University Press.

Pencavel, J. H. 1995. 'The role of labor unions in fostering economic development'. *World Bank Policy Research Working Paper* 1469.

Pinto, R. and N. Fernandes. 1996. *Murder of the Mills: An Enquiry into Bombay's Cotton Textile Industry and Its Workers*. Mumbai: Lokshahi Hakk Sanghatana.

Sartre, J.-P. 1976. *Critique of Dialectical Reason, Volume 1* (ed. F. Jameson, trans. Alan Sheridan-Smith). London: Verso.

Selwyn, B. 2012. *Workers, State and Development in Brazil*. Manchester: Manchester University Press.

————. 2017. *The Struggle for Development*. Cambridge: Polity.

Shah, A., J. Lerche, R. Axelby, D. Benbabaali, B. Donegan and J. Raj. 2017. *Ground Down by Growth: Tribe, Caste, Class and Inequality in 21st Century India*. London: Pluto.

Sharma, A. N. 2006. 'Flexibility, employment and labour market reforms in India'. *Economic and Political Weekly* (May): 2078–85.

Shyam Sundar, K. R. 2005. 'Labour flexibility debate in India: A comprehensive review and some suggestions'. *Economic and Political Weekly* 40 (22–23): 2274–85.

————. 2016. 'Labour law and governance reforms in India: A partial and misguided view of employment relations'. *Esocialsciences*, http://www.esocialsciences.org/Articles/show_Article.aspx?qs =XkEqhzvARqvilcDKHND803nggdR9eUSgpCCOf/OM24Wl86tU55x15hD89pFdO67q (accessed 2 June 2017).

————. 2019. 'The pursuit of too much labour flexibility'. *Hindu Business Line*, 25 November, https://www.thehindubusinessline.com/opinion/the-pursuit-of-too-much-labour-flexibility/article30075921.ece (accessed 11 February 2020).

Silver, B. J. 2003. *Forces of Labor: Workers' Movements and Globalization since 1870*. New York: Cambridge University Press.

Singh, G. 1995. 'Who needs an exit policy anyway?' *Economic and Political Weekly* 30(23): 1359–60.

Ste. Croix, G. E. M. de. 1981. *The Class Struggle in the Ancient Greek World: From the Archaic Age to the Arab Conquests*. Ithaca: Cornell University Press.

Teitelbaum, E. 2011. *Mobilizing Restraint: Democracy and Industrial Conflict in Post-Reform South Asia*. Ithaca: Cornell University Press.

Thompson, E. P. 1963. *The Making of the English Working Class*. London: IICA.

Wood, E. M. 1995. *Democracy against Capitalism: Renewing Historical Materialism*. Cambridge: Cambridge University Press.

World Bank. 2000. *India: Reducing Poverty, Accelerating Development*. New Delhi: Oxford University Press.

# Chapter Ten

# INVESTIGATING CLASS RELATIONS IN RURAL SOUTH AFRICA

## MARX'S 'RICH TOTALITY OF MANY DETERMINATIONS'

Farai Mtero, Brittany Bunce, Ben Cousins, Alex Dubb and Donna Hornby

## Abstract

In a much-discussed passage in the introduction to the *Grundrisse*, Marx argues that 'the concrete is concrete because it is the concentration of many determinations, hence unity of the diverse. It appears in the process of thinking, therefore, as a process of concentration, as a result, not a point of departure'.[1] This chapter discusses how this conception has informed fieldwork on class relations in rural South Africa, where households combine a multiplicity of income sources, including local and migrant wage labour, self-employment in petty commodity production (both agricultural and non-agricultural) and welfare payments by the state. In these contexts, class differentiation is constituted through complex relations and processes, involving many social forms, including income stratification, diversified livelihood strategies and social difference along lines of race, gender and generation. Households often combine a variety of class locations that also shift over time. Here, 'class' cannot simply be read off from indicators such as incomes, assets or employment status. A key focus is social relations, including relations between employers and employees, property owners and land users, migrants and households, men, women and youth, as well as between interest groups and the state. Data collection and analysis are mediated by key concepts and theories drawn from Marx, such as the production and appropriation of surplus value, accumulation and social reproduction. The chapter describes how this approach – in fact compatible with critical realism – informed research in four different fieldwork projects undertaken in South Africa and briefly reports their findings. It also discusses the challenges posed in attempting to move from simple abstractions to an adequate account of the concentrated complexities of class relations, which increasingly involve the 'fragmentation' of class identities.

---

[1]  Marx (1973: 101).

## Introduction

In this chapter we describe the application of Marxist concepts and methods to investigate complex class relations in contemporary rural South Africa. This includes drawing upon both classical Marxist analyses of the agrarian question and subsequent scholarship on processes of agrarian change to investigate ongoing capitalist transformations of the countryside.

The utility of a class-analytic approach is not self-evident. Marx's (1992) analyses of capitalism's imminent logic and the English experience of agrarian transition led him to postulate the displacement or elimination of the 'peasantry'. However, small farmers continue to exist, even amidst widespread processes of 'de-agrarianisation' and urbanisation (Bernstein 2001). Drawing on an analysis of the peasantry in pre-revolutionary Russia, Lenin demonstrated that the capital–labour relation was already manifest in tendencies to differentiation into distinct classes of agrarian capital and wage labour (Bernstein 2001). Differentiation of small farmers rarely crystallises out into clearly polarised classes of workers and owners of capital – including in the four cases presented here. Moreover, rural populations have long been observed to participate in an array of 'multiple livelihoods', through the sale of labour and its products, and are embedded in diverse cultural relations and identities that present phenomenally as stark markers of social difference (Bryceson 1999).

Certainly, the contemporary context of global capitalism is markedly different from the period when 'classical' agrarian questions were posed, and the 'answers' to these questions are likely to be different too (O'Laughlin 2009: 199). We contend that only a superficial approach to class relations evaluates the merits of class analysis on the basis of the presence or absence of 'essential' (Gibbon and Neocosmos 1985) or 'ideal-type' (Sayer 2010) categories of class, or sees class as an 'actually' (rather than analytically) and equally discrete determination among many such (Ferguson 2016). Thus, class is not an isolatable economic or social determination but is interwoven with other social oppressions, for instance, race, gender and sexuality (Bohrer 2018). Basically, 'social oppressions are historically concreted in and through one another' (Bohrer 2018: 69).

We illustrate the strength of a class-analytic approach by summarising the methods we have used to investigate class dynamics in three areas in South Africa's former 'homeland' labour reserves and in one case of land redistribution. In these contexts, the outcomes of historical processes of racially based land dispossession are a strong legacy, but rural livelihoods are also intimately shaped by wider economic transformations – evident in processes of deindustrialisation, increasing informalisation and welfarisation, declining remittances and eviction from white-owned farms (Slater 2002). In all four cases, rural households are variously implicated in exploitative relationships with 'classes of capital' (Bernstein 2010) including in state-initiated improvement schemes (Li 2007).

## Critical Realism and Marx's Method

Marx famously describes his method in the *Grundrisse*, as entailing a double analytical movement. The first is a movement from the concrete (or the chaotic observation of multiple, visible phenomena) to their simplest necessary components and relations, via abstraction. The second movement is a return to the concrete to apprehend the world as a 'rich totality of many determinations and relations' (Marx 1973: 101).

Although Marx provided little in the way of detail, this sketch of a distinctive method is consistent with critical realism, which argues that reality exists independently of us irrespective of whether we understand it adequately (our 'chaotic conception of the whole'), or whether we can empirically apprehend it. More significantly, the 'real' is the realm of objects that hold causal powers and liabilities enabling them to behave in particular ways, or with specific susceptibilities to change. Objects are part of 'structures': 'sets of internally related elements whose causal powers, when combined, are emergent from those of their constituents' (Sayer 2000: 11–14).

As in Marx's movement from the concrete to the abstract and back to the concrete, for critical realists, explanations of social reality entail more than characterising objects as they appear to us, but must instead establish what conditions necessarily prevail for phenomenal categories to be possible. Thus, grasping 'structure' is important to understanding the conditions of existence of particular kinds of phenomena and is thus essential in rigorous causal analysis. Simultaneously, it becomes possible to comprehend when such phenomena are either not possible or remain merely latent and to determine the limits beyond which a particular set of phenomenal categories are no longer valid.

## Class – A Non-Reductionist Approach

Marx's formulations on method have important implications for class analysis in contemporary capitalism. A key methodological principle is the need to be sensitive to the 'multiple determinations and relations' underlying class formation and differentiation and to their variations in different social and historical contexts (Bernstein 2010: 109). The existence of 'many determinations', however, is not simply a matter of accepting relations 'in addition to' class (Ferguson 2016). Rather, it is to accept class itself as a complex concept uniting (sometimes particular) relations of dominance and subordination (in age, gender, race and so on) with emergent structures and relations, such as those of generalised capitalist commodity production. These relations of dominance and subordination do not originate in capitalism (Bernstein 2010) and, as such, 'they are in part discrete from class, and in part mutually constituted by it' (Campling et al. 2016: 1748).

In the context of small-scale farming, the concept of 'petty commodity production' is key for integrating these complicated (and often contradictory) processes. According to Bernstein (2001: 29) petty commodity production 'specifies a form of small-scale ("family" or "household") production in capitalism engaged in a more or less specialised commodity production and constituted by a particular combination of the class places of labour and capital'. The combination generates a dynamic and necessary instability and a tendency to differentiation (Bernstein 2001: 30). The insight afforded by Lenin's (1967) schema of 'poor', 'middle' and 'rich' peasants owes less to a taxonomy of wealth stratification than as a schema that expresses the outcomes of this tendency. Here, 'poor peasants' experience squeezes on the simultaneous reproduction of their capital or labour, often expressed in dilemmas to reinvest or consume. They may be compelled to sell their labour – to proletarianise – in order to reproduce. 'Middle' peasants are able to meet the demands of simple reproduction of their labour and capital, while 'rich' peasants are those able to engage in expanded reproduction (accumulation) by increasing land and other means of production and may hire labour to supplement family labour (Bernstein 2001: 30). In addition, the class places of capital and labour are not spread evenly within family or household production. Gender and generational divisions and kinship relations often shape the distribution of property, labour and income (ibid.).

While remaining sensitive to visible hierarchies, we foreground the concept of petty commodity production to account for complex tendencies to differentiation among rural populations. In relation to this chapter, we use two interrelated methods to investigate rural class relations. First, we stratify households according to patterns in the distribution of their formal characteristics in order to inform the development of typologies suggestive of local class structures. This includes a focus on agricultural production (for sale or otherwise), as well as other income and livelihood sources and markers of social difference (expressed in gender, generation, ethnicity and so on).

Second, key mechanisms and relations implied by these patterns are investigated and progressively triangulated such that, via a process of abstraction *ala* Marx and critical realism, contextual powers and liabilities can be exposed (such as the differential interaction of off-farm income with agricultural production). This accepts that a wider contextual totality of structuring relations cannot be fully accounted for without more comprehensive study (e.g. deep ethnographies of cultural idioms; wider causes of structural unemployment and so on). However, 'context' is not treated as a simple 'backdrop', but as constitutive of the mechanisms explaining the diversity of our specific objects of study (Sayer 2010). In this way, 'class' is not narrowly understood as excluding 'other' hierarchies, nor defined merely by the immanent properties of our objects of study. As Bernstein (2010: 111) argues, 'class relations are universal but not exclusive determinants of social practices in capitalism given that they intersect and combine with other social differences in complex ways'. This approach to class analysis, we suggest, offers a parsimonious (albeit not comprehensive) and non-reductionist approach to examining 'multiple determinations' in contemporary rural realities.

## Our Methods in Context

South Africa remains a highly unequal society with deep levels of poverty disproportionately concentrated in rural areas. According to Statistics South Africa (2017), in 2015 over half of the population lived beneath the upper bound poverty line.[2] Certainly, South

---

[2]    South Africa has three poverty lines. The 'food' or extreme poverty line is based on daily calories a person needs to survive, and the threshold StatsSA uses is 2,100 calories (R547 per person per month). The lower-bound poverty line (R785 per person per month) and the upper-bound poverty line (R1,183 per person per month) include non-food items.

Africa's rural poverty is inextricably linked to historical, deeply racialised processes of land dispossession[3] and the creation of reservoirs of cheap and unskilled labour for the emerging capitalist economy, but its contemporary reproduction, its necessary links to broader economic dynamics (du Toit 2017) and the parameters of 'path dependence' (Arrighi et al. 2010) are not well understood.

Characterisations of poverty and inequality in South Africa commonly emphasise widespread labour redundancy, waning wage-earnings and a fragmented post-Apartheid politics producing palliative rather than transformative policy. Seekings and Nattrass (2015) adopt a Weberian approach to class stratification and cite 'jobless economic growth' as the general challenge confronting post-Apartheid South Africa. The uneven spatial character of the South African economy has remained a key feature, with economic activity focused on metropolitan and enclavic areas, and constituted by highly concentrated and capital-intensive industries with low labour absorptive capacity (Bank and Minkley 2005; Arrighi et al. 2010). Cousins (2007: 231) observes that this has weakened the rural poor's 'functional articulation of rural and non-rural activities and income streams [...] leading to a crisis of social reproduction',[4] resonating strongly with Bernstein's (2010) assessment of an emergent 'agrarian question of labour' in struggling capitalist economies.

In this context, our research programme has sought to examine differentiation among poor rural households in extant engagements with agricultural capital, not only to deepen understandings of the contradictory relations bedevilling unanswered questions of 'failure' or 'decline' in land reform in South Africa (Hall 2010; Lahiff 2007) and state 'improvement schemes' more broadly (Li 2007), but of the scope of potentialities of 'success' and 'growth'.

Critical realism has informed the overall schema of our research methods, specifically the iterative deploy of 'extensive' and 'intensive' methods as suggested by Sayer. The dominant strands of evidence gathered can be briefly summarised as including:

---

[3]   Repressive and exclusionary state policies associated with colonialism and Apartheid restricted class differentiation among the oppressed. However, the state-sanctioned racial oppression was by no means monolithically destructive on the African population. As a result, class differentiation was, from the outset, a key aspect of agrarian change in the former labour reserves (see Neocosmos 1993).

[4]   We use the term social reproduction in the Marxian sense to denote activities that relate to daily survival (food, shelter, clothing, etc.) and intergenerational reproduction (child care, care for the elderly and frail, etc.). Social reproduction activities have traditionally been associated with non-commodified, domestic labour that is separate from the wider capitalist economy. Yet, Marxist feminists have shown that social reproduction is an integral aspect of the capitalist society and is deeply implicated in the shifts and changes in capitalist processes of accumulation. Cousins et al. (2018) note that 'in rural economies of the Global South, small-scale farming predominates. Crop and livestock production for both domestic consumption and cash earnings including the harvesting of natural resources are an important aspect of social reproduction.' These activities are often underwritten by wage earnings from migrant labour. However, 'all of these activities are implicated in unequal and gendered divisions of labour and power relations' (Cousins et al. 2018: 1064).

(1)  Asset groups (asset ownership as an indicator of wealth status)
(2)  Wealth rankings (using local criteria)
(3)  The range of livelihood activities, sources, strategies and pathways (including agri-culture) used by rural households
(4)  'Labour exploitation': measuring the degree to which households employs others, works for others or works for themselves
(5)  Agricultural trajectories ('dropping out' of agriculture, 'hanging in' with agricul-ture, 'stepping out' of major reliance on agriculture, 'stepping up' or expanding agricultural activities and 'creeping back' into agriculture)
(6)  Livelihood trajectories ('dropping out' and becoming poorer, 'hanging in' by repro-ducing current wealth status, 'stepping out' by diversifying livelihoods, 'stepping up' and thus improving wealth status).

The combination and sequencing of these analytical tools differs across cases. Nonetheless, each has pursued a similar logic of investigation inspired by Marx's process of recursive abstraction, to not only identify, but also explain, concrete phenomena.

In each case, developing research instruments was guided first by a 'circumspective' phase of 'looking around' (Murray 2002) to subjectively (and inevitably partially and chaotically) assess the complexity of prevailing social realities. This owed much to our implicit acceptance that 'facts' are contextually embedded and empirical inves-tigation 'theory-laden', but also to our view that particular instruments and research questions could not be decided a priori. Key modifications of our research agenda included:

• For Mtero, the collapse of a state-sponsored maize scheme required reformulating questions about its interaction with processes of rural class formation;
• For Bunce, the highly differentiated outcomes of two dairy-based, Joint Venture models demanded interrogation;
• For Dubb, a key concern was the recent precipitous decline of small-scale sugarcane production;
• For Hornby, fractious conflicts associated with the collapse of particular Communal Property Associations had to be explained.

Subsequent phases of 'extensive' investigation focused on administering (similar but adapted) household surveys focused on livelihood sources, asset ownership, household structure and composition. These enabled us to obtain 'snapshots' of the breadth of social difference and to explore patterns of association among their expressions (e.g. income sources, gender, generation and ethnicity and so on).

In survey analysis, a key exercise involved creating asset groups. With chronically incomplete income data, household asset holdings (domestic, durable and agricultural) acted as important proxies for relative wealth and were found to be significantly and positively (but differentially) associated with other markers of social difference (e.g. types of and numbers of income sources, land holdings, household size and gender compos-ition and so on). For Mtero and Hornby, asset-wealth also significantly correlated with

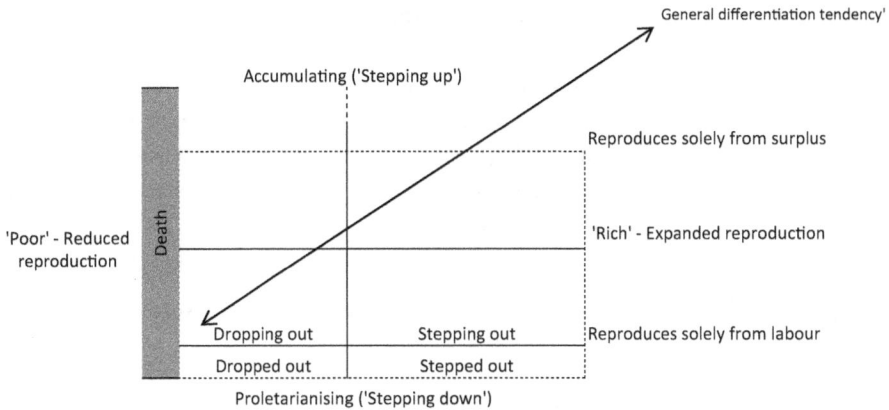

**Figure 10.1** Schematic combination of relative wealth with differentiation trajectories.

respondents' vernacular assessments of each other's relative wealth. Stratification analysis was not an end in itself, but provided important clues to the mechanisms underpinning inequalities (Sarre 1987). What they could not provide is an explanation of the patterns they revealed: how causal mechanisms operated, what differential conditions and contexts underwrote them, and the complex manner of their interaction.

Intensive research methods were crucial to moving beyond surface descriptions from quantitative analysis. Particularly important were household 'life history' interviews, encompassing a wide array of themes (such as family and marriage, farming and settlement, employment and so on).

First, life histories revealed 'longer term historical dynamics of patterns of wealth and processes of wealth generation and accumulation' (Scoones 1995: 85). In this 'retrospective approach' (Murray 2002), life histories provided an important tool to assess households' overall 'trajectory', particularly in regard to agricultural enterprises (a key research focus across our cases) (Oya 2007). Scoones et al.'s (2012) livelihood typologies (stepping up, hanging in, dropping down and stepping out) provided a key device to relate relative wealth/poverty to processes of relative accumulation/proletarianisation, across a range of livelihood sources (see Figure 10.1).

Second, life histories provided rich foundations to contextualise the substantive relations underlying these tendencies. In contrast to measuring association between contextually denuded variables in conventional survey analyses, intensive methods enabled us to examine the (often contradictory) interactions between pluri-active livelihoods and social divisions within and between households, as well as the conditions of their mechanism. Often, 'outlier' cases were particularly revealing of the limits of particular relations or combinations. Ownership, access and control of property and control of labour was often but not uniformly manifest along generational and gender lines. Employment (and other forms of 'diversification') could be leveraged to 'hang in' or 'step up' agricultural investment, but also enable some to 'step out' from agriculture altogether, and similarly could represent both expanded or reduced social reproduction. In stabilising homestead consumption, social grants could both enable the perseverance of pools of local labour and create barriers to the intensification of their exploitation.

Moreover, households' inequalities and differential trajectories could be examined as causal components of processes of differentiation, not merely as 'outcomes'. Critical were iterative processes of triangulating survey data, wealth ranking testimonies and life history interviews with further interviews between households, other state and private agencies and secondary historical materials.

## Dairy Joint Ventures in Keiskammahoek and Shiloh, Eastern Cape

The Keiskammahoek and Shiloh cases are dairy farming joint ventures on irrigation schemes in the Eastern Cape. Agribusiness firm Amadlelo Agri has partnered with customary landowners who are also labourers employed in the ventures. Divergent outcomes are most powerfully explained by differences in class structure and reveal tensions in household reproduction generated by capitalist agriculture.

The study specifically sought to develop a systematic methodology for developing class typologies from fieldwork data, involving an 'extensive' survey of 121 households and 'intensive' research entailing 29 in-depth life history interviews, 105 semi-structured interviews and ethnographic immersion (Bunce, 2018). Space constraints preclude a detailed unpacking of the process, but here we review some key features.

Patnaik's (1987) labour exploitation criterion (itself informed by Lenin's typology of 'poor, middle and rich peasants') uses 'labour exploitation' as a principal indicator to centre capital–labour relations directly, rather than inferring them from proxies such as asset ownership or size of landholding. Detailed income data were used to establish the relative degree to which households employ others, work for others or work for themselves.

Drawing on typologies developed in the sub-Saharan African context (Cousins 2010; Scoones et al. 2012; Neocosmos 1987), the labour exploitation measure was combined with income from social grants, the ownership of assets and livestock, and the contribution of agricultural production to simple or expanded reproduction (Bunce 2018). Ownership of farming assets and livestock and sale of an agricultural surplus were particularly key for distinguishing 'allotment-holding workers' and 'worker farmers' – both of which rely predominantly on wage labour, but with the latter reinvesting off-farm incomes into own-account farming on a substantial scale. Similarly, household reliance on social grants informed distinguishing 'supplementary food producers' from 'petty commodity producers'.

The resultant class typology, detailed in Table 10.1, shows households in Shiloh and Keiskammahoek to be unevenly distributed across what appear as 'hybrid' class categories. In Shiloh, petty commodity producers employ little or no wage labour and mostly exploit family labour. Supplementary food producers have no access to wage labour and rely considerably on social grants; their reproduction is especially precarious. A majority of households in Shiloh are allotment-holding workers and worker farmers (together comprising 74 per cent of the total), both relying mainly on wage labour.

**Table 10.1** Class typology for irrigation plot holders in Shiloh and Keiskammahoek (n = 121 households)

| Class typology | Shiloh (%) | Keiskammahoek (%) |
|---|---|---|
| Supplementary food producers | 7 | 0 |
| Allotment-holding worker | 30 | 15.5 |
| Worker farmer | 44 | 27 |
| Petty commodity producer/trader | 12 | 0 |
| Rent-earning rich farmers and business owners | 7 | 42 |
| Rent-earning pensioners | 0 | 15.5 |

By contrast, 57.5 per cent of households in Keiskammahoek are either 'rent-earning rich farmers and business owners' or 'rent-earning pensioners' exploiting the labour of others. The latter do not sell their labour and the former exploit hired labour more than they sell their own labour. The dynamics of labour exploitation thus differ vastly between the two cases. In Shiloh, the many intragroup conflicts that have emerged reflect a highly differentiated community, where household reproduction is under extreme pressure.

Class dynamics are not the only ones at work. They are intermeshed with many other 'determinations' and are thus complex, contingent and subject to constant change. Employing a typology based on only some key variables always involves a degree of reductionism (Scoones et al. 2012; Cousins 2010; Bernstein 2010). The class typology was therefore used in combination with an in-depth qualitative analysis to highlight historical trajectories of class formation and how class place intersects with gender, generational and other dynamics. The challenge was to make sense of how all these causal mechanisms together constituted the complex and concrete whole (Sayer 2010).

## The Besters Land Reform Project, KwaZulu-Natal

Widely hailed as a success story, the beneficiaries of the Besters Land Reform Project in KwaZulu-Natal engage in commercial beef production. The study focused on six selected farms from the total of 15 with a range of 6–28 households on each. Committees were selected to run the farm as a whole for their respective groups, constituted as Communal Property Associations (CPAs), while the state provided cattle, implements and so on (see Hornby 2015). Tensions related to the social reproduction needs of households and the aspiration to accumulate through reinvesting proceeds at CPA level were evident.

The exploratory phase entailing both key informant interviews and desktop research informed the design of a subsequent survey of 84 households (equivalent to 86 per cent of the total population of the six farms). Data on household dynamics, livelihoods and cattle production was key in developing a wealthy taxonomy in the form of asset groups. Exploring history and context became necessary in order to explain processes that gave rise to differences in asset holdings. Individual life histories with 36 informants from across the asset groups became key to exploring long-term changes in livelihoods and cattle production. Long-term livelihood changes including core events, processes,

**Table 10.2** Summary of CPA households by asset group and production trajectory highlighting key mechanisms of relative wealth (n = 84 households)

| Farming trajectories | Key common events | Asset groups | | | |
|---|---|---|---|---|---|
| | | 1 (n = 11) | 2 (n = 8) | 3 (n = 7) | 4 (n = 10) |
| Dropping out (n = 7) ↕ | Death or unemployment of household head, dependence on child grants, cattle sales | (n = 3) Cattle deaths | (n = 1) Cattle thefts, contract work | (n = 2) Cattle thefts/deaths, survivalist enterprises | (n = 1) Irregular remittances |
| Creeping back (n = 4) ↗ | Death or unemployment of household head, dependence on social grants, herd restocking through CPA disbursements and subsidies | (n = 2) Child grants only, casual work | (n = 2) Range of social grants, contract work | | |
| Hanging in (n = 11) ↕ | Herd restocking through CPA disbursements and subsidies, permanent farm work wages plus social grants | (n = 4) Death or unemployment of household head | (n = 4) Retrenchment, bride wealth payments | (n = 2) Cattle deaths/infertility, tractor hire-out, land rent | (n = 1) Cattle sales |
| Stepping up (n = 14) ↑ | Herd restocking through CPA disbursements and subsidies, range of income sources (wages, social grants and children's remittances), herd expansions | (n = 2) Delayed ceremonies | (n = 1) Delayed ceremonies, diversification into goats | (n = 3) Diversification into ceremonial oxen and goats, grazing rents | (n = 8) Survivalist enterprises, cattle purchases/inheritance, appropriation of CPA rangelands, investments in tractors, ploughs |

and adaptive strategies were key to developing differentiated livelihood trajectories (see Table 10.2) to ascertain the emerging agrarian class structure (see Scoones et al. 2012).

Livelihood trajectories were used as heuristic categories for identifying overall patterns in both accumulation and the impoverishment of households. Households may 'step up' or 'drop out', for instance, in line with changes in livestock numbers and owing to key events and turning points in their accumulation pathways. This may also depend on households negotiating tensions between the social reproduction need of households and the imperative to accumulate on the part of the CPAs.

## Small-Scale Sugarcane Production in the Umfolozi Region, KwaZulu-Natal

KwaZulu-Natal's small-scale sugarcane growers (SSGs) have been of great interest in South Africa because of their large numbers and distinctive forms of social reproduction. However, they have been subject to significant decline in recent years: from around 50,000 to 20,000 between 2000 and 2012. This was proximally attributed to low and unreliable rainfall, but was also preceded by the collapse of the Financial Aid Fund (FAF) – an industry revolving credit scheme extolled as underpinning SSGs' original growth, but also criticised for enabling 'control' of production by millers.

The Umfolozi cane supply area was selected as a revealing case for SSGs' prospects in an emerging context of relative 'independence', owing to their larger than average land holdings, better rainfall and a thinner history of FAF credit/miller interventions. However, here too, production had declined from 407,000 to 100,000 tons of cane. The specific supply-wards of Madwaleni and Shikishela were selected for study because of their rich soils and proximity to the miller-processor, thus offering a semi-control for these non-trivial factors.

Asset-wealth stratification among 74 surveyed SSG homesteads suggested a modest breadth of social difference among the majority of producers (Dubb 2015). Markers of expanded reproduction were concentrated heavily in the top asset group, and their statistical association with asset-wealth degraded heavily when restricted to groups 1–3 (see Table 10.3). Hence, nearly all SSGs were constituted from 'fragmented' classes of labour from the vantage of social reproduction and 'petty commodity producers' insofar as all mixed home-labour with casual labour, at least in cane harvesting. The only exceptions were small-scale capitalist 'contractors' – tractor-owning homesteads providing tilling, harvesting and short-haul transportation services with non-local casual labour.

'Accumulation history interviews' with 21 homesteads explicated the dynamic and contradictory relations underlying these patterns. One key vector was contractors' accumulation, premised on combining cane with contracting – enabling them to valorise tractors requiring a greater scale of production. Notably, no homesteads maintained tractors without contracting, and no contractors existed without significant cane production. Contractors also historically spurred poorer homesteads into cane via land rental/ cane establishment arrangements that enlarged their client base. But the conditions of contractors' accumulation came at a price for SSGs. Contractors emerged from a politics of regulatory change that removed preferential pricing for SSGs and encouraged millers to devolve haulage and planting services (Dubb 2015). Consequent coordination and transport constraints heavily degraded SSGs' cane, along with premiums to intensive husbandry.

Other SSGs' trajectories were best explicated by seeing shifting conditions in cane production in contradictory interactions with those of their social reproduction (see

**Table 10.3** Key socioeconomic characteristics of SSG homesteads by asset group (n = 66 grower homesteads)

| Asset group | n | Homestead size Mean | % SSGs female % | Land (ha) Total Mean | Land (ha) Cropped | Land (ha) Cane | % casual labour (cane)** | Cattle Mean | Income sources Total | Income sources Social grants | Persons with Perm. job | Temp. job | Non-agri. bus. w/out employees |
|---|---|---|---|---|---|---|---|---|---|---|---|---|---|
| 1 | 21 | 9.81 | 67 | 3.70 | 2.53 | 1.56 | 34 | 3.33 | 4.90 | 3.29 | 0.05 | 0.21 | 0.05 |
| 2 | 19 | 9.79 | 74 | 3.65 | 1.81 | 1.63 | 26 | 1.79 | 5.42 | 3.21 | 0.26 | 0.26 | 0.42 |
| 3 | 17 | 10.88 | 53 | 6.81 | 3.18 | 2.85 | 22 | 3.06 | 6.47 | 3.41 | 0.56 | 0.50 | 0.19 |
| 4 | 17 | 15.41 | 24 | 10.56 | 7.79 | 6.19 | 55 | 10.59 | 8.47 | 3.82 | 1.25 | 0.25 | 0.33 |
| Groups 1–3 Corr. | p | .232 | .175* | **.312*** | .152 | .263 | -.241 | -.059 | .335 | .145 | **.359** | .180 | .166 |
| ANOVA | F | 0.266 | | **3.521** | 1.094 | 2.493 | 0.483 | 0.664 | 1.849 | 0.036 | **4.594** | 1.220 | **4.189** |
| Groups 1–4 Corr. | p | **.433** | 0.380 | **.513** | **.463** | **.497** | **.231** | **.383** | **.486** | .177 | **.407** | .072 | .238 |
| ANOVA | F | **4.036** | | **7.701** | **8.136** | **7.702** | **2.906** | **5.197** | **3.737** | .221 | **6.480** | .917 | 2.343 |

* Refers to Cramer's V in chi-square analysis.

**Excludes cane harvest and preparation.

Bold indicates ≤0.05 statistical significance.

**Table 10.4** Frequency of case studies by asset-wealth and cane production trajectory (n = 66 grower homesteads)

| Cane trajectory / Asset group | Poorest 1 (n = 8) | 2 (n = 3) | 3 (n = 4) | Richest 4 (n = 6) | |
|---|---|---|---|---|---|
| Stepping up ↑ (n = 4) | | | 1 | 3 | Contractors |
| Hanging in ↕ (n = 2) | | | 2 | 1 | |
| Stepping out ↩ (n = 3) | 1 | | | 1 | |
| Stepping down ↓ (n = 2) | 1 | 1 | | | |
| Dropping out ↧ (n = 3) | 1 | 1 | 1 | | |
| Creeping back ↰ (n = 2) | 2 | | | | |
| Dropped out ✗ (n = 5) | 3 | 1 | 1 | | |

Table 10.4). With cane proceeds insufficient to even sustain poverty consumption levels, social grants provided a baseline for SSGs' persistence, but also limited capacities to super-exploit local labour. Similarly, while employment might assist input purchases, it also pulled homestead labour from cane. The circumstance of drought further accentuated risks that any income/labour investments would not be recovered, particularly when coincident with other shocks, such as the death of family members – common among female growers who 'dropped out'. Unusual cases of non-contracting growers 'hanging in' or 'creeping back' were marked foremost by limiting consumption to non-cane income sources, reinvesting cane proceeds in inputs and cane itself as seed, towards reaching scales where 'lump-sum' proceeds could be used for expensive purchases.

## Ongeluksnek, Matatiele, Eastern Cape

In the first phase of field research, a survey of 124 households focused on household composition, assets and livelihood sources and allowed the identification of asset groups as proxies for wealth differences (Mtero 2015). Asset groups revealed significant inequalities and important clues to the mechanisms involved, but with limited explanatory power. A subsequent participatory wealth ranking exercise explored the history, context and local meanings of wealth and poverty. The 124 survey households were then ranked in terms vernacular understandings of wealth across three groups: the poor (*Bafutsana*), the average (*Bahare*) and the rich (*Baruwi*).

As shown in Table 10.5, local criteria of wealth overlapped strongly with survey-generated asset groups. The 'poor' often experienced a social reproduction squeeze and provided labour to the rich. The 'average' exhibited a wide portfolio of livelihood activities (temporary jobs, social grants and so on) underpinning their simple reproduction (Mtero 2015). The 'rich' were defined by their claim to scarce permanent jobs, but were also notably involved in agricultural activities. In spite of wider and pervasive processes of de-agrarianisation, rich households combined dryland cropping with livestock production, mostly of cattle holdings significantly larger than average and poor households.

**Table 10.5** Cross-tabulation of Ongeluksnek households' asset group profile and wealth groups from participatory wealth ranking (n = 124 households)

| Wealth groups from participatory wealth ranking | Asset quintiles from survey data (proxy for wealth) | | | | | |
|---|---|---|---|---|---|---|
| | Q1 (%) | Q2 (%) | Q3 (%) | Q4 (%) | Q5 (%) | Total (%) |
| Rich | 11.5 | 19.2 | 11.5 | 11.5 | 46.2 | 100.0 |
| Average | 23.7 | 26.3 | 26.3 | 13.2 | 10.5 | 100.0 |
| Poor | 36.7 | 26.7 | 20.0 | 8.3 | 8.3 | 100.0 |

A subsample of 36 households was selected to explore long-term trajectories of accumulation and impoverishment of rural households. Together with data from the wealth ranking and survey exercise, a group of 90 households were analysed to identify their livelihood trajectories (Table 10.6). Scoones et al.'s (2010) typologies of 'stepping up', 'hanging in' and 'dropping out' were adapted to the Ongeluksnek context, and Dubb's (2015) 'creeping back' category was added. These typologies were critical in ascertaining the extent to which livelihood are implicated in long-term class dynamics and processes of agrarian change.

## Conclusion

In much of southern Africa, local agrarian class structures are complex, marked by diverse forms of articulation between farm and non-farm incomes within a range of pluri-active livelihoods. Sharp class differences are not readily evident. Gender, past and present processes of racialisation, generational tensions and other key social divisions also obscure class stratification. Institutionalist and anthropological perspectives have illuminated the multiple sources of livelihoods and complex modes of 'making meaning' in rural contexts, but in taking a narrow understanding of class analysis, have mistakenly portrayed it as too blunt an instrument to make sense of the evident complexity and contingency.

Yet, as we hope to have shown, Marxist class analysis is central to teasing out the key mechanisms that can explain (rather than simply describe) the diverse and complex processes of social change in each of our four study sites and to relating these to broader processes of capitalist transformation. Critical realist methods also enabled us to apprehend both the observable and epiphenomenal aspects of social reality and the underlying causal processes underlying the phenomenal categories (Sayer 2010).

Marxist methodologies, we believe, are necessary to efforts to analyse processes of agrarian change that have explanatory power. Describing observable phenomena in isolation from capitalist relations can only produce 'a chaotic conception of the whole'. But equally important is understanding class as constituted through 'multiple determinations' and evading reductionist methods focused on constructing 'ideal-types' of class categories and processes. While typologies and taxonomies are useful tools of analysis, it is in pursuit of the underlying relationships and mechanisms that class analysis yields

**Table 10.6** Comparison of Ongeluksnek households wealth stratification with overall livelihood trajectory (n = 124 households)

| Livelihood trajectories | | Rich | | Average | | Poor | | Total | | Description |
|---|---|---|---|---|---|---|---|---|---|---|
| Category | Strategy/event | n | % | n | % | n | % | n | % | |
| Stepping up (n = 16; 18%) | Formal job(s) | 4 | 18.2 | 2 | 6.1 | 0 | 0 | 6 | 6.7 | Includes mostly 'rich' households accumulating through 'sequential' or 'simultaneous' straddling, but extends to 'average' households who have mobilised resources from temporary jobs, social grants, etc. to go beyond expanded consumption and diversify for accumulation. |
| | Trading store, spaza/tavern | 5 | 22.7 | 0 | 0 | 0 | 0 | 5 | 5.6 | |
| | Livestock accumulation | 2 | 9.1 | 0 | 0 | 0 | 0 | 2 | 2.2 | |
| | Tractor/transport business | 1 | 4.5 | 0 | 0 | 0 | 0 | 1 | 1.1 | |
| | Diversification for accumulation | 1 | 4.5 | 0 | 0 | 0 | 0 | 1 | 1.1 | |
| | Homestead gardening | 1 | 4.5 | 0 | 0 | 0 | 0 | 1 | 1.1 | |
| Hanging in (n = 34; 38%) | Diversifiers | 0 | 0 | 5 | 15.2 | 0 | 0 | 5 | 5.6 | Here households were defined by 'diversification for survival': combing multiple incomes for simple reproduction. Access to social grants are key, but are orientated to immediate consumption (rather than productive investment). |
| | Combining social grants and petty trade | 0 | 0 | 3 | 9.1 | 2 | 5.7 | 5 | 5.6 | |
| | Combining social grants and farming | 0 | 0 | 0 | 0 | 2 | 5.7 | 2 | 2.2 | |
| | Combining social grants only | 0 | 0 | 2 | 6.1 | 12 | 34.3 | 14 | 15.6 | |
| | Temp jobs, casual | 0 | 0 | 8 | 24.2 | 0 | 0 | 8 | 8.9 | |
| Dropping down (n = 35; 39%) | Death/illness | 0 | 0 | 4 | 12.1 | 5 | 14.3 | 9 | 10.0 | Households marked strongly by shock events (e.g death, illness, retrenchment, stock theft, etc.). These households abandoned both field cultivation and (typically pervasive) homestead gardening. |
| | Old age | 1 | 4.5 | 1 | 3.0 | 4 | 11.4 | 6 | 6.7 | |
| | Decline of field cultivation | 5 | 22.7 | 7 | 21.2 | 1 | 2.9 | 13 | 14.4 | |
| | Livestock theft | 2 | 9.1 | 1 | 3.0 | 0 | 0 | 3 | 3.3 | |
| | Single-person households | 0 | 0 | 0 | 0 | 4 | 11.4 | 4 | 4.4 | |
| Creeping back (n = 5; 6%) | Rebuilding homestead/social grant(s) | 0 | 0 | 0 | 0 | 4 | 11.4 | 4 | 1.1 | Comprise marginalised and impoverished households returning from urban areas, or locally based people with 'new' incomes (social grant) forming households and participating in associational life (stokvels). |
| | Forming a household | 0 | 0 | 0 | 0 | 1 | 2.9 | 1 | 1.1 | |
| | Total | 22 | 100 | 33 | 100 | 35 | 100 | 90 | 100 | |

its most powerful insights. As a result, life histories were useful in investigating substantive and causal relationships underlying processes of class formation. Marx's method is well suited to grappling with social complexity, distilling the essential relations underlying diverse phenomena and uncovering their differentiated unity. It has the potential to untangle the knotty agrarian systems found in rural South Africa and elsewhere.

# References

Arrighi, G., N. Aschoff and B. Scully. 2010. 'Accumulation by dispossession and its limits: The southern Africa paradigm revisited'. *Studies in Comparative International Development* 45: 410–38.

Bank, L. and G. Minkley. 2005. 'Going nowhere slowly? Land, livelihoods and rural development in the Eastern Cape'. *Social Dynamics* 31(1): 1–38.

Bernstein, H. 2001. '"The peasantry" in global capitalism: Who, where and why?' *Socialist Register* 39: 25–51.

———. 2010. *Class Dynamics of Agrarian Change*. Halifax: Fernwood.

———. 2013. 'Commercial agriculture in South Africa since 1994: Natural, simply capitalism'. *Journal of Agrarian Change* 13(1): 23–46.

Bohrer, A. 2018. 'Intersectionality and Marxism: A critical historiography'. *Historical Materialism* 26(2): 46–74.

Bryceson, F. D. 1999. 'African rural labour, income diversification and livelihood approaches: A long-term development perspective'. *Review of African Political Economy* 26(80): 171–89.

Bunce, B. 2018. 'A class-analytic approach to agricultural joint ventures in the communal areas of South Africa'. Working Paper 103. Brighton: STEPS Centre.

Campling, L., S. Miyamura, J. Pattenden and B. Sewlyn. 2016. 'Class dynamics of development: A methodological note'. *Third World Quarterly* 37(10): 1745–67.

Cousins, B. 2007. 'Agrarian reform and the "two economies": Transforming South Africa's countryside'. In L. Ntsebeza and R. Hall (eds), *The Land Question in South Africa: The Challenge of Transformation and Redistribution*, pp. 220–45. Cape Town: HSRC.

———. 2010. 'What is a smallholder? Class-analytic perspectives on small-scale farming and agrarian reform in South Africa'. Working Paper No. 16. Belleville: Institute for Poverty, Land and Agrarian Studies.

Cousins, B., A. Dubb, D. Hornby and F. Mtero. 2018. 'Social reproduction of "classes of labour" in the rural areas of South Africa'. *Journal of Peasant Studies* 45(5-6): 1060–85.

Cousins, B., D. Weiner and N. Amin. 1992. 'Social differentiation in the communal lands of Zimbabwe'. *Review of African Political Economy* 19(53): 5–24.

du Toit, A. 2017. 'Explaining the persistence of rural poverty in South Africa'. Expert Group Meeting on Eradicating Rural Poverty to Implement the 2030 Agenda for Sustainable Development, 27 February–1 March 2017. Addis Ababa: United Nations Economic Commission for Africa.

Dubb, A. 2015. 'Dynamics of decline in small-scale sugarcane production in South Africa: Evidence from two "rural" wards in the Umfolozi region'. *Land Use Policy* 48: 362–76.

Ferguson, S. 2016. 'Intersectionality and social-reproduction feminisms: Toward an integrative ontology'. *Historical Materialism* 24(2): 38–60.

Gibbon, P. and M. Neocosmos. 1985. 'Some problems in the political economy of "African socialism"'. In H. Campbell and B. Bernstein (eds), *Contradictions of Accumulation in Africa: Studies in Economy, State and Accumulation in Africa*. Beverly Hills: Sage, pp. 153–206.

Hall, R. 2010. 'Two cycles of land policy in South Africa: Tracing the contours'. In W. Anseeuw and C. Alden Hall (eds), *The Struggle over Land in Africa: Conflicts, Politics and Change*, pp. 175–92. Cape Town: HSRC.

Hornby, D. 2015. *Cattle, Commercialisation and Land Reform: Dynamics of Social Reproduction and Accumulation in Besters, KwaZulu-Natal*. PhD thesis, University of Western Cape.

Lahiff, E. 2007. *Business Models in Land Reform*. Bellville: Institute for Poverty, Land and Agrarian Studies.

Lenin, V. I. 1967. 'The development of capitalism in Russia: The process of the formation of a home market for large-scale industry'. In *Collected Works, Volume III*. Moscow: Progress.

Li, T. M. 2007. *The Will to Improve: Governmentality, Development, and the Practice of Politics*. Durham: Duke University Press.

Marx, K. 1973. *Grundrisse: Foundations of the Critique of Political Economy (Rough Draft)*. London: Penguin.

———. 1992. *Capital: Volume I: A Critique of Political Economy*. London: Penguin.

Mtero, F. 2015. *De-agrarianisation, Livelihoods Diversification and Social Differentiation in Rural Eastern Cape, South Africa*. PhD thesis, University of Western Cape.

Murray, C. 2002. 'Livelihood research: Transcending boundaries of time and space'. *Journal of Southern African Studies* 28(3): 489–509.

Neocosmos, M. 1987. 'Homogeneity and differences on Swazi nation land'. In M. Neocosmos (ed.), *Rural Social Relations in Swaziland: Critical Analyses*, pp. 17–79. Mbabane: SSRU/University of Swaziland.

———. 1993. *The Agrarian Question in Southern Africa and 'Accumulation from Below'*. Research Report No. 93. Uppsala: Scandinavian Institute of African Studies.

O'Laughlin, B. 1996. 'Through a divided glass: Dualism, class and the agrarian question in Mozambique'. *Journal of Peasant Studies* 23(4): 1–39.

———. 2002. 'Proletarianisation, agency and changing rural livelihoods: Forced labour and resistance in colonial Mozambique'. *Journal of Southern African Studies* 28(3): 511–30.

———. 2009. 'Gender justice, land and the agrarian question in southern Africa'. In A. Haroon Akram-Lodhi and C. Kay (eds), *Peasants and Globalisation: Political Economy, Rural Transformation and the Agrarian Question*, pp. 190–213. New York: Routledge.

O' Laughlin, B., H. Bernstein, B. Cousins and E. Peters. 2013. 'Introduction: Agrarian change, rural poverty and land reform in South Africa since 1994'. *Journal of Agrarian Change* 13(1): 1–15.

Oya, C. 2007. 'Stories of rural accumulation in Africa: Trajectories and transitions'. *Journal of Agrarian Change* 7(4): 453–93.

Patnaik, U. 1987. *Peasant Class Differentiation: A Study in Method with Reference to Haryana*. New Delhi: Oxford University Press.

Sarre, P. 1987. 'Realism in practice'. *Area* 19(1): 3–10.

Sayer, A. 2000. *Realism and Social Science*. London: Sage.

———. 2010. *Method in Social Science: A Realist Approach*. Rev. 2nd ed. London: Sage.

Scoones, I. 1995. 'Investigating difference: Applications of wealth ranking and household survey approaches among farming households in southern Zimbabwe'. *Development and Change* 26(1): 67–88.

Scoones, I., N. Marongwe, B. Mavedzenge, J. Mahenehene, F. Murimbarimba and C. Sukume. 2010. *Zimbabwe's Land Reform: Myths and Realities*. Harare: Weaver.

———. 2012. 'Livelihoods after land reform in Zimbabwe: Understanding processes of rural differentiation'. *Journal of Agrarian Change* 12(4): 503–27.

Seekings, J and N. Nattrass. 2015. *Policy, Politics and Poverty in South Africa*. New York: Palgrave Macmillan.

Slater, R. 2002. 'Differentiation and diversification: Changing livelihoods in Qwaqwa, South Africa, 1970–2000'. *Journal of Southern African Studies* 28(3): 599–614.

Statistics South Africa. 2017. *General Household Survey, 2016. Statistical Release PO318*. Pretoria: Statistics South Africa.

# Chapter Eleven

# FROM MARX'S 'DOUBLE FREEDOM' TO 'DEGREES OF UNFREEDOM'

## METHODOLOGICAL INSIGHTS FROM THE STUDY OF UZBEKISTAN'S AGRARIAN LABOUR

### Lorena Lombardozzi

**Abstract**

The condition of extreme labour exploitation often observable in current global capitalism is described by many studies in social sciences as 'forced labour'. However, by depicting an ahistorical picture detached from its capitalist social forms, such definitions often reproduce shallow analyses of labour and moralistic knowledge, which conceal the structural determinants of labour exploitation. Trying to problematize the concept of labour freedom through a Marxian historical materialist perspective and drawing on mixed methods, this chapter uses the case of agrarian labour in Uzbekistan of post-Soviet independence to investigate the empirical, methodological and epistemological complexities underpinning such concept. Finally, while making explicit the policy implications the country faces to regulate and protect labour, the chapter provides some reflections on the contradictions of late capitalist accumulation in low-income countries.

## Introduction

At the end of *Capital, Volume I*, Marx defines *primitive accumulation* as the starting point of the capitalistic mode of production. Primitive accumulation can play out in different ways and under different historical settings, but, as Marx sharply points out, it requires two essential conditions: workers must be 'free' from the means of production and 'free' to sell their labour power.

> The immediate producer, the labourer, could only dispose of his own person after he had ceased to be attached to the soil and ceased to be the slave, serf, or bondsman of another. To become a free seller of labour power, who carries his commodity wherever he finds a market, he must further have escaped from the regime of the guilds, their rules for apprentices and journeymen, and the impediments of their labour regulations. (Marx 2011: 786)

Such *double freedom* makes workers obliged to sell their labour power in the market. Yet, many deviances from the double freedom characterize the contemporary capital accumulation, which shapes a continuum along various degrees of freedom (Lerche 2007). Labour is exposed to and operates through differentiated forms of unfreedom, which are contingent to institutional norms, power relations and agencies (Morgan and Olsen 2014) and which are constitutive of the unevenness of capitalist development.

Both cotton and agrarian labour were pivotal to the development of capitalism across time and space. Hence, the deployment of agrarian labour in cotton production in the Global South represents an important lens to untangle the complexity of labour unfreedom in capitalistic development today. Cotton is one of the main primary commodities of Uzbekistan and, as in other countries which experienced marketization, it has been at the centre of systematic value extraction for accumulation by the state. It was reported that children, university students and adult labour were forcibly mobilized by the Government of Uzbekistan during the cotton-picking season. This practice has been challenged for its risks attached to the recruitment process by international organizations (ILO 2017a) and labelled as 'forced labour' by media (CottonCampaign; Muradov and Ilkhamov 2014) through various 'name and shame' campaigns. However, many of these documents, by depicting an ahistorical reality detached from its capitalistic social forms (Lerche 2007), produced and reproduced shallow definitional and moralistic knowledge. This chapter contributes to the methodological, empirical and analytical Marxist scholarship on forced labour to understand the relationship between work and freedom in contemporary capitalistic development. Using the case of agrarian labour in Uzbekistan, it discusses how the *historical materialism* framework and other Marxist conceptualizations are instrumental in making explicit the material relations that enable the various degrees and forms of labour exploitation to happen in the first place.

First, it uses Marx's conceptualization of labour exploitation as a useful lens to analyse different degrees of freedom. It then unpacks the methodological implications and empirical applications to study the dimensions of unfree labour. Finally, it argues that labour exploitation cannot be understood as a social reality detached from the processes of *capital accumulation* and it cannot be solved without looking at the material and social linkages between capital and labour. In so doing, this chapter reaffirms the relevance of some key categories of the Marxian method for the study of contemporary capitalism and provides evidence into the data collection methods that can be deployed to study them concretely.

## Marx's Theories: The Barbarism of Bourgeois Civilization and the Double Freedom

*Labour exploitation* occurs under different historical conditions. Yet, Marx writes in 1844 (*Volume XXXIX*: 117) that 'the crudest modes (and instruments) of human labour reappear [under capitalism]; for example, the treadmill used by Roman slaves has become the mode of production and mode of existence of many English workers'. The dialectic and historically informed reasoning of Marx highlights that similar patterns of exploitative conditions can survive across different modes of production. The cruel natural law of labour exploitation makes history repeat itself but in different social forms proper for the specific institutional context. Nonetheless, capitalism creates unique contradictions which are represented by the coexistence of regressions to the barbarism of slavery and progress of the emancipated bourgeois civilization (Foster and Clark 2004). Such contradictions shape the unevenness of the contemporary globalized world. Making explicit this material oxymoron is useful to problematize the epistemological and ontological understanding of labour exploitation in many contexts today. Indeed, as LeBaron et al. (2018) note, the unquestioned understanding of forced labour does not point out the fact that the root causes of the worst type of labour coercion is, and will always be, the economic necessity that capitalistic mode of production creates in the first place.

Through the concept of double freedom 'Marx expresses a further contradiction, which is the freedom to sell one's labour, but that is brought into being by the "silent compulsion" of capitalist relations in the labour market' (Crane 2014). Therefore, instead of adopting totalizing categories, it is important to reflect on the fact that still nowadays, between freedom and unfreedom lie a set of 'degrees' which are shaped by coercion, power, market and non-market norms. As Crane extrapolated from Amin and van der Linden, 'it has become clear that pure "free wage labour" in the Marxian double-sense is an ideal type, the conceptual nucleus of far more complicated historical realities. Pure free wage labour [...] forms a kind of analytical core surrounded by numerous rings of labour relations that we would like to call intermediary' (1999: 7). The degree of labour coercion hence depends on the particular capitalist relations of production imposed by neoliberal capitalism and how these are absorbed and negotiated in the specific country (Lerche 2007; LeBaron 2018). In this perspective the dichotomy of what is free and unfree is dissolved in a *continuum*. Many of the *modus operandi* of labour exploitation nowadays stand across the ideal type of atomistic free labour and bonded labour. Even the most extreme forms of exploitation – and even if executed directly by the arm of the state – do not occur outside capitalism, and therefore they need to be analysed through their structural social and political mechanisms and treated as organic to capitalistic social forms.

In the Uzbek context, mainstream media generates most of the knowledge on 'forced labour' during the cotton harvest season; the way in which this issue is discussed is rather unilateral. The cotton campaign website writes[1]:

> Every year the government of Uzbekistan forcibly mobilizes over a million citizens to grow and harvest cotton. The Uzbek government forces farmers to grow cotton and deliver production quotas under threats of penalty, including the loss of the lease to farm the land, criminal charges and fines. The government forces over a million citizens [including children, university students and young workers] to pick cotton and deliver harvest quotas under threat of penalty, including expulsion from school, job loss, and loss of social security benefits.

---

[1] 'Uzbekistan's forced labor problem', http://www.cottoncampaign.org/uzbekistans-forced-labor-problem.html (accessed 15 September 2019).

Similarly, a document published by Open Society mapped the Uzbek cotton value chain to show that the government uses its power and corruption practices to control the national financial and material resource (Muradov and Ilkhamov 2014). The report states that 'the government uses forced labour of public sector employees and students, as well as resources extracted from private enterprises to reduce farmers' labour costs' (ibid.: 22) and to maximize rent, despite the decreasing yields and low efficiency due to the lack of investment with negative consequences for the cotton sector and the economy as a whole. Although it is necessary to denounce the circumstances that trigger distressful conditions of work, reporting such actions in a vacuum does not explain the social and power relations under which such agents operate and perpetuate such practices (Morgan and Olsen 2014).

Furthermore, the use of monolithic buzzwords such as 'modern slavery' or 'forced labour' risks to simplify the contradictory but structural historical-specific tensions within capitalistic social relations which are, in a way, co-determinants of the conditions of bonded or mobilized labour observable in many rural settings nowadays. In the context of Uzbekistan, the discourse on forced labour has mainly centred on a neo-institutionalist approach which emphasize client relationship and authoritarians' settings to decodify exploitation and oppression of rural labour (Ilkhamov 2007; Muradov and Ilkhamov 2014). Instead, less attention was paid to how, to what extent and why the state and social forms mediated the relationship that determined such labour surplus extractions to come about in the first place and remain politically and socially 'functional' to the capitalistic mode of production.

Also, several limitations could be observed in the methodology of these empirical studies. These reports, for instance, rarely explained the rationale behind the economic 'inefficiency arguments' used and developed a thorough and comprehensive understanding of the 'social costs' denounced. Often it is not reported how, when and if interviews have been conducted with the actors involved, neither with high-level policymakers nor with the farmers. They very often link with a thin logic forced labour, labour costs and productivity without making explicit the broader forces behind the leitmotiv of accumulation. Very few studies contextualized the Uzbek rural labour in its historical dimension or avoided to reduce all the analysis of a corrupt system, in which the role of international Western trading and financial capital is not even considered. Furthermore, whether the surplus value extracted from cotton producers by the state is transferred to other productive activities or reinvested in different forms in workers' welfare is disregarded. Those reports have simplified reality and omitted crucial aspects of the national economic system and how international capital or even labour mobility regulation contribute to increase incentives for such degrees of labour exploitation.

Far from justifying the use of exploitative and coercive practices, this analysis illustrates that a rigorous research project on the political economy of labour freedom and coercion requires a systematic and coherent process of primary data collection through fieldwork. In particular, it shows that the only way to unpack the material reality around cotton in Uzbekistan is to move away from simplistic discourses of modern slavery and study labour exploitations within the broader contours of the complex capitalist relations of production and exchange characterizing the region.

## Methodology and Methods to Unpack Degrees of Labour Freedom

As highlighted by numerous political economists, in the last decades the discipline of economics has produced knowledge on labour through highly problematic methods. Hodgson, by investigating 'How economics forgot history' (2002), explicitly denounced the need to explore the specific forms of institutions and historical specificity to understand how reality dialectically intersects with the 'economic laws' of human behaviour. Indeed, in order to be able to problematize the phenomena of unfree labour, it is necessary to keep a wide, mixed and interdisciplinary investigation. The *retroductive* approach used in many Marxist studies was particularly useful to guide the process of triangulation used in this research. Retroductive methods differ from the deductivism typical of mainstream economics, but it also differs from inductive positivism as it proceeds 'neither from observed phenomena to generalization nor from basic proposition to those that can be deducted from them' (Wilson 2015: 120). In this research, inductive investigative methods have been combined with retroductive analysis to identify theory-based patterns.

In Uzbekistan, social relationships are embedded in agrarian production and are the result of multilayer structures, agencies, technology and institutions (Polanyi 1944). Forced and bonded labour is not a monolithic object, but its forms depend on macrodynamics such as subsidies, alternative employment opportunities, forms of discrimination, gender and migration (LeBaron 2018). As mentioned above, such relationships are here analysed in a framework of social positions regulated by structure/agency model rather than individuals, and this has important analytical implications. Also, considering that means of production, commodities and labour are integrated and inseparable from social relations, a distinction between social power and social activities would be inappropriate.

There are potential ontological confounding factors that need to be considered when looking at the causal conditions of coercion of agrarian labour. The strong role of informal and non-market transactions may create difficulties in systematizing them into the research framework. For instance, in-kind transactions and informal social safety nets can have an important role in livelihood strategies. This implies that during fieldwork we should always be careful when asking questions about 'what?' because this question might be unable to capture non-standardized social or economic categories, such as the concept of employment, wage labour, labour for in-kind repayment and self-employment, including the compulsion attached to cotton-picking work (e.g. a similar point was made in a study on asset index by Johnston and Wall 2008).

Quantitative methods collect 'numbers', seek objectivity and causal explanation to deductively test prior hypothesis whereas qualitative and participatory techniques inductively value the contextual meaningfulness recognizing the contingent nature of social knowledge (Meyer 2005). Mixed methods – namely a combination of quantitative and qualitative methods – overcome the contraposition of the two, identifying a third way in which the two perspectives become complementary. The mixed method allows the research to start analysing the objects of observation and – through the deployment of interdisciplinary categories – to also develop a theoretical understanding of their material ontology. The triangulation of qualitative and quantitative methods (Bryman 2004) can reduce orientation errors (Atkinson 2005) because behind different methods lie different ontological and epistemological assumptions and data collection techniques. The divergent methodological axiology do not entail a 'communication breakdown' (Morgan 2007) but rather a complementarity (Greene 2008). The methodology implies the active role of the researcher in challenging and questioning the strengths and weaknesses of each approach and tailor the best fit for the research. Notably, the choice of methods is not only related to the particular material ontology of the object of observation but reflects the specificities of the research questions being asked.

Far from reducing the analysis of labour relations to the dichotomy of free or unfree labour, and trying to unveil the complex contradictions that leads to the context-specific degrees of labour unfreedom, I have collected different types of material. In a closed and poor economy like Uzbekistan, where the government is clearly extracting resources from agriculture to move them towards the industrial sector, understanding the way labour is organized is fundamental to understanding how capital is accumulated. Multiple methods of data collection and analysis during fieldwork allowed my research to disembed the object of observation – labour – from the ahistorical and acontextual narrative in which it is often confined, hence ensuring a rigorous epistemology for the study of unfreedom. Thus, in order to uncover the complexity of the cultural, historical and material conditions in which labour is organized and exploited, the research has been guided by multiple different sets of questions, aimed at unveiling the broader relations of production and accumulation shaping labour relations. Data collection has taken place in two rounds of fieldwork, conducted in affiliation with the Agrarian University of Samarkand. Fieldwork methods included semi-structured interviews and focus groups with key informants, a survey of farmers, observations of urban life in Uzbekistan, life histories and obviously the collection of field notes and analysis of secondary data (see Table 11.1).

The survey, by including both qualitative (open) and quantitative (closed) questions, provided with the biggest spectrum of systematic data and required a disciplined, non-reducible, time investment. The survey has gathered information on inputs access, commercialization mechanisms, assets ownership and employment relationship which challenge the stereotypical idea of homogenous labour markets. Further qualitative data supported the understanding of the quantitative results during the subsequent phases of fieldwork. The 'background stories' collected revealed nuances and filled gaps that the survey questionnaire failed to cover (Kandiyoti 1999). Qualitative data also accounted for reciprocity among individuals, their power asymmetry and social structure. Observations and unstructured interviews contributed to understand how intra-household labour and village communities interact with the compulsion of exogenous market forces and the state-led agrarian settings, but also how the Uzbek rural labour is embedded in strong customary norms based on history and culture. Life histories have also been collected often in random ways through daily life episodes such as taking a taxi, going to the bazar, and so on, but also during the survey and while living with the local family.

**Table 11.1** Mixed methods to study Uzbek agrarian Labour

| Respondents/informants | Methods | Tools | Setting |
|---|---|---|---|
| National and international stakeholders: FAO (2), ICARDA, World Bank (2), UNDP, WHO, GIZ, UNICEF, CER, Italian Embassy, EU reps, policymakers and academics | +30 semi-structured interviews | Semi-structured questions | London, Tashkent and Samarkand |
| Students | Focus group | Unstructured conversations | Samarkand |
| Farmers | Farmer survey | Questionnaire | Samarkand |
| Urban middle class | Observations | Living with hosting family | Tashkent |
| N.A. | Life histories and fieldwork notes | Informal conversations at bazars, taxi drivers, local admin offices | Tashkent and Samarkand |
| N.A. | Secondary data | | Desk research analysis |

*Source*: Fieldwork log/diary.

Yet, it is impossible to ignore the macroeconomic patterns when looking at labour relations; notably, the role of the state, global production networks and agro-industrialization processes. These aspects cannot be understood only with secondary data and have been captured instead via semi-structured interviews with high-level institutional stakeholders, academics and international organizations, local administrators and representative of the Samarkand region – like state agencies dealing with inputs supply and agrarian banks. Interviews also contributed to the understanding of the dynamics behind crops production, employment patterns and sources of capital in rural areas. They also provided useful information on degrees of mechanization in agriculture, features of contract farming and merchant capital in the region and broader policy trends. One of the most important sources of information was gathered through a focus group with university students because, having had experiences in the cotton fields as cotton pickers, they informed the research on key aspects of the Uzbek cotton mode of production. Finally, desk research of documents helped to contextualize social norms in relation to labour, power, history and geopolitics and thus played a critical role in framing the analysis. Notably, the deployment of this complex mixed method framework aimed at overcoming the distinction between micro- and macro-dynamics, by showing how these are dialectally co-constituted.

## Empirical Evidence: The Blurred Line Between Free and Unfree Labour

One of the first thing that this research unpacked was how the *historical* determinants shaped social relations of cotton production. The introduction of cotton in Uzbekistan dates to the pre-Soviet era. It was introduced from China 2,000 years ago but, after that the American Civil War impeded cotton import from the United States to Russia, Uzbekistan became the cotton basket of the Soviet Union. Thus, cotton got commodified as monoculture at the expenses of grain and foodstuff under the 'colonialization' of the Soviet Union which made Uzbekistan become, through the Soviet *kolkhoz*, the producer of 70 per cent of the cotton produced in the Soviet Union (Melvin 2000). Cotton is overall labour-intensive and historically has been an important source of subsistence for rural workers. The forced commodification of cotton in the Soviet era represents the first elements to understand how such a commodity got inserted in the relations of production of rural labour over time. Indeed, the inherited form of collective production and state-led procurement of the Soviet Union period survived and now coexists with new and more individualized forms of labour relations. The Soviet heritage that Uzbekistan holds through its history – *Tarix* – and traditions – *Rakhshat* – has hugely influenced the practice of mobilizing young generations during the cotton harvest, which dates to the pre-Soviet era. Therefore, it is clear that labour practices are determined by forms of non-economic coercion, which shows a clear path dependency with the historical practices of the Soviet Union.

Whereas across the world cotton harvest is largely mechanized, as it was in the Soviet times, in Uzbekistan (at the time of the fieldwork in 2015) cotton was still handpicked through the mobilization of labour from schools, public officials and universities between September and November of every year. State-led exploitation is uncommon among labour studies, so the Uzbek state provides surely an interesting dimension to understand the varieties of 'degrees' of free labour. In the focus group conducted with 16 university students between 18 and 21 years old living in Samarkand but coming also from rural areas, I have discovered interesting insights about their experiences as cotton pickers. They described that experience in a way that I did not expect. They obviously noted it is 'tiring' but they mentioned that there are also funny moments and occasions for socialization. Girls especially felt they did not pick enough cotton. However, they reported that food and shelter was provided regardless of their performance. The focus group unveiled important insights on the 'economic costs' of such labour. In the survey, farmers declared to pay pickers 20,000 sums per day (around US$3.5 in 2015). In order to get such amount, seasonal pickers will have had to pick around 80 kg of cotton. According to the focus group's data, students would pick daily 21 kg of cotton as a minimum, which corresponds to 5,000 sums, which raise questions about the reliability of farmers' declarations. Regardless of the reliability of farmers' response, survey findings show that women were hired ad hoc, recruited in the village, to pick cotton and were paid the same pay. Although their level of coercion is different, data triangulation showed that compensations between students and 'freely hired' pickers were similar. In fact, the ILO report on the use of child labour and forced labour in the 2016 cotton harvest in Uzbekistan noted that child labour was widely reduced and that in the case of adults, 'most pickers continue to receive their salaries or student stipends, while receiving extra payment for the amount of cotton they pick. ILO experts were told of particular efforts by the authorities this year to ensure that payments to cotton pickers were made on time at least every five days. In some instances, incentive payments were made to pickers' (ILO 2017a, b: 2). Such findings problematize the monolithic ontology of 'modern slavery' and the material meaning of labour unfreedom (Mezzadri 2016; LeBaron 2018). Also, it raises the need to investigate further, and through primary data, the epistemology of ethical labour and hiring conditions in contexts of agrarian transition.

The denunciations of the GoU's human right violations by international organizations (e.g. Muradov and Ilkhamov 2014), provide useful material to understand the differentiations of the Uzbek type of forced labour. Indeed, while it is often assumed that forced labour loses complete control of the sale of their labour power, in the Uzbek case the labour expropriated is temporally circumscribed to the cotton-picking season, which goes from September to November. Unstructured interviews confirmed that expeditions are organized as in public worker's rota and do not take place in 'absolute' opposition to social goals such as schooling and/or better paid employment. Indeed, according to World Bank data, gross school enrolment rate in grades 5–9 is over 94 per cent (2016–17[2]). Furthermore, as pointed out in other works, 'elderly respondents did not see a trade-off between child work and school, such practice being accepted as social norms across history', also considering that Uzbek school curricula include manual work such as street cleaning (Kandiyoti 2003; Lombardozzi 2019: 66; Lombardozzi forthcoming). For instance, it is reported as a common practice for children of around 10 years old to work along with the adults in the fields (ICG 2005) and be part of the 'productive' working force in a society based on extensive family work. Based on both quantitative and qualitative data, labour relations in agrarian Uzbekistan are multiple, spanning permanent skilled wage labour employed in agrofirms, unskilled permanent, seasonal, daily, family paid or unpaid reproductive work, and not least the coercively mobilized labour employed to harvest cotton. Because those relations are in constant evolution, they should be understood historically.

This research has made explicit the weaknesses of ahistorical ontological categories in understanding Uzbek's rural labour dynamics, which so far have been treated either as pre- or post-Soviet, or 'never Soviet'. Also, such complex and overlapping forms of labour challenge the dichotomy of 'free' versus 'unfree' or forced labour and instead points out that there are different and more complex degrees of coercion put in place by different social forces within relations of productions (e.g. Morgan and Olsen 2014; Lerche 2007). Another peculiar element that came out from the fieldwork was that post-harvest outputs like firing wood or seeds are often accessed as collective goods. These practices challenge the Western-centric idea of universal individual property rights and reassert the need to incorporate in the analysis also the non-economic nature of the (coercive) labour contract between the workers and the state, when the latter is the owner of the land. In fact, in Uzbekistan, labour is exploited by the state through mobilized seasonal labour but is not completely expropriated from its commons, because the state

---

[2]   http://documents.worldbank.org/curated/en/379211551844192053/pdf/Uzbekistan-Education-Sector-Analysis.pdf (accessed 15 September 2019).

(capital) has not completed primitive accumulation, at least not in the ways which Marx (2011: 787) described:

> In the history of primitive accumulation, all revolutions are epoch-making that act as levers for the capital class in course of formation; but, above all, those moments when great masses of men are suddenly and forcibly torn from their means of subsistence, and hurled as free and 'unattached' proletarians on the labour-market. The expropriation of the agricultural producer, of the peasant, from the soil, is the basis of the whole process.

Notably, this partial dispossession from the land, instead owned by the state, enable distributional mechanisms for social reproduction affecting farmers' livelihoods beyond work. At the same time, the state-based strategy of 'mobilization' of labour is an important aspect of the struggle of agrarian classes in Uzbekistan. Arguably, it also has effects on the dynamism of capitalism (Lerche 2007: 435), as the perpetuation of unfree labour may be seen as halting the formation of a proletarian class consciousness (Brass 2009) or hampering accumulation. Indeed, the economic and political mandates of the state, in this case, may always stand in contradiction. If the state stopped the mobilization of unfree labour through processes of liberalization, for instance, it could trigger new forms of accumulation based on 'free' labour that may reveal equally, if not more, exploitative. In fact, processes of value chain integration based on liberalization have hardly been less problematic for farmers or workers.

In Uzbekistan, the role the state played in shaping and managing the cotton value chain, from seeds provision to commercialization, has been paramount. After independence in 1991, the cotton sector made up approximately 25 per cent of the Uzbek GDP, (including textile industry 2.1 per cent, chemical and fertilizers 0.5 per cent) (non-public data from the government; Muradov and Ilkhamov 2014). Contrary to many countries in Africa and Asia which liberalized the sector and abolished state marketing boards, Uzbek cotton remained state-managed. The state has taxed cotton farmers through low procurement prices (being the farm gate price lower than average international market price) but has also subsidised inputs, like seeds and fertilizers (Rudenko 2008). State management has not challenged sensitive growing practices and seasonality, which entail an uneven distribution of labour requirement. Marx did note how this could lead to labour management problems (Marx 2011). In fact, it also influences the volatility of prices and supply, a point which was confirmed by interviews. Interviews also emphasized the labour-intensive nature of cotton-picking, which takes place by hand as considered cleaner and more effective (Lombardozzi 2019), commanding higher returns in the international markets. State-owned factories deal with the collection, processing and transport from the farm to the cotton airport terminals. A woman factory worker interviewed told me that her factory employed around four hundred people from September to March in three shifts per day, packaging 200 bales of 230 kg, to be exported to China and South Korea. Their salary ranges between 500,000 and 600,000 sums per month (almost US$5 per day). While exploitative, this state-led governance system has avoided the creation of a landless class of 'free' peasants, extreme poverty and inequality, debt and food insecurity which was registered in many contexts of the Global South under liberalization.

More recently, the political pressure coming from the international community to halt the use of mobilized labour in the cotton harvest, together with the economic urge to increase productivity, has led to a process of mechanization of the cotton harvest (Swinkels 2016). International organizations such as the ADB, the World Bank and the ILO have acknowledged an improvement in the minimum age of pickers and an increased openness of the GoU to collaborate on the mechanization transition (ILO 2017b). Yet, due to the coercive conditions of state-led labour exploitation, an international boycott of Uzbek cotton is still in place, involving over 314 multinational corporations which signed the Responsible Sourcing Network's pledge.[3] While well meaning, these initiatives produced questionable results. First, they prompted the GoU to divert its cotton to Asian markets like China, Bangladesh and South Korea (ICG 2005). Second, they have deepened private-led governance, organized around Corporate Social Responsibility initiatives, which are often problematic and based on a commercialized understanding of ethics (Žižek 2014; Mezzadri 2016). In fact, these initiatives empower global actors and powerful Western governments more than ensuring re-distributional gains in favour of farmers in agricultural supply chains in the Global South (LeBaron 2018). Undoubtedly, recently, the discourse around modern slavery has been deployed as a new form of protectionism, hiding instead highly strategic trading interests. Evidence shows that the global cotton market is still characterized by strong political interests, with the United States holding a leading role in regulating cotton's 'quality grading' and making competitors engage in the international market from a highly subordinated position. If the political economy of forced labour's discourse and practice should be understood in the context of regional patterns of accumulation, it also cannot be analysed in a 'local vacuum'; it has to be contextualized and linked to the international architecture of power relations.

## Conclusion

This chapter has problematized understandings of free and unfree labour based on simplistic narratives and has illustrated the relevance of the Marxian method to capture the broader capitalist dynamics incentivizing public and private actors to reproduce unfree labour as one of the main forms of exploitation (Banaji 2010; Lerche 2007) to extract surplus value. The analysis has also shown the relevance of mixed methods of enquiry to collect distinct sets of primary data to understand the perspectives and experiences of workers on the ground. Fieldwork has confirmed the need to unpack the concept of 'modern slavery' because it compresses the great varieties of exploitation across time and space into a monolithic category and does not contribute to unveil the structural underlying determinants, agencies and drivers of capital accumulation based on unfreedom. Notably, it is crucial to understand the continuities of freedom and unfreedom at a local

---

[3]   https://www.sourcingnetwork.org/cotton-pledge-signatories-complete-list (accessed 15 September 2019).

level, but it is also paramount to study how they are reproduced across the global capitalist architecture.

In terms of mixed methods deployed, the so-called Q squared approach, was the most suitable to understand the evolution of the agrarian labour relations in Uzbekistan through a political economy framework. Triangulating quantitative and qualitative evidence from multiple data collection methods has been challenging and obviously has limitations. Nevertheless, rigorousness, consistency and intuition can compensate for the uncertainties intrinsic to primary data collection. This research methodology is based on the conviction that causal relationships and events are the outcomes of different and multiple interactions (Bhaskar 1997) thus relying on several tools seems a reasonable way to detangle relevant mechanisms and explanatory variables. Focusing on the phenomena of forced labour without understanding the structural mechanisms shaping this phenomenon in the first place is a disservice to labour studies and human right advocacy. As Sven Beckert notes in his *Empire of Cotton*, 'before the factory had become a way of life, capital owners had only one model for how to mobilize vast amount of labour: the plantation economy of the Americas, built on the enslavement of millions of Africans' (2015: 180). State capitalism has often led the ways of value extraction across history, in manifold ways. The study of one of the contemporary instances in which this happens can still benefit tremendously from the Marxian method of analysis.

## References

Atkinson, P. 2005. 'Qualitative research: Unity and diversity'. *Forum Qualitative Sozialforschung/ Forum: Qualitative Social Research* 6(3): 11.

Amin, S., and M. van der Linden. 1999. 'Introduction', *International Review of Social History* 41(4): 1–7.

Banaji, J. 2003. 'The fictions of free labour: Contract, coercion, and so-called unfree labour'. *Historical Materialism* 11(3): 69–95.

———. 2010. *Theory as History: Essays on Modes of Production and Exploitation*. London: Brill.

Beckert, S. 2015. *Empire of Cotton: A Global History*. New York: Knopf.

Bhaskar, R. 1997. 'On the ontological status of ideas'. *Journal for the Theory of Social Behaviour* 27(2&3): 139–47.

Brass, T. 1999. *Towards a Political Economy of Unfree Labour: Case Studies and Debates*. London: Frank Cass.

———. 2003. 'Why unfree labour is not "so-called": The fictions of Jairus Banaji'. *Journal of Peasant Studies* 31(1): 101–36.

Bryman, A. E. 2004. 'Triangulation'. In M. Lewis-Beck, A. E. Bryman and T. Futing Liao (eds), *The Sage Encyclopedia of Social Science Research Methods*. London: Sage.

Crane, B. 2014. 'The role of bonded labour in capitalist development', https://thatfaintlight. wordpress.com/2014/09/23/the-role-of-bonded-labour-in-capitalist-development/ (accessed 29 September 2019).

Foster, J. B. and B. Clark. 2004. 'Empire of barbarism'. *Monthly Review* 56(7): 1–15.

Greene, J. C. 2008. 'Is mixed methods social inquiry a distinctive methodology?' *Journal of Mixed Methods Research* 2(1): 7–22.

Hodgson, G. M. 2002. *How Economics Forgot History: The Problem of Historical Specificity in Social Science*. London: Routledge.

Ilkhamov, A. 2007. 'Neopatrimonialism, interest groups and patronage networks: The impasses of the governance system in Uzbekistan'. *Central Asian Survey* 26(1): 65–84.

ILO. 2005. *A Global Alliance against Forced Labour*. International Labour Conference 93rd Session. Geneva: ILO.

————. 2017a. *Third-Party Monitoring of Measures against Child Labour and Forced Labour during the 2016 Cotton Harvest in Uzbekistan*. Report submitted to the World Bank by the International Labour Office, http://www.ilo.org/wcmsp5/groups/public/–ed_norm/–ipec/documents/publication/wcms_543130.pdf (accessed 15 November 2019)

————. 2017b. *Global Estimates of Child Labour, Results and Trends 2012–2016*. Geneva: ILO, http://www.ilo.org/wcmsp5/groups/public/–dgreports/– comm/documents/publication/wcms_575499.pdf (accessed 15 November 2019)

————. 2018. *Women and Men in the Informal Economy: A Statistical Picture*, 3rd ed. Geneva: ILO, http://www.ilo.org/wcmsp5/groups/public/–dgreports/–dcomm/documents/publication/wcms_626831.pdf (accessed 15 November 2019).

International Crisis Group. 2005. *The Curse of Cotton: Central Asia's Destructive Monoculture*, https://www.crisisgroup.org/europe-central-asia/central-asia/tajikistan/curse-cotton-central-asias-destructive-monoculture (accessed 17 January 2020).

Johnston, D., and M. Wall. 2008. 'Counting heads or counting televisions: Can asset-based measures of welfare assist policy-makers in Russia?', *Journal of Human Development* 9(1): 131–47.

Kandiyoti, D. 1999. 'Poverty in transition: An ethnographic critique of household surveys in post-Soviet Central Asia'. *Development and Change* 30(3): 499–524.

————. 2003. 'The cry for land: Agrarian reform, gender and land rights in Uzbekistan', *Journal of Agrarian Change* 3(1/2): 225–56.

Kaplinsky, R. 2010. *The Role of Standards in Global Value Chains*. Washington, DC: The World Bank.

LeBaron, G. 2018. *The Global Business of Forced Labour: Report of Findings*. Sheffield: SPERI/University of Sheffield, http://globalbusinessofforcedlabour.ac.uk/wp-content/uploads/2018/05/Report-of-Findings-Global-Business-of-Forced-Labour.pdf (accessed 15 November 2019)

LeBaron, G., N. Howard, C. Thibos and P. Kyritsis. 2018. 'Confronting root causes: Forced labour in global supply chains'. *Open Democracy*, https://drive.google.com/file/d/1KX7Rcfbw4SK4nh5RQmcZ-7fZho296bg6/view (accessed 15 November 2019).

Lerche, J. 2007. 'A global alliance against forced labour? Unfree labour, neo-liberal globalization and the International Labour Organization'. *Journal of Agrarian Change* 7(4): 425–52.

Lombardozzi, L. 2019. 'Can distortions in agriculture support structural transformation? The case of Uzbekistan'. *Post-Communist Economies* 31(1): 52–74.

————. Forthcoming. 'Patterns of accumulation and social differentiation through a slow-paced agrarian market transition: The case of post-Soviet Uzbekistan', *Journal of Agrarian Change*.

Marx, K. 2011. *Capital, Volume I*. Mineola, NY: Dover (reprint of The Modern Library, 1906).

Marx, K. and F. Engels. 'The economic and philosophic manuscripts of 1844 and the Communist manifesto', https://www.marxists.org/archive/marx/works/1844/epm/3rd.htm (accessed 17 January 2020).

Melvin, N. 2000. *Uzbekistan: Transition to Authoritarianism on the Silk Road, Vol. 7*. Amsterdam: Psychology Press.

Meyer, J. 2005. 'Health research'. In B. Somekh and C. Lewin (eds), *Research Methods in the Social Sciences*, 1 edn, pp. 146 53. London: Sage.

Mezzadri, A. 2016. 'Modern slavery and the gendered paradoxes of labour unfreedom: Why labour unfreedom is a more useful category than modern slavery to challenge exploitative working relations at home and abroad'. *Speri*, 26 July, comment.

Morgan, D. L. 2007. 'Paradigms lost and pragmatism regained: Methodological implications of combining qualitative and quantitative methods'. *Journal of Mixed Methods Research* 1(1): 48–76.

Morgan, J., and W. Olsen. 2014. 'Forced and unfree labour: An analysis', *International Critical Thought* 4(1): 21–37.

Muradov, B. and A. Ilkhamov. 2014. *Uzbekistan's Cotton Sector: Financial Flows and Distribution of Resources* (ed. Matt Fischer-Daly and Jeff Goldstein). New York: Open Society Foundations.

Polanyi, K., and R. M. MacIver. 1944. *The Great Transformation*, vol. 2, p. 145. Boston: Beacon Press.

Rudenko, I. 2008. *Value Chains for Rural and Regional Development: The Case of Cotton, Wheat, Fruit, and Vegetable Value Chains in the Lower Reaches of the Amu Darya River, Uzbekistan.* PhD dissertation, Hanover University.

Swinkels, R. A. 2016. Assessing the Social Impact of Cotton Harvest Mechanization in Uzbekistan. Washington, DC: World Bank Group, http://documents.worldbank.org/curated/en/753131468301564481/Assessing-the-social-impact-of-cotton-harvest-mechanization-in-Uzbekistan-final-report

Wilson, H. T. 2015. *Marx's Critical/Dialectical Procedure (RLE Marxism).* London: Routledge.

Žižek, S. 2014. 'First as tragedy, then as farce'. https://www.youtube.com/watch?v=hpAMbpQ8J7g (accessed 15 November 2019).

# Chapter Twelve

# THE LABOUR PROCESS AND HEALTH THROUGH THE LENS OF MARX'S HISTORICAL MATERIALISM

## Tania Toffanin

## Abstract

This chapter illustrates the value of Karl Marx's historical materialist approach for the analysis of the relation between capitalist development and health depletion. Tracing Marx's observations on health and exploitation in *Capital*, the chapter highlights their contemporary relevance and limitations for the study of modern and more contemporary forms of homework. The analysis focuses on the Italian case and confirms the tight interrelation between high degrees of gendered exploitation in the home and adverse health outcomes. It stresses the benefits and challenges of deploying Marx's concrete methods of enquiry in relation to health and work – often based on detailed reports by labour inspectors and doctors – in general and with reference to the case of Italian homework in historical perspective, and it points at some of the theoretical limitations of Marxian understandings of domestic labour in relation to its social longevity, structural role in capitalist development and relation to the state.

## Introduction

Among his many contributions, Karl Marx should have recognition for his ability to combine empirical analysis and theoretical elaboration with a diachronic and synchronic perspective. From the detailed analysis of the *Reports of the Inspectors of Factories*, the *Reports of the Children's Employment Commission* and the *Reports on Public Health*, Marx derives crucial elements to understand the relations of production and social reproduction in his age. Notably, Marx does not limit himself to reporting what inspectors and occupational physicians note during their work; rather he shows the interrelations between health and production by offering an analytical perspective that over time has inspired the work of generations of social scientists.

This chapter retraces Marx's observations on health in an attempt to highlight their close connection with work, and it stresses the value of the historical materialist explanation in the analysis of the connections between capitalist development and the expropriation of health. Marx's description of the working conditions in the sweatshops of nineteenth-century London are fully comparable to what happens today in sweatshops working for H&M, Zara, Benetton and other global fashion brands. Moreover, the chapter also discusses how the Marxian methodological perspective is crucial for the analysis of all types of work that statistical conventions define as 'non-standard', but which we know to be a key part of the global history of work. Among these, homework occupies a prominent place.

Industrial homework has been examined by Marx in the first book of *Capital*, in the chapter devoted to the analysis of the development of large-scale industry, where he described the impact of large-scale industry on manufacture, handicrafts and domestic industry. Marx points out that in the domestic industry the exploitation of cheap and 'immature' labour-power is higher in comparison to what happened in the factory. At home, as documented by labour inspectors at that time, the spread of poisonous substances goes hand-in-hand with the lack of ventilation, space and light. Moreover, workers' dispersion and isolation in the domestic environment made homework particularly attractive for employers. Marx's analysis of the modes of surplus extraction explains the reasons for the spread of homeworking as the industrial dimension increases.

Nevertheless, if Marx was right in stressing the attention on the functional role of homework in the development of large-scale industry, he denied the role that this form of production would have had in the international division of labour, and especially but not exclusively in the expansion of so-called light manufacturing, such as clothing, footwear or allied activities. From the nineteenth century onwards, these sectors have increased their profits with an intense use of homework, mostly done by women in rural towns across the world. Drawing from the historical case of Italy and its homeworkers, this chapter shows that although Marx did not grasp the gendered structural role played by this form of production under capitalism, the analytical perspective he offered is an indispensable tool for any analysis of relations of domination in and through work and their health effects.

## Health Under Capitalism: Historical Materialism as Method of Analysis

Since the early decades of the ninetieth-century England, the British Parliament promoted an extensive social legislation.[1] While producing growth, industrialization was also producing new poverty, as documented by Alexis de Tocqueville during his trip to England in *Memoir on Pauperism*:

---

[1]   During the first half of the ninetieth century, the British Parliament launched the following laws: The Health and Morals of Apprentices Act (1802) addressed to apprentices up to the age of 21 by preventing them from working at night and for longer than twelve hours a day while they were involved in basic education offer; The Cotton Mills Act (1819) prevented children under the age of 9 to be employed in cotton mills and established a maximum day of twelve hours of work for all children under 16; The Factory Acts (1931, 1933), first, limited the extension of the working day to twelve hours for all children under 18 (restricted to the cotton industry) and, second, established the maximum working week of forty-eight hours for children aged 9–13 (with the limit of eight hours a day) and aged 13–18 (with a limit of twelve hours a day). The 1833 Act established also the inspectorate of factories with the power to inflict sanctions for violations; The Poor Law Amended Bill (1834) was preceded by the *Poor*

The countries appearing to be most impoverished are those which in reality account for the fewest indigents, and among the peoples most admired for their opulence, one part of the population is obliged to rely on the gifts of the other in order to live. Cross the English countryside and you will think yourself transported into the Eden of modern civilisation – magnificently maintained roads, clean new houses, well-fed cattle roaming rich meadows, strong and healthy farmers, more dazzling wealth than in any country of the world, the most refined and gracious standard of the basic amenities of life to be found anywhere. There is a pervasive concern for well-being and leisure, an impression of universal prosperity which seems part of the very air you breathe. At every step in England there is something to make the tourist's heart leap. Now look more closely at the villages; examine the parish registers, and you will discover with indescribable astonishment that one-sixth of the inhabitants of this flourishing kingdom live at the expense of public charity of as necessities. ([1835] 1997: 17)

The apparently contradictory dynamics of growth and poverty are at the core of Marx's analysis developed in *Capital*, as well as Engels's illustration of the *Conditions of the Working Class in England* (1845). Marx pays some attention to the complexity of the social regulations enforced by the British Parliament at the time. However, his efforts are mainly focused on highlighting the problems produced by the industrial society. In order to examine them, he devotes considerable time to analyse the Factory Acts and the main reports concerning the working and health conditions of the industrial proletariat.

Marx's description of the exploitation shaped by industrial transformations would have certainly been partial without the analysis of documents on the conditions of the population in Victorian England. In order to show the effects of industrial exploitation he examines several key secondary sources: the *Reports of the Inspectors of Factories*, the *Reports of the Children's Employment Commission* and the *Reports on Public Health.*[2]

Marx's investigation on the living and working conditions of the population during the ongoing industrial revolution is combined with an exploration of the mechanisms of reproduction of the class structure through a more detailed analysis of the peculiar alliance between state regulation and the demands placed by the capitalist class. Although Marx did not examine the social legislation of ninetieth-century England in great detail, his approach to combine a description of such legislation with the analysis of capitalist working conditions, oppression and exploitation provides key methodological insights. His exam of the working day is paradigmatic. In the history of capitalist production, Marx observes, the establishment of a norm for the working day presents itself as a struggle between opposite interests, namely those of the class of capitalists and those of the working class. It is exactly the awareness of this dialect relationship shaping the regulation of working time that drives Marx to engage in a detailed exam of the

---

*Law Report* (1834). This Act was addressed to introduce the control of central government in the treatment of the poverty; The Public Health Act (1848) created a General Board of Health that supervised the implementation of municipal sanitation projects (concerning water and sewage systems). The Act supported also the creation of local boards of health with the authority to manage water supplies, sewerage, trades, quality of food, streets, garbage and all the sanitary concerns (Fee and Brown 2005).

2   See *Capital, Volume I*, chapters 10 and 15.

dynamics surrounding the different Factory Acts launched between 1833 and 1850; the strategies used by capitalists to circumvent laws; and the effects these laws had on working conditions.

In *Capital, Volume I*, chapter 10, Marx devotes almost one hundred pages to the analysis of the working day. In particular, he examines the factual extension of the working day regardless of the legislation launched by the Parliament. What is interesting here is the use of the reports made by the factory inspectors in order to attest the formation of surplus value by surplus labour. Marx examines these reports some years after the enforcement of the Factory Act of 1850. This Act established that the legal working day for all young persons and women had to be comprised between six in the morning and six in the evening. Moreover, it fixed an hour and a half for meals. On Saturdays, workers were allowed to work only from 6 a.m. to 2 p.m. With this Act, the employers gained two hours per week: instead of fifty-eight hours, they could spread the production over sixty hours. Despite the increase of the weekly working hours this new law produced, employers obsessively chased the extraction of more surplus labour through 'small thefts of capital from the workers' meal-times and recreation times [...] described by the factory inspectors as "petty pilferings of minutes", "snatching a few minutes" or, in the technical language of the workers, "nibbling and cribbling at meal-times" ' ([1867] 1992: 352). Labour inspectors wrote:

> The fraudulent mill-owner begins work a quarter of an hour (sometimes more, sometimes less) before 6 a.m., and leaves off a quarter of an hour (sometimes more, sometimes less) after 6 p.m. He takes 5 minutes from the beginning and from the end of the half hour nominally allowed for breakfast, and 10 minutes at the beginning and end of the hour nominally allowed for dinner. He works for a quarter of an hour (sometimes more, sometimes less) after 2 p.m. on Saturday [...] An additional hour a day gained by small instalments before 6 a.m., after 6 p.m., and at the beginning and end of the times nominally fixed for meals, is nearly equivalent to working 13 months in the year [...] If you allow me (as I was informed by a highly respectable master) to work only ten minutes in the day over-time, you put one thousand a year in my pocket [...] *Moments are the elements of profit*. (1992: 349–52, emphasis added)

Notably, the Factory Act of 1850 regulated the majority of factory workers but left the work performed by children aged from six to thirteen still under the regulation of the Factory Act of 1844. This prescribed a working day from 5.30 a.m. to 8.30 p.m. As observed by von Plener (1873), this discrepancy allowed employers to use child labour for a longer time than the new working day established by the Factory Act of 1850 allowed. The different regulation of labour based on age highlighted the advantages recognized to employers at that time. Other advantages were recognized to employers in branches of the English industry left out of the Factory Act regulation.

Marx dedicates many pages of the chapter on the working day to the analysis of working conditions in industries that are not affected by the mechanization process. These industries, labelled as 'light manufacturing' in contemporary times, were – and still are – characterized by an intense use of manual work, extreme attention to details and by the seasonality of production. In these sectors, working conditions are far worse than they are in large industries affected by the mechanization of the production process. Marx examines the *Third Public Health Report* and the *First Report of the Children's Employment Commission*. In the pottery industry of Staffordshire, the manufacture of matches, the manufacture of wallpaper, the baking trade and the fashion industry, the working conditions were characterized by a structural and severe exploitation of labour, especially to the detriment of minors. The attention Marx places – also in many other occasions – on working conditions in the fashion industry is particularly significant. Already in the mid-nineteenth century, he captures what much of the social sciences can hardly grasp in our times: the extraordinary extraction of surplus value by employers. Historically, the fashion industry has always been characterized by bad working conditions, in terms of work intensity, wages and harassment against workers. In this industry, the use of child labour and the practice of homeworking have always been structural ways of lowering labour costs. Deaths produced by overwork were frequent among women employed in the lace making, as already observed by Engels in *The Condition of the Working Class in England* (1845). Lace making, as many other activities related to the fashion industry, needs an extreme attention to details, fast fingers and high flexibility. Fashion changes continuously, more in our time than in the nineteenth century. However, the low technological investment demanded and the modest skills required for entrepreneurship in this sector have always been crucial variables for the business start-up.

Marx reports the death from overwork of Mary Anne Walkley, 20 years old, employed in a dressmaking workshop and who worked uninterruptedly for 26½ hours, with sixty other girls, thirty in each room. The rooms provided only one-third of the necessary quantity of air, measured in cubic feet ([1867] 1992: 364). These working conditions were widespread among needlewomen, as reported by Dr Richardson, a senior physician at one of the London hospitals.[3] Arguably, such conditions are still present in the readymade garment sector. In 2013, the collapse of the Rana Plaza building in Dhaka, Bangladesh, which gathered five garment factories employing mainly women working in hazardous conditions, caused the killing of more than a thousand

---

[3]  See *Capital, Volume I*, p. 365. Marx quotes here the article of Dr Richardson, 'Work and overwork', in *Social Science Review*, 18 July 1863: 'With needlewomen of all kinds, including milliners, dressmakers, and ordinary sempstresses, there are three miseries – over-work, deficient air, and either deficient food or deficient digestion [...] Needlework, in the main [...] is infinitely better adapted to women than to men. But the mischiefs of the trade, in the metropolis especially, are that it is monopolised by some twenty-six capitalists, who, under the advantages that spring from capital, can bring in capital to force economy out of labour. This power tells throughout the whole class. If a dressmaker can get a little circle of customers, such is the competition that, in her home, she must work to the death to hold it together, and this same over-work she must of necessity inflict on any who may assist her. If she fail, do not try independently, she must join an establishment, where her labour is not less, but where her money is safe. Placed thus, she becomes a mere slave, tossed about with the variations of society. Now at home, in one room, starving, or near to it, then engaged 15, 16, aye, even 18 hours out of the 24, in an air that is scarcely tolerable, and on food which, even if it be good, cannot be digested in the absence of pure air. On these victims, consumption, which is purely a disease of bad air, feeds.'

people.[4] As was the case in nineteenth-century London, these deaths triggered narrow debates on safety standards, rather than leading to a wider condemnation and questioning of capitalist models of production (today export-oriented and led by multinationals) which provide poorly paid, unsafe jobs. However, safety at work is not a technical issue but a political one.

In fact, the analysis of working conditions and their health implications in the English industry, without legal limits to exploitation, drives Marx to questions going well beyond occupational health. At this point of the exam of the working day and considering employers' avid appetite for surplus labour, Marx wonders in rhetorical terms *what the limits of the working day are*, answering that 'it is self-evident that the worker is nothing other than labour-power for the duration of his whole life, and that therefore all his disposable time is by nature and by right labour-time, to be devoted to the self-valorization of capital' ([1867] 1992: 375). The examination of the working conditions emerging from labour inspectors' reports also leads Marx to observe that the apparent condition of freedom with which the worker is represented in the labour market – as the owner of the commodity 'labour-power' – clashes with the coercion permeating the employment relationship.

In this analysis of working time, as Seccombe (1974) points out, Marx treats the consumption of the means of subsistence and the reproduction of labour-power as two aspects of the same process. For Marx, the wage form governs labour within industry: the removal of domestic labour from the domain of surplus appropriation prevents the law of value from also controlling domestic labour. However, in this way, domestic labour's economic function is entirely occulted.[5]

## Invisibilized Labour through the Lens of the Marxian Enquire

Marx's analysis of the structure of capital and labour in ninetieth England mostly addresses the effects produced by the diffusion of large-scale industry and by machinery on workers' conditions. The involvement of all the family members in industrial work expands the degree of exploitation as the result of the surplus labour produced, rather than increasing the household's budget. However, Marx observes that the transformations occurring in production concern both the large-scale and the domestic industry. He described the latter as follows:

> This modern 'domestic industry' has nothing except the name in common with old-fashioned domestic industry, the existence of which presupposes independent urban handicrafts, independent peasant farming and, above all, a dwelling-house for the worker and his family. That kind of industry has now been converted into an external department of the factory, the manufacturing workshop, or the warehouse. Besides the factory worker, the workers engaged in manufacture, and the handicraftsmen, whom it concentrates in large masses at one spot,

4   For an extensive analysis of the sweatshop system, see Mezzadri (2016).
5   Among the most important literature on this topic, see Federici (1975), Dalla Costa and James (1975), Malos (1980), Mies (1982, 1986) and Vogel (1983).

and directly commands, capital also sets another army in motion, by means of invisible threads: the outworkers in the domestic industries, who live in the large towns as well as being scattered over the countryside. ([1867] 1992: 591)

Isolation and invisibilization (rather than invisibility) are structural characteristic of homework. Homework is a form of production carried out in private households, mainly by women. However, since the domicile is private and therefore removed from the work of supervisory bodies like the labour inspectorate, children and other members of the family have often worked alongside women. As mostly performed by women, working isolated in their homes, this work is hardly considered by unions. In fact, the structural exposure of this part of the workforce to dangerous working conditions has often been denied. However, despite the little attention received by unions, homework is a paradigmatic form of production: it has always existed, to varying degrees, within pre-capitalist and capitalist societies.

Homeworking has been often represented as a phenomenon marked by a conditional nature and entirely dependent on economic cycles. Instead, it is a substantial part of the economy and has endured four industrial revolutions, demonstrating great capacity to adapt to various national and international contexts. This premise is essential to deconstruct the hegemonic narrative around many forms of production, defined as 'non-standard'. Often, the definition of 'non-standard' or 'atypical' includes all contractualized forms of subordinate work that are not full-time or permanent, within a subordinate employment relationship. It refers to a complex whole that includes fixed-term work (seasonal, intermittent), dependent self-employment and part-time work (ILO 2016). However, if we look closely at the histories of work at a global level, we realize that these forms, defined by international statistical conventions as 'non-standard' and 'atypical', are in fact perhaps the most common and typical forms of employment. In fact, it is the experience of what many conventions defined as 'standard' and 'typical' work that seems, both in historical perspective and with reference to the contemporary world of work, to be the exception.

In the first book of *Capital*, Karl Marx highlights the structural relations between this form of production and national economies. He points out that the spread of homeworking is directly proportional to the growth in the size of the business, to the point that this specific part of the workforce becomes an 'external department of the factory' (see quote above). Many advantages explain the structurality of homeworking and its global spread. Marx had already grasped them in his time, once again by carefully examining the reports of the labour inspectors, collected in the *Reports of the Children's Employment Commission*, as described below:

The workers' power of resistance declines with their dispersal; because a whole series of plundering parasites insinuate themselves between the actual employer and the worker he employs; because a domestic industry has always to compete either with the factory system, or with manufacturing in the same branch of production; because poverty robs the worker of the conditions most essential to his labour, of space, light and ventilation; because employment becomes more and more irregular; and, finally, because in these last places of refuge for the masses made 'redundant' by large scale industry and agriculture, competition for work necessarily attains its maximum. ([1867] 1992: 591)

These few lines, written in the nineteenth century, contain all the major problems intrinsically present in homeworking: (1) the dispersion of workers that affects their ability to resist the employer; (2) the presence of intermediaries who operate by lowering the wages of homeworkers; (3) the high competition between homeworkers and factory workers; (4) the miserable working conditions, due to lack of space, light and ventilation; (5) the irregularity of the working activity that makes this portion of the workforce in extreme competition for work.

Marx's analysis of the *Reports of the Children's Employment Commission* offers us a lesson on how to deal with the study of working conditions through the analysis of official sources that in this case, in addition to providing data, also contain excerpts from interviews particularly useful to investigate the world of work. The analysis reveals that the spread of homework, far from producing new jobs, is a formidable means of excluding the workforce employed at home from the social protection, albeit modest, granted to workers employed in factories. Unlike the trend of much sociology of work that denies the relevance of the relationship between norms and reality, through the examination of the regulation produced by the Factory Acts, Marx shows that limitations of the working day constituted one of the decisive variables for the diffusion of homeworking. In addition, one must consider that in Victorian England as in many countries of the world today, labour inspections are not allowed in homes. The remuneration through the piecework system enables increases in self-exploitation, also thanks to the presence of family members who collaborate in the work activity.

In spite of the enormous advantages it brought to capital, according to Marx – erroneously – homeworking was destined to play a marginal role within the growing capitalist dynamic. Marxian analysis of homework, moreover, leaves some crucial nodes unresolved. As highlighted by Mies (1982), when Marx calculates the rate of exploitation of industrial labour, he thinks that 50 per cent of the work time is composed of necessary labour and the other 50 per cent of surplus labour time. However, through homework, capital extorts necessary labour from women workers. Piecework rates are not necessarily subject to negotiation between employer and homeworker. The power asymmetry in the employment relationship is so high as to preclude calculations of piecework rates meeting the needs of women workers' reproduction.

Ultimately, while providing some initial key insights on its features, Marx's analysis of homeworking neither capture the gender characterization of this form of production, nor it explains its persistence over time. What Marx and many scholars have not fully grasped is capital's great interest in promoting the spread of homeworking. Observing the development of this form of production in diachronic terms and across the world, it is evident that it remains prevalent in many countries or regions; particularly those lacking adequate services to support care work and dominated by patriarchal ideology. Historically, the employment of women at home in such contexts – through the free provision of care work they ensure – has allowed substantial savings of resources to governments. In this sense, the resilience of homework should also be read as based on the alliance between state, capital and patriarchy. It is this alliance that has supported the diffusion of homeworking on a global scale. The next section explores these themes by looking at the case of Italy in historical perspective. The narrative also highlights the benefits and challenges of deploying the Marxian method – especially in relation to the documents, reports and records he utilized – for the study of this form of work in modern or contemporary settings.

## Homeworking in Italy: A Historical Materialist Interpretation

The analysis of the Italian context is particularly interesting for the diffusion that this form of production experienced in the last century. Contrary to the little attention paid to it, its expansion has played a crucial role in the development of the Italian textile, clothing and footwear industry. It would indeed be very difficult to grasp the rise of the 'Made in Italy' at global level without considering the contribution of Italian homeworkers, in the same way in which it would be hard to understand the dynamics of contemporary globalized production without acknowledging the contribution of millions of homeworkers worldwide.

Notably, the number of workers employed at home in Italy has always been uncertain. In 1903, according to the census of factories and industrial enterprises, there were 295,223 looms working at home, without, however, any reference to the workers involved in domestic production. In 1927, according to national census, there were 34,219 workers employed in the various industries at home. The role played by fascist ruralism in the structuring of the Italian labour market and, in particular, in defining the patterns of gender segregation (not merely the gender division of labour) should be underlined as one the key issue to understand the territorial dispersion of the workforce (De Grazia 1992: 85). This territorial dispersion found in Italy a fundamental ally in the Catholic church. If fascist anti-urbanism was functional to a tight control over the labour force, it also allowed for the concealment of unemployment rates and reinforced the limitations of women's participation in paid work. Patriarchal ideologies reproducing an imagery of women as mothers have been widely mobilized both by the Catholic church and the fascist regime. As observed by Maria Vittoria Ballestrero (1979), during Fascism, labour laws concerning women had a double characterization: both 'protective' and 'expulsive', and these two aims were only apparently conflicting. Rising unemployment was brought under control through bans on the participation of women and children in paid work outside the home.[6] These dynamics promoted homeworking among Italian women in the whole post-war period.

---

[6]  See Ballestrero (1979: 64–65). With Law no. 653 of 26 April 1934, concerned with the protection of women and children at work, the work of women was coupled with that of children with the result of reinforcing the rigidity female labour supply while with Law No. 1347 of 5 July 1934 on the protection of motherhood, women were particularly limited in working activity.

In 1954, the parliamentary inquiry on the conditions of workers in Italy estimated that homeworkers were between 800,000 and 1 million. In the 1970s, other estimates, from surveys of extraparliamentary left-wing groups, disclosed the presence of 1 million 600 workers employed at home (Nanni 1970; Brusco 1973). What emerged from the analysis of census and documents on homeworking is that from the end of the 1930s to the 1990s, this work disappeared from the censuses of the Italian National Institute of Statistics concerning the labour force survey (Toffanin 2016). That means that, in effect, it has been absent from the national accounting of the workforce during the period of its maximum expansion. Unfortunately, for the study of Italian homeworking, we cannot rely on the detailed reports produced by labour inspectors in ninetieth-century England so carefully studied by Marx. However, we can count on many documents and epidemiological investigations that offer a comprehensive illustration of working conditions at home; in short, we can actually learn from and deploy Marx's method of study exploitation through the mapping of its health implications.

In post-war Italy, occupational physicians, trade unionists and activists placed growing attention on the toxic substances adopted in homework activities and their effects. The control of economic activities carried out at home – despite the rhetoric of the 'inviolability of private homes' – became a key issue in the struggle to achieve the introduction of laws to protect homeworkers. In fact, industrial homework implies the transfer of harmful conditions normally present in factories to the domestic environment. The dwelling as a pillar of private property is excluded from the control that inspection bodies carry out within companies. When work is undertaken at home it becomes part of the domestic life in a dimension people are very familiar with. At home, long working hours and harmful substances are reconstructed as less problematic. This aspect in particular explains what has driven many Italian entrepreneurs to outsource some stages of the production process to homeworkers; especially those involving the use of hazardous or toxic materials.

Particularly in the footwear industry, the use of glues based on organic solvents has always been related to high health risk for workers, due to their toxicity. In the 1970s, the disease associated with the use of glues was given a name; polyneuropathy, directly associated with of shoe factory work. In 1974, following the frequent occurrence of deaths caused by vinyl chloride, the experts of the International Agency for Research on Cancer reviewed the studies carried out by Enrico Vigliani, who in 1938 had already discovered the link between the benzene contained in the glues used in the production of footwear and the onset of cancer. Epidemiological investigations further confirmed the connection between the use of these glues and cases of leukaemia among workers exposed to benzene (Blanc 2007: 69). The epidemiological investigations carried out in Italy also revealed the onset of significant psychophysical alterations in the bodies of the workers most exposed to the solvents in use in the footwear and leather industries; malformations, paresis, tumours, leukaemia and anaemia were spread among workers using glues (Paci et al. 1988). These investigations soon revealed that polyneuropathy, or polyneuritis, caused by glues based on organic solvents, was produced by the inhalation of various harmful substances; the benzene contained in these glues is believed to be the crucial element causing the onset of polyneuropathy. From 1957 to 1978, 538 cases of polyneuropathy were recorded in Italy among factory workers. In 1963, a law limiting the content of benzene in glues was launched. Since then solvent was allowed with a concentration not exceeding 2 per cent of weight. In 1971, the International Labour Organisation introduced Convention 136 on the protection against the risk of intoxication due to benzene, which imposed on the ratifying states a strict control over its use.[7] However, the carcinogenicity of benzene was not officially established until 1981 (McMichael 1988).

Homeworkers, however, isolated and secluded in their homes were hardly subject to any epidemiological investigation. The few studies carried out on this topic revealed a high exposure to health risk among homeworkers (Discalzi et al. 1988; Bartolucci et al. 1991). In fact, although many years had already passed since the entry into force of Law 877/1973 in Italy, prohibiting the use of dangerous substances in the home, the epidemiological investigations carried out in the nineties among homeworkers revealed the following problems: (1) the gluing operation still involved the use of adhesives in which as many as nine different types of solvents were found, including n-hexane[8]; (2) this process was normally carried out in the kitchens of homes. The absence of ventilation and other preventive measures means that exposure to the risk involved all family members; (3) exposure to solvents did not end when work was interrupted: the absence of ventilation produced a concentration of harmful substances that needed special devices in order to be limited.

During the 1970s, feminist and left-wing movements raised several public complaints to highlight the pathologies found among homeworkers. The committees set up at that time were aimed at initiating preventive action and providing for early diagnoses, care and assistance and re-employment. Women affected by polyneuritis would often develop chronic diseases that required continuous care and treatment.[9] In addition to polyneuritis caused by adhesives, other pathologies have affected Italian homeworkers, such as the exposure to leather dust from the leather industry; the inhalation of textile fibres in the production of carpets; diseases affecting the ulnar nerve and carpal tunnel due

---

[7] In Italy the use of benzene was further regulated following the enactment of Law 146/1994 entitled 'Provisions for the fulfilment of obligations deriving from Italy's membership of the European Communities – Community Law 1993'. Article 35 regulates the use of benzene and its homologues (toluene and xylene, which are also used in the footwear and leather goods industry) during work activities. Ministerial Decree 707/1996 subsequently implemented what had already been established by Decree 626/1994. In fact, it prohibits the use of benzene and substances and preparations containing benzene in a concentration equal to or greater than 0.1 per cent by mass. Finally, Legislative Decree 81/2008, modified and supplemented by Legislative Decree 106/2009, intervened to regulate the use of benzene and its homologues.

[8] N-hexane is a chemical made from crude oil. It is highly flammable, and its vapours can cause an explosion. N-hexane is used as a solvent in the extraction of vegetable oils, production of glue and in rubber, and in the shoe industry. See also Jokanović (2009: 761–62).

[9] As reported by feminist newspapers, because of the difficulty in relating the symptoms reported by homeworkers to their working conditions, often physicians diagnosed the less serious cases as nervous breakdowns, which were treated with Optalidon and Valium (Cutrufelli and Vatta 1976).

to the frequent use of the sewing machine and repetitive movements in the processing of leather or fabrics; and eye diseases due to prolonged effort in extremely precise processing.[10]

The invisibilization of homework in Italy, as in many other countries, is paradigmatic of the attempt to conceal a part of the workforce that has been crucial to companies but also to governments who, through care work effectively offered free of charge by women, have been able to save huge amounts of resources which would have otherwise have to be allocated to social policies. Yet, homework continues to challenge academics, trade unionists and legislators on the same issues: the analysis of working conditions even in the presence of difficult fieldwork; the representation of dispersed workers; gender bargaining and the protection of work in all its forms. This chapter has suggested that, despite its theoretical and methodological limitations and challenges, still much can be learnt from Marx's method of analysis of working conditions premised on health outcomes.

## Conclusion

Despite Marx failing to recognize the role and value of domestic labour, as argued by many feminist theorists, his work is still crucial for the general scientific theory of the history formulated and for the concrete methods of enquiry he deployed to illustrate exploitation in practice. The idea that 'the mode of production in material life determines the general character of the social, political and spiritual processes of life' (Marx [1859] 1904: 11) means that in order to study the labour process you need to consider the relations of production as inseparable elements. Considering that production plays a key role in the reproduction of society, the analysis of the relationship between production and health must be central to every radical investigation of the labour process and its effects on workers. In these terms, Marx's analysis continues to play a pivotal role for generations of scholars dealing with labour issues.

First, Marxian analysis – and here is where its enduring relevance lies – starts from what materially happens in the sphere of production to understand the reproduction of society. The processes of division of labour that Marx described when observing his own contemporary reality are, in fact, at the basis of the tendencies towards the general degradation of work later described by Braverman (1974) and many other scholars. Work-related pathologies and health issues are always closely linked to the worker's loss of control over his work. In fact, today, this trend no longer concerns only manual work but also intellectual work.[11]

Second, Marxian analysis is particularly useful for a better understanding of all forms of exploitation, including homeworkers' super-exploitation. Despite the advancement in setting labour standards, this super-exploitation remains a structural component of the capitalist system. As already during Marx's time, the examination of the relationship

---

[10]  For a more detailed account, see Toffanin (2016).

[11]  Among the relevant literature, see Eurofound and ILO (2017) and Graham et al. (2017).

between the work regulation enforced by governments and the production of new forms of exploitation remains paramount. The examination of working conditions carried out by Marx after the launch of the Factory Acts is paradigmatic: during historical phases characterized by the intensification of labour exploitation, laws apparently aimed at improving working conditions are instead often bent to the interests of capital.

Finally, the Marxian method carefully indicating the interweaving between work and health outcomes offers us with endless possibilities for further research on the world of work, deploying tools going well beyond those generally acknowledge in much of labour process theory. Ultimately, the historical materialism deployed by Marx invites us to observe the factual reality of capital and labour considering the synchronic and dia-chronic dimension of social processes. This double perspective is necessary in order to avoid, on the one hand, an epiphenomenal analysis of society and, on the other hand, an analysis that is focused to the historical unfolding of some events but disregards factual reality.

The analysis of homeworking in Italy through the lens of Marx's historical materi-alism is crucial to understand how the Italian economic miracle developed and, above all, what were the social costs of economic growth as it unfolded in the country after the Second World War. The Italian case confirms that Marx certainly grasped the advantages of the dispersion of the labour force across homes for capital. However, he did not fully grasp its gendered aspects, nor that its segregational features meant that, besides working for capital, women homeworkers also effectively work for the state, replacing its services with their unpaid care work; a taxing process depleting their health and that of their families.

## References

Ballestrero, M. V. 1979. *Dalla tutela alla parità. La legislazione italiana sul lavoro delle donne*. Bologna: Il Mulino.

Bartolucci, G. B., G. Gori, G. Boscaro, L. Vianello and E. De Rosa. 1991. 'Inquinamento da solventi nel lavoro calzaturiero a domicilio'. *Giornale degli igienisti industriali* 3: 73–83.

Blanc, P. 2007. *How Everyday Products Make People Sick. Toxins at Home and in the Workplace*. Berkeley: University of California Press.

Braverman, H. 1974. *Labor and Monopoly Capital: The Degradation of Work in the Twentieth Century*. New York: Monthly Review Press.

Brusco, S. 1973. 'Prime note per uno studio del lavoro a domicilio in Italia'. *Inchiesta* 3(10): 33–49.

Cutrufelli, M. R. and A. Vatta. 1976. 'Il veleno in cucina. C'è ma non si dice'. *Noi Donne* 35: 31–32.

Dalla Costa, M. and S. James. 1975. *The Power of Women and the Subversion of the Community*. Bristol: Falling Wall.

De Grazia, V. 1992. *How Fascism Ruled Women. Italy 1922–1945*. Berkeley: University of California Press.

Discalzi, G., G. Perrelli and I. Pavan. 1988. 'Rischio da solventi nel lavoro domiciliare'. *Medicina del Lavoro* 79: 234–36.

Engels, F. [1845] 2009. *The Conditions of the Working Class in England*. London: Penguin.

Eurofound and ILO. 2017. *Working Anytime, Anywhere: The Effects on the World of Work*. Luxembourg: Publications Office of the European Union; Geneva: International Labour Office.

Federici, S. 1975. *Wages against Housework*. Bristol: Power of Women Collective and Falling Wall.

Fee, E. and T. M. Brown. 2005. 'The public health act of 1848'. *Bulletin of the World Health Organization* 83: 866–67.

Graham, M., I. Hjorth and V. Lehdonvirta. 2017. 'Digital labour and development: Impacts of global digital labour platforms and the gig economy on worker livelihoods'. *Transfer: European Review of Labour and Research* 2: 135–62.

ILO. 2016. *Non-standard Employment around the World: Understanding Challenges, Shaping Prospects.* Geneva: International Labour Office.

Jokanović, M. 2009. 'Neuropathy: Chemically-induced'. In *Encyclopedia of Neuroscience.* London: Academic, pp. 759–65.

Malos, E. 1980. *The Politics of Housework.* London: Allison and Busby.

Marx, K. [1859] 1904. *A Contribution to the Critique of Political Economy.* Chicago: Charles H. Kerr.

———. [1867] 1992. *Capital. A Critique of Political Economy, Volume I.* London: Penguin.

McMichael, A. J. 1988. 'Carcinogenicity of benzene, toluene and xylene: Epidemiological and experimental evidence'. *IARC Scientific Publications* 85: 3–18.

Mezzadri, A. 2016. *The Sweatshop Regime. Labouring Bodies, Exploitation, and Garments Made in India.* Cambridge: Cambridge University Press.

Mies, M. 1982. *The Lace Makers of Narsapur. Indian Housewives Produce for the Word Market.* London: Zed.

———. 1986. *Patriarchy and Accumulation on a World Scale. Women in the International Division of Labor.* London: Zed.

Nanni, S. 1970. *Il lavoro a domicilio negli atti della commissione parlamentare di inchiesta sulle condizioni dei lavoratori in Italia 1955–1958.* Roma: Camera dei Deputati, Archivio storico.

Paci, E., E. Buiatti, L. Miligi, A. S. Costantini and S. Annalisa. 1988. 'Mortalità tra lavoratori di un calzaturificio a Firenze in relazione all'esposizione di benzene'. In *Atti del 51° congresso nazionale della società italiana di medicina del lavoro e di igiene industriale*, Florence, 13–16 December. Bologna: Monduzzi, pp. 945–48.

Plener, E. E. von. 1873. *The English Factory Legislation.* London: Chapman and Hall.

Seccombe, W. 1974. 'The housewife and her labour under capitalism'. *New Left Review* 1(83): 3–24.

Tocqueville, A. de. [1835] 1997. *Memoir on Pauperism.* Chicago: Ivan R. Dee.

Toffanin, T. 2016. *Fabbriche invisibili. Storie di donne, lavoranti a domicilio.* Verona: ombre corte.

Vogel, L. 1983. *Marxism and the Oppression of Women: Toward a Unitary Theory.* New Brunswick: Rutgers University Press.

# Chapter Thirteen

# MARX AND THE POOR'S NOURISHMENT

## DIETS IN CONTEMPORARY SUB-SAHARAN AFRICA

### Sara Stevano

## Abstract

Across *Capital*, Marx is attentive to food consumption and nourishment as conditions of the reproduction of labour and as manifestations of the immiseration of the working class. In chapter 25 of *Volume I*, Marx illustrates the general law of capitalist accumulation by analysing the living conditions of labourers in Britain in 1846–66. Drawing on public health investigations, Marx discusses the deficient diets of labourers as resulting from expanding capital accumulation as well as capital centralisation and concentration. Marx reports nutrient tables indicating low consumption of food rich in nitrogen (i.e. meats, fish and fruit and vegetables) among the working class, with agricultural labourers and women suffering from the most deficient diets. This chapter builds on Marx's analysis of nutrition and health depletion of the poor occurring through the expansion of capitalist production with two aims. First, it investigates whether food consumption among the poor in contemporary sub-Saharan Africa presents similar patterns to the British labourers' diets described in *Capital*. Using primary data collected in Mozambique and Ghana, it shows that scarce consumption of protein-rich food continues to be a defining feature of the poor's diets. However, another key aspect is the penetration of packaged and processed food, which is a manifestation of a globalised food regime and the expansion of capital in food production. Second, this chapter provides insights on the methodological approach used to collect data on food consumption and the linkages with the food system, which requires multiple levels of analysis and data sources.

## Introduction

In the past few decades, the study of nutrition has come to be dominated by medical sciences, which promote a biomedical, individualised and technical understanding of nutritional outcomes (O'Laughlin 2013; Jaspars et al. 2018). Nutrition narratives have become detached from the analysis of systems of commodified food production, trade policies and labour regimes, endangering our understanding of nutritional issues. Further, the expropriation of nutrition of its socioeconomic and political content has paved the way to the entrance of the food industry in shaping nutrition narratives on a global scale, which contributes to deepening the problem, precipitating a crisis of malnutrition (Winson 2013; Street 2015; Sathyamala 2016). It is necessary to re-embed the study of nutrition and diets in the underlying determinants, through a political economy approach aimed at uncovering the socioeconomic, political and cultural processes furthering the polarisation of nutrition outcomes.

Across *Capital*, Marx is attentive to food consumption and nourishment as conditions of the reproduction of labour and as manifestations of the immiseration of the working class. In chapter 25 of *Volume I*, Marx illustrates the general law of capitalist accumulation by analysing the living conditions of labourers in Britain in 1846–66. Drawing on secondary data collected through public health investigations, Marx discusses the deficient diets of labourers as resulting from expanding capital accumulation as well as capital centralisation and concentration. Marx reports nutrient tables indicating low consumption of food rich in nitrogen (i.e. meats, fish, milk, fruit and vegetables) among the working class, with agricultural labourers and women suffering from the most deficient diets.

This chapter builds on Marx's analysis of nutrition and health depletion of the poor occurring through the expansion of capitalist production with two aims. First, it investigates whether food consumption among the poor in contemporary sub-Saharan Africa presents similar patterns to the British labourers' diets described in *Capital*. Drawing on evidence from Mozambique and Ghana, it shows that scarce consumption of protein-rich food continues to be a defining feature of the poor's diets. However, another key aspect is the penetration of packaged and processed food, which is a manifestation of a globalised food regime and the expansion of capital in food production. Second, this chapter provides insights on the methodological approach used to collect data on food consumption and the linkages with the food system, which requires multiple levels of analysis and data sources.

The chapter is structured as follows. The next section discusses how the study of diets and nutrition can provide a lens to analyse transformations in global capitalism, drawing on Marx's writings and other insightful literature investigating the socioeconomic and political determinants of food and nutrition. The following sections present and analyse the empirical evidence on diets in Mozambique and Ghana and then reflect on key methodological issues.

## Diets and Nutrition as a Lens to Analyse Global Capitalism

In a recent piece that reclaims the importance of Marx as a *food theorist*, Foster (2016) takes issue with a stream of literature in the sociology and anthropology of food that dismisses the contribution of Marx to the study of food. To the contrary, Foster argues, Marx was very concerned with the nourishment of the working class and articulated an analysis of the system of food production as becoming *industrial* under the pressure of capitalism, which led to increased agricultural productivity but produced a *metabolic rift* that impoverished the soil (ibid.). Thus, Foster portrays Marx as anticipating the notion of food regime and contemporary debates on ecology. Indeed, it is necessary to acknowledge the influence of Marx on much of the later literature on food regimes, conceptualised as linking 'international relations of food production and consumption to forms of accumulation broadly distinguishing periods of capital transformation since 1870' (Friedmann and McMichael 1989: 95). Insights from and interpretations of Marx have been central to debates on the structuring of food systems, processes of agrarian change and capital's relations to nature (Bernstein 2016).

Furthermore, among the literature on food consumption, we find contributions that emphasise how the geography and the systems of food provisioning underpin consumption practices and, therefore, approach the study of consumption through a historical materialist analysis (Fine et al. 1998; Freidberg 2003). In particular, Fine et al. (1998: 2) conceptualise the *system of provision* as 'an integral or unified set of structures and processes that determine the way in which consumption is socioeconomically and culturally organised' (Fine et al. 1998: 2). Central to this understanding is the material basis of the cultural manifestations of food consumption practices and food knowledge as interrelated with, and ultimately produced by, the systems of provision (Fine 2002, 2007). For instance, Freidberg (2007) argues that the concentration of information and power in the hands of Western supermarkets is contributing to the spread of *imperial* knowledge on food quality with enormous implications for the practices of food producers in the Global South.

While these bodies of literature offer essential insights for the study of food, especially as a lens through which looking at the dynamics of global capitalism, specific considerations on nutrition have become less prominent in the social sciences as nutrition narratives came to be dominated by medical sciences (Jaspars et al. 2018). The advances in nutrition sciences created an image of nutrition as a technical, biomedical and individualised issue (Winson 2013; Sathyamala 2016). O'Laughlin (2013) reminds us that the key debate on the determinants of health is about how the relations between the biological and the social are framed: either positioning the individual at the centre or starting from the society individuals live in. Nutrition became an international policy concern in the context of the 1930s crisis, when the League of Nations Health Organisation (LNHO) was tasked with investigating the gaps between overproduction and underconsumption of food (Sathyamala 2016). However, falling to political pressures, the LNHO soon abandoned the documentation of the linkages between socioeconomic policies and the prevalence of hunger and turned to the development of technical reports that framed malnutrition as an issue of eating the wrong types of food. Thus, Sathyamala (ibid.) argues, the dichotomisation of food and nutrition began to obscure the structural determinants of hunger.

In light of the subsequent proliferation of *sanitised* approaches to nutrition, stripped of its socioeconomic and political content, it is even more revealing to uncover Marx's interest in the welfare of the labouring classes, in particular their diets, nutritional intake and housing conditions. He contextualises the living conditions of the working class in the analysis of the law of capitalist accumulation, discussed in chapter 25 of *Volume I*. In this chapter of *Capital*, Marx explores the implications of the expansion of capital for the labouring classes. He argues that, to grasp the implications of capital growth, we need to look at the composition of capital, constituted by a constant component – the means of production – and a variable component – the labour power. Marx notes that, through the production of surplus-value, the constant component of capital grows more rapidly than the variable component. The overall effect is to displace workers, that is the creation of a *surplus labouring population*. Marx articulates a poignant critique of theories of wage determination as being based on movements of labour supply and demand and posits that it is the movements in the reserve army of labour that determine wages.

Looking at the striking difference in the average age at death between the upper middle class and the labouring class, 38 years old for the former and 17 years old for the latter in Manchester, Marx observes that the proletariat faces social needs that are different from those of other classes. For example, he ascribes the practice of early marriages among the working class to the shorter life span due to the poor living and working conditions. Thus, Marx embeds a perspective on the conditions of poverty in which the working class lives into the analysis of the processes of capitalist accumulation and states:

> The greater the social wealth, the functioning capital, the extent and energy of its growth, and, therefore, also the absolute mass of the proletariat and the productiveness of its labour, the greater is the industrial reserve army [...] But the greater this reserve army in proportion to the active labour army, the greater is the mass of a consolidated surplus population, whose misery is in inverse ratio to its torment of labour. The more extensive, finally, the lazarus layers of the working class, and the industrial reserve army, the greater is official pauperism. This is the absolute general law of capitalist accumulation. (Marx 1887: 451)

Marx's interest in the labourers' diets and dwelling conditions is in pursuit of a 'full elucidation of the law of capitalist accumulation' (ibid.: 456). Against this backdrop, Marx draws on public health investigations commissioned by the Privy Council and conducted by Dr Smith and Dr Simon in 1862 and 1863, respectively.[1] These studies targeted agricultural labourers and various categories of factory workers and concluded that English agricultural labourers, women and children were those with the poorest diets. Labourers' diets were characterised by insufficient intake of nitrogen – that is, derived from foods containing protein, such as meat, fish and dairy. Although bread was the main food for the working class, at times even the intake of carbon – that is, carbohydrates – was insufficient. The cost of food in relation to workers' wages suggests that the labouring class could afford very poor diets. Based on Dr Simon's investigation, Foster (2016) reports that the diet of the working class was based on carbohydrates and fat and was lacking in protein, milk and fresh vegetables. To highlight the deficiencies of the working-class diet, Marx reports nutrient tables showing that the diets of the labourers had lower nutrient intake than those of convicts in prison.

Foster (2016) argues that Marx does not stop at the description of nutrient intakes but, across various writings, shows an interest in the various transformations occurring to food as a commodity. In particular, he was concerned with the problem of degradation of food fed to the working class and the transformations of British agriculture, becoming industrialised and shifting from the production of cereals and grains for human consumption, especially important in the labourers' diets, to animal farming, directed at the upper classes' consumption (ibid.). On the other hand, as it emerges from Marx's discussion of the law of capitalist accumulation, the penetration of capital into agricultural production has the effect of 'freeing' more labour in the countryside and increasing

---

[1]   The cotton famine occurred in 1862.

the reserve army, with further detrimental effects on the working and living conditions of labourers as a whole. Thus, the key contribution of Marx's perspective on the nourishment of the labouring class in Britain is that diets and nutrient intakes are depicted as manifestations of labour regimes, agrifood systems and, ultimately, of processes of capitalist accumulation. These are the foundations for the development of a political economy of diets, reconnect the study of nutrition and that of food and re-embed it in the social sciences, to capture the underpinning economic, social and political determinants.

## Diets in Contemporary Sub-Saharan Africa: Evidence from Mozambique and Ghana

To reflect on the relevance of Marx's analysis of the working-class diet in contemporary Africa we first need to address the meaning of class analysis in the African context. A rich literature on colonial and postcolonial trajectories of development in Africa has documented how patterns of capital accumulation have not led to dualistic class formations, such as a landless rural proletariat and commercial farmers, but rather to 'classes of labour' (Bernstein 2010) engaging with combinations of wage, unwage work and cash-earning activities (O'Laughlin 2002). Thus, social differentiation exists among farmers and labourers and processes of proletarianisation have unfolded in complex ways, leading some households to adopt the practices of both capital and labour. O'Laughlin (1996) suggests that in Africa processes of social differentiation are to be distinguished into practices of livelihood diversification, on the one hand, and trajectories of class formation, on the other, as these processes may not proceed in parallel. Thus, while emphasising the relevance of class analysis in Africa to capture differentiation, it is necessary to recognise the existence of multiple classes of labour and intraclass inequality (Peters 2004).

The fuzziness of class divides creates questions on how to categorise farmers and rural households in different settings in Africa, which have been addressed, for example, by classifying households depending on their ability to reproduce themselves through agricultural production (Cousins et al. 1992) and by employing a set of criteria including ability to hire labour and capital intensification (Oya 2004). Possibly even greater challenges arise when seeking to analyse both rural and urban contexts, as much recent literature grapples with the contested phenomenon of the rise of the middle class in African cities seeking to pin down the existence of such social formation using a variety of indicators, including consumption patterns and identity (Lentz 2015; Melber 2017).

To gain an understanding of socioeconomic stratification in the studies conducted in Mozambique and Ghana, we relied on a combination of criteria. In Mozambique, where we collected data on land ownership and labour-hiring or selling, it was clear that the ability to hire labour vis-à-vis the necessity to sell labour remains a critical divide in rural areas and, to some extent, in urban areas too. However, important aspects of differentiation within the categories of labour-hirers and labour-sellers need to be considered. As a proxy for wealth, in both Mozambique and Ghana, an asset index was used to capture the durable goods possessed by the household. In Ghana, the asset index was combined with data on neighbourhood of residence and type of school attended. In both

**Table 13.1** Summary of case studies, Mozambique and Ghana

| Study | Mozambique (province of Cabo Delgado) | Ghana (Accra Metropolitan Area) |
|---|---|---|
| Research participants | Women, families, communities | Children in junior high schools |
| Research sites | 3 districts: Pemba (urban), Metuge (rural), Mueda (rural) | 4 junior high schools (1 public in low-income neighbourhood, 1 public in lower-middle-income neighbourhood, 1 private in upper-middle-income neighbourhood, 1 elitist private) |
| Methods for primary data collection | Ethnographic methods, semi-structured qualitative interviews, household survey (120 respondents) | Interviews with key stakeholders in the food sector, focus groups with children, student survey (139 respondents) |

*Source:* Compiled by the author

contexts, data on food consumption is revealing and captures variation in welfare across classes of labour.

Evidence from primary research conducted in Mozambique (2011–12) and in Ghana (2015–16) is only juxtaposed as these are studies with different scopes and not designed in a comparative fashion, despite having a common concern with food practices. The details are summarised in Table 13.1.

The province of Cabo Delgado, in northern Mozambique, faces a severe problem of chronic malnutrition, measured by the levels of stunting.[2] More than 50 per cent of children in Cabo Delgado are stunted: 56 per cent in 2008 (MICS 2008), which was the highest level nationally, and 52 per cent in 2011 (Demographic Health Survey 2011). The available food consumption data suggests that 36 per cent of the population in Cabo Delgado has inadequate diets, characterised by poor dietary diversity (World Food Programme 2010).[3] Indeed the lack of diversity in types of food consumed is confirmed by the data collected in 2011–12. The household dietary diversity indicator incorporated in the household survey shows that diets are overly dependent on cereals (91 per cent), mostly maize and rice, vegetables (72 per cent), legumes (56 per cent) and, to some extent, cooking oil (51 per cent), while consumption of vitamin A-rich vegetables, fruit, meat and milk is extremely low. In particular, the percentages of non-consumption of meat and milk were above 90 per cent.

Although many rural households have at least a few chickens and sometimes some goats, livestock tends to be kept as an asset, eaten on special occasions, such as funerals,

---

[2]  According to the WHO, children are defined as stunted if their height-for-age is more than two standard deviations below the WHO child growth standards median.

[3]  The household dietary diversity indicator records the types of foods consumed by the household in the 24 hours before the interview and is considered to be a good proxy for food quality (Ruel 2002; Swindale and Bilinsky 2006).

**Table 13.2** Meat consumption in the previous month

|  | No. of households | Per cent of households |
| --- | --- | --- |
| No consumption of meat | 52 | 43.3 |
| Rarely (1 or 2 times) | 41 | 34.2 |
| Sometimes (between 3 and 10 times) | 26 | 21.7 |
| Often (more than 10 times) | 1 | 0.8 |

*Source:* Based on survey data collected by the author.

or prepared for guests. Meat is considered to be a prestigious food and is eaten with parsimony. As Table 13.2 shows, consumption of meat is very low, with almost half of the sample reporting no consumption at all in the previous month and only one respondent reporting high consumption (i.e. more than 10 times) in the same time period. Among the households with higher consumption of meat were the wealthier ones, while the poorer were concentrated among those that reported no consumption of meat in the previous month.

Poor households face both income and time constraints that limit their ability to produce, acquire and prepare food. While household production continues to be an important source of food, households are not able to meet their food needs in full and resort to food purchase, which is a ubiquitous aspect of food provisioning for urban and rural households alike.[4] As meals have two components: the staple (typically maize, rice or cassava) and the relish (sauce made with vegetables, beans, fish or meat), at least the preparation of the relish, requires purchased ingredients. While the staples may be domestically produced and/or bought in bulk, the relish is acquired daily and how much a household can spend for the relish differentiates between wealthier and poorer households. Daily food expenses can range between 10 and 20 MT – sufficient to buy a few tomatoes, a very small quantity of 'small' fish or some leaves – to 80 or 100 MT, in a few cases even 200 MT – which allow for purchasing bigger quantities of vegetables and fish, but also vegetable oil, *Rajah* (curry powder), meat and other foods that can be eaten outside the principal meals.

Both daily food practices and the organisation of agricultural production, structured by casual labour relations, compulsion to diversify livelihoods and seasonality, shape households' access to food. On the one hand, it emerged that a common practice is to repeat the same meal twice in a day due to either *lack of money* to buy a different relish or *lack of time* to prepare a different relish, owing to fluctuating incomes, multiple occupations and clashes between work and food preparation times. On the other hand, household facing food shortages are forced to seek piece-rate wage work in other people's fields at times of the year that coincide with the need for the most intense agricultural work on their own fields, which jeopardises their ability to produce food for the following

---

[4] All the survey respondents said they (or someone else in their household) bought some food in the month before the interview. The survey was conducted between April and June 2012, which is (early) harvest time in Cabo Delgado.

**Table 13.3** Nutrition in Ghana and Greater Accra Region (percentages)

| | Child nutrition (under 5) | | Women nutrition | |
| --- | --- | --- | --- | --- |
| | Stunting | Overweight | Underweight | Overweight |
| National average | 18.8 | 2.6 | 6.2 | 40.1[a] |
| Greater Accra Region | 10.4 | 3.2 | 4.5 | 57.3 |

*Source*: Compiled by the author using WHO and DHS data.
[a]The national average for both women and men is 33.6 per cent.

year. These dynamics are at the core of the (re)production of food vulnerability (see Stevano 2019).

An image of diets as monotonous and lacking, combined with poor consumption data, contributes to neglecting an important aspect of food practices in northern Mozambique: the growing pervasiveness of packaged and processed foods.[5] For instance, *Rajah*, a brand of curry powder produced by Unilever, is considered to be essential to give flavour to any type of relish. In wealthier households that have already become accustomed to the use of *Rajah* in cooking, a relish without *Rajah* is considered to be tasteless. By the same token, 91 per cent of the survey respondents believe soft drinks and packaged biscuits are good for children's health and 40 per cent of the respondents said that they bought soft drinks or biscuits for their children in the month before the interview. The gap between those who can afford to buy these foods (more or less) regularly and those who would buy them but cannot afford it suggests that (extra) cash earnings are likely to be spent on foods considered to be enticing. Higher and more regular cash incomes do ensure greater food security and dietary diversity but, at the same time, higher consumption of sugar-rich and nutrient-poor packaged and processed foods.

The importance of packaged and processed foods emerged, even more strongly, in the study in Accra. A key difference in the background information available on Mozambique and Ghana is that, while in the northern Mozambique context the literature is mostly concerned with food insecurity and poorly diversified diets, studies of Ghana embody the growing attention paid to the process of dietary change that is leading to the rise of overweight and obesity alongside persistent undernutrition. Table 13.3 shows that the Greater Accra Region has lower, but nonetheless non-insignificant, levels of stunting and underweight compared to the national averages, but higher levels of overweight among children and women.

The dietary diversity indicator integrated in the student survey we conducted in 2016 captures high consumption of cereals (99.3 per cent), oils and fats (65.5 per cent), sweets (50.4 per cent), meat (48.2 per cent), vegetables (48.2 per cent) and dairy products (43.9 per cent). Instead, very low levels of consumption were recorded for vitamin A-rich

---

5   Importantly, this is also linked to a longstanding and flawed narrative that depicts rural households as reliant on subsistence agriculture and, therefore, outside of the circuits of commodification and food purchase (see O'Laughlin 1996).

**Table 13.4** Frequency of Fan Milk snacks consumption in the previous week, by wealth quintile (percentages)

| Consumption frequency | 1st quintile (poorest) | 2nd quintile | 3rd quintile | 4th quintile | 5th quintile (richest) |
|---|---|---|---|---|---|
| 0 | 31.3 | 34.4 | 15.8 | 17.2 | 33.3 |
| 1 | 34.3 | 34.4 | 21 | 24.1 | 33.3 |
| More than 1 | 34.4 | 31.2 | 63.2 | 58.7 | 33.4 |

*Source*: Created by authors.

fruit (3.6 per cent) and nuts/seeds (9.4 per cent). Dietary diversity grows with wealth, as measured by the asset index, and, in particular, it can be observed that consumption of dairy and vegetables is higher among the children in the wealthiest group and gradually decreases through the wealth quintiles. However, for other food items the association with wealth is not clear-cut. In particular, this appears to be the case for foods and drinks that are consumed as snacks. We find that consumption of packaged foods, such as soft drinks and snacks, is high across all wealth groups in our sample and peaks in the middle wealth group.

The WHO survey of students in Ghana finds that 55.8 per cent of children in junior high schools have carbonated drinks on a daily basis (WHO 2012). Packaged snacks and soft drinks are sold by food vendors on the schools' premises or in surrounding areas and are among the cheapest foods available at school or on the road. The food industry ensures availability, affordability and desirability of its products. An important channel for availability is the use of both formal and informal ways for distribution. Packaged foods are not only found in supermarkets, but also in food markets, mobile and stationary food stalls. Companies that target children rely on networks of distribution that can reach children at school. An example is provided by Fan Milk International, a Danish multi-national operating in Ghana since the 1960s and acquired by Danone and The Abraaj Group in 2013, which dominates the market for packaged frozen snacks. Fan Milk's distribution structure relies on thousands of *self-employed* mobile street vendors operating particularly in urban areas. In interviews conducted with Fan Milk vendors, it emerged that many go to public schools at break times and at the end of the school day because Fan Milk snacks are popular among children. In our survey, we found that 72.7 per cent of children had eaten Fan Milk snacks in the previous week, with the highest consumption frequency found in the middle wealth quintiles, as shown in Table 13.4.

Affordability is also crucial to ensure purchase. Food companies resort to strategies such as miniature packaging in order to maximise their ability to tap into most segments of the market. In the case of Fan Milk snacks, vendors may cut the snacks in half so that two children can share the cost. In our mapping of food products and outlets across Accra, it was clear that the same branded product is packaged in a range of sizes, then sold in different food outlets. Street vendors sell the smallest packages, with one-portion powdered drink mix, such as Nestlé's Milo, being a popular food stall item. Street food is especially prominent in the diets of children from the poorer and middle wealth quintiles.

Thus, by drawing on the evidence on food practices collected in Mozambique and Ghana, we can observe that the diets of the poorest continue to be characterised by overreliance on carbohydrates and fat and poor consumption of animal foods, such as dairy and meats, and fresh vegetables. The poorest often rely on various forms of casual wage and self-employment and, owing to multiple and fragmented occupations, they face the most significant income and time constraints to producing, acquiring and preparing adequate food. However, in addition to this, we see that packaged and processed foods feature prominently in the diets of the poor in contemporary sub-Saharan Africa. Consumption of these foods appears to be peaking for the middle wealth groups while shaping the aspirations of poorer groups. This is a manifestation of the growing presence of multinational food corporations across the Global South, which began with the structural adjustment programmes and gave rise, according to Winson (2013), to a third *dietary regime* characterised by the spatial colonisation of nutrient-poor products of new food environments, such as poorer countries in the South.[6] Although much literature focuses on supermarkets, fast-food chains and the growth of the 'middle classes' (e.g. Winson 2013), it is clear that the food industry makes widespread use of informal distribution channels, aggressive marketing strategies and relatively low prices, which are mechanisms to reach not only the wealthier, but also the poorer strata of the population.

Through concentration of power in the systems of commodified food production, the food industry shapes consumption, but also aspirations and knowledge about food in ways that reveal how the material conditions of food production and distribution underpin cultural relations to food. Furthermore, the food industry appropriates nutrition narratives through, inter alia, advertising the health and nutrient properties of food products, at times added to them. The focus on the nutrient composition of food as a biomedical issue, detached from socioeconomic and political processes, has paved the way to the entrance of capital in the production of nutrients (Sathyamala 2016). Thus, the food industry positions itself as addressing the nutrient deficiencies that are in fact created, or aggravated, by the expansion of capitalist accumulation on a global scale. Although diets look more diversified in appearance, it can be argued that they have undergone a process of degradation due to the loss of quality and nutrients (Winson 2013), which affects overwhelmingly the diets of the working classes, comprising of low and middle wealth groups.

## Bridging Micro–Macro Divides in the Analysis of Diets

When exploring the methodological issues entailed in the collection and analysis of data on diets within a Marxist framework, it is necessary to consider the type of necessary data and its quality and how to bring different types of data together to substantiate a political economy analysis. The availability of reliable data on food practices and diets is an

---

[6]  Winson (2013) introduces the concept of dietary regime, which, drawing on that of food regime, seeks to provide an emphasis on the constitution, reproduction, crisis and transformation of mass diets.

essential starting point. While data on individual nutrition outcomes – that is, anthropo-metric measures – is now collected regularly in most countries through the Demographic Health Surveys and others, data on diets tends to be fragmented, lacking detail and of poor quality, thus not equipped to support an in-depth analysis. The bias towards meas-urement of nutrition outcomes, instead of diets, demonstrates the prevalent approach to nutrition as a biomedical issue. However, understanding how people source and prepare food and the types of food they consume is essential for a political economy analysis. Thus, it may be necessary to engage in primary data collection to gather this informa-tion, as we did in Mozambique and Ghana.

Collecting data on food practices is a challenging exercise due to their complex and multilayered nature. Often information is not entirely accurate because of recall bias and a tendency to withhold detailed information about every food and drink somehow acquired and consumed. For instance, in Mozambique, it emerged that it is common to consider the main staple as 'food', which leads to omitting many foods consumed outside the principal meals. Thus, questions need to be detailed and allow the respondent to locate food events in the daily activities. Indeed, the observation of everyday life practices and knowledge of the food environment are fundamental to guide the formulation of questions that can yield meaningful data. Ethnographic methods, observation, mapping of foods available and secondary literature that can help build an understanding of the food landscape are all important components of exercises of data collection on food and diets.

One important limitation of available data is the lack of information on processed and packaged foods. At the aggregate level, the statistics on trade of packaged and processed foods are not publicly or immediately available, as the most accurate data is retained by the food industry. The Food and Agriculture Organisation provides national estimates on food production and trade for various foods, but not specifically for processed and/or packaged foods. On the other hand, large scale surveys have not been equipped to gather data on consumption of processed and packaged foods because, often using the household as the unit of analysis, they focus on household-based food consumption, at the expense of food consumed away from home (Farfan et al. 2015). Thus, although we know about the rise of supermarkets and the growth of food multinationals, we do not have matching consumption data. Small-scale or ad hoc surveys may be a better way to have a quantitative basis for data on food practices. In Mozambique, a food module was included in the household survey questionnaire and, in Ghana, the questionnaire used for the student survey was focused on food consumption, knowledge and acquisition.

To develop a political economy analysis of diets is best to draw on different data sources: primary and secondary, qualitative and quantitative. The triangulation can help minimise data inaccuracies and, importantly, bridge different levels of analysis. The most significant challenge is that there is a separation between the study of nutrition – which mostly remains at the micro level based on data on individuals or, at best, households – and that of food systems, which takes a macro approach. To further a political economy of diet and nutrition is necessary to bridge this micro–macro divide and offer an inter-pretation of data on nutrition and diets in the context of globalising food systems, labour regimes and everyday life practices of organisation of productive and reproductive work.

Arguably, the most accomplished study in this respect is O'Laughlin's (2013) investigation of the production of affliction in southern Africa, which looks at how class, gender and race relations of power underpin the reproduction of health inequalities through the colonial and postcolonial regimes of capital accumulation. Indeed, a historical materialist analysis is necessary.

## Conclusion

Drawing on Marx's investigation of the nourishment of the British working class in the second half of the nineteenth century, this chapter explored diets in contemporary sub-Saharan Africa, in particular among differentiated classes of labour and wealth groups in Mozambique and Ghana. It is striking to note how some features of the working-class diet, in particular the reliance on carbohydrates and fat and the lack of meat and dairy, are apparent in the diets of the poorest in contemporary sub-Saharan Africa. Consumption of meat among the poorer in Mozambique is either absent or very low and meat is considered to be a food for special occasions. In Ghana, consumption of dairy tends to increase with wealth. Differently though, a significant, and often neglected, aspect of diets across sub-Saharan Africa is the ubiquitous presence of packaged and processed foods, such as snacks, soft drinks and cooking stocks. Consumption of these foods is high across the board, peaking among the middle wealth groups, a finding that emerged clearly in the Ghana study. Poorer people have aspirations for these foods and do purchase them, when they can afford them. Thus, it is clear that the expansion of capital in food production is driving dietary transformations, with the rise of multinational food corporations shaping diets in globalised food systems.

In *Capital*, Marx discusses the living conditions of the working class in the context of the law of capitalist accumulation, thus he links poor diets with the regime of capital accumulation that depletes the working and living conditions of the labouring class through the creation of the surplus labouring population. In doing so, Marx puts forward an understanding of diets that is embedded in trajectories of capitalist development and the configurations of labour regimes. This approach provides the foundations for reintegrating the study of diets and nutrition into the social sciences, so as to explore the socio-economic, political and historical determinants of dietary change and food inequalities. However, developing a contemporary political economy of nutrition requires engaging in primary data collection to generate detailed and accurate evidence on food practices and then to triangulate different data sources to articulate a multilevel analysis that can bridge micro–macro divides. It is necessary to consolidate thorough analyses of food consumption and nutrition data in the frame of organisation of everyday life practices, concentration of capital in agrifood systems and systems of production, distribution and trade, and map the mechanisms through which these processes come to shape what food is available, how it sourced and consumed.

## References

Bernstein, H. 2010. *Class Dynamics of Agrarian Change*. Halifax: Fernwood.

————. 2016. 'Agrarian political economy and modern world capitalism: The contributions of food regime analysis'. *Journal of Peasant Studies* 43(3): 611–47.

Cousins, B., D. Weiner and N. Amin. 1992. 'Social differentiation in the communal lands of Zimbabwe'. *Review of African Political Economy* 19(53): 5–24.

Demographic Health Survey. 2011. *Moçambique Inquérito Demográfico e de Saúde 2011*. Calverton, MD: Ministerio da Saude; Instituto Nacional de Estatística; ICF International.

Farfan, G., M. E. Genoni and R. Vakis. 2015. 'You are what (and where) you eat: Capturing food away from home in welfare measures'. World Bank Policy Research Working Paper No. 7257.

Fine, B. 2002. *The World of Consumption. The Material and Cultural Revisited*. London: Routledge.

————. 2007. 'From sweetness to McDonald's: How do we manufacture (the meaning of) foods?' *Review of Social & Economic Studies* 29(2): 247–71.

Fine, B., M. Heasman and J. Wright. 1998. 'What we eat and why: A socioeconomic approach to standard items in food consumption'. In A. Murcott (ed.), *The Nation's Diet: The Social Science of Food Choice*, pp. 95–111. London: Longman.

Foster, J. B. 2016. 'Marx as a food theorist'. *Monthly Review* 68(7): 1–22.

Freidberg, S. 2003. 'French beans for the masses: A modern historical geography of food in Burkina Faso', *Journal of Historical Geography* 29(3): 445–63.

————. 2007. 'Supermarkets and imperial knowledge'. *Cultural Geographies* 14(3): 321–42.

Friedmann, H. and P. McMichael. 1989. 'Agriculture and the state system: The rise and decline of national agricultures, 1870 to the present'. *Sociologia ruralis* 29(2): 93–117.

Jaspars, S., T. Scott-Smith and E. Hull. 2018. 'Contested evolution of nutrition for humanitarian and development ends'. Report of an international workshop.

Lentz, C. 2015. 'Elites or middle classes? Lessons from transnational research for the study of social stratification in Africa'. Working Paper of the Department of Anthropology and African Studies No. 161. Mainz: Johannes Gutenberg Universität.

Marx, K. 1887. *Capital. A Critique of Political Economy*. First English edition. Moscow: Progress.

Melber, H. 2017. 'The African middle class(es): In the middle of what?' *Review of African Political Economy* 44(151): 142–54.

MICS. 2008. *Multiple Indicator Cluster Survey (MICS) 2008*. Maputo: Instituto Nacional de Estatística.

O'Laughlin, B. 1996. 'Through a divided glass: Dualism, class and the agrarian question in Mozambique'. *Journal of Peasant Studies* 23(4): 1–39.

————. 2002. 'Proletarianisation, agency and changing rural livelihoods: Forced labour and resistance in colonial Mozambique'. *Journal of Southern African Studies* 28(3): 511–30.

————. 2013. 'Land, labour and the production of affliction in rural southern Africa'. *Journal of Agrarian Change* 13(1): 175–96.

Oya, C. 2004. 'The empirical investigation of rural class formation: Methodological issues in a study of large- and mid-scale farmers in Senegal'. *Historical Materialism* 12(4): 289–326.

Peters, P. E. 2004. 'Inequality and social conflict over land in Africa'. *Journal of Agrarian Change* 4(3): 269–314.

Ruel, M. T. 2002. 'Is dietary diversity an indicator of food security or dietary quality? A review of measurement issues and research needs'. FCND Discussion Paper 140. Washington, DC: International Food Policy Research Institute.

Sathyamala, C. 2016. 'Nutritionalizing food: A framework for capital accumulation'. *Development and Change* 47(4): 818–39.

Stevano, S. 2019. 'The limits of instrumentalism: Informal work and gendered cycles of food insecurity in Mozambique'. *Journal of Development Studies* 55(1): 83–98.

Street, A. 2015. 'Food as pharma: Marketing nutraceuticals to India's rural poor'. *Critical Public Health* 25(3): 361–72.

Swindale, A. and P. Bilinsky. 2006. *Household Dietary Diversity Score (HDDS) for Measurement of Household Food Access: Indicator Guide*. Washington, DC: Food and Nutrition Technical Assistance Project.

WHO. 2012. *Global School-Based Student Health Survey. Junior High Schools Report.* World Health Organisation.

Winson, A. 2013. *The Industrial Diet. The Degradation of Food and the Struggle for Healthy Eating.* New York: New York University Press.

World Food Programme. 2010. *Comprehensive Food Security and Vulnerability Analysis, Republic of Mozambique.* Maputo: World Food Programme.

# Chapter Fourteen

# MARX IN UTERO

## A WORKERS' INQUIRY OF THE IN/VISIBLE LABOURS OF REPRODUCTION IN THE SURROGACY INDUSTRY

### Sigrid Vertommen

**Abstract**

What can the work of Marx tell us about surrogacy and vice versa; what can the work of surrogacy tell us about Marx? My research on commercial surrogacy in Georgia offers an interesting case study to reassess the relevance of Marxist research frameworks, as it uncomfortably disrupts capitalist dualisms of production versus reproduction, family versus market, gift versus commodity and waged versus unwaged work. Today, Georgian surrogates are paid for putting their reproductive biologies and gestational bodies to work in the (re)production of babies, family happiness and surplus value in the surrogacy industry. Yet, neither in classic political economy accounts nor in its Marxist counterpart are they seen as 'real' workers. On the contrary, surrogates and their 'labour of love' are made invisible and relegated to the hidden abodes of reproduction. In this chapter I use the work of Marx and his disobedient feminist 'granddaughters' to analyse and politically translate the invisibility of reproductive work in the global surrogacy industry.

## Marx and the (Re)production of Material Life

*The first premise of all human existence and, therefore, of all history, [is that humans] must be in a position to live in order to be able to make history. But life involves before everything else eating and drinking, a habitation, clothing and many other things. The first historical act is thus the production of the means to satisfy these needs, the production of material life itself. (Marx and Engels [1845] 1987)*

I conduct research on the political economy of assisted reproductive technologies (ARTs), at the crossroads of ongoing histories of (settler)colonialism and (bio)capitalism. Over the past years, I have been focusing on mapping the booming transnational surrogacy chain between Israel/Palestine and Georgia. I follow the reproductive trail of infertile Israeli couples and their fertility brokers who are increasingly traveling to Georgia where they hope to recruit affordable surrogates who can make their dreams of genetic parenthood come true.

I hear the reader thinking: why on earth would Marx be relevant for studying contemporary processes of baby- and family-making? How can the work of the bearded
old man from Trier – who spent most of his intellectual/political life thinking, reading
and writing about the horrors of industrial capitalism – inform our analysis of surrogacy and assisted reproduction? Marx himself – unlike his comrade in crime, Friedrich
Engels – has not written that much on the biological reproduction of life and the gendered role of the (nuclear) family under capitalism (Hartsock 1983; Hartman 1986;
Federici 2018).[1] Particularly in his magnum opus *Capital*, he remained conspicuously
silent on the workings of gender and reproduction in the circuit of commodity production. If Marx were to live now, it is unlikely that he would know his way around
the fertility clinic or the surrogacy agency. As a father of eight children (seven children
with his wife Jenny Von Westphalen and one with their lifelong housekeeper and friend
Helene Demuth[2]), it is even more unlikely that he would have needed to. Yet, in my
qualitative research on transnational surrogacy, Marx has proven to be a fertile source
of inspiration, especially through the work of his disobedient granddaughters, that is,
Marxist and autonomist feminists such as Silvia Federici, Maria Mies, Angela Davis,
Ariel Salleh and Kathi Weeks who have examined the value of women's reproductive
work under capitalism. For them, as for me, Marx's work has been an indispensable
yet insufficient tool for understanding and overcoming gendered forms of exploitation
under capitalism.

To his praise, Marx's historical materialist approach has assisted me in understanding
reproduction not merely as a cultural *or* biological matter but as a *material relation* that
*dialectically* takes shape in and through its 'intra-actions' (not interactions) with capital,
nature/biology and labour (Barad 2007; Brown 2013; Moore 2015; Battistoni 2017;
Lewis 2019). As the opening quote from *The German Ideology* (1987) illustrates, Marx's
understanding of 'material life' was not rooted in the binarization of biology versus
society or nature versus nurture, as is often presumed. Instead, he viewed these apparent
dualisms as *dialectical* moments of the whole, which are always historically situated and
mediated through *labour*, a key insight for (some) Marxists. Marx went on to explain in
*Capital, Volume I* (2013: 120):

> Labour is, in the first place, a process in which both man [*sic*] and Nature participate, and
> in which man, through his own actions, mediates, regulates and controls the metabolism
> between himself and nature. He opposes himself to Nature as one of her own forces, setting

---

[1]  In her recent book, Heather Brown (2013) posited that Marx has developed important insights
    on gender, feminism and the family (most crucially through his dialectic method) scattered
    throughout his work, although it 'occasionally evinced signs of Victorian morality'.

[2]  Although most sources confirm that Marx was indeed the father of Helen Demuth's illegit-
    imate baby, it remains a contentious issue. It is certain, though, that soon after his birth the
    boy, who was named Frederick after Friedrich Engels, was placed with a working foster family
    in London (Wheen 2001). I thank Noëmi Willemen for pointing out this detail, which seems
    relevant in a book chapter on the invisible labours of reproduction.

in motion arms and legs, head and hands, the natural forces of his body, in order to appro-priate Nature's productions in a form adapted to his own wants.

Unfortunately, Marx's understanding of labour under capitalism has always been a rather productictivist one, referring to the waged work of the industrial worker who produced com-modities for the market and not to the unwaged work of the housewife's who reproduced life in the household. As Maria Mies (2014: 46) poignantly remarked in her ecofeminist critique of capitalist patriarchy:

> The instruments of wage labour are the hands and the head but never the womb or the breasts of a woman. Thus, not only are men and women differently defined in their interaction with nature, but the human body itself is divided into truly human parts (head and hand) and natural or purely animal parts (genitalia, womb).

Surrogacy is an interesting case study to re-assess the relevance of Marxist research frameworks in explaining how the world works, as it uncomfortably disrupts capitalist categorizations of production and reproduction, family and market, waged and unwaged work. Today, Georgian surrogates are paid for putting their reproductive biologies and gestational bodies to work in the (re)production of babies, family happiness and surplus value in the surrogacy industry. Yet, neither in classic political economy accounts nor in its Marxist counterpart, are they seen as 'real' workers. On the contrary, their work is made invisible and relegated to the hidden abodes of reproduction. Before further unpacking how I started from Marx to look beyond Marx in analysing and politically translating the invisible labours of reproduction in the global surrogacy industry, let me first position my work within the existing scholarship on surrogacy.

## State of the ART: Towards a Workers' Inquiry of Surrogacy

Gestational surrogacy is a reproductive practice in which a woman gestates an embryo and delivers a baby for intended parent(s) with infertility issues. First, the embryos are created in the lab through in vitro fertilization, a technology that fertilizes the oocytes from an intended mother or egg cell donor with the sperm from an intended father or sperm donor. The embryo(s) are then transferred to the uterus of the surrogate, who is hormonally prepared to gestate the foetus and eventually birth the baby (Vora 2019).

Over the past two decades gestational surrogacy has transformed from a rather small-scale intimate practice into a booming transnational industry in which women started commodifying their reproductive bodies, biologies and capacities by working as surrogates and egg cell providers. According to recent studies, the global fertility market is estimated to reach between US$36–40 billion in revenue by 2026, with commercial surrogacy being one of its most lucrative services (Frost and Sullivan 2019; Kowitt 2020). In several states in the United States, Canada, Israel and India it has developed into a flourishing 'baby business' involving various actors and stakeholders such as surrogacy agencies, fertility clinics, genetic counsellors, law firms specialized in family and migra-tion law, shipping and logistics companies, hospitality services (hotels, restaurants, tourist industry) and, of course, a global army of reproductive workers including egg vendors and surrogate carriers but also nurses, nannies and drivers (Vertommen and Barbagallo, under review).[3]

As an increasingly popular and evocative fertility procedure, surrogacy has drawn plenty of scholarly attention across disciplines over the past decades. This has resulted in an ever-growing and fascinating body of work, in which Marx, however, remains largely absent. Much of the early anthropological research focused on how surrogacy is organized in specific national and cultural settings. It also addressed how surrogacy enabled the emergence of new family and kinship structures and novel parental identities and subjectivities, such as gay dads and surro-moms (Ragoné 1994; Teman 2010). Other research approached surrogacy from a bioethical or legal stance, discussing whether surrogacy is a morally acceptable reproductive practice, and whether it should be regulated through a gift regime (altruistic surrogacy) or through a market regime (commercial surrogacy) (Shalev 1991; Shenfield et al. 2005).

What was still missing, though, was a broader political economy analysis of how surrogacy was integrated into a capitalist 'bioeconomy', structured around the global flow of reproductive tissues, technologies, workers, mediators, investors and consumers. Recently, feminist and science and technology studies scholars began studying the incorporation of reproductive processes, bodies, data and practices in capitalist projects of commodification and rent-making (Franklin and Lock 2003; Rajan 2006; Helmreich 2008; Birch and Tyfield 2013; Cooper and Waldby 2014; Pavone and Goven 2017; Van de Wiel 2018). While some scholars emphasized the competitive advantage of techno-scientific innovations (from test tubes to automated biobags) as sources of valorization and others foregrounded the growing importance of rent and assets (via intellectual property monopolies), I call on Marx to shift our attention again to the *regimes of labour* that are at the heart of processes of valorization in the fertility industry. In advancing a workers' inquiry of surrogacy, I have prioritized different kinds of questions on who does what kind of work in the fertility industry. How are these divisions of labour gendered, racialized and classed? Which activities and services are considered as work? And how are these paid and valued?[4]

Notably, a workers' inquiry is a method that was developed by Marx and later picked up by Marxists such as C. L. R. James and Selma James, Raya Dunayevskaya, Grace Lee Boggs, Claude Lefort and Mario Tronti to assess the labour conditions of the working class.[5] The idea behind a workers' inquiry is that workers are not passive subjects to

---

[3]  In the United States with fertility power par excellence, the market for infertility services and technologies is expected to grow from approximately $6 billion in 2019 to $8 billion in 2023. In China, revenues could double to over $7 billion by 2023 (Frost and Sullivan 2019).

[4]  I got inspired to rethink surrogacy/mothering through the methodological lens of a workers' inquiry and, vice versa, to rethink workers' inquiries through the lens of surrogacy/mothering during a talk with Camille Barbagallo, Jamie Woodcock and Eoin O'Cearnaigh on contemporary workers' inquiries at May Day Rooms in September 2017.

[5]  For a comprehensive account of the theoretical and methodological genealogies of workers' inquiries, see Haider and Mohandesi, *Viewpoint Magazine*, 27 September 2013, https://www.viewpointmag.com/2013/09/27/workers-inquiry-a-genealogy/ (accessed 8 February 2020).

be researched, but the most pivotal and best situated actors in describing and thus transforming their own conditions (Marx 1880; James 1972; Woodcock 2017). As Marx (1880: 636, quoted in Haider and Mohandesi 2013) stated: 'It is the workers in town and country alone [who] can describe with full knowledge the misfortunes from which they suffer.' Following in the footsteps of feminist scholars like Sharmila Rudrappa (2015), Amrita Pande (2014), Kalindi Vora (2015), Michal Nahman (2013) and Sophie Lewis (2019), my research uses the experiences and perspectives of surrogates on their paid and unpaid reproductive work, as a lens to understand broader capitalist processes.

## The Hidden Abodes of (Re)production

*You must never regard cleanliness and order as something secondary, for health and cheerfulness depend upon them. Insist strictly that your rooms are scrubbed frequently and fix a definite time for it – and you, my dear Karl, have a weekly scrub with sponge and soap. (Letter from Henriette Pressburg to her son Karl Marx, 1836)*

For many Marxists labour is the pivotal entry point into a materialist analysis of the capitalist world economy (Weeks 2011). It is seen as the 'father of all wealth' and the 'secret of profit-making' (Marx 2013). When Marx wrote *Capital* in 1867, it was meant as a critique of bourgeois political economy that viewed market-based exchange between buyers and sellers of commodities as the central motor of capitalist value creation. In his quest to explain how capitalism actually operated, Marx followed an inspiring method that has also been useful in my own research. He always started from things that were *visible*, such as commodities – or in my case, a healthy surrogacy babies – and then moved to the 'hidden' social relations that had to be revealed or made visible through scientific research.

In a much-cited passage in *Capital, Volume I* on the buying and selling of that 'peculiar' commodity labour power, Marx (2013: 118–19) described how on the marketplace 'the very Eden of innate rights', the owner of money and the owner of labour power appear as equals who exchange money for labour power. Yet, in order to reveal how and where capitalist valorization takes place, Marx invites us to leave the site of the analysis from market-based exchange to wage-based production. He (2013: 118–19) wrote:

> Let us therefore, in company with the owner of money and the owner of labourpower, leave this noisy sphere, where everything takes place on the surface and in full view of everyone, and follow them into the hidden abode of production, on whose threshold there hangs the notice 'No admittance except on business'. Here we shall see, not only how capital produces, but how capital is produced. The secret of profit-making must at last be laid bare.

According to Kathi Weeks (2011: 6), what Marx accomplished by altering the focus of the study and descending into the hidden abode of production is to publicize the realm of waged work and to expose it as the 'lifeblood' of capitalist production rather than a 'peripheral byproduct or natural precursor'. Once we arrive in the realm of production,

---

For a contemporary take on precarious workers' inquiries, see the *Notes from Below* collective and journal https://notesfrombelow.org/ (accessed 8 February 2020).

Marx (2013: 119) noted a 'change in physiognomy of our dramatis personae'. They didn't appear as equals anymore.

> He, who before was the money-owner, now strides in front as capitalist; the possessor of labour-power follows as his labourer. The one with an air of importance, smirking, intent on business; the other, timid and holding back, like one who is bringing his own hide to market and has nothing to expect but – a hiding.

Since the 1970s Marxist and autonomist feminists have been critiquing classic Marxian frameworks for not paying enough attention to all the nurturing, caring, emotional, reproductive labour that is required for producing that special commodity labour power (Dallacosta and James 1972; Federici 1975; Davis 1981; Vogel 1983; Fraser 2014; Bhattacharya 2017, Mezzadri 2019; Ferguson 2019). They argued that the vital work of keeping the worker alive and reproducing the next generation of workers is mostly performed in unwaged capacity by women at home or in the community. These feminists have pushed the analysis of capitalist modes of production from the factory to the kitchens and the bedrooms, revealing a whole realm of gendered exploitation and oppression that remained invisible in Marx(ism): domestic work, mothering, sex and reproduction (Barbagallo and Federici 2012; Curcio 2020).

In her plea for a feminist historical materialism, Nancy Hartsock (1983) took on board Marx's suggestion to follow the worker from the marketplace to the workplace, but she pushed his argument further. She proposed to follow the worker into the even more hidden abode of reproduction, the homeplace, where according to Hartsock (1983: 234) another change occurs in the dramatis personae.

> He, who before followed behind as the worker, timid and holding back, with nothing to expect but a hiding, now strides in front, while a third person, not specifically present in Marx's account of the transactions between capitalist and worker (both of whom are male) follows timidly behind, carrying groceries, baby, and diapers.

Yet, for Marx, what women did when they were birthing, changing diapers, cleaning, cooking and having sex was not so much work, but part of nature and therefore taken for granted. Acknowledging that labour was not the only source of wealth creation under capitalism, Marx (2013: 23) cited William Petty in *Capital* to clarify its gendered differentiations when writing that 'labour is the father [of wealth] and the earth its mother'. Social reproduction was at best considered as a component of primitive accumulation, but never as a source of surplus value in and of itself.

Today, much of the domestic housework that was once performed by slaves as forced labour or by housewives as 'a labour of love' is now incontestably paid labour. Increasingly, reproductive labour has been commodified into 'an immediate point of accumulation' that can be bought and sold on the labour market (Federici 2012: 112). However, as the case of surrogacy clearly demonstrates, the social conditions under which reproductive work is performed on the market remain as pernicious as ever. It is precarious, undervalued, invisible, often criminalized work, that is still not viewed as 'real work'. During my fieldwork research on surrogacy in Georgia, I used Marx to go beyond Marx, in exploring the invisible labours of reproduction.

## The Invisible Wombs of the Market: Housewifization of Georgian Surrogates

A recent report by UN Women (2018) investigated the causes of Georgian women's 'economic inactivity' and their high levels of informal employment. According to the UN statistics only 50 per cent of the Georgian women participate in the labour force, and half of them are employed in the informal sector. The study clarified that Georgian women face a gender pay gap of more than 40 per cent on the formal labour market and spend on average 45 hours per week on unpaid care work at home (compared to only 15 hours for men) with no affordable childcare services available. The report concluded that these obstacles should be removed *in order to* economically activate Georgian women on the labour market.

One of these supposedly 'economically inactive' women, was Elena,[6] a single mother from Tbilisi who was eight months far in her surrogacy pregnancy when we first met. Like thousands of other women, Elena was trying to make a living in Georgia's fractured economy by carrying a baby for a foreign couple. Elena explained that she would have to work three years as a laboratory assistant to earn the same amount – US$15,000 – as she does now while 'doing nothing, except for being pregnant' (interview with Vertommen, Tbilisi, 21 June 2018).[7] 'Being' a surrogate also allowed Elena to stay at home with her 2-year-old son, as she could not afford to pay for childcare when she worked outside of the house.

Surrogacy is legal in Georgia, but it is not considered as work. Elena signed a surrogacy contract with the commissioning parents to officialize the agreement. Yet, this was not a labour contract that was regulated by the Georgian labour code. Although Elena was paid for her gestational services, she was not given a salary or a wage, but rather a fee or financial compensation. If something were to happen to her during the procedure, this would not count as a work accident, but as an ordinary health issue. Furthermore, when interviewing her surrogacy agent, it was remarkable how the language of donation and altruism was used to promote fertility services, even though surrogacy has undeniably transformed into a commercial industry. Elena was not recruited as a gestational worker, but as a gift-giving angel (see extract from an interview held in Tbilisi, 12 May 2018):

**Agent:** The whole procedure costs 30.000 dollar, 36.000 with egg donation. The agency fee is 4.500 dollars, the whole process from the start until the end, the

---

[6]   The arguments developed in this section have been further developed in an article I have written with Camille Barbagallo on 'Invisible wombs of the market: The dialectics of waged and unwaged reproductive labour in the global surrogacy industry', currently under revision.

[7]   In 2018, the average annual income for women was US$1.830 (GEL 4.517) compared to US$3.110 for men, suggesting a pay gap of 41 per cent (UN Women 2018).

surrogate gets 15.000 dollars, during the pregnancy she gets 400 dollar per month and then 11.400 after delivery, the egg donor gets 1000 dollar.

**Me:** Is the money for the surrogate considered as a salary?

**Agent:** No, it's seen as a compensation.

**Me:** So, it's not seen as a job?

**Agent:** No, it's like a financial help from the parents in return of their gift.

When asking Elena whether she considered surrogacy to be her work, she resolutely answered 'no' (interview, Tbilisi, 21 June 2018). Despite all the physical and emotional labour involved in gestating the foetus and the time she spent on medical appointments and skype conversations with the intended parents over the past year, she refused to describe surrogacy as her work. She clarified:

> Pregnancy is an automatic thing; it's just happening on its own. I am just being a mother and a housewife, and I am doing this because I desperately need the money.

Nargiza, another surrogate who was in the sixth month of surrogacy pregnancy when I interviewed her, got visibly annoyed when I asked her whether she considered surrogacy as her work (interview, Tbilisi, 2 June 2018). She replied:

**Nargiza:** Have you ever been pregnant?

**Me:** Not really

**Nargiza:** That's why you are asking this question. We can return to this discussion after you have had a baby (laughing). You need to go through pregnancy to understand it. Pregnancy is just a state that you are in. It's not a good or a bad job. it's not a job. I chose to be a surrogate because I need to be a good mother. The wellbeing of my daughter means everything for me.

'Being' a good mother was not only an important reason for Elena and Nargiza to become surrogates, but it was also a crucial requirement. Elena's surrogacy agent explained that only women who have already birthed their own children were accepted to become surrogates as this diminishes the chances of a scenario in which the surrogate would want to keep the surrogacy baby after birth (interview, Tbilisi, 12 May 2018). It also provides proof of the optimal functioning of their reproductive biologies and gestational bodies. While the work of motherhood is the condition of surrogacy's possibility in Georgia, the fertility sector merely treats it as an unpaid internship.[8] Similarly, while the Georgian surrogacy industry is highly dependent on the closely intertwined and mutually formative work of motherhood, pregnancy and surrogacy, for Elena and Nargiza both the unwaged reproductive work of mothering and the paid reproductive work of gestating were viewed as a natural state of being, rather than a performative state of labouring.

---

[8]  Thanks to Camille Barbagallo for this insightful comment.

To make sense of this dialectal relation between the unseen work of motherhood and surrogacy, Marx's insights have been useful but not sufficient. For this, I turned to the work of scholars like Jason Moore (2015), Kalindi Vora (2015), Sophie Lewis (2019) and Maria Mies (2014) who have provided sharp analyses of the historical value of unpaid work of women, slaves, colonized peoples and nature under capitalism. In her research on Indian women's involvement in lace making, Mies (1982: 110) introduced the concept of 'housewifization' to explain that despite their full incorporation into a capitalist export-oriented production system as wage labourers, 'the lace makers' integration was premised on their self-understanding as housewives'. In her later work Mies (2014: 116) clarified that 'women are the optimal labour force because they are universally defined as housewives, not as workers'. Similarly, I argue that profitability in the fertility industry largely depends on the housewifization of Georgian surrogates. From this perspective, the work of surrogacy is highly exploitative, badly paid and suffers from poor labour conditions, precisely because the work of pregnancy and motherhood is not recognized and valued as work at all. As Moore (2015: 54) succinctly puts is: 'Value does not work, unless most work is not valued.'

This housewifization of surrogates is even further enhanced by the fact that they perform their gestational labour alone 'at home'. Surrogacy is taboo in Georgian society, and surrogates are often judged for presumably 'selling their own children'. Contrary to Indian surrogates who were grouped together by the fertility agencies in so called surrogacy hotels to avoid stigmatization in their home communities, Georgian surrogates remain isolated, divided and invisible in the homeplace. Not even their own homeplace, but a new home, where they feel safe from moral judgements.

Every time I met Elena, for instance, it was in the new flat she moved into during the seventh month of her pregnancy, to avoid gossip from her neighbours. Even when I interviewed her during the day, the curtains of the apartment would be closed, and she wore baggy clothes in order to hide her bump. Nargiza quit her job as a barista once she became a surrogate, because she did not want her colleagues to know about it. She continued to wear a wedding ring when leaving the house, although she had been divorced for many years. 'To avoid nasty comments by strangers,' she said (interview, Tbilisi, 23 May 2018).

## Seizing the Means of Reproduction: Between Theory and Praxis

*Wages for housework is only the beginning, but its message is clear: from now on they have to pay us because as females we do not guarantee anything any longer. We want to call work what is work so that eventually we might rediscover what is love and create what will be our sexuality which we have never known. We are housemaids, prostitutes, nurses, shrinks [...] From now on we want money for each moment of it, so we can refuse some of it and eventually all of it. (Federici 1975)*

There are methodological, ethical and political challenges in conducting a workers' inquiry of a job that is not considered as 'real' work', in a workplace that is not perceived as a 'real' site of labour, with participants who do not identify as 'real' workers. As with Selma James's (1972) workers' inquiry of housewives, this also became apparent during my fieldwork with surrogates in Georgia when discussing the 'appropriateness' of a labour perspective on surrogacy/motherhood. This struggle between appearance and reality, falsehood and authenticity is precisely one of the main theoretical arguments I develop, that is, that the work of reproduction is naturalized, made invisible and therefore devalued, not only by the bosses, but also by 'the mother workers'.

On the one hand, this invisibility is tactically deployed by Georgian surrogates to remain under the radar; to avoid being seen and shamed by nosey neighbours, to circumvent taxation by the state and to protect themselves against the surveillance of pushy commissioning parents or surrogacy agents. On the other hand, this invisibility is enforced on them and one of the structural reasons why surrogates, like prostitutes, mothers and other reproductive workers, do not easily identify and organize as workers. There are no unions or cooperatives of surrogates where Georgian surrogates are seizing their means of reproduction. This *refusal* of workers' consciousness and identity has in turn deepened processes and practices of exploitation in the fertility industry. Georgian surrogates remain absent on birth certificate of the baby. They are not allowed to decide about the number of embryos that are transferred to their wombs, how to give birth, whether to breastfeed or to perform an embryo reduction or abortion. This is decided by the commissioning parents and the fertility agents and doctors. They also miss out on collective negotiating power over their wages, health and life insurance and so on. Marx (2013: 355) once wrote that 'it is not a piece of luck to be a productive labourer, but rather a misfortune'. True, but it surely does help to be identified and to identify as one. Therefore, more workers' inquiries of/by paid and unpaid reproductive workers (sex workers, mothers, fathers, egg cell providers, housewives, altruistic surrogates, commercial surrogates, nurses, teachers, midwives, cleaners and so on) could help us, on the one hand, rethink crucial Marxist terms such as value, class (composition), the working day, the work floor and, on the other hand, reimagine crucial Marxist organizing tactics such as the strike, the union, the party and so on.

It is through Marxist and autonomist feminist perspectives on capitalist valorization, that I have come to understand both surrogacy and motherhood as work. This body of work helped me to examine the dialectical relation between paid and unpaid reproductive labour that is required in the (re)production of babies and profit. This is contrary to what UN Women, the Georgian state, the fertility industry and many surrogates themselves claim. For them surrogacy does not count as work, and, as Jason Moore (2015) rightfully remarked, this is precisely how capitalists get rich, by not paying their bills and devaluing most work.

The most important lesson that I take from Marx is that we need to understand how capitalism works in order to overcome it, and that we need to develop the necessary conceptual tools to understand the world in order to change it. This is a double process of 'creative destruction'. First, it means that we must be fierce and radical in our critiques of capitalist society and bourgeois knowledge production. But critical deconstruction is only the first step of this process of creative destruction and often the easiest one for academics who are taught to build ivory towered careers by critiquing the work of others. What is too often forgotten, though, is the second step, that is, the need to be generous and generative in what we offer in return. The intellectual ammunition we co-create should ultimately make sense in the lives of the people we study. Marx himself has dedicated his life to critiquing bourgeois political economy by uncovering wage-based production as the driving force of capitalism. This analysis has enabled people who are selling their labour power to make sense of their role and power as workers and to ultimately change the conditions under which they are building their lives and making history.

Despite disagreeing with Marx on notions of what constitutes 'productive work', Marxist and autonomist feminists have done much of that inspiring work of 'creative destruction'. They have uncovered how capitalism appropriates processes and practices of reproduction by externalizing and naturalizing it. This feminist insistence on the denaturalization of reproduction has been uncomfortable for many people, including working-class housewives and mothers. For many women it was and is still shocking to frame love as unwaged work, or to ask money for every smile they are asked to give, as the opening paragraph of the *Wages for Housework* manifesto suggests them to do. Yet, this provocation has been generative for introducing reproductive labour as an organizing principle. This has enabled me, for instance, to see the (dis)continuities between the work struggles of Georgian surrogates, outsourced cleaners at my university and disenfranchised sex workers and mothers in London who are the driving force behind the Women's Strike Assembly in London. There are no doubt limits to a labour perspective on surrogacy and other reproductive practices and processes, as Susan Himmelweit (1995), Kalindi Vora (2012) and Kathi Weeks (2011) have poignantly argued, albeit from different angles. Yet, the reproductive labour perspective has made it possible to forge comradely practices of solidarity between groups of people who have been excluded in malestream political economy accounts from being seen and from seeing themselves as political subjects.

## Acknowledgements

The research behind this essay is funded by the Belgian Fund for Scientific Research (FWO) via a postdoctoral fellowship on 'Global fertility chains: A feminist political economy of outsourced reproduction from Israel to Ukraine and Georgia'. I am grateful to my research participants in Georgia and Israel/Palestine, to my Women's Strike comrades in London and Ghent and to my former ReproSoc colleagues at the University of Cambridge for showing me what it means to put reproduction centre stage. I would also like to thank Alessandra Mezzadri for sharing her valuable notes and thoughts on Marx and *Capital* with me.

## References

Barad, K. 2007. *Meeting the Universe Halfway: Quantum Physics and the Entanglement of Matter and Meaning.* Durham: Duke University Press.
Barbagallo, C. and S. Federici. 2012. 'Care work and the commons'. *Commoner* 15.
Battistoni, A. 2017. 'Bringing in the work of nature: From natural capital to hybrid labor'. *Political Theory* 45(1): 5–31.
Bhattacharya, T. 2017. *Social Reproduction Theory: Remapping Class, Recentering Oppression.* London: Pluto.
Birch, K. and D. Tyfield. 2013. 'Theorizing the bioeconomy: Biovalue, biocapital, bioeconomics or … what?' *Science, Technology and Human Values* 38(3): 299–327.

Brown, H. 2013. *Marx on Gender and the Family: A Critical Study*. London: Haymarket.

Cooper, M. and C. Waldby. 2014. *Clinical Labour: Tissue Donors and Research Subjects in the Global Bioeconomy*. Durham, NC: Duke University Press.

Curcio, A. 2020. 'Marxist feminism of rupture'. *Viewpoint Magazine*, 14 January, https://www.viewpointmag.com/2020/01/14/marxist-feminism-of-rupture/ (accessed 4 February 2020).

Dalla Costa, M. and S. James. 1972. *The Power of Women and the Subversion of the Community*. New York: Pétroleuse.

Davis, A. 1981. *Women, Race and Class*. London: Women's Press.

Engels, F. [1891] 1972. *The Origins of the Family, Private Property and the State*. London: Penguin Classics.

Federici, S. 1975. *Wages against Housework*. Bristol: Power of Women Collective and Falling Wall.

———. 2012. *Revolution at Point Zero: Housework, Reproduction, and Feminist Struggle*. Oakland: PM Press.

———. 2018. 'Marx and feminism', *Triple C* 16(2): 468–75.

Ferguson, S. 2019. *Women and Work: Feminism, Labour and Social Reproduction*. London: Pluto.

Franklin, S. and M. Lock. 2003. *Remaking Life & Death: Toward an Anthropology of the Biosciences*. Sante Fe: Sar Press.

Fraser, N. 2014. 'Behind Marx's hidden abode'. *New Left Review* 86.

Frost and Sullivan. 2019. 'The fertility business is booming'. *Economist*, 8 August, https://www.economist.com/business/2019/08/08/the-fertility-business-is-booming (accessed 4 February 2020).

Haider, A. and S. Mohandesi. 2013. 'Workers' inquiry: A genealogy'. *Viewpoint Magazine*, 27 September, https://www.viewpointmag.com/2013/09/27/workers-inquiry-a-genealogy/ (accessed 8 February 2020).

Hartman, H. 1986. 'The unhappy marriage of Marxism and feminism: Towards a more progressive union'. In L. Sargent (ed.), *The Unhappy Marriage of Marxism and Feminism: A Debate on Class and Patriarchy*, pp. 1–41. London: Pluto.

Hartsock, C. M. N. 1983. 'The feminist standpoint: Developing the ground for a specifically feminist historical materialism'. In S. Harding and M. B. Hintikka (eds), *Discovering Reality*, pp. 283–310. Dordrecht: Springer.

Helmreich, S. 2008. 'Species of biocapital'. *Science as Culture* 17(4): 1998–2008.

Himmelweit, S. 1995. 'The discovery of "unpaid work": The social consequences of the expansion of "work" '. *Feminist Economics* 1(2): 1–19.

James, S. 1972. 'A woman's place'. In M. D. Costa and S. James (eds), *The Power of Women and the Subversion of the Community*, pp. 58–64. London: Falling Wall .

Kowitt, B. 2020. 'Fertility Inc.: Inside the big business of babymaking', https://fortune.com/longform/fertility-business-femtech-investing-ivf/ (accessed 4 February 2020).

Lewis, S. 2019. *Full Surrogacy Now: Feminism against family*. London: Verso.

Marx, K. 1880. 'Enquête ouvrière and workers' questionnaire'. In *Marx-Engels Collected Works, Volume 24*. New York: International.

———. 2013. *Capital: A Critical Analysis of Capitalist Production*. Ware: Wordsworth Editions.

Marx, K. and F. Engels. [1845] 1987. *The German Ideology*. London: Lawrence and Wishart.

Mezzadri, A. 2019. 'On the value of social reproduction. Informal labour, the majority world and the need for inclusive theories and politics'. *Radical Philosophy* 2(4): 33–41.

Mies, M. 1982. *The Lace Makers of Narsapur: Indian Housewives Produce for the World Market*. London: Zed.

———. [1986] 2014. *Patriarchy and Accumulation of a World Scale: Women in the International Division of Labour*. London: Zed.

Moore, J. 2015. *Capitalism in the Web of Life: Ecology and the Accumulation of Capital*. London: Verso.

Nahman, M. 2013. *Extractions: An Ethnography of Reproductive Tourism*. Hampshire: Palgrave Macmillan.

Pande, A. 2014. *Wombs in Labor: Transnational Commercial Surrogacy in India*. New York: Columbia University Press

Pavone, V. and J. Goven. 2017. *Bioeconomies: Life, Technology, and Capital in the 21st Century*. Cham: Palgrave Macmillan.

Ragoné, H. 1994. *Surrogate Motherhood: Conceptions of the Heart*. Boulder: Westview.

Rajan, K. S. 2006. *Biocapital: The Constitution of Postgenomic Life*. Durham: Duke University Press.

Rudrappa, S. 2015. *Discounted Life: The Price of Global Surrogacy in India*. New York: New York University Press.

Shalev, C. 1991. *Birth Power: The Case for Surrogacy*. New Haven: Yale University Press.

Shenfield, F., G. Pennings, J. Cohen, P. Devroey, G. de Wert and B. Tarlatzis. 2005. 'ESHRE task force on ethics and law 10: Surrogacy'. *Human Reproduction* 20(10): 2705–7.

Teman, E. 2010. *Birthing a Mother: The Surrogate Body and the Pregnant Self*. Berkeley: University of California Press.

UN Women. 2018. *Women's Economic Inactivity and Engagement in the Informal Sector in Georgia: Causes and Consequences*. Tbilisi: UN Women Georgia Office.

Van de Wiel, L. 2018. 'Prenatal imaging: Egg freezing, embryo selection and the visual politics of reproductive time'. *Catalyst* 4(2): 1–35.

Vogel, I. 1983. *Marxism and the Oppression of Women: Toward a Unitary Theory*. New Brunswick: Rutgers University Press.

Vora, K. 2012. 'Limits of labour: Accounting for affect and the biological in transnational surrogacy and service work'. *South Atlantic Quarterly* 111(4): 681–700.

Vora, K. 2015. *Life Support: Biocapital and the New History of Outsourced Labor*. Minneapolis: University of Minnesota Press.

———. 2019. 'After the housewife: Surrogacy, labour and human reproduction'. *Radical Philosophy* 2(4): 42–46.

Weeks, K. 2011. *The Problem with Work: Feminism, Marxism, Antiwork Politics, and Postwork Imaginaries*. London: Duke University Press.

Wheen, F. 2001. *Karl Marx: A Life*. New York: W.W. Norton.

Woodcock, J. 2017. *Working the Phones: Control and Resistance in the Call Centres*. London: Pluto.

# Chapter Fifteen

# MARX, THE CHIEF, THE PRISONER AND THE REFUGEE

Gavin Capps, Genevieve LeBaron and Paolo Novak in
Conversation with Alessandra Mezzadri

**Abstract**

This chapter preliminarily interrogates the potential relevance of Marxian analysis and
methodology for the study of what would appear as 'marginal' categories in the study of
political economy, namely those that are either often (mis)represented as remnants of a pre-
capitalist or a non-capitalist past, or inaccurately theorised in residual or exclusionary terms
vis-à-vis the main working logics of global capitalism. The chapter gathers the reflections of
three scholars of, respectively, South African tribal chieftaincy, prison and forced labour, and
refugees and border studies, on the possibility to deploy Marxian methods and categories
to capture the features of three main figures: the tribal chief, the prisoner and the refugee.
Crucially, in the process of thinking about these figures, which takes the narrative form of a
collective interview, we learn both what Marxian political economy can offer as well as what
are its main methodological shortcomings.

## Introduction by Alessandra Mezzadri

As explained in the general introduction, the contributions included in this volume
explore the potential of bringing *Marx in the Field* through three different lenses. The first
lens implies analysing some key categories and tropes in Marxian analysis that are crucial
for the study of our global present (e.g. Jan, Hanieh). The second lens entails, instead,
exploring how Marxian main categories and concepts may appear concretely in the field,
in ways that may seem fairly distinct – yet analytically and logically compatible – with
those historically sketched by Marx in his work (e.g. Bernstein, Selwyn). Indeed, learning
from Jairus Banaji (2010), when researching and 'doing' political economy, we should
always distinguish logics from history. Finally, the third lens involves an engagement with
actual methods of enquiry – either those deployed by Marx to study, for instance, accumulation and/or exploitation (e.g. Toffanin, Stevano), or those one could deploy today to
produce an analysis consistent with Marx's method (Mtero et al., Harriss-White). In effect,
as we have seen towards the end of this volume, all contributions adopt at least two out of
these three lenses to explore the usefulness of Marx for historical and contemporary field
research. Many, then, also analyse how Marxian analysis could/should be 'contaminated'
with insights from other theoretical traditions (e.g. Mezzadri, Lombardozzi).

Some contributions develop the agenda of *Marx in the Field* with a focus on what can be defined as more 'traditional' objects of enquiry in Marxian analysis, such as accumulation, exploitation, class formation or class struggle. Others, instead, engage with it on the basis of areas of enquiry that have been traditionally far less explored by radical political economy, such as child labour, nutrition, health or surrogacy. This chapter continues mapping some other counterintuitive areas of enquiry for Marxian analysis. In fact, it sketches some of the benefits and perils of adopting Marxian methods of enquiry for the study of categories that have not figured prominently in political economy, but which have been often been portrayed as lying outside or beyond its primary scope. The first category briefly analysed in the chapter is that of the African chieftaincy. In significant parts of the Global South, including in emerging economies, chieftaincies remain a key organisational form of socioeconomic life. Modernist accounts may portray them as symptoms of backwardness and remnants of the past, and Orientalist accounts may romanticise them as enclaves untouched by the logics of capitalist life. However, these realities are instead contemporary, coeval to capitalism and, in fact, often fully integrated into capitalist logics. Can Marx come to the rescue, against these reductionist depictions?

The second category addressed is the prisoner. In effect, studies of labour unfreedom have benefited from an engagement with Marxian analysis (as also argued by Lombardozzi in this volume) – despite critical voices in the debate remain hardly numerous, and liberal (ahistorical) depictions of 'modern slavery' are increasingly taking centre stage (for a critique, see O'Connell Davidson 2015). However, far less studies discuss unfreedom and its link to labour or labouring within contexts of legal coercive institutions. When it comes to the actual wholly unfree subject, namely the prisoner – body locked up in a correctional facility – can Marxian ideas of unfreedom still help guiding the analysis at all, and if yes how?

Finally, the third figure briefly explored here is that of the refugee. Arguably, given its mobility beyond national boundaries and complex legal status, the refugee has often escaped Marxian theorisations in its own right and has instead only been either tangentially or instrumentally addressed by political economy. What are the main features of this instrumentalism, and to what extent can it be overcome? Below, three scholars whose work has focused on these three figures answer three questions each on the possibilities and challenges of bringing Marx – respectively – to meet the chiefs, to visit a prison or in refugee camp. Obviously, given its length and structure, the chapter hardly hopes to map definitive answers. Rather, it aims at initiating a debate to be continued elsewhere and at confirming – once again – the usefulness of interrogating our present through Marx's method, to reveals both its strengths and flaws.

## Marx and the Chiefs: Three Questions to Gavin Capps

***Question 1.*** *There has been a tendency to represent tribal structures and kinship relations in large swathes of the Global South as lying outside the logics of capitalism and hence beyond the reach of the Marxian method of analysis. What are the limits of this approach?*

There are certainly numerous studies which have fallen into this trap. Some may have developed analyses opposed to or aimed at overcoming Marx. Others may not reject Marxist analysis but nonetheless theorise capitalist and kinship/customary structures as separate yet articulated spheres. However, Marx comes to the rescue against such dichotomies. Marx's essence/appearance distinction, in particular (see also Bernstein, this volume) can transcend ideal-typifications of capitalism, either by contemporary opponents of Marx or by some overly schematic Marxist approaches.

For instance, my work has shown the benefits of placing the modern African chieftaincy within Marxism, by developing a category appropriate for its concrete analysis within historical materialism. This ambition was prompted by two reasons. The first was practical and due to the resurgence of the chieftaincy as both a political and economic actor in the context of the new scramble for Africa's natural resources (Bernstein 2014). The second was theoretical and followed the publication of key works that in different ways argued that the chieftaincy (in its combined features of tribal structures and kinship relations) was beyond the conceptual reach of Marx's critique of political economy and hence could not be explained in terms of value relations (e.g. Mamdani 1996; Berry 2018).

Indeed, the key problem of these works was that in their attempt to rightly oppose the ideal-typification of capitalism by orthodox Marxists, they actually embraced it. For them, if within a context capitalism does not appear as it 'should' (or, rather, as 'Marxism' narrowly understood expects it should) then it must be something else – an assumption which itself is associated with various intellectual and political traditions claiming heritage from Marx, most particularly the once-fashionable 'articulation of modes of production' approach, which was dealt its decisive blow by Jairus Banaji (1977) but also Gibbon and Neocosmos (1985).

Yet, Marx draws a critical distinction between the phenomenal forms and essential relations of capitalism, arguing that the former not only systematically obscure the latter, but that they can also assume a variety forms in concrete social formations, which do not necessarily correspond to those deployed by Marx for illustrative purposes in his analysis of capitalism in *Capital*, but can nevertheless be explained by it. Two crucial points follow. First, that Marx deploys a very specific method of abstraction for moving between phenomenal forms and essential relations, a method which rests on establishing the hierarchy of mediations that connect them, mediations that must necessarily vary in each case and therefore which most not only identify the conditions of existence of these phenomena but explain why they assume the specific forms that they do and with what effects. This is where the science is. And this can be found in the structure of *Capital* itself, as earlier assumptions are modified and reworked through the method of 'progressive complication' (or 'dosed abstraction') that runs through the text and which moves us from the fundamental dynamics of capitalism to the forms it assumes on the surface of society (Callinicos 2001: 239).

And second, in any case, Marx himself made no claim that the 'Western' experience of capitalist development would be identically repeated elsewhere and indeed spent the latter part of his life appropriating greater swathes of material about the development of capitalism on a global scale and the diverse forms it was taking. So, the question I had to ask myself was how can we extend the abstract categories of *Capital* to the social form of the modern African chieftaincy, using this method and hence how could or indeed should I develop the appropriate mediations? The answer was to be found in the concrete specifics of my case.

**Question 2.** *Let's get to these specifics. You have studied in-depth the BaFokeng chieftaincy in South Africa. Can you describe the concrete case you analysed, and identify which concepts/passages in Marx were crucial for this analysis?*

The modern chieftaincy, in many parts of Africa, has been largely treated as a symptom of pre-capitalist relations. Some theorisations have highlighted its contemporary features and roles; however, they have tended to see the chieftaincy as a mainly political phenomenon. Its development and exercise of local political power was theorised as an expression of the colonial bifurcated state attempting to resolve 'the native question' (e.g. Mamdani 1996); and its exercise of control over communal land was seen as a form of rent-seeking (Berry 2018).

However, the modern chieftaincy has always exercised also a key economic role – and covered a specific class function in African political economy. In fact, in many instances it covered a compatible role of that of landlordism in relation to the capitalist transformations mapped by Marx. One concept developed by Marx is particularly useful to understand the chieftaincy – that of modern 'landed property' and its monopoly over ground rent. Marx develops this concept in *Capital, Volume III*, although obviously the concept is crucial for its discussion of primitive accumulation in *Volume I* (Marx 1974a).

For Marx, the rise of modern landed property is crucial to the historic genesis of the capital relation, as it operates the separation of producers from the means of production. It is the violent imposition of new property relations effectively 'based on the monopoly of certain persons over the definitive portions of the globe, as exclusive spheres of their private will to the exclusion of others' (Marx 1974b: 615) – that decisively separates the mass of the direct producers ('peasants') from their means of livelihood and hurls them on to the labour market as 'free and "unattached" proletarians' (Marx 1974a: 669) (see Capps 2016: 458).

Now: obviously there are differences between Marx's new capitalist landlords and the African chiefs; however, this difference is phenomenal, not essential. On the other hand, Marx himself would have never expected otherwise, as he clearly writes that 'wage-labour and landed property, like capital, are historically specific social forms; one of labour, and the other of the monopolized earth, both in fact being forms corresponding to the same economic formation of society' (Marx 1991: 954).

The issue is, does the chieftaincy cover a role similar to that of capitalist landlords? The answer is yes, albeit obviously historically the form in which the relation appears is hardly that described by Marx.

Since colonial times the chieftaincy mobilised migrant labour through customary channels for the support of the white settler-colonial productions. In fact, chieftaincies were central to the support and reproduction of the Migrant Labour System, which supported mining across southern Africa (O'Laughlin 1996). It was chiefs who collected the taxes that compelled peasants to produce marketable surpluses or engage in wage labour outside the communal land, or again imposing the cultivation of some crops (forced cropping). They were key brokers of the colonial systems, and the chieftaincy itself was crucial for the reproduction of this process of 'accumulation without dispossession' that represented what Jairus Banaji (2003) would define as the specific 'form of exploitation' characterising many southern African regions. In short, the chieftaincy did not only resolve 'the native question'; it also actively managed 'the labour question' (Capps 2018). As such, chieftaincies should be understood as embedded in value relations, not simply as political rent-seeking agents.

BaFokeng, in particular, should be conceptualised as a 'tribal landed property', that is, a form that internalised, expressed and mediated the contradiction between the imperatives of colonial capitalist accumulation and exploitation in Africa, and the communal landed property relations supposedly embedded in and reproducing customary relations. Compared to other regions, in BaFokeng, the power of the chieftaincy to mediate access to land and control the labour force has not only been based on rent; rather, it has been further complicated by the presence, within the region, of platinum reserves. In other regions, especially gold-rich regions, (white) industrial settler-capital and the 'customary' chieftaincy were spatially separated, the former in key mining areas and the latter in rural areas, together with the cheap labour reserves. In BaFokeng, this spatial separation did not exist, as mining reserves crossed chieftaincy's communal land. Hence, here the chieftaincy could not only claim ground rent for mining extraction, but also mining royalties (Capps 2012a, 2016).

While royalties were initially mediated by the apartheid state, which worked as trustee according to South African law, in the 'New' South Africa the African National Congress (ANC) changed approach with its move to 'Black Economic Empowerment' (BEE). At this point, the BaFokeng chieftaincy, whose royalty fee was forcibly reduced by the apartheid state during a previous confrontation with Impala, the regional platinum company, used the newly established 'BEE agenda' to claim a role as stakeholder in the mining company, de facto using its function as 'tribal landed property' to get a more direct share of surplus value – not merely rents – generated through mining. With the new BEE agenda, ironically, the ANC policy had abolished the rule of 'tribal landed property' in BaFokeng (Capps 2012b), only to turn the chieftaincy into a full-fledged capitalist agent, which soon started diversifying out of its historical dependence on mining, while reconstituting itself as a distinct fraction of newly established black economic elite (Capps and Mnwana 2015).

Notwithstanding the dangers of generalisations, the case of BaFokeng shows that a full range of Marx's categories of political economy may be extended to circumstances where they were previously thought not to apply due to the communal – or better, phenomenal – form of land tenure (Capps 2016, 2018). This entails exciting possibilities to continue deploying Marx for the study of our present.

**Question 3.** *In terms of practical methods of enquiry, how would you describe your approach to data collection, and which lessons would you derive for a future generation of fieldworkers in the twenty-first century?*

As Lenin puts it, historical materialism can only be based on 'the concrete analysis of the concrete situation' (Ali 2017). However, the concrete hardly comes from nowhere; it must also be studied in its historical instantiation. The study of any concrete category must also be historical, to capture the development of the form in motion, its trajectory. Moreover, it must be multidimensional, to capture its many determinations (see Mtero et al. on class, in this volume).

Studying the chieftaincy as the synthesis of many determinations and relations in their historical materialist form, has meant the need to rely on fieldwork methods capable of grasping and exploring these determinations in both their own specific trajectories – allocating them analytical/explanatory weight – as well as in their totality. Hence, I worked on multiple sources and on multiple fronts: archival, historical and field-based. Mostly, in BaFokeng, where I conducted my research for several years, I had to recognised and navigate the complex power relations that structure and pervade fieldwork in highly unequal rural settings (Breman 1985), and this led me to uncover a long history of group land-buying, which, it later transpired, is not only critical to grasp the contemporary politics of the area I explored, but also of similar cases.

In the field, my starting point was that a study of social relations should, in the words of Wendy Olsen (1992: 58), 'examine both sides of each relationship'. In the BaFokeng case, this meant gaining access not only to the tribal administration but also to a range of other actors, organisations and institutions situated at different levels of a complex political economy and locked in shifting relations of conflict and alliance. Moreover, it meant doing so in a fieldwork situation dominated by a highly sophisticated local elite, which was at once aggressively mindful of its public image, alert to the potential power of academic work, and presumptive that I would share its worldview. From the onset, this presented considerable methodological and ethical challenges which had to be politically thought through (Capps 2007).

The actual data collection methods I deployed were fourfold. First, detailed interviews with key informants in each of the main organisations and institutions identified as relevant to the study; second, intensive local level research in a small sample of BaFokeng villages, including through a structured household questionnaire; third, research in the archives of key government departments; and, finally, a quasi-ethnographic commitment to living locally in a BaFokeng village and participating in the community's more politically significant gatherings and events (Capps 2007). It is as a result of all these combined methods of analysis that I managed to bring *Marx in the Field*.

## Marx and the Prisoner: Three Questions for Genevieve LeBaron

**Question 1.** *You have worked extensively on prison labour and labour unfreedom in general. In your view, where does prison labour sits in classic Marxian debates on unfreedom?*

In the contemporary economy, prisoners produce goods ranging from artisanal foods sold in high-end grocery stores to luxury motorcycles. They fight fires, roast coffee beans and build furniture for college and university dorm rooms. Prisoners are sometimes paid just pennies a day, or nothing at all; in some jurisdictions, they are paid minimum wage but the government is allowed to appropriate wages towards covering the costs of incarceration. Prisoners are some of the most vulnerable and unfree workers in the economy, given the extent of control that corrections officers wield over their lives and bodies, given that they are often legally mandated to work with no say over their pay or conditions, and given the serious challenges they face in organising (LeBaron 2015; LeBaron 2018a; LeBaron 2012). Nevertheless, in 2018, prisoners across the United States went on strike, in part to protest the labour conditions they describe as modern-day slavery (cf. Johnson 2018).

Prison labour is often overlooked within debates on forced and unfree labour in the global economy. Broadly speaking, especially where Marxist perspectives are concerned, debates about contemporary unfree labour have tended to focus on unfree labour that takes place within the private economy where workers are being exploited by recruiters, producers and private businesses (LeBaron and Phillips 2019), as well as forms of unfreedom that relate to what is often described as 'deproletarianisation' (Rioux et al. 2019). Where prison labour has been examined, it is often described in relatively generic terms, as an interchangeable form of contemporary slavery motivated by corporations' insatiable demand for a cheap, exploitable workforce (LeBaron 2018a, 2015).

The unique dynamics of unfreedom involved in prison labour, and its unique place within the capitalist economy, warrant more nuanced and extensive investigation. Prison labour is legally possible in the United States because of a loophole in the Thirteenth Amendment to the US constitution which banned slavery and involuntary servitude except 'as a punishment for crime whereof the party shall have been duly convicted' (US National Archives 2019). Unlike private forms of unfree labour, the main architect and beneficiary of prison labour systems is typically the state. In the United States, for instance, the vast majority of prisoners work for the government, including state-level and federal government corporations, as well as towards prison maintenance and facilities work – not for private companies. Even where states loan their prison workforces to corporations, they typically bring in income since companies are often mandated to pay minimum wage (though may receive other benefits that lower their costs of production, ranging from tax cuts, discounted or free space and electricity, and assistance with worker surveillance and management).

Since the early days of US capitalism, prison labour has been used as a tool of social, market, and racial discipline and terror, and to habituate the bodies of prisoners into the dictates of the waged labour market. It has played different roles in different eras and geographies of capitalist development, but across the board, it has been an important tool of state efforts to create and forge capitalist labour markets and push those whose labour is worth the least into reliance on wages. It has always involved complex interplay between race, class, gender and criminal justice status. As such, it doesn't fit neatly into existing Marxist debates on unfreedom. It presents an especially major challenge for those theorists who see unfree labour as incompatible with capitalism (Rioux et al. 2019); these theorists have tended to overlook prison labour rather than confront its widespread usage in some countries across multiple centuries of capitalist development. It's time for that to change.

*Question 2. In the concrete study of the what first Angela Davis and then Ruth Wilson Gilmore (2007[BIB-028]) have called the 'prison industrial complex', how do gender and race interplay with unfreedom, and to what extent does Marxian understandings of unfreedom capture this process?*

Labour unfreedom has always been deeply intertwined with race and gender, since the very onset of capitalism. As put by Marx (1991: chapter 13, 925), 'the veiled slavery of the wage workers in Europe needed, for its pedestal, slavery pure and simple in the new world'. Race and gender also crucially shape the prison labour system. It is hard to think of a prison labour system anywhere in the world, or even in any previous era of capitalism, where the majority of those subjected to prison labour are not racialised populations, immigrants or ethnic minorities.

In some prison labour systems, racial logics and forms of discipline are especially overt. For instance, in the 1990s, in the state of Alabama, correctional officers publicly attached inmates who refused to work on chain gangs to the hitching post, which Tessa Gorman has accurately described as a 'reminder of racial terrorism' from slavery that 'consists of an iron collar that was closed by a bolt, attached to an upright bar or post' (Gorman 1997). In the state of Louisiana, an almost entirely African American prison population is required to labour on Angola prison farm, which is a former slave plantation. Prison labour is a highly racialised mode of domination and exploitation and it cannot be understood in isolation from wider dynamics of race and racialised forms of social control present in any given era of capitalist development.

The gendered dynamics of prison labour are also important. For much of the history of global capitalism, prison labour has been pretty male because incarceration rates for men vastly outweigh incarceration rates of women. However, this has begun to change in the neoliberal era, as women have been incarcerated at higher rates amidst a 'global lockdown' of women (Sudbury 2005; Roberts 2016). Beyond the gender of individual prisoners, gendered power relations and dynamics surround prison labour regimes. For instance, in the state of Texas, male inmates have been made to wear pink prison outfits and underwear and feminised in various ways, as part of a broader strategy to humiliate prison workers. In the same county, all-women chain gangs have been compared to dogs. Gender dynamics are underexplored within studies of prison labour and certainly warrant further exploration.

Marxist understandings of unfreedom are not currently optimised to grasp these dynamics. Indeed, barring some important exceptions (cf. Mezzadri 2017), Marxist work on unfree labour has been surprisingly gender and race blind. I say surprisingly because it is clear – even in official statistics – that women and girls, people of colour, indigenous people and migrants are disproportionately vulnerable to unfree labour in the contemporary global economy. Yet, aside from in feminised industries (e.g. sex and care work) where gendered vulnerability is often emphasised and analysed (LeBaron and Gore 2019), there are major analytical and empirical blind spots with respect to how race, gender and sexuality shape workers' vulnerability to unfreedom. There is a need for analysis of unfreedom and unfree labour, within prisons and far beyond, that grasps race and gender as a key part of the story – of how and why workers are vulnerable (or not) to unfreedom, of their conditions and experiences within unfree labour, as part of the overall logics of unfree labour systems and as forms of power and inequality that are reproduced through unfree labour.

**Question 3.** *In terms of data collection, which are the key challenges in researching prison labour, and which are the most effective methods to study it through a Marxian lens?*

The key challenges in researching prison labour are threefold: practical, ethical and methodological.

Researchers will confront a number of practical challenges in researching prison labour. Perhaps most critical are the difficulties in accessing prisoners, who are the most reliable source of information on prison labour conditions and dynamics. States and companies are usually hesitant to grant researchers access to their prison populations and workforces. Even where there is access, privacy law combined with highly regimented prison schedules can make it difficult for researchers to get the information they need to construct meaningful samples and recruit research participants. Gaining access to former prisoners is often difficult for similar reasons. The greatest challenge, then, is getting into prison to access workers so as to interview and observe them, or locating those with relevant experience once they've left prison.

Most of the research on prison labour, therefore, relies on other types of data and evidence. Some journalism on prison labour, such as recent exposés of labour conditions within internment camps in Xinjang, China, relies on satellite imagery. Other research relies on documentary evidence, such as documents obtained through Freedom-of-Information requests or company websites. However, this information is often patchy and can be time-, resource- and labour-intensive for researchers to obtain.

As well, like all research involving workers who are unfree and vulnerable to retribution by employers, researching prison labour poses ethical challenges (LeBaron 2018b). In this case, the stakes are especially high given the multifaceted retribution that could be unleashed by the entire criminal justice system, from sentence extension to solitary confinement, and ethical considerations are especially pronounced given that it is typically not possible to interview workers privately and offsite without their employer or a prison official listening. To fully understand prisoners' experiences, the conditions under which they are working and the factors that shape their entry and exit from prison labour, there is a need for in-depth research among prison workers themselves.

Yet, this needs to be done in an ethical, respectful and empowering way, without putting prisoners – who already experience serious constraints on their freedom – at risk, including their risk of losing their prison employment (since they often depend on this to cover fees imposed for their costs of incarceration), or being assigned a less desirable form of prison labour. Overlapping challenges intertwine and further complicate these obvious ethical challenges, including the need to carefully safeguard and anonymise sensitive data and create a protocol for what happens if the researcher uncovers or is told about illegal activity.

Finally, researchers confront a series of methodological challenges in collecting data on prison labour. These include, for instance, ensuring the credibility, representativeness and high quality of data in the face of the serious obstacles to these, and balancing the need for anonymity and protection of research participants.

## Marx and the Refugee: Three Questions to Paolo Novak

*Question 1. The refugee has been theorised either in relation to a core of capitalist relations, or as residually lying at the margins of such relations. In your view, why do Marxist analyses struggle so much to accommodate the refugee institution?*

Marx never gave us a definitive method for the study of institutions and the state, and it is thus challenging to apply the concepts he developed to the study of the refugee, a quint-essentially state-centred legal institution. Perhaps for this reason, political economy analyses never study the refugee institution in its own terms. Some contributions approach refugee law *à la* Mieville (2005), that is, as a subset of international law whose constituent forms are the constituent forms of global capitalism and, therefore, of imperialism. Through this lens one obtains crucial insights on some of the forces that structure the refugee institution, but the latter is reduced to a mere by-product of imperialism, leaving little space for political engagement other than hoping for all international law to be abolished (ibid.: 318). Other contributions approach refugee law as a subset of a broader range of legal instruments and institutions that shape the inclusion of migrants into labour markets a mediating the insertion of migrants into labour markets. Once again, this is insightful, as it brings to the fore the functionality of migration laws in constituting a mode of appropriation of labour power premised on hyper-precarious migrant labour (Ferguson and McNally 2014), but dilutes the specificity of the refugee institution.

In my research, I try to study the refugee institution as a productive force for social change caught up in, but at the same time in excess of, these relations (Novak 2015).

So, one can say that the main problem lies in the fact that the refugee, for most political economy analyses, is not necessarily studied in its own terms. but always in its functional role in relation to one or more 'traditional' key concerns of political economy – such as accumulation, imperialism, labour or class. Often, refugees are conceived as the product of imperialism and its related patterns of dispossession; or in their role and mobilisation as particularly vulnerable labour, subject to particularly intense forms of exploitation. Through these lenses one may still obtain crucial insights, but it is still not the same thing as developing an analysis centred on the refugee as the main 'protagonist' of the narrative.

*Question 2. If you had to pick one Marxian concept epitomising both the possibilities and limitations in dealing with the institution of the refugee in political economy, which concepts would you choose?*

The concept of imperialism is perhaps the stronger contribution of conventional Marxist analyses to the study of refugees – and, at the same time, its weakest spot. Traditionally, these analyses have deployed the concept of imperialism to capture refugee-related dynamics in two ways. First, international refugee law and refugee-related interventions across the globe are seen, through this concept, as a ruse by imperialist states to project their power. And obviously these analyses have a point. Since its inception the international refugee regime has never been (exclusively) driven by humanitarian concerns, with powerful states' interests always structuring its key analytical units, relations and hierarchies, as well as its contextual operations. This was so during the Cold War, when interventions in support of refugees escaping from Soviet-supported regimes across Africa and Asia were lavishly funded and often constituted an all-pervasive and cross-cutting axis of conflict. This is so today, when the militarised management of refugee migration to countries in the Global North functions as a way to project the latter's power and influence far away from their borders. The definition, transformation and interpretation of refugee law, as well as refugee-related interventions by national states or the so-called international community have always been deeply implicated with attempts to establish and reproduce imperialist forces, globally and at regional level (Chandler 2006; Foster et al. 2008).

Second, studies of the refugee institution informed by the concept of imperialism help us move away from its legal form, as an individual who lacks the protection of the state that s/he belongs to, based on race, religion or political affiliation. Rather, they locate 'bourgeois' refugee law and the relation between states and citizens it expresses in the historical and material contexts that explain and justify its development, linking the legal form of the refugee institution to the interests of classes and particular groups within inter/national societies. In this way, refugee displacement is explained by reference to imperialist proxy wars and the violence and destruction that ensue them, to processes of primitive accumulation and/or the pauperisation of countries in the Global South through predatory lending and land grabs. The root causes of displacement stem from the ongoing production of underdevelopment across the world and from the need to expand and then defend global markets and the consequences. Forced displacement is a by-product of the economic relationships of imperialism (Petras 2007).

The great contribution of these analyses, thus, lies in their bringing to life (some of) the social relations that shape the content of the refugee institution, exposing the false separation between the political and the economic, and the fallacy of the distinction between 'voluntary' and 'forced' migration that is constitutive of migration law and migration management institutions. Yet, in conceiving all instances of refugee displacement and of refugee-related interventions as the ultimate expression of the economic relationships of imperialism, these approaches don't offer many practical insights for the purposes of field research. Indeed, through the prism of imperialism, the concrete mechanisms through which the refugee institution is heterogeneously declined in different geographical contexts and historical moments, the socially and subjectively differentiated outcomes and effects that it produces on displaced populations, and the latter's situated contestations, struggles and avoidance tactics, that is, the ways in which the refugee institution is rendered concrete and reproduced in context, all appear as parochial analytical interests. Ultimately, a field-based investigation of refugee dynamics that is defined by theories of imperialism can at best offer a confirmation of the significance of these theories rather than novel insights. I find this to be a major limitation.

*Question 3. Based on your field experience, are there ways to bring Marxian analysis into the study of refugees – that is, to bring Marx in a refugee camp?*

Absolutely. The positions sketched above are but the most conventional Marxist engagements with the field of refugee studies. More recent analyses, while not necessarily challenging the above tenets, have explored refugee dynamics through exciting and empirically driven studies. There is a growing awareness, for example, about the significance of asylum and refugee law for the insertion of migrants into labour markets, with interesting studies offering insights on the 'refugeeisation' of the European agricultural labour force (Dines and Rigo 2015). Captivating ethnographic accounts have described the process of 'step-wise' migration from West Africa into Spanish labour markets, disentangling the relation between asylum-seekers and un/free labour (Cross 2013). The transformation of refugee laws and directives governing asylum in Europe has been ethnographically linked to variegated forms of neoliberalism (Novak 2019). And so on. These new trajectories of Marxian engagements with the refugee institution import into refugee studies Marxian concerns with exploitation and labour struggles, which are crucial to capture the significance of refugee law in relation to labour markets and to the experiences of refugee-hood; they underline how the migration regime aims at containing, channelling and impeding refugees' right to seek asylum under the rubric of 'irregular migration'; perhaps most importantly, for the purposes of this discussion, they offer theoretical contributions that are driven by field research, rather than using field research to confirm already existing theorisations.

Yet, they perhaps, once again, shift our attention away from the refugee institution as such, from the processes that explain its design, emergence and transformation. These processes are central to my research, as I arrive at these debates from the classical tropes of refugee studies and their foundational question – namely 'who is a refugee?' Yes, the refugee institution is structured by the economic relationships of imperialism, but not only by them. Yes, refugee law and the broader gamut of legal and institutional devices developed for the purposes of migration controls, increases the rate of exploitation for migrants across the world, but its emergence and transformation cannot be reduced to capital's imperatives. Yes, refugees may well escape from the ravages of imperialist wars and the spread of market relations, but their political subjectivities are irreducible to any synthetic representation. I need more tools to answer the above question.

For this reason, my research on refugees is, instead, deeply informed by the Marxian concept of commodity fetishism. This is because, much like a commodity, the refugee 'appears, at first sight, a very trivial thing, and easily understood. Its analysis shows that it is, in reality, a very queer thing' (Marx 1867). The queerness of the refugee institution emerges through field research investigations that are concerned with the processes that explain its contextual (re)production. The latter is of course structured by imperialist states, as much as by employers who prey on the legally subordinated inclusion of refugees into labour markets. But, at national level, it is also carefully crafted and deployed by host governments, the Ministries and agencies dealing with refugees, local administrations, the police, civil servants and the state apparatus at large, in ways that are functional to the interests of the constituencies they represent. It is rendered concrete by humanitarian agencies, their variegated mandates, the experts that drive their practices and the humanitarian workers that contextually adapt and implement them. It is dynamically transformed by refugees themselves, who resist, evade and reappropriate it. The refugee institution benefits landowners, community leaders, brokers, helpers and all those who manage to use it to reproduce their privileged status. The social relations that define the ever-changing form of the refugee institution and its contextual declinations cannot remain tied to any given content. Rather, the refugee institution is contextually produced by the articulation between these forces and agents, and the queer ways in which they transform and are in turn transformed by it. They need to be investigated contextually.

The fetishism of the commodity/refugee institution has its origins in the peculiar social character of the labour that produces it. Only an investigation that defetishises the refugee, that is, that unveils the relation between the producers of that institution as opposed to presenting it as a relation between each of them and the product of their labour, the secret character of the refugee is unveiled. Such an investigation may require 'corrupting' classic political economy methods, infusing them, for example, with post-structuralist gazes that are concerned with the regimes of power knowledge that inscribe refugee spaces, or with deconstructions that capture the social excesses that characterise refugee law (Novak 2015).

Indeed, many Marxist will despair at the ways in which I have appropriated the concept of fetishism and at the ways in which I used the words labour and producers. I think, however, that in order to study a 'queer thing', queer methods are required.

## References

### Introduction

Banaji, J. 2010. *Theory as History: Essays on Modes of Production and Exploitation*. Chicago: Haymarket.
O'Connell Davidson, J. 2015. *Modern Slavery: The Margins of Freedom*. New York: Palgrave Macmillan.

### Marx and the Chiefs

Ali, T. 2017. *The Dilemmas of Lenin: Terrorism, War, Empire, Love, Revolution*. London: Verso.
Banaji, J. 1977. 'Modes of production in a materialist conception of history'. *Capital and Class* 3: 1–44.
———. 2003. 'The fictions of free labour, contract, coercion, and so-called unfree labour'. *Historical Materialism* 11(3): 69–95.
———. 2010. *Theory as History: Essays on Modes of Production and Exploitation*. Chicago: Haymarket.
Bernstein, H. 2014. '"African peasants and revolution" revisited'. *Review of African Political Economy* 41(1): S95–107.
Berry, S. 1993. *Chiefs Know Their Boundaries. Essays on Property, Power and the Past in Asante 1896–1996*. Oxford: James Currey.
———. 2018. 'Chieftaincy, land, and the state in Ghana and South Africa'. In J. L. Comaroff and J. Comaroff (eds), *The Politics of Custom: Chiefship, Capital, and the State in Contemporary Africa*, pp. 79–109. Chicago: Chicago University Press.
Breman, J. 1985. 'Between fieldwork and immiserisation: The partiality of fieldwork in rural India'. *Journal of Peasant Studies* 13: 5–36.

Callinicos, A. 2001. 'Periodizing capitalism and analyzing imperialism: Classical Marxism and capitalist evolution'. In R. Albritton, M. Itoh, R. Westra and A. Zuege (eds), *Phases of Capitalist Development*, pp. 230–45. London: Palgrave Macmillan.

Capps, G. 2007. 'Lenin in the field? Researching class and 'taking sides' in BaFokeng, South Africa'. Paper presented to the Fourth Historical Materialism Conference, SOAS, 9–11 November.

———. 2012a. 'Victim of its own success? The platinum mining industry and the Apartheid mineral property system in South Africa's political transition'. *Review of African Political Economy* 39(131): 63–84.

———. 2012b. 'A bourgeois reform with social justice? The contradictions of the Mineral Development Bill and the black economic empowerment in the South Africa platinum mining industry'. *Review of African Political Economy* 39(132): 315–33.

———. 2016. 'Tribal-landed property: The value of the chieftaincy in contemporary Africa'. *Journal of Agrarian Change* (Special issue: 'The political economy of Agrarian change: Essays in appreciation of Henry Bernstein') 16(3): 452–77.

———. 2018. 'Custom and exploitation: Rethinking the origins of the modern African chieftaincy in the political economy of colonialism'. *Journal of Peasant Studies* 45(5–6): 969–93.

Capps, G. and Mnwana S. 2015. 'Claims from below: Platinum and the politics of land in the Bakgatla Traditional Authority Area'. *Review of African political economy* 42(146): 606–24.

Gibbon, P. and M. Neocosmos. 1985. 'Some problems in the political economy of "African socialism"'. In H. Bernstein and B. Campbell (eds.), *Contradictions of Accumulation in Africa*, pp. 153–206. London: Sage.

Mamdani, M. 1996. *Citizen and Subject. Contemporary Africa and the Legacy of Late Colonialism*. London: James Currey.

Marx, K. 1974a. *Capital, Volume I*. London: Lawrence and Wishart.

———. 1974b. *Capital, Volume III*. London: Lawrence and Wishart.

———. 1991. *Capital, Volume III*. London: Penguin.

O'Laughlin, B. 1996. 'Through a divided glass: Dualism, class and the agrarian question in Mozambique'. *Journal of Peasant Studies* 23(4): 1–39.

———. 2000. 'Class and the customary: The ambiguous legacy of the Indigenato in Mozambique'. *African Affairs* 99: 5–42.

Olsen, W. 1992. 'Random sampling and repeat surveys in South India'. In S. Devereux and J. Hoddinott (eds), *Fieldwork in Developing Countries*. London: Harvester Wheatsheaf.

Pradella, L. 2015. *Globalisation and the Critique of Political Economy: New Insights from Marx's Writings*. London: Routledge.

## Marx and the Prisoner

Gilmore, R. W. 2007. *Golden Gulag: Prisons, Surplus, Crisis, and Opposition in Globalizing California*. Berkeley: University of California Press.

Gorman, T. 1997. 'Back on the chain gang: Why the Eight Amendment and the history of slavery proscribe the resurgence of chain gangs'. *California Law Review* 85(2): 441–78.

Johnson, K. R. 2018. 'Prison labor is modern slavery. I've been sent to solitary for speaking out'. *Guardian*, https://www.theguardian.com/commentisfree/2018/aug/23/prisoner-speak-out-american-slave-labor-strike.

LeBaron, G. 2012. 'Rethinking prison labor: Social discipline and the state in historical perspective'. *WorkingUSA* 15(3): 327–51.

———. 2015. 'Slaves of the state: American prison labour past and present', 23 April, https://www.opendemocracy.net/en/beyond-trafficking-and-slavery/slaves-of-state-american-prison-labour-past-and-present/

———. 2018a 'Prison labour, slavery, and the state'. In L. Brace and J. O'Connell Davidson (eds), *Revisiting Slavery and Antislavery: Towards a Critical Analysis*. Cham: Palgrave Macmillan.

——— (ed.). 2018b. *Researching Forced Labour in the Global Economy: Methodological Challenges and Advances*. Oxford: Oxford University Press.

LeBaron, G. and G. Ellie. 2019. 'Gender and forced labour: Understanding the links in global cocoa supply chains'. *Journal of Development Studies* 56(6): 1–23.

LeBaron, G. and P. Nicola. 2019. 'States and the political economy of unfree labour'. *New Political Economy* 24(1): 1–21.

Marx, K. 1991. *Capital, Volume I*. London: Penguin.

Mezzadri, A. 2017. *The Sweatshop Regime: Labouring Bodies, Exploitation, and Garments Made in India*. Cambridge: Cambridge University Press.

Rioux, S., L. Genevieve and V. Peter 2019. 'Capitalism and unfree labour: A review of Marxist perspectives on modern slavery'. *Review of International Political Economy*, doi: 10.1080/ 09692290.2019.1650094.

Roberts, A. 2016. *Gendered States of Punishment and Welfare: Feminist Political Economy, Primitive Accumulation and the Law*. Abingdon: Routledge.

Sudbury, J. (ed.). 2005. *Global Lockdown: Race, Gender and the Prison-Industrial Complex*. New York: Routledge.

US National Archives. 2019. 'The constitution of the United States', https://www.archives.gov/ founding-docs/constitution

### Marx and the Refugee

Chandler, D. 2006. *Empire in Denial: The Politics of State-Building*. London: Pluto.

Cross, H. 2013. *Migrants, Borders and Global Capitalism: West African Labour Mobility and EU Borders*. London: Routledge.

Dines, N. and E. Rigo. 2015. 'Postcolonial citizenships and the "refugeeization" of the workforce: Migrant agricultural labor in the Italian Mezzogiorno'. In S. Ponzanesi and G. Colpani (eds), *Postcolonial Transitions in Europe: Contexts, Practices and Politics*, pp. 151–72. London: Rowman and Littlefield.

Ferguson, S. and D. McNally. 2014. 'Precarious migrants: Gender, race and the social reproduction of a global working class'. *Socialist Register* 51: 1–23.

Foster, J. B., H. Holleman and R. W. McChesney. 2008. 'The U.S. imperial triangle and military spending'. *Monthly Review* 60(5): 1–19.

Marx, K. 1867. *Capital, Volume I* (chapter 1, section 4), https://www.marxists.org/archive/marx/ works/1867-c1/ch01.htm#26a (accessed 30 January 2020).

Mieville C. 2005. *Between Equal Rights: A Marxist Theory of International Law*. Leiden: Brill.

Novak, P. 2015. 'Refugee status as a productive tension'. *Transnational Legal Theory* 6(2): 287–311.

———. 2019. 'The neoliberal location of asylum'. *Political Geography* 70: 1–13.

Petras, J. 2007. *Rulers and Ruled in the US Empire: Bankers, Zionists, Militants*. Atlanta: Clarity.

# Chapter Sixteen

# POSTCOLONIAL MARXISM AND THE 'CYBER-FIELD' IN COVID TIMES

## ON LABOUR BECOMING 'WORKING CLASS'

### Subir Sinha

## Abstract

Interrogating Indian labour's political subjectivity through the lens of postcolonial Marxism during COVID times, this chapter draws on evidence from the 'cyber-field' to explore the fraught processes through which labour may 'become' working class. Reflecting on Marx's various writings on the formation of collective political subjects, the chapter traces the uniqueness of the Indian case and the ways in which such uniqueness has abruptly surfaced during the disruptions generated by the COVID-19 lockdown, which has suddenly displaced the lives of millions of migrant workers, forcing them on the move to reach their rural homes. The analysis also reflects on the merits and limitations of studying social processes from afar, using the cyberspace as a novel archive and field-work terrain.

## Introduction: The Field and the Archive in COVID Times

On 25 March 2020, Indian Prime Minister Narendra Modi appeared on national television at 8 p.m. and declared a complete and indefinite national lockdown in effect from midnight. This resulted in an immediate closure of factories, workshops, shops and all other sites of work, and also all vehicular, rail and air transport. Hardest hit were millions of labourers who migrate seasonally or for longer periods from some of India's most 'economically backward' regions to centres of high growth. From the announcement of the lockdown to now, images and voices of, and information on, migrant labourers have received extensive coverage in media and social media. While this is too immediate an event, and the experience, one could say, is too 'raw', this moment of rupture from the ordinary presents an opportunity to reflect both on 'field-based research' and on certain elements of Marx's writings as they relate to the collective political subjectivity of 'labour' becoming 'working class'.

In 'normal', that is, pre-COVID times, questions on migrant labour, their relation to capital, to the state, to unions, their conditions of work, their contract, their social and everyday life, their relation to new technology, their migration itself and so on would have been investigated via ethnography and time spent in 'the field': However, 'locked down' indefinitely, the 'field' is not accessible to us for fieldwork or ethnography.

For scholars who are not citizens of the country in which their research is located, accessing 'the field' – it is not usually acknowledged – is always subject to geopolitical factors (see Ellison 2019 for a rare account). The denial of visas (as in the celebrated cases of Gerald Berreman for India, and Benedict Anderson and, later, Jeffrey Winter in Indonesia) is a tool wielded by states to control who can produce knowledge about 'the field', and to create a degree of compliance and a holding back on critique. In India, ruled by Modi's Bhartiya Janata Party (BJP), the current thinking, informed by a crude critique of the production of knowledge by 'Western scholars', gatekeeping and surveillance of research has now become common, and research visas are not something researchers can take for granted. Without mobility, the field cannot be accessed, and in a world in which sharp authoritarian populism is on the rise, criticism of political leaders and policies threatens that mobility.

But it is not only geopolitics that curtails access to the field: the current global lockdown in the face of the coronavirus pandemic has resulted in severe restrictions to travel. This has oriented ongoing thinking on 'partial ethnography' as well as provided the context for early thinking on 'patchwork' ethnography: issues that were once of 'research ethics' have become those of dealing with the crisis of knowledge production in an age of indefinite global travel restrictions: how does one talk about 'the field' when one cannot 'go to' or 'immerse' oneself in the field? Research in the time of a global COVID-19 lockdown on travel necessitates breaking down other foundational assumptions of 'home' and 'away' that underpins much ethnography and fieldwork, and rethinking how to use what is available to us, 'at home', in times when 'the field' is not accessible.

What is available to us is a 'cyber-field' – a composite of the internet, media and social media with a global reach and an interrupted, discontinuous set of images, videos, voices and reports that make up a wholly new kind of archive. In lockdown conditions, it is impossible to do fieldwork in one site, let alone follow influential suggestions for 'multisited fieldwork' (Marcus 1995). Ethnographic imaginaries that conceive of the 'field sites' on which research must be conducted must themselves be recalibrated. Airoldi (2018) details how one might learn from 'conventional ethnography' to study 'meta-fields' and 'contextual fields', using the technological architecture of digital platforms to study the formation of collective identities. My concerns are different here, and less technical. I suggest, and later in the paper document, the creation of a 'cyber-field': a space of flows – of images, voices, reports and information – posted on social media platforms by migrant labourers, activists and solidarity groups, and news agencies. I searched for relevant hashtags (e.g. #migrantworkers, #migrantlabourers and #migrantsontheroad) on Twitter, whose algorithmic logic based on data of my past usage of the platform displayed footage and news coverage of migrant workers under COVID-19 lockdown. Additionally, I was invited to Facebook and WhatsApp groups exchanging such information for activist and relief purposes. I take these platforms as the 'field sites' on which I explore the collective political subjectivity of migrant labourers, and I take posts on social media to constitute a 'cyber-archive'.

## Migrant Labourers and Working Classes: Between Marxism and Postcolonial Theory

The emergence and collective political subjectivity of the working class is central to Marxist anticipations of communism: produced by capitalism, this class is the agent for its annihilation. Marx's account of the emergence of a radical working class due to the rule of capital precedes his account of the workings of capital itself. In *The Communist Manifesto*, written 19 years prior to *Capital, Volume I*, Marx and Engels note that 'the history of all hitherto existing society is the history of class struggle', and that in the 'epoch of the bourgeoisie' a 'simplified antagonism' exists between two great classes, 'the bourgeoisie and the proletariat'. An 'early' work from 1848, the *Manifesto* sees the working class as already fully formed, under the leadership of the communist parties would act out 'laws of historical development' that would play out to their inevitable denouement. Against this revolutionary optimism about the already fully formed political agency of the working class, it is instructive to read the prefaces to the subsequent editions, which note national variations in degrees and modes of capitalist development and of corresponding differences in the composition, nature and political potential of the working class.

To see the origins of 'working class' in Marx's writings, let us consider some passages from Marx's chapters on primitive accumulation in *Capital, Volume I*. The dissolving of links between agricultural producers and the land is key in Marx's account because, as he notes in chapter 26, 'the capitalist system *presupposes* the *complete* separation of labourers from *all* property in the means by which they can realise their labour' (emphasis added), and the 'so called primitive accumulation therefore is nothing more nothing else that historical process of divorcing the producer from the means of production'. This is important as 'the immediate producer could only predispose of his own person after he had ceased to be attached to the soil and ceased to be the slave, serf or bondman of another'.

What happens during the passage of time between agricultural producers' separation from the land and the emergence of the working class of the *Manifesto*? Working in urban factories, and struggles against capitalists, over time created a 'class' identity that overrode other possible identities. Marx's observes in *Capital, Volume I*, chapter 27 that 'by the 19th century the very memory of the connexion between the agricultural Labour and communal property had vanished'. Since, for Marx, in its 'classic' English form, the processes of separations last over four centuries, this amnesia of the brutalities of separation from the land did not form part of the 'class consciousness' of what became the 'pure' industrial and urban working class. However, where these processes are both compressed in time and incomplete, and the separations are ongoing, it is important to ask how they inform the formation and consciousness of the Indian working class.

How 'universal' are these processes of 'separation' of producers from the means of production that give rise both to capitalism, and of the working class, and the forgetting of the links with the land of the process of brutal dispossession? There is ambiguity and contradiction in Marx's writings on whether there a *singular* path to capitalist development, exemplified in the passage in the preface of *Capital, Volume I* that 'the country that is more developed industrially only shows, to the less developed, the image of its own future', which suggests a logic of replication of the 'classic' path of England and western Europe (though even here he notes differences). But in many places in the same text, and in other writings, Marx asserts process of capitalism becoming universal necessitates different 'national' paths: for example, Marx notes at the end of chapter 26, this process is not uniform across countries: 'the history of this expropriation in different countries assumes different aspects and runs through its various phases in different orders of succession and at different periods', and that only 'in England is it the classic form'.

Prefaces of later editions of the *Communist Manifesto* show considerable movement away from the imaginaries of the working class presented in the original 1848 edition. In the preface to the 1872 German edition, Marx and Engels admit that the twenty-five years in the interim have rendered their predictions of working-class action 'antiquated' for a variety of reasons. They go further in the preface of the 1882 Russian edition:

> In Russia we find, face-to-face with the rapidly flowering capitalist swindle and bourgeois property, just beginning to develop, more than half the land owned in common by the peasants. Now the question is: can the Russian *obschina* (peasant commune), though greatly undermined, yet a form of primeval common ownership of land, pass directly to the higher form of Communist common ownership? Or, on the contrary, must it first pass through the same process of dissolution such as constitutes the historical evolution of the West?

This idea that the dissolution of the commons was *not* necessary for passages to communism, and therefore that a revolutionary working class *could* exist without peasants being separated from the common lands, is also contained in Marx's 1881 *Letter to Vera Zasulich*. One can see this underlying idea, of a peasantry being led by the working class, both in Kautsky's 'political' agrarian question and the Leninist political programme of a party of the working class exercising leadership over the peasantry in a transition to communism in conditions where capitalism has advanced even as a substantial peasantry attached to the land exists.

The evidence of 'differences from the classic English path', scattered but widespread in Marx's (and Engels's) writings, complicates the idea of universality of capitalism and of the working class, its composition and its political subjectivity. In many of the prefaces quoted above, Marx and Engels note that the working class only worked to install the bourgeoisie to power in national settings, and also that their organisational status and the political fields in which they operated were variable in relation, chiefly, to the levels and forms of capitalist development – in other words not 'confronting' the bourgeoisie but actively accepting its hegemony. The idea of 'difference' is already there in Marxist texts, in which capitalist development happens in a compressed timeframe than in the 'classic English path', and the emergence of a working class coexists with large peasantries, even of commons. This difference is a possible basis for studying how those leaving the villages as migrant labour become 'working class'.

A large literature suggests that the separation of agricultural producers from the land in contemporary India is not as 'complete' as in the classic form of England, and the 'immediate producer' is has not 'ceased to be attached to the soil', nor 'ceased to be the slave, serf, or bondman of another'. What are some reasons for this incompleteness?

For Chakrabarty (1988), there is no reason to expect a transition to supposedly 'pure working class' consciousness and that elements of 'culture' would remain. Sanyal (2007) argues that an agrarian transition would not materialise in settings like India because, due to democracy and development interventions, primitive accumulation will go hand-in-hand with mitigations of its effects. For Bernstein (2010) under conditions of con-temporary capitalism, the 'agrarian question of labour' would not be resolved as in the classic cases: instead of becoming 'labour', peasants would be engaged in petty com-modity production.

While there is an element of truth in these postcolonial (Chakrabarty), Marxist (Bernstein) and postcolonial-Marxist (Sanyal) approaches, none of them captures the liminality and hybridity of migrant workers and their consciousness: located between agriculture and industry, between village and city, part-worker and part-peasant. Nor do they give agency to the working classes of postcolonial settings from attempting to fight the processes of separation: migrant workers themselves sustain small-holder agriculture via their remittances and attempt to keep complete separation from land at bay by in the face of evidence of shrinking size of holdings, which in turn indicates that dispossession and differentiation are in extended play. How to research these aspects of Indian labour in COVID times?

## The Cyber-Field, the Cyber-Archive and Researching Migrant Workers in COVID Times

The global COVID-19 lockdown has separated researchers from the field sites on which such questions would normally be investigated – the farm, the factory, the transport hub, the labour *naka* and places-in-motion, such as the migrant trains and means of transport. In the absence of access to 'the field', can the online terrain function as one? Could we treat social media as a new archive in conditions when pandemics, increasingly turbu-lent expressions of climate change, global political volatility and events yet unforeseen may close off access to 'the field' for extended periods of time, but to use this terrain for research. There are, of course, many deficiencies in the online world as a 'field' on which to conduct research: we are used, in fieldwork, to inhabit, as much as possible, the same material realities as the subjects of our research, and there is an expectation of some intimacy between the researcher and the researched, attempting to 'become the other', or to represent in academic language experiences that are fundamentally alien to 'our own'. Some of the best fieldwork has been produced by scholars who have returned to 'the field' over time. Such immersive experiences, sharing of the material world and repeated returns are not possible in the context of the online field, which is by definition, remote, where interactions can be intimate but at a remove, and which is ephemeral: no 'return' to the field is possible, as 'the field' does not have the relative stability as in 'normal fieldwork'.

Social media archives are produced for online consumption, while being rooted in 'lived' experiences and materialities. Digital archives on social media are, but by their very nature, produced outside the control of the researcher: research is NOT the pri-mary purpose for the creation of social media artefacts such as the video clips I explore below: it is much more anarchic, lacking any central coordination that other archives have when they curate certain collections. For my purposes, it is important to note that video clips are produced and archived in real time, they are 'raw' data of a sort, and there is, in the case of the clips produced by workers themselves, unmediated central command. We may label them 'autoethnography' after the fact, but the purpose of these clips is to reach authorities for immediate relief. Video and text are also produced and posted by privately owned news agencies, activists, NGOs and newly formed networks of 'civil society' and civic associations. This archive on the state of India's migrant workers emerged in the context of the coronavirus lockdown and provides a unique snapshot, allowing tentative answers to the questions I pose above.

Around a hundred million migrant labourers have been working in sprawling Indian cities in a very wide array of activities and sites of production: factories, but also homes, hospitals, street vendors, hawkers, roadside eateries, small-scale repair and so on.[1] All these activities came to sudden halt on 25 March, leaving them with little cash in hand (their trades are based on cash and on small payments) and consequently no food stocks. Over the next weeks, they started to leave the cities for their home villages in their millions: with all transport networks also shut down, they were filmed walking up to a 1,000 km on foot, often with no food. Some clips show food being distributed by good Samaritans and religious groups and NGOs. Video clips were also posted of them being assaulted by police on the way: India's corona lockdown was also a crackdown by state agencies and vigilantes connected to the ruling BJP.

Once the images of their exodus could no longer be ignored, bus and train services were arranged for migrant labourers. However, they were prevented in some cases by force from leaving, by locking them up, not retuning their identity cards, or withholding wages.[2] In Gujarat, travel agents connected to the ruling BJP duped workers desperate to go home.[3] During this period, Indian courts ruled that firms should not be forced to pay wages to workers, as long as food was made available.[4] Some states, while the exodus was ongoing, hastily moved to remove labour protections on wages and hours and their right to organise.[5] Curfew-like conditions were imposed by the Government of UP, a state that is a major source of migrant workers and a terrain that must be traversed by others going to their villages east of it. Returning to their villages, migrant workers faced immediate problems of availability of food and work. Still, they often resolved never to go back to

---

[1]   This number is from https://news.un.org/en/story/2020/06/1065662 (accessed 15 June 2020).

[2]   See https://www.wsj.com/articles/indias-migrant-laborers-begin-heading-home-as-coronavirus-lockdown-eases-11589196559 and https://www.newindianexpress.com/states/kerala/2020/jun/13/employers-withhold-id-cards-deny-wages-to-detain-migrants-2155903.html (accessed 15 June 2020).

[3]   https://thewire.in/labour/surat-migrant-workers-bjp-ticket (accessed 15 June 2020).

[4]   https://www.telegraphindia.com/india/if-meals-are-given-why-do-they-require-wages-supreme-courts-query-during-coronavirus-lockdown/cid/1762977 (accessed 15 June 2020).

[5]   https://www.thehindubusinessline.com/news/national/up-government-suspends-all-labor-laws-except-three-to-lure-industrialists/article31531867.ece (accessed 15 June 2020).

the cities: 'they treated us like dogs', they are reported to say, about their employers and state authorities.[6] In some cases they are shown as returning to the cities but demanding improved wages and conditions of work.[7]

Let me provide a sequential narrative to the materials in the new archive: what do the video clips show at the outset of the corona lockdown, and what changes in the content of these clips between then and now? What can we read from this material about the status of class formation and class consciousness of migrant labourers? And to what extent does working on this new digital field – the internet, social media platforms, closed and encrypted communication apps, and so on – allow us to explore the relevance and limits of Marx's writings on these questions?

Video clips made by migrant workers began to appear on Indian social media within a week of the lockdown, showing them clustered in small rooms, their voices and faces captured by their smart phone cameras weary and fearful. They say they have run out for essential food items. Some do not themselves have accounts on open platforms – they ask 'someone' to post it on social media. Some say that they do not have much balance left in their phone account and are anxious about the isolation they would face once it runs out. All this suggests a double precarity: their ability to feed themselves and to communicate their condition to state authorities, and their access to communication apps.

While some identify the sector of the economy they work in – 'we work in construction in Mumbai' – overwhelmingly the video clips of the first phase do not use occupational or class identifiers: looking tentatively into the camera, the overwhelmingly male groups give the name of the village, district and state to which they belong, and how many of them are rooming together. They plead for help, but at this time to no one in particular (*koi hamari madad kare*: someone please help us). Invariably, their homes are located in the poorest regions of India: Bihar, Bengal, eastern and central Uttar Pradesh, Madhya Pradesh, Chhattisgarh, Jharkhand, Odisha.[8] These clips showing labourers from the same village – possibly also of the same religion and caste – rooming together suggests that 'community' identity trumped class. Correspondingly, pleas for help from good Samaritans, rather than demands for rights, indicate that labourers located themselves within a moral economy.

Some clips show workers state that they had not been paid for weeks – this is corroborated by a study by the Stranded Workers' Action Network (a group that emerged during the pandemic to deal with workers' issues) from the time that 50–90 per cent of workers in the informal sector, depending on location, had not received payments, and

---

[6]  https://www.nationalgeographic.com/history/2020/05/they-treat-us-like-stray-dogs-migrant-workers-flee-india-cities/ and https://www.indiatoday.in/india/story/migrant-workers-walking-hometowns-tiresome-journey-coronavirus-covid19-lockdown-1678954-2020-05-17 (accessed 15 June 2020).

[7]  For example, https://thefederal.com/states/south/telangana/employers-try-to-woo-migrant-workers-with-hefty-wages-flight-tickets/ (accessed 15 June 2020).

[8]  See Das and Sahu (2019) for origins of workers in Surat, from where many videos were loaded.

96 per cent did not receive emergency food rations from government agencies.[9] When demand for food was made, it was made from local authorities, not from the Modi government, which had imposed the lockdown. From late April, clips were in circulation showing workers in Surat, a major migrant worker hub, demanding payment of withheld wages.[10] These wages were, in any case, pitifully low, and labourers described being defrauded by employers.[11] When trade unions took the matter to court, the Supreme Court ruled that firms too were facing a crisis caused by the lockdown, and as long as food was arranged for migrant labourers, there was no need to pay wages.

One element of informality that emerged in these videos was that, due the many concatenations that mediate the relation of labourer to capitalist, in some locations up to 90 per cent of workers were not aware of the name of their employer. A labour organiser from Tiruppur, a long-time centre for export-oriented garment manufacture, participating in a webinar featuring voices of workers organised by the Praxis Institute of Participatory Research (an activist organisation dedicated to labour issues), noted that labourers were not aware of government schemes for their benefit, or of social security contributions their employers were required to make for them by law. Both these examples show not only a lack of consciousness of their rights, but also of the relative failure of left-wing parties and unions to generate it. The Hind Mazdoor Sangh, affiliated to the Hindutva right wing and the largest trade union in India in terms of membership, took up some issues with the government.

Once migrant labourers took to the road to get back to their villages, the video clips of their exodus took the tone of an epic unfolding tragedy. Silent files of hundreds walking, telling those filming them that they had no water, no cash, no food for days. Some decided to walk on rail tracks, and eight labourers were killed when they slept on them, exhausted. Others showed badly blistered feet. A team of labourers who set off for a 1,000 km journey on bicycles spoke of extortionate prices they had to pay, draining their meagre savings. News media reported one case that a labourer who stole a bicycle left a heart-rending note apologising to the owner on the grounds that he had no other means of transport. The radical wing of the bourgeoisie – progressive civil society – took several actions on their behalf. New associations sprung up on social media on the issue of providing immediate relief, transport, food and cash to stranded workers. Muslim and Sikh religious organisations, as well as those connected to the Hindutva right, also undertook food distribution, though here Hindutva groups were shown to prevent Muslim groups from doing this.

Moved by the harrowing video of their struggle home, some middle-class Indians intercepted them on the roads and donated food, water, cash and footwear. Of course,

---

[9]  https://www.thehindu.com/data/data-96-migrant-workers-did-not-get-rations-from-the-government-90-did-not-receive-wages-during-lockdown-survey/article31384413.ece (accessed 15 June 2020).

[10]  https://thewire.in/rights/surat-migrant-workers-covid-19-lockdown-wages (accessed 15 June 2020).

[11]  https://scroll.in/article/959428/across-india-workers-complain-that-employers-used-lockdown-to-defraud-them-of-wages-they-are-owed (accessed 15 June 2020).

this was not the most prominent of the middle-class responses: that remained a sort of 'soul searching' and feelings of collective guilt for some, again reinforcing the 'moral economy' lens through which they saw the condition of migrant labourers. For members of the ruling Hindutva right- wing, the exodus was another moment to make the distinction between Muslims and Hindus, the central axis of their politics. This involved assaulting street vendors who were Muslims. A Hindutva post circulated on WhatsApp had a caption over the picture of returning migrants: 'look at them, they are loyal to the nation, unlike those others. They suffer with dignity, but they do not protest against Modi', a cynical though accurate comment on the lack of class consciousness among migrant workers. That caste and religious identities remained strong among migrant labourers, who have been targeted by Hindutva organisations now for over a decade, also emerged from other clips, showing refusal of food from Muslims, or, once they reached a corona quarantine centre, refusal of food cooked by Dalits.

In mid-May, video clips emerged of enraged labourers in Gujarat and Bengaluru, among other places, going on a rampage over the issue of transport back to their villages. The anger stemmed partly from the fact that agents of their employers tried to prevent their return by force, locking them up inside their dormitories. In Surat, workers rampaged against local BJP officials they suspected of having taken extortionate fares for seats on non-existent trains. News circulated of trains that left for certain destinations, but were found meandering hundreds of miles away, according to rumours at the behest of employers colluding with BJP politicians who realised, too late, what the labour exodus meant for the Indian capital. On the trains themselves, video clips showed extremely poor conditions, and news of workers who died on these trains, of hunger and the by-now 40-plus-degrees heat.

The last set of video clips relate to migrant labourers once they reach back to their villages and their plans for return. Recall that their places of origins are located in some of the most 'economically backward areas', and that they come from backgrounds of agrarian distress. We know from already existing research that most became seasonally migrant workers to be able to raise money for repaying debts, to provide necessary cash for small-scale family agriculture, for health and other incidental expenses. Several clips show anger with elected officials, statements that government did nothing for them, but still only muted criticism of Modi. Statements on their treatment by employers and officials maintain a moral framing of their outrage: no one came to our help, they treated us worse than dogs, but not: what about our rights? Some resolve never to return to the cities for work and to stay in the relative security of the village, even though there is poverty there and lack of work: 'If I have to die, I will die in dignity with my own people. At least we will have something to eat here.'

Others are negotiating with their employers: they will return only if their wages are increased, payments are regular and direct, and facilities are improved, a sort of stirring of class consciousness. In Punjab, where migrant labour is necessary for agriculture, clashes have broken out, as migrant workers demand a rate for planting rice paddy that is about 15 per cent higher than what landowners are willing to give.[12]

---

[12]  https://thewire.in/agriculture/punjab-paddy-farmers-labourers (accessed 15 June 2020).

## Conclusion

The pandemic as an extraordinary event revealed the ordinary truths and workings of India's informal economy and the relations between labour, capital and the state. Millions of migrant labourers went through unprecedented but predictable pain, and relations of exploitation and repression, so far hidden in plain sight, were laid bare. But arguably, migrants' political subjectivity is not of a 'working class' that is conscious of itself as a class and which is in battle with the bourgeoise and the state for its rights. There is also an absence of the political party of the working class, leading the process of it becoming a 'class for itself': political analyst Aditya Nigam notes the relative absence of India's communist parties from the scene.[13] In the absence of workers' own organisations, it was left to elements of bourgeois civil society and bourgeois parties to fight for their rights and to provide relief.

The pandemic exposed what Engels (2008), in the context of the condition of the English working class in the late nineteenth century, called the bourgeoisie's 'art of hiding the distress of the working class'. For the vast majority of India's middle classes, experience of migrant labourers' presence is limited to their lifeworld: the domestic worker, the fruit and vegetable vendors below their housing blocks, those running local eateries, delivery people and so on. Themselves organically connected to Indian capitalism, they were unaware of the structural position of migrant workers within it. Unless involved in targeted initiatives and associations, such as Gurgaon Nagrik Ekta Manch, Stranded Workers' Action Network or the many action groups sprouting on social media, the middle classes remained clueless about workers and their struggle: in one case, when a 13-year-old girl carried her ailing father on the back of her bicycle and pedalled nearly a 1,000 km to get to her home village, some suggested that the Indian Olympic Association groom her for a career in competitive cycling events.

Reading these excerpts, we capture a necessarily fragmented picture of labour–capital relations and of the relations between labour and the middle classes, between workers and the state and between them as 'the peasantry' from which they come. Put together, however, these excerpts do say something significant about capitalism's Indian iteration, relating to the questions posed at the outset to explore what the 'online field' suggests at a time when fieldwork has to be remote, partial and patchwork.

A certain trajectory, I had suggested, can be drawn between the processes of primitive accumulation Marx describes in the later chapters of *Capital, Volume I*: from the 'separation' of workers from the means of production in agriculture to their dispossession; to their 'freedom' to sell their labour power and move to urban industry to their amnesia about their connections with agriculture; moving on their coming to consciousness as a 'class', involving recognition of commonalities with other labours and formation of their representative organisations (unions and parties) in struggle with factory owners and the state; and, finally, to their confrontation with the 'other great class, the bourgeoisie'.

---

[13]  https://kafila.online/2020/06/18/crisis-of-working-class-politics-challenges-for-rebuilding-the-left/ (accessed 15 June 2020).

Although the temporal sequence is inverted, the working class as the collective political subject of the *Communist Manifesto*, who will take the world to a communist horizon, is a product of these processes described in *Capital* and other works.

It is a feature of postcolonial capitalism in locations like India that 'advanced capitalism' and 'backwardness' may exist in a symbiotic relationship: what A. P. D'Costa (2014) refers to as 'compressed capitalism'. Earlier writings on 'postcolonial capitalism' (Sanyal 2007; Chatterjee 2008; Samaddar 2018; Sinha 2016, among others) had emphasised the difference between trajectories such as India's and the earlier 'classic' trajectories by pointing, among other factors, to the necessary limits put on capitalist deepening and expansion, by the very fact that the victims of primitive accumulation-like processes had the right to vote and a semblance of constitutional political equality, which forced the state to take ameliorative and welfare measures and led to the emergence of a 'need economy'. But the COVID-19 pandemic and the cyber-fields and digital archives that emerged in its wake indicate that the rights and welfare measures that these writings suggested ameliorated and even 'reversed' the processes of separation from land and primitive accumulation more generally couldn't support livelihoods during an acute capitalist crisis.

Apart from arson and rioting in Surat, Bengaluru, Mumbai and Delhi–NCR, the anger of migrant workers at their abandonment by employers, the state and society at large did not find political expression. Working class rebellion was rare. Was this because, as Jean Dreze (2020) argued, 'when people are hungry and feeble, they are not well placed to rebel'? Or could one argue that these events depicted in the video clips happened at a time when, and in places where, the parties of the working class have been considerably weakened? It is instructive to note that the two of the larger trade unions that 'pleaded' with the Modi government for relief for migrant workers are affiliated with the Hindu right, which disavows any structural contradiction between labour and capital under the ideology of 'integral humanism'. These moves sought to resolve the migrant labour crisis within the Modi project, rather than in opposition to it.

But despite the 'moral economy' framing of the migrant crisis, including by migrant workers themselves, their migration process remains a social movement (*Viewpoint Magazine* 2018) with subversive and even transformational potential. Ashraf (2020) reads the exodus of the workers itself as a kind of resistance, a 'weapon of the weak'. Even though migrant workers did not express themselves in terms of a working class, their employers and the state recognised them as such. The moves to curtail their rights by the Uttar Pradesh government to enforce a 12-hour working day were withdrawn.[14] With migrant workers widely reported to be reluctant to go back to cities, employers are now offering higher wages, payment for trips home and improved conditions of work. Neither based on class-for-itself action and working-class consciousness nor led by strong working-class parties and organisation, the massive and disorganised exodus of migrant

---

[14] https://economictimes.indiatimes.com/news/politics-and-nation/uttar-pradesh-govt-withdraws-controversial-order-of-12-hour-shifts-for-workers-in-industrial-units/articleshow/75772375.cms (accessed 15 June 2020).

workers has brought about 'reforms' that, in the original paths to capitalist transition, were achieved after decades of sustained class struggles.

## References

Airoldi, M. 2018. 'Ethnography and the digital fields of social media'. *International Journal of Social Research Methodology* 21(6): 661–73.

Ashraf, A. 2020. 'Exodus as resistance', https://www.mid-day.com/articles/exodus-as-resistance/22790245 (accessed 15 June 2020).

Bernstein, H. 2010. *Class Dynamics of Agrarian Change*. Halifax: Fernwood & Kumarian.

Chakrabarty, D. 1988. 'Class consciousness and the Indian working class: Dilemmas of Marxist historiography'. *Journal of Asian and African Studies* 23(1–2): 21–31.

Chatterjee, P. 2008. 'Democracy and economic transformation in India'. *Economic and Political Weekly* 43(16): 53–62.

D'Costa, A. P. 2014. 'Compressed capitalism and development: Primitive accumulation, petty commodity production, and capitalist maturity in India and China'. *Critical Asian Studies* 46(3): 317–44.

Das, B. and G. B. Sahu. 2019. 'Coping with cities and connecting with villages: Migrant workers in Surat city'. *Indian Journal of Labour Economics* 62: 89–112.

Dreze, J. 2020. 'When people are hungry and feeble, they are not well placed to revolt'. *Caravan Magazine*, 30 March, https://caravanmagazine.in/policy/no-one-should-be-condemned-to-starvation-jean-dreze (accessed 15 June 2020).

Ellison, S. H. 2019. 'Ethnography in uncertain times', *Geopolitics*.

Engels, F. [1892] 2008. *The Condition of the Working Class in England in 1844*. New York: Cosmo.

Marcus, G. 1995. 'Ethnography in/of the world system: The emergence of multi-sited ethnography'. *Annual Review of Anthropology* 24: 95–117.

Marx, K. [1867] 1882. *Capital, Volume I*, https://www.marxists.org/archive/marx/works/download/pdf/Capital-Volume-I.pdf (accessed 15 June 2020).

Marx, K. and F. Engles. 1848. 'The Communist Manifesto', https://www.marxists.org/archive/marx/works/1848/communist-manifesto/ (accessed 15 June 2020).

Marx, K. and V. Zasulic. 1881. 'Letters', https://www.marxists.org/archive/marx/works/1881/zasulich/index.htm (accessed 15 June 2020).

Nigam, A. 2020. 'Crisis of working class politics: Challenges for rebuilding the left', https://kafila.online/2020/06/18/crisis-of-working-class-politics-challenges-for-rebuilding-the-left/ (accessed 15 June 2020).

Samaddar, R. 2018. *Karl Marx in the Postcolonial Age*. London: Palgrave.

Sanyal, K. 2007. *Rethinking Capitalist Development: Primitive Accumulation, Governmentality and Post-colonial Capitalism*. New Delhi: Routledge

Sinha, S. 2016. ' "Histories of power", the "universalisation of capital" and India's Modi moment: Between and beyond Marxism and postcolonial theory'. *Critical Sociology* 43(4–5): 529–44.

*Viewpoint Magazine*. 2018. 'The border crossing us'. *Viewpoint*, 7 November, https://www.viewpointmag.com/2018/11/07/from-what-shore-does-socialism-arrive/ (accessed 15 June 2020).

# NOTES ON CONTRIBUTORS
## (IN ORDER OF APPEARANCE)

**Alessandra Mezzadri** is Reader in Global Development and Political Economy at SOAS, University of London, UK. Her research interests focus on global industrial circuits and labour regimes; the global garment industry; labour standards, CSR, Modern Slavery and ethical consumerism; feminisms in development and social reproduction approaches; India's informal economy, and the political economy of COVID-19. Her research has been financed by ESRC-DfID and British Academy and is published in journals such as *Development and Change, Geoforum, Third World Quarterly, Progress in Development Studies, Oxford Development Studies*, and *Global Labour Journal*, among others. It has also featured in several media outlets. She is the author of *The Sweatshop Regime: Labouring Bodies, Exploitation and Garments 'Made in India'* published by Cambridge University Press (2017, 2020).

**Henry Bernstein** is Professor Emeritus of Development Studies at SOAS, University of London, UK, and Adjunct Professor at the College of Humanities and Development Studies, China Agricultural University. He is best-known for his work in agrarian political economy, and with T. J. Byres was for many years editor of the *Journal of Peasant Studies* and founding editor of the *Journal of Agrarian Change*. His 'little book on a big idea' *Class Dynamics of Agrarian Change* (2010) has been translated into several languages.

**Barbara Harriss-White** is Professor Emeritus of Development Studies, and Emeritus Fellow of Wolfson College, Oxford, UK. She has used fieldwork to research the economics of agricultural markets, India's socially regulated capitalist economy and corporate capital; the malnutrition caused by markets and other aspects of deprivation, such as poverty, gender and health inequality, disability, ageing, destitution, and caste discrimination. She has a long-term interest in agrarian change in southern India. She has advised the UK'S Department of International Development (DfID), the French Foreign Ministry and seven UN organisations. She has authored, edited and co-edited several books, including *India Working: Essays on Economy and Society* (Cambridge University Press India, 2003); *Rural Commercial Capital: Agricultural Markets In West Bengal* (Oxford University Press India, 2008); *Middle India and Urban-Rural Development, Four Decades of Change* (Springer India, 2016) and *The Wild East* (UCL Press 2019).

**Muhammad Ali Jan** is Assistant Professor at the Information Technology University, Lahore, Pakistan, and Junior Research Fellow, Wolfson College, University of Oxford, UK. He has degrees in Development Studies and International Development from SOAS and Oxford and works on the political economy of agrarian change in Pakistan. His research interests also include the politics of development in South Asia and the institutions regulating the informal economy in Pakistan. His work has appeared in academic journals like *The Journal of Agrarian Change* and *Economic and Political Weekly*. He is currently preparing a manuscript on the agrarian sociology of Pakistani Punjab, focusing on class and status struggles between merchants, landlords and peasants in two districts of the province.

**Adam Hanieh** is Professor of Political Economy and Global Development at IAIS, University of Exeter, UK, and Joint Chair at the Institute of International and Area Studies (IIAS) at Tsinghua University, Beijing, China. Prior to joining Exeter, Adam taught at SOAS, and at Zayed University, United Arab Emirates. From 1997-2003, he worked in the NGO and public sectors in Ramallah, Palestine, where he completed an MA in Regional Studies at Al Quds University. He holds a PhD in Political Science from York University, Canada. His research interests include political economy of the Middle East; labour migration; class and state formation in the Gulf Cooperation Council; Palestine. His work has been published in numerous international journals, like *Development and Change, Antipode* and *Capital and Class*. He is the author of *Money, Markets, and Monarchies: The Gulf Cooperation Council and the Political Economy of the Contemporary Middle East* (Cambridge University Press, 2018), *Lineages of Revolt: Issues of Contemporary Capitalism in the Middle East* (Chicago Haymarket, 2013) *Capitalism and Class in the Gulf Arab States* (New York: Palgrave Macmillan, 2011).

**Susan Newman** is Professor of Economics at the Open University, UK. She held prior posts at the University of the West of England, at the Institute of Social Studies (ISS) in The Hague, Netherlands, and at the University of Witwatersrand, Johannesburg, South Africa. Susan has published articles on the political economy of agricultural commodity chains as well as post-Apartheid industrial development in South Africa. Her work critically engages with mainstream economic approaches and draws from various traditions in classical political economy, including Marx. It has been published in numerous academic journals, like *Development and Change, Economic Geography, Journal of Social and Economic Policy and Review of Radical Political Economics*. She has contributed to the *Elgar Companion to Marx's Economics*.

**Benjamin Selwyn** is Professor of International Relations and International Development in the department of International Relations at the University of Sussex, UK. His research and writing engages with relations between evolving class relations and the formation and reproduction of global value chains. He is author of *The Struggle for Development* (2017), *The Global Development Crisis* (2014), *Workers, State and Development in Brazil: Powers of Labour, Chains of Value* (2012) and co-editor of *Class Dynamics of Development* (2017).

**Satoshi Miyamura** is a Senior Lecturer at the Department of Economics, SOAS, University of London, UK. He currently works on patterns of industrial restructuring, labour market institutions and labour-management relations in a range of manufacturing sectors, including jute and cotton textile, engineering and pharmaceutical industries in various regions of India, including West Bengal, Maharashtra, Gujarat and the Delhi/ National Capital Region. More generally, his research interests are in the political economy of development in India and Japan; economics of labour and institutions; economic history and history of economic thought. His work has been published in several international journals including *Third World Quarterly The Journal of Peasant Studies* and *New Political Economy*.

**Farai Mtero** is a senior researcher at the Institute for Poverty, Land and Agrarian Studies (PLAAS) at the University of the Western Cape, where he undertook research for his PhD. He is currently leading a research project on land redistribution in South Africa.

**Brittany Bunce** holds a PhD from the Institute for Poverty, Land and Agrarian Studies, University of the Western Cape. She is currently a research associate at PLAAS. Brittany's research focuses on the political economy of agrarian change, land reform, inclusive business models and smallholder farmers.

**Ben Cousins** is an Emeritus Professor at the Institute for Poverty, Land and Agrarian Studies at the University of the Western Cape, and undertakes research on agrarian change, land reform, property rights and smallholder agriculture in Southern Africa.

**Alex Dubb** is a PhD candidate at the Institute for Poverty, Land and Agrarian Studies (PLAAS) at the University of Western Cape, focusing on the grain-livestock complex in South Africa. He has published extensively on the sugar industry in Southern Africa.

**Donna Hornby** is currently a post-doctoral researcher at the Institute for Poverty, Land and Agrarian Studies (PLAAS), University of the Western Cape. She has been a land and agrarian researcher and activist in KwaZulu-Natal, South Africa for over 20 years, working on issues of land reform, smallholder farmers, customary tenure systems and rural development.

**Lorena Lombardozzi** is a Senior Lecturer in Economics at the Open University and has held teaching positions at SOAS and City, University of London. She received her PhD in Economics at SOAS with a thesis focusing on the state, market transition and food consumption in Uzbekistan. Her work is published in various journals including *Capital and Class*, *Review of International Political Economy*, and *Political Quarterly*. Lorena has also worked as a development economist in Argentina and Uruguay in 2014, in Uzbekistan for UNODC Central Asia from 2010 to 2012, and between 2007 and 2010 with the European Commission and the Italian Ministry of Foreign Affairs. Her research interests include theories of international political economy; growth and distribution in post-Soviet spaces, planned economies, and Europe; and feminist economics, labour and industrial policy.

**Sara Stevano** is a development and feminist political economist, with interdisciplinary skills in the field of anthropology. She is a Senior Lecturer in Economics at SOAS, London, UK, after holding different teaching and research positions the University of the West of England (UWE), Bristol, and King's College, London. Her areas of study are the political economy of labour, food and nutrition, social reproduction, gender analysis and research methodology (including mixed methods) for political economy. Her work focuses on Africa, in particular Mozambique and Ghana, and has been published in international journals including *The Journal of Development Studies*, *Cambridge Journal of Economics*, *Feminist Economics* and *World Development*. She is the co-author with Sara Cantillon and Odile Mackett of *Feminist Political Economy: A Global Perspective* (Agenda Publishing, 2023).

**Tania Toffanin** is a feminist labour sociologist. She is currently Research Fellow at the National Research Council (Institute for Studies on the Mediterranean, ISMed) in Naples. She has an M.A. in Political Sciences from the University of Padova, where she also taught before joining ISMed, and a Ph.D. in Labour Studies from the University of Milan. She was the 2015 Fernand Braudel Fellow at the Collège D' Études Mondiales (Fondation

Maison des Sciences de l' Homme) where she worked on 'Luxury and Capitalism'. She is the author of *Fabbriche Invisibili: Storie di Donne Lavoranti a Domicilio* (*Invisible Factories: Stories of Women Homeworkers*, Ombre Corte, 2016) that will be soon translated into English.

**Sigrid Vertommen** is a postdoctoral fellow at the Department of Conflict and Development Studies in Ghent University and an affiliated scholar at the Sociology of Reproduction Research Group (ReproSoc) in the University of Cambridge. She is conducting qualitative research on the political economy of global fertility chains between Israel/Palestine, Ukraine (egg cell provision) and Georgia (surrogacy), with a particular interest in understanding the role of egg cell providers and surrogates through the lens of reproductive labour. Her work has been published in various journals such as *BioSocieties* and *New Genetics and Society*. She is member of the Slow Science and the Women's Strike collective at Ghent University.

**Gavin Capps** is Senior Lecturer in Economics at Kingston University, London. He held previous academic positions in South Africa, where he was Senior Researcher in the Society, Work and Politics Institute (SWOP) at the University of the Witwatersrand. Here, he led the Mining and Rural Transformation in Southern Africa (MARTISA) project. His work has been published in a number of journals, including the *Journal of Agrarian Change* for which he won the Bernstein and Byres prize for the best article in agrarian political economy in 2016. He is currently working on a book-length study of the political economy of the platinum industry in post-apartheid South Africa.

**Genevieve LeBaron** is Professor and Director, School of Public Policy, at Simon Fraser University's (SFU) Vancouver campus. Before joining SFU, she was Professor of Politics and Co-Director of Sheffield Political Economy Research Institute (SPERI) at the University of Sheffield. She has been researching forced and unfree labour in the global economy for over a decade, and has published books on the topic with *Polity*, *Oxford University Press*, and *Cambridge University Press*, as well as articles in journals including *Journal of Development Studies*, *Review of International Political Economy*, *New Political Economy*, and *Brown Journal of World Affairs*. She is Principal Investigator of the Global Business of Forced Labour project funded by the UK Economic and Social Research Council.

**Paolo Novak** is Senior Lecturer in Development Studies and Co-Chair of the Centre for Migration and Diaspora Studies, at SOAS, University of London, UK. His research is located at the intersection of critical borders, migration, and development studies, and is concerned with studying the socio-spatial tension between the abstract cartographies defined by borders, and their fluid and dynamic embodied manifestations. He has conducted field research in Pakistan, Meghalaya (India), Egypt and Italy. His last research project is titled "Asylum seekers reception: taxonomies and location" and was funded by the British Academy.

**Subir Sinha** is trained as a historian at Delhi University and as a Political Scientist at Northwestern University. He is Reader in the Department of Development Studies at SOAS, London. He writes on Marxism and Postcolonial theory, populism, agrarian questions and social movements. His work on the global fish-workers' movement has been awarded the Bernstein and Byres prize in agrarian political economy by the *Journal of Agrarian Change*. He is currently finishing a book on The Postcolonial Commons and is analysing the impact of the COVID-19 pandemic on international development and on India's migrant labour through 'cyber-fieldwork'.

# INDEX

www.ingramcontent.com/pod-product-compliance
Lightning Source LLC
Chambersburg PA
CBHW020238290326
41929CB00044B/232